INSIGHT GUIDES

Created and Directed by Hans Höfer

WATERWAYS OF EUROPE

Edited by Lyle Lawson
Photography by Lyle Lawson and others

Editorial Director Brian Bell

APA PUBLICATIONS

The book you are holding is part of the world's largest range of guidebooks. Its purpose is to help you have the most valuable travel experience possible, and we try to achieve this by providing not only information about countries, regions and cities but also genuine insight into their history, culture, institutions and people.

In 1970, when I created the first Insight Guide – to Bali – it was already becoming clear that mass tourism could inflict great damage on a destination. I believed then that, with insight into a country's people and culture, visitors would both enhance their own experience and be accepted more easily by their hosts. Now, in a world where ethnic hostilities and nationalist conflicts are all too common, such attempts to increase understanding between peoples are more important than ever.

Insight Guides:
Essentials for understanding

Because a nation's past holds the key to its present, each Insight Guide kicks off with lively history chapters. These are followed by magazine-style essays on the people's culture. This essential background information gives readers the necessary context for using the Places section, with its comprehensive run-down on things worth seeing and doing. Finally, a listings section contains all the information you'll need on travel, hotels, restaurants and opening times. The pictures, for which Insight Guides have become so celebrated, are just as important. Our photojournalistic approach aims not only to illustrate a destination but to also communicate visually and directly to readers life as it is lived by the locals.

No single writer can capture the essence of a destination after a short visit. So we rely heavily on locally based writers and journalists, who provide both lively prose and frank, authoritative assessments. This local input, filtered through our worldwide network of editors, ensures that the books are truly international, free of an outsider's prejudices. For this reason, the destination dictates the version of English used, British or American spelling. So our guide to New York has all the authority of an American guidebook, our book on Paris is as dependable as a French guidebook and our book on Hong Kong is as trustworthy as an Asian guidebook.

From edition to edition, our team of correspondents works hard to keep the 190 titles in the series up-to-date. As new museums open and old attractions close, as volcanoes erupt and presidents fall, as travel patterns change and new frontiers open, we bring the information to you. We take this job very seriously and, because we operate our own printing plant in Singapore, we are able to update and reprint best-selling books as often as needed.

Compact Guides
The "great little guides"

As invaluable as such background information is, it isn't always fun to carry an Insight Guide through a crowded souk or up a church tower. Could we, readers asked, distil the key reference material into a slim volume that would answer their on-the-spot questions? Our response was to design Compact Guides as an entirely new product, with original text carefully cross-referenced to detailed maps and more than 200 photographs. In essence, they're miniature encyclopedias, concise and comprehensive, displaying reliable and up-to-date information in an accessible way.

Pocket Guides:
A local host in book form

However wide-ranging the information in a book, human beings still value the personal touch. Having complimented our editors on the quality and comprehensiveness of a book, our readers would often bombard them with questions. Where do *you* go to eat? What do *you* think is the best beach? What would you recommend if I have only three days? This gave us the idea of asking our local correspondents to act as "substitute hosts" by telling us about their preferred walks and trips, listing the restaurants they go to and structuring a visit into a series of carefully timed itineraries. The result was our Pocket Guides, complete with full-size fold-out maps. The 100-plus titles in this companion series help readers plan a trip precisely, particularly if their time is short.

Exploring with Insight:
A valuable travel experience

In conjunction with co-publishers all over the world, we print in up to 10 languages, from German to Chinese, from Danish to Russian. But our aim remains simple: to enhance your travel experience by combining our expertise in guidebook publishing with the on-the-spot knowledge of our correspondents.

We also rely on readers who tell us of their travel discoveries. So please get in touch: our contact numbers are listed below.

See you soon.

Hans Höfer, Publisher
APA Publications

CONTACTING THE EDITORS

As we make every effort to update Insight Guides as often as possible, we would appreciate it if readers would call to our attention any errors or out-of-date information by contacting:

**Apa Publications, P.O. Box 7910, London SE1 8ZB, England.
Tel: (44) 171 620 0008.
Fax: (44) 171 620 1074.
e-mail: insight@apaguide.demon.co.uk.**

ENGLISH LANGUAGE DISTRIBUTORS

USA, the Caribbean, Latin America: Houghton Mifflin Company, 222 Berkeley Street, Boston, MA 02116-3764, USA. Fax: 351 1109.

Canada: Thomas Allen & Son, 300 Steelcase Road East, Markham, Ontario L3R 1G2. Tel: (1 905) 475 9126. Fax: 475 6747.

Great Britain & Ireland: GeoCenter International (UK) Ltd, The Viables Centre, Harrow Way, Basingstoke, RG22 4BJ, England. Tel: (44 1256) 817987. Fax: 817988.

Netherlands, Belgium, Luxembourg: Uitgeverij Cambium, BV, Gildenveld 50, 3892 DJ Zeewolde, The Netherlands. Tel: (31 3242) 5170. Fax: 5175.

Denmark, Norway: Politikens Forlag Ltd, 26 Vestergade, DK-1456 Copenhagen K, Denmark. Tel: (45 33) 112122. Fax: 932152.

Sweden: Study & Travel, Box 17552, 11891 Stockholm, Sweden. Tel: (46 8 452) 9696. Fax: 9797.

Italy: Inter Orbis S.p.A. Via B. Croce, 4-20094, Corsico (MI), Italy. Tel: (39 2) 486931. Fax: 48693214.

Cyprus: K.P. Kyriakou, Panagides Building, 3 Grivas Digenis Avenue, P.O. Box 159, Limassol, Cyprus. Tel: (357 5) 368508. Fax: 371706.

Israel: Steimatzky Ltd., 11 Hakishan St., P.O. Box 1444, Bnei-Brak 51114, Israel. Tel: (972 3) 579 4579. Fax: 579 4567.

South Africa, Namibia: Faradawu CC, 76 Barnato St., Berea 2198, South Africa. Tel: (27 11) 484 2701. Fax: 484 2852.

India, Nepal: IBD, 107/108 Arcadia, 195 Nariman Point, Bombay 400 021, India. Tel: (91 22) 225220. Fax: 287 2531.

Pakistan: Paramount Books (Pvt) Ltd., 152/0 Block 2, PECHS, 75400, Karachi 29, Pakistan. Tel: (92 21) 455 1630. Fax: 455 3772.

Sri Lanka: Lake House Bookshop, 100 Sir Chittampalan A, Gardinas, Mawatha, Colombo 2, Sri Lanka. Tel: (94 1) 432104. Fax: 432104.

Japan: Charles E. Tuttle Co. Inc., 2-6 Suido 1-Chome, Bunkyo-Ku, Tokyo 112, Japan. Tel: (81) 3 38117106. Fax: 44 8220413.

Australia: Simon & Schuster Ltd., P.O. Box 507, East Roseville, NSW 2069, Australia. Tel: (61 2) 4170299. Fax: 4173188.

New Zealand: David Bateman Ltd., P.O. Box 100-242, North Shore Mail Centre, Auckland 1330, New Zealand. Tel: (64 9) 4157664. Fax: 4158892.

Thailand, Myanmar, Vietnam: Apa Publications (Thailand) Ltd., 2220/31 Soi Ramkhamhaeng 36/1, Ramkhamhaeng Road, Huamark, Bangkok 10240, Thailand. Tel/fax: (66 2) 3752669.

Hong Kong, Macau, China, Philippines: Apa Publications (HK) Ltd., 804-805 Kinox Centre, 9 Hung To Road, Kwun Tong, Kowloon, Hong Kong. Tel: (852) 23 57 48 83. Fax: 23 44 83 31.

Taiwan: Lai Lai Book Company, 4F-1 No 271, Sec 3, Taipei, Taiwan ROC. Tel: (886 2) 363 4265. Fax: 362 5366.

Singapore, Malaysia & rest of world: Höfer Communications (Pte) Ltd., 38 Joo Koon Road, Singapore 628990. Tel: (65) 861 2755. Fax: 861 6438.

OTHER LANGUAGE EDITIONS

Chinese: Formosan Magazine Press Ltd., 6th Floor, No 189 Yen Pin S Road, Taipei, Taiwan. Tel: (886 2) 361 2151. Fax: 382 1270.

Danish: Politikens Forlag Ltd. (see above).

Dutch: Uitgeverij Cambium, BV, Gildenveld 50, 3892 DJ Zeewolde, The Netherlands. Tel: (31 3242) 5170. Fax: 5175

French: Editions Gallimard, 5 Rue Sébastien Bottin, 75007 Paris, France. Tel: (33 1) 49 54 42 00. Fax: 45 44 39 46.

German: Langenscheidt KG, Neusserstraße 3, 80807 München, Germany. Tel: (49 89) 360960. Fax: 363862.

Italian: Zanfi Editori, Via Emilia Ovest 954, 41 100 Modena, Italy. Tel: (39 59) 871700. Fax: 891701.

Spanish: El Pais-Aguilar, Juan Bravo 38, 28006 Madrid, Spain. Tel: (34 1) 3224770. Fax: 3224771.

Since no single book, however ambitious, can hope to cover in depth all the canals, navigable rivers and lakes in the entire continent, *Insight Guide: Waterways of Europe* sets out to inspire. Those who have a rather limited idea of what this kind of trip involves will discover a glorious variety of possibilities. Those who need no introduction to vacations afloat will find many new options they had not previously considered.

Many boating aficionados, inevitably, will howl that their favorite waterway or canal has been omitted. True: there wasn't room for all, and the authors had to make some tough choices. Except for a short stretch when the Seine flows through Paris, we've left out that great river, as well as the Rhône and the Rhine (the subject of its own Insight Guide). Only those rivers which are more recreational than commercial (or form part of a pleasure route) have been explored, because we have concentrated on the waterways which cater to the waterborne explorer.

Project Editor and primary photographer **Lyle Lawson** (a contributor to many Insight Guides including India, Burgundy, Turkey, the Baltic States and Sicily) says she was born with an incurable disease: "itchy feet", one that never seems to go into remission and only gets worse as time passes. Even before she graduated from Parsons

Lawson

School of Design in New York City, that passion for travel had taken her to many parts of the globe. An assignment from *Modern Photography* magazine to photograph and write about Bicentennial America brought domestic travel, and the start of a career in photojournalism. Since then, her work has appeared in many international publications. Between assignments, Lawson runs "Shuttertrips", a US-based outfit that operates photography tours which explore the world.

A blue-water sailor for many years, Lawson became an inland waterway convert after a cruise along the Canal du Midi (Southwestern France is still her favorite area to barge, second is Burgundy). Other journeys followed, and the knowledge gleaned is shared with this book's readers.

Anthony

The first person to join the writing crew was **Carmen Anthony**, who contributed the chapter on Ireland. A native of Los Angeles and a graduate of the University of Southern California, Anthony worked as a reporter for United Press International in Denver, and later Madrid. During those years in Spain, she made the first of many trips to Ireland where she fell in love with the country and its friendly, gentle people. Now a New York-based freelance writer, Anthony writes primarily about the hotel and travel industries.

Marcus Brooke has had a life-long love of the sea and all connected with it. As a 10-year-old in Glasgow, he would, after school, walk the two miles to the vast docks which made the city a great maritime power and gaze at the giant cargo ships from faraway places which he longed to visit. Brooke fulfilled his dreams and now writes about and photographs those places, yet he retains a warm spot for Britain, which he knows from top to bottom.

Brooke

Grayling

Evans

Harryman

Lasley

This has resulted in his many contributions and photographs to the British section of this book.

Christopher Grayling, author of *The Bridgewater Heritage*, a biography about the father of Britain's canal network, writes about the Duke's waterways. After graduating from Sydney Sussex College, Cambridge, he ran a small publishing company before joining the British Broadcasting Corporation. He went on to produce a daily business program on television, although writing remained a primary interest. His remarkable knowledge of all the pubs along the waterways was gleaned when he wrote *Manchester Ales and Port* and *The History of Oldham Brewery*.

An 11-year stint in Britain's Royal Navy left **Richard Evans** with an unending love of travel, and his writing assignments now return him to many of the places where he once cruised as a lieutenant. Captaining a hotel barge for two years on the Thames left him uniquely qualified to write about that river. He also supplied the glossary of boating terms and the descriptions for lock passage that appear in the Travel Tips section.

Elizabeth Harryman and **Paul Lasley**, Los Angeles-based husband and wife travel writers, contributed the Alsace-Lorraine and Burgundy chapters. But European travel is just one of their specialities: they jointly write a syndicated food column, and he is Travel Editor of *Ranch and Life*, while she heads the same department of *Palm Springs Life*.

Peter Spinks, an English writer living in Holland, guides the mariner on a journey through part of that country, **Eric and Ruth Bailey** chart the Somme River, and **Pit de Jonge** co-authored the Belgium chapter.

To help photograph the chapters on Great Britain and Ireland, Lawson approached two of England's most respected photographers, **Derek Pratt** and **Dennis Mansell**. Pratt is a commerical and industrial photographer whose special love is inland waterways, and he travels throughout the British Isles photographing them. He is also author of *Southern Inland Waterways*, and *Discovering London's Canals,* which are illustrated by his photographs. Mansell decided at a very young age that he wanted to be a photographer; during a 40-year career, he has worked for the Associated Press and national daily papers. Now he concentrates on advertising and travel photography, and his work appears in publications around the world.

Tom Kelly's photographs were in *Insight Guide: Ireland* and he was the main photographer for *Insight Guide: Dublin*. **Douglas Corrance**, a top Scottish photographer, has spent many years capturing every aspect of that part of the world, and was primary photographer for *Insight Guide: Edinburgh*. **Hugh McKnight's** massive archives yielded a treasure trove of historical pictures and modern photographs.

Pratt

Mansell

The Travel Tips section was compiled by **Rosemary Schade**. Horizon Cruises provided help in Europe to writers and photographers. Proofreading and indexing were completed in Insight's London editorial office by **Rosemary Jackson Hunter**.

Preceding pages: England's Oxford Canal; on the Canal du Nivernais, Burgundy; English narrowboat in Bath.

Maps

Plate III.

Theory of Navigable Canals.

THE RISE OF THE CANAL

Europe's canals form a curious cobweb. A modern map of these waterways literally seems a cobweb, rendered irregular by the centuries of their use, abandonment and revival. Just as the courses of the canals trace complex paths across one's map, so also their history is an interweaving of the slow and haphazard development of inland waterways for the spread of commerce and civilization throughout Europe.

Historians trace the use of canals back at least 5,000 years, when Pepi I ordered Uni, the Governor of Upper Egypt, to build navigation canals to bypass the first cataract of the Nile near Aswan. The advantages of river and wind transport were obvious in ages when transport otherwise meant the pace of men and beasts of burden.

The roster of European canal builders reads like a course in European history: the Greeks, Romans, the Swedes (working in what is now Russia and Turkey), the French, the English, the Hanseatic League, the Dutch, the Italians. The tracing of these threads of each nation's contributions has been the subject of much scholarly study, but here we highlight development of the oldest canals and those waterways which today await the traveler who wishes to explore something old, something new; scenes both historical and full of insight into the countries through which these ribbons of water weave a web of leisure and adventure.

The Egyptians did not stop with their first canal: a second was constructed around 1700 BC near Wadi Halfa, adding to the Nile's navigational length. In the 2nd century BC, Rameses II built the most famous of the Egyptian waterways, linking the Nile near Cairo to the Great Bitter Lake and giving access to the Red Sea. Rameses' great canal had a length of 59 miles (95 kms), a width of 146 ft (45 meters), and a depth of 16 ft (5 meters), but constant flooding altered the

dimensions. History records major renovations to it, the last one in AD 640. Under the Arab Governor of Egypt, Amr ibn-'As. This canal, and others of the period, were not the modern waterways of today and were little better than troughs cut through the earth. Because of soil type, constant dredging and weeding out of the ubiquitous reeds was necessary. The flood stage (or lack of it) of the Nile caused additional problems: barges floated easily or else had to be pulled through the sluggish waters, and seasonal rains caused numerous course changes. Eventually, the cost became too great, and cheaper means of transportation were adopted.

An Asian connection: Necessity created the first Chinese canals: in that vast country, most of the major rivers run parallel to each other, and if China were to take advantage of these natural means of transport, then north-south canals linking the west to east-flowing rivers had to be built. The Pien (Bian) Canal in Henan linked the Yellow River with the Huaihe. The Yellow River was a grain growing area, and the Huaihe needed the harvested wheat. Built in the 4th century BC, the Pien was a precursor of one of the world's most famous early waterways, China's Grand Canal.

A project of the Sui Dynasty in the late 6th century AD, the Grand Canal started near Hangzhou, crossed the Yangtze and Yellow Rivers on its northward journey, and ended near Beijing. In the course of its thousand-mile run, some rise in elevation occured. To compensate for the loss of water at either end, the waters of two small rivers were diverted into the elevated area, making the Grand Canal the earliest recorded summit level canal design.

The Romans expand: While the Egyptians and Chinese were developing their canal networks, the Romans were also looking at ways to utilize the waterways of their huge empire. It was the sea routes which gave Rome its great power; radiating from the Mediterranean, the easiest way to enter a country was to follow the rivers that flowed into that sea. When these became impassable or ran too far from the desired destination, the Roman solution was to link the rivers.

Troops could then be transferred from one district to another without a long and wearying land journey, and goods which added to Rome's quality of life could be taken to market more easily.

The Romans also built canals to supplement rivers, and to by-pass the often-flooded roads. In the 1st century AD, the Rhine, always a source of transport, was linked by the Romans at its three outfalls by a canal. The Fossa Corbulinis (now the Vliet Canal), ran just inside the coast and linked northern Ijssel to Utrecht, and Leiden with Helinium in the south, and its primary function was to shunt goods north or south.

That same century continued the massive

ters during this time were small, no more than 39- to 48-ft (12- to 15-meters) long, six-ft (two-meters) wide and flat-bottomed so that they could enter most waterways. They were also rudimentary craft with little cover for the boatmen.

The first boats depended upon wind, sea or man to propel them. In the Dark Ages, before the harness was invented, teams of oxen were used; later horses and donkeys filled the same function. Depending upon water current, hundreds of men and women could be used, or as few as half a dozen. If working against a tide, 30 pairs of oxen or up to 400 pairs of men would be needed to bow-haul one boat. When barges started traveling in

Roman canal-building program. Darius conceived the 9-mile (15-km) long Fossa Drusian, which linked the Rhine and Ijssel. To avoid the tricky waters of the Rhone Delta, Caius Marius dug the Fossa Mariana. The Iron Gates of the Danube, which had long posed a navigational barrier, were surmounted when Trajan cut a canal near Sip. Boats could be towed by oxen in either direction, eliminating lengthy portages. In England, the Fosse Dyke linked the Trent and Witham Rivers near Lincoln; further south, Winchester was given sea access with the Itchen Dyke.

Most of the boats that plied the local wa-

trains, up to 80 pairs of horses pulled seven to 10 vessels.

By the start of the 20th century, steam tugs and motorized boats had all but replaced horse power. Only the two world wars brought a brief return of the horses, and in Europe today all *péniches* (standard 123-ft/38.5-meter barges) and the smaller *flûtes* are *automoteurs*, moving under their own diesel-powered engines.

Over the centuries, many types of boats carried cargo; some were even peculiar to one waterway only, and are extinct today; for instance, the *allège* was found on France's Charente River. Often, the type of barge identified its home area, such as the *Roannaise* which described a boat from Roanne working the Loire River. Other names were generic: the *galiot* was a barge about 10 tons, a *galion* used sail power, and the *gabre* was a single masted, 65 to 113 ft/20 to 30 meters long barge carrying 80 to 200 tons. *Sapines* had sails and carried up to 170 tons; *sapinettes*, smaller and faster, held no more than 60 tons. Passenger boats, called *coches d'eau* (water carriages) traveled as fast as the owners wanted to schedule them.

England, Ireland, Holland and Belgium had their own variation on this theme. The boats came, worked and went, and with the revival of inland waterways for pleasure

one of wood or logs lashed together, a steering wheel for a rudder, and coats of paint and comfortable furnishings instead of bare planks, distinguishes the modern canal barge from its older cousin.

The Dark Ages: After the fall of Rome, and the attendant strife in Europe, commercial use of waterways declined. Most large estates were self-sufficient, and the trading which did exist was conducted within the confines of a small area. This was an era of low productivity on farms, where plows and the use of animals as beasts of burden were virtually unknown due to the lack of proper harnesses. The invention of a horse collar during the reign of Charlemagne, and then of

boating, they're returning again, albeit in fiberglass and aluminum this time.

Width and length: In many respects, canal boat design has changed little through the centuries. They are, for the most part, shallow draft, and although their length may extend beyond 123 ft (38 meters), their draft still remains approximately what it was. Only the eventual substitution of an engine for sail or horse power, cabins for staff and guests instead of an open deck, a steel hull for

Left, in the 18th century, horses or people powered barges. **Above**, early locks were crude structures made of logs.

horse-shoes, enabled those animals to carry many times their weight.

The introduction of the iron scythe produced a bigger, more efficient harvest, meaning the excess had to be traded or sold. With horses, man didn't have to rely upon himself or the vagrancies of the wind to get produce to market. Horses were also less expensive to keep than men, fewer were needed for haulage, and water freight prices became competitive.

As countries began to loosen themselves from the shackles of the agrarian Dark Ages, rivers became the focus of power for a mini-Industrial Revolution. True, there was no steam power (that in itself would cause the eventual downfall of the rivers as money-spinners); but man began to harness the water's natural energy. By the 11th century, instead of using water power to solely run mills for grinding wheat and corn into flour, the churning water ran machines that, among other things, smelted and forged iron, and sawed timber.

The men who owned the industries generated by water usually controlled the same waterway. The intrusion of barges and the flash locks needed to transport them through different water levels meant a cessation of work. Consequently, most barge traffic was confined to the large rivers which did not

need locks, and to very heavy cargoes, such as marble, timber and wine, which could not be carried overland. Then, as always, the problem was how to create a safe and easily navigable waterway through hills and valleys, raising or lowering water levels when necessary without disrupting local life.

Locking up the water: The original solution was to unload cargoes at the barrier (whether it be dam, rapids or waterfall), and reload onto another boat beyond the problem. (Many cities have started this way. In the United States, settlers heading westward down the Ohio River had to change boats where a series of waterfalls made further navigation impossible. This site became Louisville, now Kentucky's primary city.) This transfer was time-consuming, and more than one cargo was lost or damaged.

The Egyptians created flash locks, so called because they allowed a flash of water to pour from or into a pool, thus raising or lowering the pool's water level. For a descending boat, the process was simple; as the water spewed outward, it gave an easy passage over the water. An upward journey was more difficult: the barge had to be pulled or winched along, and might even need to wait while the canal filled sufficiently. This was adequate for relatively flat lands like Egypt and the Low Countries, but in hilly, even mountainous countryside, the problem was more acute where numerous flashes were needed for the shortest distances.

The Greeks had another answer. Around 600 BC, Periander created a ship-railway across Greece's Isthmus of Corinth. Operation was simple: ships were loaded onto flatbeds which rolled along grooves cut into cobbled roadways. Not a canal because no water was involved, it was, however, the forerunner of today's Corinth Canal and remained in use for about 1,000 years.

The inclined plane also enabled the transfer of boats from one elevation to another. Called *overdragen* by the Dutch, these slipways were placed over dams; cables were tied to each end of a boat which was drawn over the slipway. Some of these planes were made of logs placed so boats could roll over them.

A gate of some sort to block the water was another idea. Early designs were simple: a board that could be raised or lowered according to need was placed in the canal, river or lake. This not only kept the water a certain level, but fulfilled a second purpose, that of containing the canal water within certain boundaries.

The earliest Chinese designs had wood or stone fitted in each side of the canal. Vertical grooves were then cut into opposite sides of the bank, and trees, either singly or bound together to form a solid gate, were fitted into each of the grooves. The water could be raised or lowered by altering the height of the tree-gate with the help of pulleys and counterweights. These maneuvers got the boats through the waterjam, but still took too much time.

Impounding ponds: In AD 984, a Chinese engineer, Chiao Weo-Yo, invented the first pound lock for use on the Grand Canal. Water could be impounded by building two gates, one at each end of the area which was to be enclosed. Both ends would be shut, water flowed in (or out), and when the desired level was reached, the gates at the end which matched the outside water level were opened, and out sailed the boat.

The creation of the pound lock enabled larger boats to traverse the waterways. The only inhibitions were the width and depth of the canals, and the length between the two impounding gates. It was from this seemingly simple design that all future lock construction would stem, whether they were

town which built a true pound lock on the River Lek in 1373.

Unfortunately, during the early Middle Ages, and before pound locks, disagreements were constant between shippers and those who controlled the waterways. One way of keeping traffic down was taxes. Individuals who owned the water rights had the power to levy whatever taxes traffic would bear, and if a boat passed through a multi-tax waterway, many a shipper might find his taxes outstripping the cargo's selling price.

Consequently, as taxes rose, waterway use declined, freight tonnage declined, and the rivers and canals fell into disrepair. There were, however, some exceptions: around

LE PANORAMA DE BÉZIERS. — LE CANAL AUX 9 ÉCLUSES.

stair-steps or an interlinking series of gates.

Another variation on this theme was the creation of boat basins. An enormous one was built in Utretch in 1373 with three gates on the Lek River between it and Vreeswijk, divided by a flood gate at one end and the canal at the other. Built to hold 20 to 30 boats, the basin is erroneously credited with being the first European pound lock. That distinction belongs to Gouda, another Netherlands

1100, a stretch of the Aa River between St Omer and Gravelines went from six-ton boat capacity to be able to accommodate those 50 times larger in just 60 years.

One forward-looking monarch, Henry I (1100–35) revived one of England's Roman Canals, the Fosse Dyke. In the mid-1300s England's Edward III (1327–77), and his son, the Black Prince, dredged part of the Lot River in southwestern France, and shipped wine from Cahors downstream to the Garonne and the sea.

Medieval giants: The Hanseatic League, one of the largest trading groups of the Middle Ages, was formed by a group of

Left, Pierre-Paul Riquet, the genius behind the Canal du Midi. **Above**, turn-of-the-century view of Béziers' stair-step Fonseranne Locks.

merchants who definitely believed in their name, *Hansa* (defensive association). At its height, the League controlled trade routes that ranged from England to Russia and from Hamburg to Marseilles. Begun in 11th-century Germany, and first based in Hamburg and Lübeck, the League reached its apogee in the 14th century. Centering primarily on the great European rivers, the Rhine, Seine, Elbe, Volga and Thames, these men encouraged waterway developement, and marine technology. In return, the Hansas obtained the right to freely navigate "their" rivers, to develop ports where they wanted and charge whatever tolls their charter or the traffic warranted or would bear.

again: the charging of road tolls. Taking a cue from their canal brethren, towns and villages began to place their own taxes on roads running through their territories. Competition began when the canal owners, sensing a means of increasing business, lowered their rates to a level just below those of the roads. Inspired by increased business, a spurt in canal improvement began.

The Italian connection: Construction of the Cathedral of Milan in 1386 was genesis for the first pound lock on an Italian canal, and eventually involved Leonardo da Vinci with inland waterways. The quarries were near Lake Maggiore, and floating the marble blocks on log rafts down the Naviglio

One important canal developed during this time is still in use: the Utrecht-Vecht. Starting at Muiden on the Zuiderzee, it went southward. At Maarseen, cargoes could be transhipped to ocean going ships, but otherwise the boats continued on into the sea of islands that were the forerunner of modern Holland. (These islands have now been formed into land by the use of the country's massive dike system.) Antwerp was terminus for both ocean-going ships and the canal boats that flowed northward from Brussels, Ghent and northern France.

In the late Middle Ages, a surprising twist made waterways commercially viable

Grande Canal seemed the easiest way of getting them to the building site. Because of the changes in ground level, many flash locks were needed, and when they were in use, the city's water supply was cut off.

By 1420, this so enraged the citizens that work on the Cathedral stopped while two engineers, Fillipo da Modena and Fioravante da Bologna devised a different system. The city's moat (which ran alongside the Cathedral) was about 6 feet (2 meters) higher than the Naviglio; the two were connected via a short canal. The engineers' solution was to place gates at either end of the joining canal, making one long pool whose depth could be varied, thus eliminating any further need to disrupt Milan's water supply.

In 1482, Leonardo da Vinci was appointed a state engineer in Milan. At first concerned only with later work on the Cathedral, his fascination with things mechanical soon drew him toward the canals. He oversaw the planning and building of several, and some studies in *Codex Atlantis* made many people believe the artist had invented the pound lock. This is not true, but Leonardo did bring together all the elements: masonry walls to replace dirt ones, chamber floors built on piles and supported by wooden crossbeams, gates that pivoted instead of working vertically, windlass-operated canal gates and paddles set into those

A Renaissance: By chance, Leonardo's death ushered in one of the greatest canal-building periods. During the previous centuries, despite the work of some enlightened groups, waterways were still a difficult means of transport.

Silt had filled the mouths of many rivers; undrained land contributed to ever-shifting channels, and spring flooding, unchecked by dams or locks continued to wreak havoc with trade. But the undaunted persevered, aided by two factors: road travel was exceedingly uncomfortable, and coastal shipping was subject to pirate raids. One of France's first projects, canalization of Brittany's River Vilaine started in 1539; 15 pound locks and

gates, but operated more easily from above.

In 1515, Leonardo went to France at the behest of François I; one of the projects the King desired more than anything was a canal between the Atlantic and Mediterranean. Alas, even the great da Vinci could not conquer the contours of the Midi, and he died in 1519 at the Château Amboise 162 years before the Canal du Midi became a reality.

Left, before electricity, feet were used to guide boats through tunnels. **Above**, the Arzvillier Inclined Plane on the Marne au Rhin Canal can handle one commercial barge or over half a dozen smaller boats.

47 years later, it finally was completed.

The acceptance of Catholicism by Henri IV in 1598 ("Paris is worth a Mass", the monarch was quoted as saying.) brought peace to France after the Wars of Religion. One of Henri's first schemes was to link Paris with the provinces through a series of canals. The Briare, started in 1605, was the first, and joined the Seine and Loire rivers. Part of today's Central Canals system, the Briare was notable because its construction proved that a summit level canal could be built through difficult terrain.

The Genius of Riquet: Perhaps the greatest 17th-century waterway construction was the

150-mile (240-km) long Canal du Midi. Traversing untraversable land, the mechanics of its going from dream to reality was a nightmare that had confounded the best engineering brains. Its birth was due to the brilliant perseverance of one man, Pierre-Paul Riquet. Upon completion in 1681, the Canal du Midi ran from the Etang du Thau on the Mediterranean, rising 614 ft (189 meters) through 75 locks spread over 114 miles (184 km) to the summit reached beyond Castelnaudary. After a run of three miles (five km), the waterway fell 205 ft (63 meters) in less than 33 miles (51 km) through 26 locks to its end at a junction with the Garonne River.

In addition to breaking old construction

precepts with the seven-lock rise near Béziers and the 523-ft (161-meter) long Malpas Tunnel, Riquet changed the basic lock design. Before, they were constructed with straight sides; to withstand earth pressure, Riquet replaced the rectangular shapes with long ovals (still in existence).

The Midi's success opened a floodgate; more rivers were joined, canals dug, and tonnage leaped upward. And passenger load sizes were not far behind. Daily steamer services left Paris for points throughout the country, and there seemed no end to waterway growth.

Of all construction during this period, one

is still commercially paramount: the linking of the Somme and Oise rivers in 1738. At first, traffic was light, as was revenue, and thought was given to closure. Wiser heads prevailed and today that waterway, then called the Canal de Picardie, forms the basis for the Canal de St Quentin, one of Europe's most important north-south canal routes.

The English start to build: In England, 1709 and the first smelting of iron and coke by Abraham Darby brought the Industrial Age to that country. Fifty-two years later the Bridgewater Canal, England's most famous purpose-built waterway, arrived.

But artificial cuts and pound locks to control unruly waters were not new: in the mid-1560s John Trew built the first lock on the Exeter Canal (a short waterway lateral to the Exe River). After that, taming of rivers seemed a national pastime, and by 1760, over 700 miles (1,125 km) of controlled rivers were added to those running naturally.

The Duke of Bridgewater, known as the father of the British canal system was inspired by a vist he made to the Canal du Midi. The Duke returned home full of enthusiasm for the possibilities offered by man-made waterways. At last, he could have a direct route from his coal mines to the cities where the fuel was needed without expensive overland or roundabout river journeys.

Bridgewater worked with James Brindley to create the canal that is erroneously credited with being the first purpose-built waterway in Great Britain. (That distinction belongs to the Newry, which opened in 1742 and ran for 18 miles/29 kms from Upper Bann to Newry Harbor in Northern Ireland.) The Bridgewater joined the Worsley coal mines to Manchester, and was the first of many waterways that Brindley would design over a career that lasted over 50 years.

Other innovative canal designers and engineers followed: Thomas Telford lived between 1757 and 1834; younger than Brindley, his works were of the last era of canal growth, and among his masterpieces are Birmingham and Liverpool, the Shropshire Union and Scotland's Caledonian. William Jessup specialized in aqueduct architecture; the Pontcysyllte is his, and among canals, the Grand Union and Ireland's Grand are to his credit. John Rennie specialized in widebeam waterways, the Kennet and Avon being among those he built.

These men oversaw the dramatic increase of Great Britain's inland waterways. The numbers are staggering: from the opening of the Bridgewater in 1760, 830 miles (1,330 km) were added within 30 years. By 1810, another 1,206 miles (1,930 km) had come into being. When canal building ended in the 1850s, England and Wales had over 4,000 miles (6,400 km) of navigable waterways.

The Trent, Mersey, Severn and Thames were interlinked. The Pennines were crossed; so too, Scotland, with the Caledonian Canal, and union of the rivers Clyde and Forth. In Ireland, The Grand Canal brought Dublin to the Shannon River. All this and much more happened in the span of

A combination of the inclined plane and a boat lift was devised. The lift is just what it sounds like: a boat is placed into a tub or cradle and hoisted straight up or down from one water level to another by pulleys or counterweights. In Europe, the first one went into operation in 1789 at the Churprinz Works Canal near Dresden. Despite several attempts, it was not until 1838 that England had something similar. It was on the Grand Western Canal and was capable of carrying two eight-ton boats at the same time as they travelled in opposite directions.

The inclined plane had been in existence for centuries, but unlike the first one in Corinth which was waterless, or later ones

50 years, a period which finally ended in 1810 when the River Thames was linked to Bristol via the River Avon.

English innovations: As canal design became more sophisticated, and steeper land traversed, the need for more economical and quicker lock passage became necessary. In this and other mechanical creations, the British were the most innovative engineers and designers of the 18th century.

Left, the Duke of Bridgewater, father of the English Canal system. **Above left**, James Brindley and **right**, Thomas Telford were two of the most innovative English canal engineers.

where a boat was pulled directly up or down to different levels, the newest combined the best of lift and plane: a boat was put in a water-filled cradle, and carried in either direction. Size now was no limit, and larger and larger boats could work English canals. 1788 saw England's inclined cradle on the Ketley Canal, followed in 1792 by steam powered ones on the Shropshire Union.

Tunnels and aqueducts also were needed, and in this, the English again led the way. By the 1850s when the final spurt of canal building ended, the country had a total of 36 miles (58 km), more than the rest of the world combined. The Pontcysyllte Aqueduct rose

123 ft (38 meters) above the valley as it carried the Llangollen Canal into the Welsh hills.

Unlike other countries where governments oversaw all facets of canal work from planning to financing, building and running, England was the land of free enterprise. Industrialists linked rivers and cut canals to suit themselves. The purpose was simple: money. Closer and more-easily reached markets meant lower production costs and higher profits.

This lack of a central authority was to have devastating long-term effects. Because there was no standard size, some waterways were limited to narrow, 30-ton boats, others could transport wide-beam barges. Many areas

which raged between 1558 and 1648. Armed resistance, however, did not begin in earnest until 1579 when seven northern (and Protestant) provinces declared themselves autonomous. Two years later an edict made the arrangement official, and the seven became known as the Alliance of Utrecht.

The 1648 Treaty of Westphalia brought final capitulation by Spain, and the Northern Netherlands formally became a separate republic, remaining one except for a brief period between 1792 and 1813 when it was part of Napoleon's Empire. The Southern Provinces stayed under outside domination until 1830 when the Kingdom of Belgium was declared a separate country.

were over-canalized, those with fewer natural resources to exploit were ignored. With no forward or unified thinking, barge passage within the country was limited since waterways could not be linked without expensive renovation. And who would pay for it? The canals were privately owned, and no individual would spend his own money to enrich a rival. This led, eventually, to a curtailment of waterway growth.

Holland and Belgium: While the French and English had been following their own independent course, Spain, hereditary ruler of The Low Countries saw the Dutch fight for independence become the Eighty Years War

During the late 1550s, the war between the Dutch and Spain did not interfere with commerce: canals were cut between the inland towns of Brussels, Ghent, and Bruges, connecting them to the Schelde. And the rivers which flowed through the Low Countries were joined by purpose-built waterways, enabling the cheap, safe and easy transportation of goods between Rhine cities and Amsterdam and the sea. In Amsterdam, the Single Canal was in place by the early 1500s, but the final three canals of its ring system weren't completed until a century later.

The Treaty of Westphalia hit the Belgian shippers hard; as a separate country, the

Dutch had the right to close off their waterways to foreign traffic. This the Calvinist northerners did to their Catholic neighbors. The Schelde Estuary was shut to all Belgian shipping, forcing a return to inadequately-harbored Bruges. A canal was finally cut to Ostend for sea access, and a treaty that the Belgians (then the Spanish Netherlands) signed with France in 1675 allowed free passage of each other's ships.

Although a country of many natural waterways, most Dutch ones were tidal, and subject to dangerous sailing conditions. After several major accidents, *trekvaartens* (waterways with towpaths) seemed to offer an answer. These would have no current to

Continental Europe was poised on the brink of greater prosperity; more cargo to carry meant more trade, more jobs. Throughout the continent, countries were expanding, and building more artificial waterways. Passenger service was of good quality, and one could easily travel from city to city.

A setback: The French Revolution in 1789 put paid to further canal building in that country for some two decades. Only the Canal de Bourgogne, started in 1774 by the luckless Louis XVI was finished, finally opening in 1793. Everything else, including, additions to the Central Canals system, the Midi network and northern industrial routes had to wait until the 19th century for work to

worry about, and therefore be safer. One of the first operated between Amsterdam and Haarlem; opened in 1631, boats carried passengers and cargo easily and cheaply. Other *trekvaartens* followed, and the rage to build Europe's first mass transportation system lasted through the late 1660s. The boats running on this network were probably the first to operate on a schedule and to distinguish between comfort levels: a small compartment was set aside for those willing to pay a first class supplement.

<u>Left</u>, today, barges are homes for some... and, <u>above</u>, hotels for others.

recommence on them.

Napoleon did just that, and for several reasons: to restore national unity, develop the country, and create a more efficient military force. This latter brought completion of the Breton canals, which enabled his ships to safely pass through the peninsula instead of being at the mercy of hostile vessels lurking off-shore. A plan was drawn and rejected for the Canal du Nord (finally dug in 1965), but one for the 1810 extension of the Canal de St Quentin was successful.

Peace and prosperity: The Congress of Vienna in 1815 ended the Napoleonic Age, and with it, his expansionist Empire. The Treaty also gave free passage to ships of all the nations through which a river passed or formed a boundary, from the upper navigation limits to the sea.

With Europe relatively peaceful, the Industrial Revolution flowered. The years between 1815 and the start of the Suez Canal in 1859 saw some further waterway digging in Europe. Amsterdam, Rotterdam, Ghent and Antwerp expanded their artifical waterways to give access to larger ships; governments enlarged existing canals and drew up specifications for new ones. In spite of good road networks throughout most of Continental Europe, the steamboat companies responded by inaugurating express services: two to four galloping horses (instead of one walking) shortened journeys, and a river boat cabin was more comfortable than a seat in a rocking road carriage. It seemed as if transport centered about rivers and canals would continue forever.

Steam and trains: The arrival of the railroads shattered that dream. The Liverpool and Manchester Line opened in the 1830s, and by 1900 the faster rail service made water transport obsolete. What had taken centuries to develop was overtaken in less than 100 years. Waterway use for commercial haulage of heavy or bulky goods limped on through two world wars, but the rapid rebuilding of Europe (and the explosion of highway construction after the second) seemed to doom even the most resilient canals and rivers. Many were struck off the list of official waterways, locks were allowed to fall apart, some canals were filled in and macadam poured where water once flowed. England and Ireland were particularly hurt because there was no commercial value to any of their waterways. Only the big transit routes serving the major rivers (Rhine, Rhône and Seine) seemed inviolate.

The 1970s, fortunately, brought a Renaissance; spurred on by a small band of enthusiasts who lobbied and spread the word of a canal journey as vacation, people began to awaken to the treasures at hand. Happily, the disintegration process is being reversed, the inland waterways of Europe are in another flowering and should be available for generations ahead to savor and enjoy.

<u>Right</u>, 18th-century engraving of a sailing barge on the Midi Canal.

Inland Waterways Of Europe

300 km

SHETLAND ISLANDS

Bergen

NORGE

Oslo

Atlantic

Ocean

HEBRIDES

⑲ SCOTLAND

Glasgow ⑲ Edinburgh

North Sea

DANMARK

Skagerrak

GREAT BRITAIN
AND NORTHERN IRELAND

Belfast

Irish Sea

Leeds

Liverpool ⑰

EIRE

⑳ Dublin

ENGLAND

⑱
⑱

Birmingham
WALES

⑭ ⑯

⑮

Hamburg

Elbe

Hannover

Amsterdam

⑨ ⑪

NEDERLAND

London

The ⑬
Thames

Rotterdam ⑩

Essen

Dortmund

Southampton

Bruxelles ⑫

Köln

Bonn

BUNDESREP.

English Channel

Strait of Dover

BELGIQUE

LUXEMBOURG

Frankfurt

DEUTSCHLAND

CHANNEL
ISLANDS

le Havre

la Seine ③

Brest

NORMANDIE

Nürnberg

BRETAGNE ①

le Mans

② Orléans

④ Paris

Nancy ⑤

Rhein

Stuttgart

München

Nantes

la Loire

⑥

Dijon

⑧ Zürich

FRANCE

BOURGOGNE

Bern

SCHWEIZ

Bozen

1. Brittany
2. Mayenne/ Sarthe
3. The Somme
4. Ile De France
5. Alsace/ Lorraine
6. Waterways of Burgundy
7. The Charente
8. Between Two Seas
9. Holland
10. The Randstad Cities
11. Friesland
12. Belgium
13. The Thames
14. Grand Union and Oxford Canal
15. The Norfolk Broads
16. The Fens
17. Leeds to Liverpool Canal
18. The Midlands/ Wales
19. Scotland
20. Irish Canals

⑦

Limoges

Clermont-
Ferrand

Lyon

ALPES

Milano

Bordeaux
GUYENNE

Golf of
Biscay

Garonne

⑧

Grenoble

Torino

ITALIA

Genova

Firenze

San
Sebastián

GASCOGNE

Toulouse

Nimes

Rhône

PROVENCE

Marseille

Pisa

PYRENEES

Zaragoza

ESPAÑA

Mediterranean

Sea

CORSE

Barcelona

CRUISING THROUGH EUROPE

Thomas Jefferson, an ambassador to France before he became the third President of the United States, was a man who was always ahead of his time. So it should come as no surprise that, almost 200 years before canal holidays became popular, he wrote to a friend, "You should not think of returning to America without taking the tour I have just taken." Jefferson was talking about France's Midi Canal, but his words could apply equally well to any part of Europe's inland waterway network.

Each country and waterway have their own special quality. Want to fish, try Ireland's Shannon River or Erne Waterway. Do cities enchant? Look no farther than the canals of London, Paris or Amsterdam. Ornithology a hobby? England's Norfolk Broads or France's Camargue come quickly to mind.

Wine? Burgundy, the Garonne and Bordeaux, or Champagne country are the answers. Cathedrals and history? England's River Thames or the Fens, the Ile de France, or Belgium are the obvious choices. Solitude? Brittany's Finistère Canal seems to be the most underpopulated waterway in France. Like to sail? Friesland in Holland and Scotland's Caledonian Canal have the right conditions.

And a canal journey is unique, offering the traveler several precious gifts: time, choice , and the opportunity to meet the locals.

Time and choice are of one package. What appeals? Spending an extra day in a place that attracts, or moving on? Overnighting in the shadow of a castle, or under a spreading tree? How glorious not to be shackled to a plane or train timetable!

But the most important advantage an inland waterways cruise can give is the unparallel opportunity to meet those who live along the rivers and canals. Because the total distance traveled during a cruise is so short, usually 50 miles (80km) or less, there is more opportunity to learn something about the people who live along them, and they about you.

Waterway folk are traditionally a welcoming crowd, and "boat" is a language spoken by everyone. A friendly "hello" when docking can help find the town's favorite restaurant. Later, sharing regional dishes and local wines can spark an evening's conversation, and help glean a greater understanding and knowledge of another culture. Morning means leaving newly-found friends, but also knowing that others may lie at the next lock or town. Best of all, each night brings a new location – without leaving "home".

Whether to help you choose, or, to guide you as you explore, these are the sights, the stops, the temptations, the treats, of cruising through Europe by boat.

Preceding pages: Amsterdam at night; Ireland's River Shannon by day; boats on the Llangollen, Wales; sunset over England's Great Ouse River.

FRANCE

Not only does France offer the familiar sybaritic delights of outstanding food and wine, it also has one of the world's most diverse waterway networks.

Will it be the southwest and a country cruise along Pierre Paul Riquet's masterpiece, the Canal du Midi, where the waterway twists and turns in a never-ending delight of landscapes and small villages. Or Burgundy, and a stately gavotte down one of three waterways, the Central, Yonne and Nivernais or Burdundy; with each offering a superb selection of wines, restaurants and rolling countryside. An even quieter change of pace is offered by the Mayenne and Sarthe where the only overnight visitors might be a herd of dairy cows.

But what, you may be asking, can compare with the excitement of sharing a waterway with the enormous *péniches* that carry cargoes up and down the Oise, Seine, and Somme rivers. Or, the Alsace-Lorraine, which offers an irrestible combination of French and German cuisine and architecture along with delightful waterway travel.

Rememberance of madness past is in France as well; the battlefields and cemeteries of two world wars are scattered throughout the Ile de France. But, so too are the vineyards of its champagnes, those effervescent reaffirmations of life and happy moments.

And Brittany. Thrust into the Atlantic, a part of France, yet not of it, its waterways offer windswept vistas, magnificient castles, and some of the friendliest waterside residents to be found in France.

Visit the cathedrals where the kings of France were crowned and buried; where Joan of Arc led her army against the hated English, and where those English once ruled in France. All this, and more, awaits the marine traveler.

Preceding pages: Angers' château overlooks the Maine; a helping hand with the lock. **Left,** Laval sits on the Mayenne River.

FROM THE MEDITERRANEAN TO THE ATLANTIC

From Mediterranean-facing Les Saintes-Maries-de-la-Mer to Bordeaux, where the Garonne meets the Atlantic-flowing Gironde, this beautiful land between two seas has welcomed visitors since earliest times. For the romantic sailor, the gentle breezes, bright sunshine, and the generally temperate climate have always been an irresistible lure. Fortunately, for the traveller who must fit the journey into a modern workaday world, it is an exploration which can be accomplished in small steps.

The landscape is diverse: sand dunes and salt marshes at one end, rolling hills and vineyards at the other. History, too, lives among the cobbled streets and narrow lanes of the region's small towns and large cities.

And the food. And the wine. The traveler cannot starve or die of thirst. Many of France's earthiest and most robust cuisines are found along these waters, and the wine ranges from hearty local *crus* to some of the finest vintages the country has on offer.

Le Petit Rhône: Those who enjoy stark beauty will certainly relish a journey down this 35-mile (57-km) lock-free stretch of water into the Camargue. (If renting a boat, check the contract and verify that it permits passage onto the **Petit Rhône**. Some companies get very nervous when their property is taken into rivers with tidal flows.) Although Le Petit commences just above Arles, the navigation markers can be confusing: they're measured from Lyon and match those on Le Grand Rhône.

The river scenery is not exciting: the treeless landscape is flat, reeds line the sometimes muddy banks. To avoid flooding, these are high, obscuring the view beyond.

Some sightseeing does exist: from **Albaron** (marked by a huge 16th-century tower), **Mas du Pont de Rousty** and its **Camargue Museum** are some 4 miles (6 km) away. Otherwise, there are

only five bridges and one cable ferry crossing to negotiate, and except for a few houses and the occasional fishermen nothing intrudes.

The pot at the end of this dubious rainbow is **Les Saintes-Maries-de-la-Mer**, a lively and historical town on the Mediterranean and the center of Camargue life. (To cruise into town means a short stretch of open sea; best to dock at the river's **Port Dromar** and bicycle the 3 miles/5 km. If staying the night, use pontoon moorings: water levels vary with the tides.)

Not content to name their town after one Mary, the City Fathers decided to triple-bless it by choosing three: first, Mary, the Virgin Mary's sister, also known as Marie Jacobé; the second was Marie Salome, mother of James and John; and finally Mary Magdalene (who really needs no introduction).

Why these three? All were present at the Crucifixion, and all, according to legend, lived for awhile in Stes-Maries. This story, first told in the 9th century, relates how the three women along with

Left, the Petit Rhône begins at Arles. **Right**, the "Round Lock" of Agde.

Mary Magdalene's siblings, Lazarus and Martha, and Saints Maximin and Sidonius plus a black servant named Sarah, left the Holy Land in a boat without any navigation aids or propellants. Miraculously, the group landed where Stes-Maries stands today, and to thank the Virgin for guarding their lives, built an oratory to her.

The group did not remain together: Martha found a home in Terascon, the two male saints headed for Aix, and Lazarus and Mary Magdalene ended up converting heathens at Ste Baume. Only the remaining Marys and Sarah stayed in Stes-Maries and when each died her remains were interred in the Oratory. Whether the story is legend or fact, it does not matter to the local inhabitants or to those who have made Stes-Maries a place of pilgrimage and pious belief throughout the centuries.

The steeple of the **church** (climb the ramparts for views over the Camargue) is visible from miles away. The present structure is of the 12th-century, replacing one built in the 9th. Romanesque in design and heavily fortified, from afar it could easily be mistaken for a military structure.

Inside the church, fierce imagery continues: statues of two lions which support the south porch are depicted gobbling up their kill. In the chancel, the capitals of the columns are carved in a variety of secular and religious themes. The north wall has niches hollowed into it; look for one containing the boat used during the pilgrimages, another holds a piece of marble known as the **Saint's Pillow**. In 1448, King René of Aix had the remains of the two Marys enshrined, and their reliquaries are in the upper chapel.

And what of Sarah? Her statue is in the crypt, surrounded by an ancient altar and reliquary. The gypsies of Provence adopted her as their patron saint, and every 23 May thousands gather from far and wide for the festival of the black Madonna, when a statue is carried into the sea surrounded by white horses.

There are two other pilgrimages during the year: on the next to last Sunday

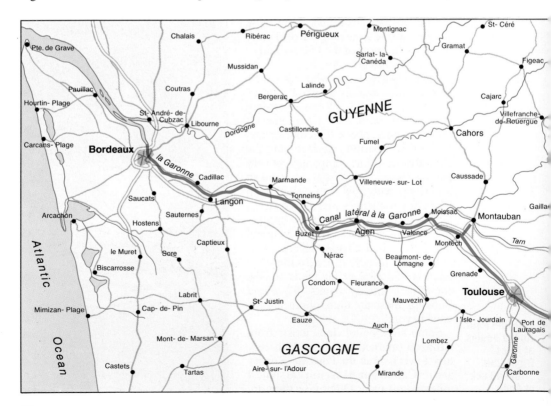

in October and on the first Sunday in December.

On the first night, the crypt is the scene for an all-night vigil. The next day a special mass is said for the Marys in front of their Reliquaries which have been lowered to the main altar. Then the saints' shrines and their statues are placed in the boat, and a procession of magnificently dressed celebrants takes it to the seashore. Floated into the water, the bishop blesses boat and sea. The final day is like a county fair; there are games and rides, dances, performances, and rodeo events and other displays of horsemanship.

Van Gogh visited Stes-Maries in 1888, and brought fame with his paintings of sail boats on the beach and impressions of the village. (One of these is in the Kroller-Muller Museum in Holland.) The **harbor** is still stacked with sailing (and motor) vessels of all sizes, working and pleasure. In the morning, watch the catch unloaded.

Unfortunately, innumerable *frites* stands, souvenir shops and glass-fronted hotels blot the town's seafront; but, a few streets from the water, good taste returns. Several stables offer tours on horseback, and the whitewashed stone cottages with their reed roofs are great to photograph.

The **Baroncelli Museum** (good views from its terrace) is devoted to the Camargue and its history. It's divided into 18 sections, each depicting a different facet of local life which range from a *ferrade* (rodeo) to a kitchen. The nearby **Etang de Vaccarès** forms the center of the Camargue National Reserve, and ornithologists will want to stop at **Pont de Grau Bird Sanctuary** (migration season brings a bonanza). Excursions can be arranged to other nearby *étangs* to see the herds of wild bulls and flamingoes which make the area their home.

Méjanes has an amusement park dedicated to Camargue farm life and an electric railway takes visitors through the countryside.

From Port Dromar, it's a 20-mile (33-km) cruise to Ecluse St Gilles and the short Rhône transfer canal.

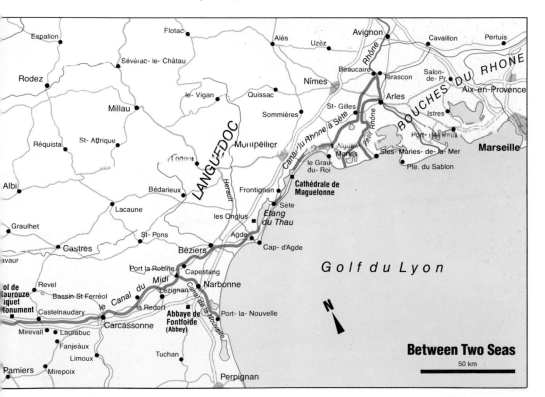

Between Two Seas

50 km

Le Canal du Rhône à Sète: One delight of this 60-mile (98-km) long canal is the absence of locks! There's only one: Nourriguier, 5 miles (8 km) from Beaucaire. Junctions are made at St Gilles lock with Le Petit Rhône, and the Mediterranean is accessed through Le Grau du Roi, and other small canals. Beyond Sète, a further 11 miles (18 km) across the Etang de Thau from Séte, and the Canal du Midi arrives.

The Rhône à Sète generally traverses a wilderness graced only by vineyards, vegetable fields and vast salt lakes interspersed with small towns of historical interest. This voyage will bring memories of sunsets over the Etangs, walking a medieval wall, umbrella pines lining the distant shore, and hours of lovely solitude.

The earliest form of canal was dug here during the late 17th century when channels were dredged from the Etang de Thau towards Aigues-Mortes. Originally the canal was named Canal des Etangs, more than a century of to-ing and fro-ing occurred before a plan was adopted in the 1770s to build a another section from Aigues-Morte to the Rhône at Beaucaire. During the Revolution work stopped, but by 1800 work had recommenced, and when finished some 10 years later, the canal was given its current name.

The lack of railroads in this area meant that commercial barge traffic remained fairly constant over the years, and as late as 1974 over 250,000 tons were carried on the waterway. Four years later, in 1978, this had shrunk to 22,000 tons and when freight haulage climbed to 70,000 tons in the early 1980s, it was hoped that with improved waterways and dredging, the tonnage could be maintained or increased.

For the vacationer, this is mixed news: although increased commercial traffic means more of the black monsters jockeying for space on the canal, it also means increased revenues with which to maintain the waterway.

Where the Rhône flows between Tarascon and Beaucaire, medieval castles stand sentinel on each side of the **Tarascon's castle dates from the 12th century.**

river. (During the years of conflict between France and the Holy Roman Empire, and when the Rhône was a boundary between them, the helmsman's cry might not only save a ship from the shoals, but also keep it safe from enemy capture. Instead of the standard port and starboard calls, the cry became "Empire" and "Kingdom".)

To the west of the bridge, mostly hidden behind flood walls, sits **Beaucaire**, beginning (or end) of the canal. (Until the mid-1970s a lock allowed access from the Rhône into the canal here, but when the river levels altered, the locking system had to be changed and now the transit point is located further south off the Petit Rhône near the town St Gilles.)

Beaucaire is a town of arches and hidden courtyards, flower pots on every window sill and terrace, a place tucked away from the world. Yet a glance at a map shows Beaucaire near enough to Arles, Avignon and Nimes to make it a sightseeing base (trains from the local station or Tarascon's). The old narrow

White thatched-houses are a Camargue tradition.

streets are fun to explore; there's a friendly atmosphere, and part of the fun of docking in the marina is the possibility of finding a working barge moored alongside at night.

Now a forgotten backwater, Beaucaire was once one of the major river ports, with ships bringing and taking goods to and from Mediterranean and Atlantic cities. So great was its reputation that each July the city was host to one of the largest fairs in Europe. Over 300,000 people would descend upon it; vendors set up booths throughout the town and on ships anchored in the river. A carnival was positioned on ground between the castle and the river; performers, human and animal, provided the entertainment.

The fair died out in the 19th century, a victim of changing times. At the **Museum of Old Beaucaire**, memories of the "good old days" are on display, and each Ascension Day, a smaller version of the fair is celebrated.

Cardinal Richelieu had the **castle** of Beaucaire (and many others) destroyed

in the 1630s, and only its 11th-century walls (it's possible to walk partially around them) remain. Inside the gates the Romanesque **chapel** sports a carved tympanun and a twin-bayed belfry. A climb to the top of the **Triangle Tower** allows views of Beaucaire, Tarascon, and the pine and cypress-shaded children's playground below.

The 10th-century frieze on the outside of **Notre Dame des Pommiers** (Our Lady of the Appletrees) is awkwardly situated, making it hard to study the figures. Inside, the 18th-century domed church is unremarkable.

Legend has it that in the Middle Ages, **Tarascon** was terrorised by a half-fish, half-dragon monster known as the *tarasque*. It lived in a cave along the riverbank, devouring children and livestock. Those trying to row across the river were at risk, too, and the city was shunned like one in the grip of a plague. According to legend, all was made well when St Martha killed the beast with a traditional sign of the cross.

In 1474, King René of Aix started a festival to commemorate this miracle, and today, a model of the grotesque creature is trundled about the town during a festival held on the last Sunday in June.

Terascon's **castle** was started in the 12th century, but not finished until the 15th. Once seat of the Dukes of Anjou, Counts of Provence, and Kings of Naples and Sicily, it went to Louis XI in 1481 when he inherited the province. After the Revolution, the castle served as a state prison until 1926.

Restored to its former glory, square towers connect walls which rise 150 ft (48 meters) above the Rhône. A **seigneurial lodge** sits inside them, its ceilings vaulted and decorated. A climb to the **terrace** is rewarded with magnificent views up and down the river valley. **St Marthe's** chruch is near the castle; the vastly restored building originated in the 12th century and the saint's crypt is in her name-chapel.

Would-be Camargue cowboys and Nimes matadors should visit the milkbar across the road from the castle. All the paraphernalia necessary to look like one of the real things are for sale inside.

St Gilles, 15 dreary miles (24 km) from Beaucaire and a western gateway to the Camargue, was once a major seaport, visited by ships from all parts of the Mediterranean; now only pleasure boats and the occasional barge pass through town. There's a wine processing plant to visit near the tarted-up waterfront and most of the restaurants feature the local speciality, *boeuf à la gardiane*, (a casserole of beef cooked in red wine).

The town derives its origins from an 8th-century legend. St Gilles, giving up a pampered life in Greece, sailed aimlessly through the Mediterranean, ending up in Provence. Gilles's only friend in his new environment was a deer; one day while man and beast were together in the forest, a hunting party stalked the pair. Gilles saved the deer from the arrow of a Visogoth king; the king, moved by the devotion of Gilles to the animal, offered to build an abbey on the spot. Gilles agreed.

Gilles then traveled to Rome, hoping

The flags are for marking nets below water.

to persuade the Pope to recognize the abbey. The prelate's gift was two enormous doors which Gilles launched down the Tiber. Lo and behold, they floated into St Gilles just as the saint arrived overland.

The atrocities of the Albigensian Crusade had their beginnings in 1209 when the Papal Legate was assassinated in front of the Abbey's doors. Any destruction not wrought during this period was continued during the Wars of Religion in the 1500s with the Revolutionists getting their turn to wreak further havoc in the 1790s.

The **west front** is the reason to visit; this superb example of Provençal- Romanesque art was carved between 1180 and 1240, and the facades of the three doors feature scenes from the life of Christ. The 12th-century **crypt** in the 17th to 19th-century church holds St Gilles' tomb.

Tables await customers in Aigues-Mortes.

Just beyond town is the lock of the same name which leads to the Petit Rhône. From here to Aigues-Mortes it's a straight and narrow run; the **Etangs de Scamandre**, **de Grey**, and **du Charnier** are visible in the distance, and at **Gallician**, the tower of Aigues-Mortes comes into view. During the migration season, this area is mobbed by birds and ornithologists.

Also in this marshy, delta area are many side canals which drift off the main route. Some are short-cuts between major navigations, but most are for irrigation purposes and very narrow. Their sometimes abrupt dead ends may preclude turning around. Any wise navigator who plans an adventure off the known routes is advised to have a complete set of charts.

Cruising into **Aigues-Mortes** is like sailing into the Middle Ages. Approached via the long, straight canal, the fortified city slowly rises from the coastal plain, its walls reflected in the calm waters. Meaning "dead waters", the Roman town of Aquae Mortuae probably got its name because of the marshpools and lagoons in the vicinity.

Located on the western border of the Camargue, it was once a thriving sea-

port; now, however, Aigue sits 3 miles (5 km) inland, a lonely sentinel surrounded by salt flats and marshes.

Louis IX was responsible for the **Tour de Constance**; it was built to protect the harbor and town, departure point for his 1248 and 1270 Crusades. (The first was marginally more successful than the disastrous second. Fighting in Egypt, the King was captured and ransomed; after marching to Palestine, he was marched out, and returned to France in 1254. Undaunted, St Louis tried again, but he died of plague at Tunis and never saw France again.)

The tower was begun in 1241, finished seven years later, and is 107 ft (33 meters) high with walls 23 ft (seven meters) thick. From the top are views toward the distant Cévennes Mountains. The **St Louis Chapel** is reached via a spiral staircase.

The **Knight's Hall** was used more as prison for the King's foes than home for his defenders. Many distinguished people were incarcerated here; one devout Huguenot, Marie Durand, lived in the

room between 1730 and 1768. Note the huge oven in the Guard's Room.

The **ramparts** are of later kingships, those of Philip the Bold and Philip the Fair, and were constructed between 1272 and 1300. It's possible to walk around the outside of the 36-ft (11-meter) high walls which link five main towers, and numerous half-towers. A limited number of gates are there to relieve the long lines of stone. The resulting fortress forms a rectangle with a grid-like pattern of streets. (Some interior rampart walking is possible but only for short stretches.)

In the **main square** is a statue of St Louis by Jacques Pradier, and the restaurants surrounding it serve the local delicacy, *moules*, in a variety of ways. A **Musée Municipal** contains a small collection of local artifacts.

Five miles (8 km) down the **Canal Maritime** is an afternoon's excursion to seaside **Le Grau du Roi**. Entering its busy Port du Pêche one cannot mistake the town's role: commercial marinas and dry docks outnumber pleasure facilities. The picturesque fishing town is noted for its *bouillabaisse*; it's possible to dock alongside one of the many canal-side restaurants, but lack of space makes overnight moorings hard to find.

This is part of France's "other Riviera", a resort for the less wealthy, but for those who still want a Mediterranean holiday. Stretching out on either side of Le Grau like the tentacles of an octopus are an astounding number of oddly-shaped and ugly hotels. The ubiquitous funfair provides additional diversion and a nearby bull-fighting arena offers that spectacle. (The bull is unharmed.)

Boats with a draft of less than 4 ft (1.2 meters) and headroom of no more than 6 ft (1.8 meters) can avoid returning to Aigues-Mortes by traveling to the Canal du Rhône à Sète via the **Vidoule River**. Entry to the canal is controlled by traffic lights and guillotine gates.

The medieval joy of Aigues-Mortes offers no prepartion for the next few distressing miles. To one side is **Etang de Mauguio Ou de L'Or**; on the other a series of completed, almost completed and contemplated apartment/hotel sites, **Graphic signs in the Midi.**

60

a highway connecting all. Speed quickly past. **Caron** and **Palavas** do, however, offer access to the sea by boat and **Montpellier** by land.

Beyond Palavas, a treat: the concrete-banked canal is a separate ribbon, floating on its own through an open body of water with pine tree covered dunes to the left offering protection from the ocean's waves. Some of the loveliest beaches are here; rough tracks make road access difficult, and nudists will enjoy the areas set aside for them.

On this delicious bit of water is **Maguelonne**, site of a Phoenician port dating from the 2nd century. Like many ancient cities, it has seen a parade of masters who destroyed and rebuilt: Romans, Saracens, Protestants, Catholics, and so on. Richelieu disestablished the cathedral in 1622, and all that remains today is the former cathedral, a 19th-century restoration of a Romanesque-Gothic building. To visit, dock near the **Arc de Triomphe**, a lonely miniature of the large one in Paris.

Race through **Frontignan** and its belching oil refineries. The center also of Muscat wine, the vineyards must only survive because of their more inland position.

Sète, dominated by **Mont St Clair** with **Fort Richelieu** perched on top, is noted for its setting rather than historic buildings. The town got its leg up in the world when it was chosen (after the usual political wrangles) to be the eastern terminus of the Canal du Midi. Colbert, Louis XIV's finance minister, provided the money and engineering was by Pierre-Paul Riquet.

In the 19th century, a basin and access canal for seagoing vessels were dug, making Sète a major French port (on the Mediterranean, it's second only to Marseilles). Tuna and sardines are the primary catch, and oyster beds are on the nearby Etang de Thau.

The **Old Port** beckons those in search of local color and restaurants. With the elegant, honey-colored houses bordering it, the port is a very quaint place. The poet, Paul Valéry made the **Sailor's Cemetery** famous; his grave lies there

Water seeps through a lock gate as grass grows on its inside.

now, and the **museum** contains a room of Valéry memorabilia; also a fine collection of Impressionist paintings. An **Aquarium** is at Station Biologique.

Jouets Nautiques is held here (as in other French towns) every summer. This is a medieval jousting contest between costumed young men of the area, in which boats are the steeds. The craft are elaborately painted and decorated; flags and banners float from every prow, brass bands play. As the boats are rowed towards each other, each side tries to unseat the other. The last dry participant is the winner.

Getting in and out of Sète can be confusing; do not deviate from channel markings. Transient space is limited; try for one at **Société Nautique** in the **Vieu Bassin** (all facilities).

Crossing the **Etang de Thau** can be intimidating. Once a lagoon, it's now only separated from the Mediterranean by a large sandbar called **Le Toc**. Over 20,000 acres (8,000 hectares) of water with a circumference of 34 miles (55 km), it's lined with a succession of small towns with attractive harbors.

Some words of warning: constantly shifting shoals make depth markers almost obsolete; boats which draw more than 3 feet (1 meter) will have to visit some of these towns by other transport. Until the wind blows, the Thau is a peaceful waterway, but because it's shallow, the water is whipped up faster than other places. On the western side, the income-producing shellfish beds must be avoided.

Balaruc-les-Bains sits at the tip of a peninsula on a direct line from Sète; a small resort, it has the only skin-diving center in the Thau. **Bouzigues** is an old fishing village with white-washed stone houses, **Mèze** is a lively and colorful town with a protected port.

Marseillan is noted for its oysters and the *aperitif* Noilly-Pratt, a blend of Languedoc wines and something else known only to the management. Cellars are quay-side; visitors are always welcome. **Les Onglous**, beginning of the Canal du Midi, is little over a mile's straight cruise from here.

A lockkeeper's daughter.

Le Canal du Midi: Pierre-Paul Riquet, the designer and planner who inspired the Canal du Midi, did not live to see the opening of his masterpiece. He died in 1680, less than six months before its inauguration, almost bankrupt from pouring his own money into the project. This celebrated canal, however, (probably the most popular in France), remains as his enduring legacy to the world.

But this magnificent creation took a long time in arriving. The Roman Tacitus first described the possibility of a canal linking the Mediterranean and the Atlantic, and early kings of France wanted an inland waterway to by-pass unfriendly territories found along the route. The landscape was even more unfriendly, and baffled a series of astute designers and engineers – including Leonardo da Vinci, who discussed the project with François I in 1516.

Before that, in the 8th century, Charlemagne made the first recorded survey; then Charles IX and Henri IV were frustrated in their desires to build the canal. After François I, Louis VIII had preliminary engineering specifications drawn to no avail.

What the great Leonardo could not accomplish, an unknown inspector of salt taxes, Baron Bonrepos (Pierre-Paul Riquet, an engineer by avocation only) finally did. Riquet was born to a family of modest background; an auspicious marriage at 19 gained him enough wealth to purchase the Bonrepos estate and title. The origin of Riquet's obsession with the Canal du Midi is lost to history, but he became a man possessed. The canal project became such an *idée fixe* that Riquet began spending enormous sums of his own money on surveys and models.

The completion of the Briare Canal linking the Loire and Seine Rivers in 1646 convinced Riquet that a canal of many levels was possible, and that his waterway, originally called *Canal des Deux Mers* (Canal of Two Seas), might become reality.

One problem still perplexed: a secure and constant water supply. The Midi

Sewing in the lockside sunshine.

had wet winters, and spring rains could flood any canal, yet prolonged summer droughts which could leave the canal bereft of water, were common. A ditch could be dug, but a ditch without water is not a canal.

During revenue-collecting travels, Riquet made a series of surveys of the lakes and streams above the proposed waterway. A central area where water could flow east and west, and be held or dispersed to the canal as needed was necessary.

A natural basin did not exist so one would have to be built. St Ferréol, north-west of Castelnaudary was finally chosen, and more models were crafted. (When finished, St Ferréol was the largest irrigation project of its time, and the reservoir, covering 170 acres/70 hectares, was created by an earth-filled dam 2,600-ft/800-meters long, over 100-ft/30-meters high, and 450-ft/138-meters thick at the base.)

As wealthy as he was, Riquet did not have the funds to complete the canal alone. Money – lots of it – was needed,

and for this, he first approached Boulmont, Archbishop of Toulouse in 1662. The churchman inspected the models built on Riquet's estate along with the preliminary plans and drawings. Boulmont turned towards the Crown; Louis XIV's finance minister, Colbert, was impressed. This waterway would complement the planned naval port in Rochefort (at the mouth of the Charente on the Atlantic), giving ships a faster and safer way of traveling between it and Toulon on the Mediterranean.

In October 1666 a Royal Charter was granted and Le Canal Royale du Languedoc company was formed. The waterway would run from the River Garonne at Toulouse to Agde and then to Sète via a channel across the Etang du Thau. The Central Government, the Languedoc Local Authority, and Riquet became the financers with profits to come from future canal tolls.

Le Canal Royal was to be another star in the the already crowded crown of Le Roi Soleil; in other words, money was no object. The lack of any income for

Signs on each lockhouse indicate distance to the next one.

many years did not seem to worry Colbert, who poured countless francs into the ditch and by 1672 the waterway was navigable eastward from Toulouse for 30 miles (50 km).

But 1677 produced a different thought: the Crown, dismayed by delays and escalating costs, finally decided to call it a day, and withdrew all state funding. Undeterred, Riquet, who was now a man of 73, continued to pour his own money into the waterway; fatigue, mounting debt and frustration killed him in October 1680.

Riquet was buried with honors in Toulouse's cathedral. His waterway opened on 15 May 1681, and is still in operation over 300 years later. His vision, his drive, his obsession, transformed the southwest of France: the benefits from increased trade and modern tourism cannot be measured.

Sadly, the only real losers were the Riquet family. They made no money on the canal until 1724, and with the French Revolution in 1789, lost their rights to any future revenue.

In 1834, steam tugs started hauling trains of barges, and by 1838 there were over 270 vessels regularly working on the Midi. In the 1840s a steam voyage only took four days between Sète and Toulouse; when night passage was allowed, the non-stop journey could be made in just 36 hours.

Because of the vagaries of the Garonne River, sea-going vessels have never plied the Midi. The opening of the Canal Latéral à la Garonne in 1856 partially solved the problem; but by then, the railways and bigger ships had arrived, making the original purpose of the Midi obsolete.

The railroads stopped whatever progress might have continued. By a quirk of fate, the Toulouse-Bordeaux connection was opened the same year as the Latéral. Big business being big business, the railroad negotiated a lease in 1857 allowing them control over the Midi and Latéral Canals. Benign neglect became the policy, and both waterways went into a severe financial and physical decline.

When the pact expired in 1898 and the State resumed control, repairs were made and tolls were abolished in order to increase traffic. Tonnage has fluctuated through the 20th century; usually toward the minus side. Few commercial barges remain; many have been reborn as floating hotels.

Little has changed on the canal in the 300 years since its inception. The most promising recent event happened in 1978 when a program of lock lengthening was announced. When finished, the new locks would allow passage of the standard 123-ft (38-meter) long commercial French barges instead of the current 95-ft (30-meter) Midi limits. Sadly, little has been accomplished since then.

Two outstanding engineering feats still amaze: the seven-tier Fonseranne locks outside Béziers and the Malpas tunnel just beyond them. The world's first water tunnel, the "Mal", at 542 ft (167 meters) is minute when compared to others, but before its construction, skeptics doubted it would work. Both lock and tunnel advanced the body of canal-building knowledge and made the

Capestang's St Etienne church beckons through the trees.

creation of other waterways through equally impossible terrain possible.

Scenically, the Canal du Midi offers something for everyone: beaches and marshland, rolling hills covered with vineyards or grain, somnolent villages of grey stone and black slate, wild iris and cultivated geraniums decorate waterside and gardens, and south of the plane tree-shaded waterway, the snow-capped Pyrénées are usually in view. (These plane trees with which the canal is forever associated, and which provide a shady tunnel, were not planted for aesthetic reasons: their root system keeps the banks from eroding, and their leaves reduce evaporation by keeping direct sunlight from the water.)

Although the lock-houses are all similar (built to a single standard by Riquet), each is as different inside as the owners, and decorated accordingly. In summer the locks are kept open seven days a week, and the tow path is generally in good shape although some stretches are in need of repair.

The lighthouse at **Les Onglous**, 150 miles (240 km) and 99 locks from Toulouse, marks the Midi's official beginning, but ask most locals where they think it starts and the answer will be the **Ecluse Ronde**. The round lock of **Agde** isn't truly round any more – a recent enlargement made it a semi-oval – but the name has stuck. This lock (five miles/nine km through marsh and reed from Les Onglous) is equipped with three pairs of gates: two are for through-canal transit, the third gives access to the **Hérault River**, Agde (facilities available) and the Mediterranean. Not wanting to leave the canal, moor just beyond the Round Lock; the marina is a 10-minute walk from Agde.

The Greek *Agathe*, (which means good fortune) matches its name; founded in the 6th century by Phoenicians, Agde is a charming town with hilly, narrow streets climbing from the waterfront. The 12th-century **Cathedral of St Etienne** is built of volcanic rock; local artifacts and underwater archaeological treasures are found at **Musée Agathois**, and a statue on the quayside celebrates **Rent it yourself or…**

the city's love affair with water. The Thursday market, held under the cathedral's squat tower, is a great place to provision.

Nudist beaches are near **Cap d'Agde**; those more inhibited will discover compatible areas, too. **Le Grau-d'Agde** is the fishing port; those wanting local color will find it enchanting.

The journey towards Béziers begins inauspiciously: flat, rather dull countryside. Relief arrives with the **River Libron** crossing. This curious arrangement of sluice gates was devised because the countryside's lack of elevation prevented construction of a proper aqueduct over the river.

Port Cassafières is a purpose-built marina with all services; a beach is about a mile away. **Villeneuve** has more easily reached provisioning than hilltop Béziers. The scenery starts to change as the windswept Camargue is left in the boat's wake; the ubiquitous plane trees begin to shade the waterway, and rolling hills replace marshland.

The **Cathedral of St Nazaire** is

...join others on a hotel barge.

Béziers' beacon. Romans called the town *Baeterrae Septimanorum* and their Seventh Legion called it home. Pierre-Paul Riquet was born here, and wine and tourism are today's principal income producers.

The first atrocity of the Albigensian Crusade took place in front of the cathedral in 1209. Pope Innocent III, angered by the heretical preaching of the Cathares (from the Greek *catharos* meaning clean) who differed from strict Catholic dogma, used the slaying of his Legate in St Gilles *(see page 58)* to order the destruction of the cathedral. More than 25,000 townspeople were slaughtered here, both believers and non-believers. When asked why no distinction had been made between the two factions, the Catholic reply was supposed to have been: *Tuez les touts; Dieu reconnaîtra les siens.* (Kill them all; God will recognize his own.)

The essence of Catharian doctrine was a belief in reincarnation and the double rejection of the Old Testament and Christ as deity. The strictest adher-

ents spurned the world, living on a diet consisting of non-sexually produced food (no meats, eggs, etc).

The movement began in Abli (an hour's drive north of Toulouse, hence the name); at first the Roman Catholic church ignored the heretics, but as the winds of change blew through the Languedoc, the pope felt the blasphemers had to be stopped, and declared an internal Crusade. Simon IV de Montfort was the leader of a covey of greedy barons (hungry for new property?), bishops and other assorted thugs and bullies who pillaged, plundered and devastated the countryside.

Montfort was killed in the siege of Toulouse in 1218, but that didn't stop the carnage. Louis VII finally did, by leading his army south, placing trusted generals as seneschals in major cities. A treaty was signed in 1229, Languedoc was annexed to France, and by 1244 the last stronghold of Albigensian resistance, Montségur, fell after a long siege, although the Inquisition continued its devilish work until the late 1250s.

The present structure is 13th-century; inside, the 15th-century rose window is very impressive. From the nearby parapets are views of the **Orbs River**. Incorporated into the font of 13th-century **St Aphrodise** is part of a Roman sarcophagus. The bronze figure of Christ is by a local artist, Injalbert.

Musée des Beaux Arts, in **Hôtel Fabregut**, has the usual painting and sculpture collections. **Musée du Vieux Biterrois et du Vin** offers intriguing displays of Greco-Roman antiquities, local ethnology, and viticulture.

Riquet's statue is on his name street, a broad plane tree-shaded boulevard; on Friday, the weekly market spreads out along the wide center divider. An amphitheater is less than a mile from it; Nimes-style bull fights are held here.

Beyond moorings at Béziers' **Port Neuf** (services available) lies **Pont-Canal sur Orb** which was opened in 1857 replacing an earlier, less reliable transit of the river. As the boat glides across the aqueduct, and before it enters the **Fonserrane staircase locks'** basin,

The lake of Montady seen from the Oppidium d'Ensérune.

take a last look back at Béziers. The seven-lock chain is perhaps the best known engineering feature of Riquet's canal. The total rise (or fall) is over 43 ft (13 meters); up and down movements take place during designated hours (check locally for time), and a late arrival means an overnight stop at the locks.

During the early 1980s a waterslope was built adjacent to the present "steps". Based on the design of the one at Montech *(see page 81)*, it consists of a concrete flume on a five-degree slope. Barges are intended to be floated into a large water-filled tub which will be pulled up or pushed down the slope by two electric engines. Unfortunately, this marvel of engineering has not been used to date because of some missing essential parts.

At the top of the stairs, **Le Grand Bief**, a 33-mile (54-km) lockless run begins. The longest canal reach in France is a twisting, turning stretch of water where every curve brings a change in scenery.

Colombiers has a delightful ambience, and many feel it ranks among the top three places on the canal; certainly, in springtime the horse chestnut trees add a special feeling. Note the old arched bridge with its attendant *lavoir* (laundry stone). The **château** is now a restaurant; its old **stables** housed the barge-towing horses. It was known as a *relais* (relay point) because barge owners changed pulling teams here.

Malpas Tunnel is associated with several legends; one asserts it was completed in six days in order to meet a financial deadline. Perhaps this is where the tunnel got its name: *mal* (bad) and *pas* (pass).

The **Oppidum d'Ensérune** (dock along the canal bank below it – there's a breath-taking walk to it, and wonderful views) was an Iberian-Greek city founded during the 6th century BC and some columns and house foundations are open to view. The **Archaeology Museum** contains a magnificent collection of pre-Roman antiquities. The curious land formation below and to the north is the drained **lake of Montady**;

Vineyards of the Minervois.

the drains form an unusual pattern, radiating out from the center. The result looks something like a sliced pie with none of the pieces removed.

On approaching **Capestang**, the spires of 14th-century **St Etienne** are first seen through the trees; its stained-glass windows depict Biblical scenes and the prophets. Tuesdays, Thursdays and Saturdays are market days.

The canal now goes into a frenzy of S curves, Z curves and sundry variations, at one time almost doubling back on itself. Nearing **Port La Robine** brings a respite, but only barely. (The Canal de la Robine heads south from here.) Vauban designed the **Pont-Canal sur la Cresse** aqueduct in 1686 to replace a less successful river crossing.

Le Someil is another of the Midi's prettiest villages; now home to three restaurants, one of them reputedly aiming for national recognition. Several artists have set up studios in the old ivy-covered houses; permanently moored boats make an attractive counterpoint, and there's adequate transient mooring

space. On the south bank, a bookstore caters to bibliophiles with a dusty selection of new, used and out-of-print books, old maps and other publications about the canal and the Midi.

The oldest canal aqueduct on the Midi is the **Pont-Canal sur la Répudre**. Built in 1676, the 35-ft (11-meter) span carries the canal over this tributary of the Aude in a U-turn. The charming town of **Paraza** with its small château then comes into view.

Ecluse d'Argens marks the end of lockless cruising, and the beginning of a series of locks that are fairly close together, including a right-angle turn between **Ecluse Garde de la Ognon** and the double **Ecluses d'Ognon**.

Many also claim that hilltop-situated **Argens-Minervois** is the most charming village on the Midi. If not, it comes close to it. An old château dominates; originally built by the Bishop of Narbonne, it looks as deserted as the village. If electric wires didn't run into each stone house, it could all be transported 200 years into the past.

Left, 17th-century carvings on a Market Square building. **Below**, the cemetery of Carcassonne.

Homps is not very attractive nor very distinguished but it's possible to fill both boat and stomach. From here it's a little over 7 miles (12 km) north to the fortress village of Minerve. The ride, through the rolling vineyard-filled hills is mostly up, meaning it's easier coming home. (Taxis are available for the faint of heart.)

From afar, **Minerve** can't be seen. Has the journey been for naught? Stopping at the viewpoint near the town, one finds there is much ado about something. The town perches on top of an enormous rock, a honey-golden island amid vineyards. Entrance is through one of two bridges; fortifications date from the 12th century, which during the Albigensian Crusade helped to successfully defend Minerve during sieges. The **church** and **museum** are interesting; photographers should note that the town is ideally an afternoon picture.

La Redort offers facilities and overnight anchorage; the canal's half-way point comes near **Marseillette**. Approaching **Trèbes** is a three-rise lock.

La Cité rises above the vineyards.

Beyond the town is the **Orbiel Canal Bridge**, a 1686 addition to the canal's original design, and the 113-ft (35-meters) span has been declared a national monument.

After **Ecluse Evèque** come the early 19th-century **Fresquel locks** and **aqueduct**. When the Midi was about to become a reality, those cities which wanted to be "on line" had to pay for this privilege. Carcassonne's citizens were either too cheap or shortsighted to do so, and the canal followed the Fresquel River away from the town.

Only when other waterway towns started making money did Carcassonne's leaders change their mind. But it was too late, and the 3-mile (5-km) deviation to the town which starts here didn't open until 1810.

After one passes **Ecluse de St Jean** and the avenue of cypress trees surrounding it, **Carcassonne** is little over a mile away. Moorings (all facilities) are near the train station, and it's a 10 to 15-minute walk across the **Aude River** and uphill to La Cité.

In the years following Viollet-le-Duc's restoration of **La Cité**, there has been a constant murmur of protest: does this neo-Gothic 19th-century fairy-tale castle represent the true soul of the original? In the end, perhaps it doesn't really matter. This uniquely spectacular, romantic, skyline-dominating fortress with more than 50 towers and 3 miles (5 km) of walls is France's largest walled medieval city, and without peer in the country, perhaps also in Europe.

From a distance, the scale of this splendid city is breathtaking; it rises from a sea of vineyards, a double ring of walls with black slate roofed conical towers thrusting into the Languedoc sky. Even on a day of pouring rain, the sight never fails to stir, and at night when the walls are illuminated, they can be seen from miles away.

Occupied by the Romans, who made it an important stop on their trade routes, Carcaso was a busy town before the 1st century BC. The Visogoths arrived in the 5th century, building the first defensive walls. Charlemagne and the Franks took Carcassonne in the 8th century, and then came the Counts of Toulouse, who continued the fortifications which mark the city today.

Carcassonne saw much devastation during the Albigensian Crusade (Simon de Montfort headquartered here). The Ville Basse (lower town) was built by Louis IX; the Black Prince burnt it down in 1355. Two Philips, the Bold and the Fair, rebuilt most of the fortifications between 1270 and the early 1300s.

Until the Treaty of the Pyrénées, Carcassonne was the southernmost border boundary of France; when peace with Spain came in 1659, and a fortress was no longer required, homes were created using stones from the walls. As the population grew, the wall decreased in size, and it wasn't until the 19th century that Viollet-le-Duc was hired to restore La Cité.

Enter La Cité through one of **two gates**, the **Narbonne** or **Aude**. Clustered along the cobbled streets (where parking is reserved for residents' cars only) are homes of the fewer than 500

The Grand Basin of Castelnaudary.

residents. Wander to the **Château Comtal**; its **Musée de la Cité** includes local artifacts and costumes of the medieval and Renaissance periods.

The **ramparts** offer views of **Ville Basse**, the **Pyrénées** and the **Montagne Noire**; walking between the two sets of walls (the lists) gives an idea of their construction and defense capabilities. The **Basilica of St Nazaire** has beautiful rose windows; count the statues in the Gothic choir: there should be 22.

On the downside, there are endless souvenir stands, *crêperies*, cafés, and wine tasting shops where the local Corbières wines may be sampled. Down the hill from La Cité, Ville Basse's thrice weekly market adds much to shopping ease.

Before sailing, consider an excursion along **La Route Dominicaine** to **Montréal**, **Fangeaux**, **Laurabue**, and **Mireval**. It's too far to bicycle; rent a taxi and take a day to explore the area where a young Spanish priest, Domingo de Guzman, stood firm in his orthodox Christian beliefs amid a sea of Dualism. He braved the Albigensian heretics by living among them in Fangeaux, and spent the years from 1206 to 1216 trying to reconvert the local population to the real faith. His singular belief was dually rewarded: his name is carried by the Dominican Order and he was eventually canonized.

The countryside offers vistas in all directions, the villages have half-timbered houses and ancient churches.

Between Carcassonne and Castelnaudary the canal rises 123 ft (38 meters) in fewer than 6 miles (10 km) along countless curves. The towns are farther from the waterway; for companionship, the 15 lock-keepers on this stretch will more than make up for the lack of villages.

To visit **Pezens**, tie up just beyond the bridge. Walk the half mile or so to the church of **St Madeleine**; its choir and apse are 10th-century. **Villesequelande** sits behind a vineyard. There's an ancient church with a cluster of typical Midi houses around it.

The **Grand Bassin of Castelnaudary** is approached through the four-rise **Ecluse St Roch**. Opened in 1673, it was originally designed by Riquet as a harbor for barges and a water supply for the locks. Today, however, the Bassin is synonymous with the Canal du Midi. Entering the harbor on a late summer's day with the sun shining on the white-washed houses around it is even a non-photographer's dream.

For a peaceful looking place, "Castel", has seen a great deal of turbulent history: it was besieged during the Albigensian Crusade; the English Black Prince set fire to it almost 150 years later in 1355; in the 1630s the local governor, Duc Henri de Montmorency, led an uprising of noblemen who felt Louis XIII's brother Gaston d'Orléans would be a better king. Richelieu thought otherwise, and the governor was eventually captured here.

Walk up the hill past the 14th-century **St Michel church**; just beyond it is **Moulin de Cugarel**, last of the breed that once populated the plains below. A **Museum of Pharmacology** is in **St Jacques Hospital**. Food-wise, the town is known throughout France as the birth-

place of *cassoulet* a dish of beans, sausage, lamb, and spices, simmered for several days in an earthenware pot. A huge Monday market gives much choice of supplies.

From Castelnaudary, the **Bassin de St Ferréol** the great reservoir which forms the canal's water supply is about an hour's drive north. It's a recreational area, and certainly a mecca for locals in the summer.

Leaving Castelnaudary one enters an agricultural area, and from here to Toulouse, towns are not, with rare exceptions, canal-side. Supplies are harder to get although some of the lock-keepers will have provisions to sell from their gardens or vineyards; a general rule is to stock up whenever a shop appears along the way.

At **Ecluse de la Méditerranée**, look for an old potter's workshop near the lock, and at **Le Ségala**, note the washing stones near the bridge. Cruising toward the summit lock, the **obelisk** ahead on the right is a memorial to Pierre-Paul Riquet. Just before the lock is **Col de**

Naurouza, one of the first reservoirs designed by Riquet. The stream flowing into it is **Rigole de la Plaine** which carries water from Ferréol. **Ecluse de l'Océan** marks the canal's summit, 624 ft (192 meters) above sea level. It's a short reach of less than 2 miles (3 km) before the descent begins.

Port Lauragais is a multi-purpose rest stop. Autoroute travellers can use it as well as boats travelling on the Midi. Of particular interest is the **Centre Pierre-Paul Riquet**, a museum devoted to the canal and its builder; the multimedia exhibit devotes most of its space to Riquet, but others who worked on the canal's development are featured, too. The cafeteria serves mediocre regional cuisine; the bookstore sells only French language publications.

Moor at **Ecluse de Renneville** to visit **Avignonet**; although the Languedoc church tower is the only reminder, this sleepy village saw great violence during the Albigensian Crusade, and one grisly event was the massacre of Papal officials by heretics.

Observe the small building near **Ecluse Négra**; it's a **chapel** dedicated to sailors of the canal. **Aygues-Vives** is worth the half-mile walk from the canal; taking its name from the Latin *Aquavit* (living waters) the old town seems equally alive today. The **church** has a *cloche-mur*, a belltower which looks like a backless wall and is typical of the area. Climb **Montgisard's church tower** for a 180-degree view of the surrounding countryside.

Port Sud is a purpose-built marina with every facility available; from here, the rolling hills depart and the suburbs and industry of the Toulouse put in their first appearance.

Toulouse, France's seventh largest city, also known as *La Ville Rose* (Pink City), has short-term moorings near **Port St Sauveur**, and **Ecluse de Bayard**; for longer visits, dock at **Port de la Embouchure** (straight ahead after **Ecluse Bérnais**).

Once the third largest city in Gaul, Tolosa was also the Visogoth's capital, and for four centuries was governed by the Counts of Toulouse. Its most infa-

Strolling in Narbonne.

mous era was during the Albigensian Crusade when the Count of Toulouse led the heretics against Rome. During the fighting Toulouse was besieged, sacked and ruled by both sides; peace came after the death of Simon de Montfort in 1218, but a true return to normality did not return until the middle of the century.

A marriage between a daughter of the last Count of Toulouse and the brother of Louis IX brought Languedoc to France, albeit as a separate duchy. With the Revolution, it was broken into small departments, but Toulouse remains the economic center of the region.

Toulouse's reputation as center for much of the French aircraft industry is not new. One of the earliest test pilots, Saint-Exupéry, flew from the local airport; 1919 brought airmail service to Morocco, and the first passenger service to South America was inaugurated here in 1930. Concorde was born in the city, and today European Airbuses roll off the production line.

Toulouse's heart is the **Old Town**.

Bordered by the Garonne River and Canal du Midi, it is a mass of criss-crossing cobbled streets, aristocratic houses, churches and museums, all constructed in the dusty red brick for which the city is famous.

A fine Renaissance palace, the Hôtel d'Assezat, on Rue de Metz near Place du Capitole (daily open-air market), is an elegant colonnaded square, also boasting the 18th-century Hôtel de Ville, now the Opera House. Other old houses are on Rues du Languedoc, de la Dalbad, and Gambetta.

The **Eglise de Jacobins**, the first Dominican convent church, is considered a textbook example of Languedoc Gothic. Founded in the mid-12th century as a monastery, after the Revolution it became a stable, and remained so until 1865.

Restoration was completed only in the late 1970s; except for two 14th-century rose windows, new stained-glass by Max Ingrand has been fitted into the Gothic frames, but no changes have been wrought on the intricate and deli-

Swirling at a canalside fun fair.

cate palm-tree vaulting and ribbing. In 1974, the relics of Thomas Aquinas were placed under the main altar.

A visit to the **Cloisters** should not be missed; destroyed during army occupation, they've been restored to their 13th-century design. Fragments of the original frescoes are found on the walls of the chapel and *salle capitulaire*.

The **Basilica of St Sernin** (named for the man who brought Christianity to the city in the 3rd century) is one of the finest examples of Romanesque architecture in southwestern France. Building started in 1080; restorations over the centuries included one by Viollet-le-Duc in 1855. A massive building, its tower is more than 210-ft (65-meters) high, the double-aisled interior runs 375-ft (115 meters) long and its vaulting arches meet 65 ft (20 meters) above the floor.

The interior is gloomy, and even the baroque sculptures behind the 11th-century marble altar do not lift the oppressive feeling. Note the Romanesque **Porte Miégeville**, its tympanum and capitals carved with well-known stories from the Bible.

Riquet is buried in the **Cathédrale de St Etienne**. His tomb is marked by a black marble tablet at the base of a pillar near the altar. The building was started in the 11th century, which makes it the oldest structure of its kind in southern France, but today it displays no distinctive architectural style.

Museum lovers will wallow in the offerings of Toulouse: a 14th-century cloister house; the **Musée de Augustins** with a collection of fine paintings by noted artists; **Musée St-Raymond**, near St Sernin, displays Roman antiquities. Ethnology enthusiasts will want to visit **Musée du Vieux Toulouse**, and **Musée Paul Dupuy** pays homage to applied arts through the ages. **Musée d'Historie Naturelle** is near the University in the **Jardin des Plantes**.

To join the Latéral canal, make a right turn when leaving L'Embouchure. (A left leads toward the **Canal de Brienne**, used only for supplying water to the two canals.)

St Pierre is Moissac's treasure.

Le Canal Robine: Sometimes called **La Nouvelle**, this 21-mile (37-km) waterway runs south from Port la Robine on the Canal du Midi to the Mediterranean. Completed in 1776, its main purpose was to give shippers from the central Midi a shorter distance to the sea. Even without cruising all the way to the last town, Port la Nouvelle, the 8-mile (14-km) voyage to Narbonne makes a pleasant detour on your journey.

Leaving the Midi, the **Robine** runs in a straight line for 3 miles (5 km). Just after **Ecluse St Cyr** is a barge-turning area, and at **Salles d'Aude**, the canal, very much in the way railroad tracks bisect small towns, divides this one. After passing through the **Ecluse du Gailousty**, the **River Aude** enters the canal for a short distance. (It is advisable to pay strict attention to navigation markers: the current is tricky, there are ferry cables and a weir to avoid, and after rainstorms, the channel can be especially difficult until **Ecluse de Moussoulens** is reached.)

Ecluse du Gua marks the outskirts of **Narbonne**, and the canal's route cuts through the city's heart. Founded as Narbo Martius around 600 BC, Narbonne was formally colonized in 118 BC, and became the most important city of Gallo Narbonnensis. Even then it was a busy port; large ships anchored in a nearby lagoon and a branch of the river Aude, both now silted up.

Two emperors of Rome were born here, and Marcus Antonius was one of the city's governors. The architectural excellence of the city was celebrated in literature by Ausonius in the 4th century and by Sidonius Apollinaris in the following century.

From 413 to 720 the city was ruled by the Visogoths; it was besieged by the Saracens for two years before finally falling to them. Pepin le Bref was the next who desired Narbonne: the Saracens had him at their gates for seven years. Between then and 1355, when the Black Prince was turned away from the walls, the city was under the leadership of Comte of d'Auvergne and of Comte de Toulouse.

The silting up of the harbors, the effects of war and diverging political alliances, contributed to a decline in Narbonne's fortunes. Today, few remnants of its illustrious past remain, but the city emits a distinct charm and a sense of welcome.

Narbonne, with a population of around 43,000, is a peaceful city: plane trees abound on either side of the canal and the river banks have been landscaped to provide a pleasant setting of umbrella-shaded tables and park benches all around.

The most convenient moorings are found along the concrete quays within sight of the Cathedral. There are mooring rings, sidewalks and stairs for easy access, and fresh produce is available at a large **indoor market** just east of the canal. There are also public lavatories (avoid berthing near them; they do a rip-roaring business at very disagreeable hours), and between the canal and the cathedral is a large commercial area, filled with up-market and down-market restaurants where the local wine, Corbières, can be sampled.

Fontfroide Abbey matches its name: "cool fountain".

The **Cathedral of St Just** is largely unfinished; constructed in the fortified style, building commenced in 1272 with additions in the 18th and 19th centuries. Entering is a chilling and chilly experience: the interior is austere and gloomy. The choir and stained-glass windows deserve attention and in the **Treasury** is a museum of Christian art with objects ranging from the 7th century onward. It would have been a magnificent church if it had been finished, Stendhal remarked when he saw it in 1838.

A **city museum** is in the former Archbishop's Palace and includes an interesting collection of French pottery, porcelain, paintings and other finds of local antiquity. Next-door, the mock-Gothic **Hôtel de Ville** was designed by Viollet-le-Duc.

One of the fun things about passing through Narbonne is cruising under the housebridge, the **Pont des Marchands**, a "tunnel" less than 50 ft (16 meters) long. One caution: boats with a superstructure of more than 9 ft (3 meters) cannot slip through.

Before leaving Narbonne, consider a visit to the **Abbey of Fontfroide**, a 9-mile (15-km) ride from town. Nestled in an oasis of cypress trees, the Abbey dates from the 12th and 13th centuries when it flourished under the Cistercians. After the Revolution, it fell into disrepair, and was not restored until early in this century and is now privately owned. Note especially the modern stained-glass windows in the chapel, the graceful buildings, and carefully planned gardens which very aptly echo its name, "cool fountain".

As one heads toward the sea from Narbonne, the landscape changes from fields filled with vineyards, grain, or grazing animals into an area of marsh lakes and reedy stretches reminiscent of the Camargue. There are small towns at a distance, but in general the canal cruises in a solitary manner between two enormous lakes, the **Etangs des Bages** and **de l'Ayrolle**. Although the treeless waterway is well defined, it is narrow and the reeds along the banks sometimes appear to choke it.

The last lock before entering **Port la Nouvelle** is **Ecluse Ste Lucie**. The many other small boats in the port are mostly involved in the fishing trade. Some large ocean-going cargo vessels pick up bulk wine and other goods brought by canal barges. Fuel and water may be obtained and cranes for stepping masts are available.

Although the town boasts few tourist attractions, there are several nearby beaches and resorts. For those who enjoy nudist bathing, there is an official area at **Les Montilles** a few miles southwest of Port la Nouvelle.

Le Canal Latéral à la Garonne: Two centuries younger than the Midi Canal, **The Latéral** was built to replace the very uncertain navigation of the Garonne River downstream from Toulouse. Work started in 1838 and by 1843 regular passenger services began operating between Montauban and Toulouse. By 1850 navigation extended to Agen and finally in 1865 the last lock at Castets was completed.

A few working barges still regularly ply the waterway; usually carrying bulk **A quiet park in Toulouse.**

wine or grain. All the original locks have been rebuilt to Freycinet standards (123 feet/38 meters); when the same thing happens on the Midi, and barges from any part of France can transit them, perhaps additional commercial traffic will result.

Seen immediately after the Canal du Midi, the 120-mile (193-km), 93-lock waterway can first disappoint. However, after enduring the relatively dull stretch to Montech (25 miles/40 km), it's a charming waterway, one that runs through one of the most productive fruit-growing regions in France. In the spring and early summer blossoms blanket the hillside, and late summer brings wheat ripening to a deep gold, fields of corn swaying in the breeze.

This is a region noted for its food and wine, and the restaurants encountered maintain that reputation at less cost than places further east. And towards Bordeaux, some of the great vineyards of the world are within a short ride away. Also on the plus side: most visitors congregate on the Midi, but on the

Farming along Le Canal Latéral.

Latéral an entire day may pass without sight of another boat.

When compared to the multi-contoured Midi, the Latéral appears to run in an almost straight line. Lock operation is easier here, too, and access is by traffic-lights activated by turning a pole suspended over the water at points about 900 ft (280 meters) on either side of the lock. Instructions in French, German and English add to the operation's ease.

One negative cannot be ignored: the railway. It runs alongside the canal from Toulouse almost to Montech, reappears before Castelsarrasin and doesn't finally disappear until Agen.

Leaving Toulouse is like entering it, drearily industrial. Only when **Ecluse 6**, **St Jory**, arrives does any sort of countryside begin to appear.

The river flowing below the aqueduct just before **Ecluse 7**, **Hers**, bears the same name. The town above the next lock is **Castelnau d'Estrctcfonds**, marked by a large château.

From Montech, **Montauban** is a 6-mile (11-km) cruise. (The nine locks

aren't manned; check with lock-keeper in Montech before proceeding.) The canal is elevated so it appears the boat is gliding on top of the world. The deserted waterway passes the village of **Lacourt**, an old château peers from the trees, farmers till their fields, and even sight of the autoroute doesn't diminish the sail's pleasure.

The cut originally connected the canal with the **Tarn river**; now the joining lock is closed, and the Tarn is only suitable for canoes and rowboats. The small mooring basin is adjacent to the lock, and Montauban's historical area a short walk across the river.

Montauban, another pink-brick city, was founded in the 1140s by the Counts of Toulouse. From the river, the old city looks walled; this is an optical illusion created by its hillside position and *bâstide* construction. Heart of the **Old Town** is the **Place Nationale** (site of a weekly market) with arched porticos leading from the square's corners.

St Jacques church, built in the fortified style, is off the west exit; originally the cathedral, it was superceded in 1739 when **Notre Dame** was built. Inside the cathedral, note the painting by native-born artist, Ingres. Titled *The Vow of Louis VIII*, it brings to mind one incident of the Huguenot strife. The king was not able to take the strongly Protestant city, even after a siege lasting three months, so Louis moved onto easier pickings.

Seven years later, with the last of the troublesome cities converted or destroyed, Louis returned to Montauban, and in 1628, the city, with no other options left, quietly capitulated.

More paintings and drawings are on display in the **Ingres Museum**. Housed in a former **Bishop's Palace**, look for the Black Prince's chamber in the 14th-century basement. Before returning to the canal, observe the row of 17th-century houses alongside the Tarn. A few years ago, many were in a state of severe dilapidation; now renovated and restored they've been transformed into multi-use buildings.

Montech brings two-lane traffic to

Playing boules: who came the closest?

the canal. One lane (which pleasure craft must use) passes through a series of five locks spread over less than a mile and a half. Commercial traffic, however travels the fast lane in a 1,440-ft (443-meter) long concrete waterslope. The slope, which has a three-degree slant, began operating in 1973, and is like the one in Béziers *(see page 69)*. Other than this curiosity, Montech has little of interest to the waterborne tourist.

As the canal approaches **Moissac**, it crosses the Tarn via the great stone aqueduct which has a span of 1,157 ft (356 meters). Immediately reaching "dry land", the canal makes a sharp left turn and two locks later flows into the center of a most charming city. Just beyond the second, a two-step lock to the left allows access to the river (it joins the Garonne shortly downstream of Moissac) and/or a, full-service marina. A delightful facet of Moissac is that the canal, instead of skirting the town, drives through the middle of it. Substantial brick houses with flower-potted windows look down on boats; traffic is

halted when passing through the **Pont St Jacques** swing bridge. (Toot to attract the keeper's attention.)

Pride of Moissac is the 7th-century **Abbey Church of St Pierre** which, despite repeated attacks from Arabs, Normans, English, and the French during their Revolution, remained standing, only to face the possibility of its being torn down in the mid-1800s to make way for a new railway station. Sanity, in the form of the Beaux Arts Association intervened, and the church's safety was assured.

The carved south doorway dates to the early 12th century, and is considered one of the finest examples of French ecclesiastical art. Depicting the vision of the Apocalypse according to St John, the intricate stone carvings are remarkable. In the center of the tympanum, Christ is shown surrounded by symbols of the four evangelicals: man, bull, eagle and lion, with other seated figures facing Him. Note the interesting center post between the doors: on one side are three overlapping lions, the other side

has designs representing the prophets.

The only other remnant of the original church is the bottom part of the tower; the balance is 15th-century. Inside the church proper, disappointment fills the gloom: drab should not follow such magnificence.

The **cloister's** pillars are made from multi-colored marbles, and the gallery they form is a necklace for the lone cedar standing in the middle of a grass carpet. Their capitals are extraordinary: bibical scenes, figures grotesque and graceful decorate each one.

The pedestrian mall leading to the church is lined with the ubiquitous tourist shops, fast-food restaurants, and other purveyors of dubious treasures. But spending an afternoon at one of the café tables near the church, watching the light work changes of color on the stone, is an undeniable pleasure.

On the secular side, Moissac has a great selection of restaurants. The **Moulin de Mougonnne Hotel** offers the most elegant dining and overlooks the Tarn, but others near the town square

serve equally good regional cuisine. A morning market on the same square is typical of southwest France, and on the square above the cloisters, *boules* games are often in progress.

Leaving Moissac, the wide expanse of water below the canal is part of a hydro-electric project further downstream. From **Ecluse 26**, **Espagnette**, look left for views of the enormous lake formed by the dam (it and the nuclear power station are beyond **Valence d'Agen**). In that town, note the public washhouse; a useful facility when built in the 19th century, its use has declined as women have acquired their own washing machines.

Styling itself as the prune capital of the world, the title is hard to dispute after tasting the many varieties available in shops throughout **Agen**. There's a large mooring at the **Halt de Tourisme** with the amenities that make life so pleasurable, and sightseeing is just across a pedestrian bridge that spans the railroad tracks.

A modern city, Agen sits at the southern end of the Plain of Agenais, a fertile district with mild winters. Yet it is also an ancient town: recent excavations found the remains of a Roman amphitheater comparable to the one in Saintes-sur-Charente, and during the Hundred Years War, the city was taken and retaken by the French and English with alarming regularity.

Place de l'Hôtel de Ville is heart of the old quarter. A **City Museum** is housed in a series of interlocking Renaissance mansions; the collection ranges from Gallo-Roman remains to paintings by Goya and Sisley. The **Cathédrale de St Caprais** was founded in the 11th century as a collegiate church, but has been restored and decorated in a rather gloomy way.

Almost immediately after leaving the boat basin, one of the longest (1,750 ft/ 539 meters) aqueducts in France carries the Latéral over the Garonne. After crossing the 23-arched bridge a series of four locks lowers the canal over 40 ft (12 meters).

The Latéral wanders on its own for the next 12 miles (20 km) through shaded

Flowers decorate most...

glens; a red-tiled farmhouse or two appear in the distance, but except for **Ecluse 38, l'Augignon**, nothing intrudes upon the solitude.

The **Baïse River** is traversed via a short aqueduct before **Ecluse 39, Baïse**. Just before Buzet-sur-Baïse is a cut-off into the river just crossed. (This 3-mile/5-km canal leads to the Garonne River, and after turning left, provides a navigation to the canal junction at Castets about 50 miles/80 km away. The newly-opened route provides an 85-mile/135-km circuit from Agen to Castets on the Latéral and a return on the Garonne to the Baïse and back to Agen, or vice versa.)

Buzet is a mariner's dream, offering all supplies including a large wine cooperative. The suspension bridge above the canal at **Mas d'Argenais** spans river and canal, and the view from the garden next to the local château covers the entire Garonne valley. Unfortunately no shops can be found at the water's edge, but marine repairs, water, gas and oil are available. **Pont de Sables** is

...windows in Southern France.

especially inviting. There is a restaurant as well as a rowing club; weekends bring out the colorful shells and the crowds.

The next reach is also attractive, shaded but with sun dappling through the trees creating dancing sparks on the water. Seen from the road, a boat passing in the elevated canal appears to float through the trees like an apparition.

Meilhan, just beyond **Ecluse 47, Gravières**, is one of the loveliest towns on the canal. From it are views over the valley: pastures mixed with forests and the meandering river moving through them like a snake.

Castets en Dorte and the lock connecting river and canal arrive without warning. The town is high on a hill; so, unless desperate for supplies, wait until Langon to reprovision.

La Garonne: Unlike their country cousins of the Midi, the great Bordeaux vineyards do not line the banks of the **Garonne River**. During its 35-mile (56-km) lockless run from Castets to Bordeaux, these are generally hidden in the

hills beyond the water's view, but one or two may be easily visited from towns located along the river.

Because the river is tidal, cruising to Bordeaux can be difficult. If determined, check with the lock-keeper at Castets for local high tide time, then take advantage of the current for the journey to Bordeaux. With the constant shifting of sand banks and shoals, it is most important to pay strict attention to channel markers.

Due to fluctuating water levels, a day journey is advised. This is easily possible: making no en-route stops, the downriver cruise should take less than six hours; sightseeing should add no more than that. Moorings along the waterway are few, although with the increase of pleasure boating in the past 10 years, more and more towns, are upgrading old facilities and building new ones.

Langon, first port of call after leaving the Canal Latéral à la Garonne, has a large, recently-opened pleasure boat harbor. The great **Sauternes** vineyards are about 6 miles (10 km) south of here; **Château Filhot** is one of those offering tours and tasting.

More energy? Swing down Rte D-126 for 3 miles (5 km) to **Roquetaillade** where one of the fortresses built by Pope Clement V sits in a well-preserved state. The triangle is completed by returning to Langon, and a number of restaurants can fill the empty stomach and slake a parched mouth.

From the Garonne, the walls and turrets of the 15th-century **Château des Ducs d'Epernon** in **Cadillac** are clearly visible. Originally a bâstide, the 14th-century walls still enclose much of the town. **La Porte de Mer** (Sea Gate) provides dramatic evidence of the sometime wayward river: plaques mark the great floods of 1770 and 1930. The château was ransacked during the Revolution; it later became a prison. Note particularly the richly carved fireplaces. An assortment of restaurants attest to the town's popularity, and the marina offers pontoon moorings for overnight visitors.

Fishing nets along the Garonne.

Cambès has waterpoints, no fuel. Don't attempt the southern channel around **Ile de La Lande** during low tide or the boat may be there until the next high water. Beyond here, a number of châteaux, all privately owned, decorate the low hills.

Although 60 miles (100 km) inland, **Bordeaux** is considered a major international seaport, capable of receiving large ships. For the sailor in a small boat, those ships and the 1,300-feet (400-meter) wide Garonne can be an intimidating experience.

There are two places for transients to dock, on the left bank near **Pont St Jean** and the **Service de Navigation** office (most convenient, but best only for short stays) or in the non-tidal **Floating Basin**. This is reached through a lock on the south side beyond the 17-arched **Pont de Pierre** (built in the early 19th century), but before the modern suspension bridge.

Bordeaux, whose population now exceeds 212,000, was an important commercial port and wine center from its earliest days, though the first wines shipped out of Roman Burgadilia were not from their *côtes*, but the Midi's. Vines were planted locally some time in the first century; thereafter, no matter who or what was governing the region, the vines grew and thrived.

Nothing except the vines (and some columns and arches found in **Palais Galien** southwest of Place Gambetta) remain from Roman occupation; the Visogoths arrived a little after AD 400; the Dark Ages brought the Saracens (730ish), Vikings (840s), and an assortment of other visitors, first rising to power, then falling.

Bordeaux's big break arrived when the Duke of Aquitaine's daughter, Eleanor, was repudiated by Louis VII, but still allowed to keep her dowry lands. Eleanor married the soon-to-be Plantagenet King Henry II and thus began the marriage of England and western France, a territory that ranged from the Pyrénées northward to the Channel. The monopoly on wine exports was held by the English and they (and Bordeaux) profited greatly.

For the English their defeat in 1453 may have only ended their presence in France, but for the burghers of Bordeaux, it almost caused financial ruin: the primary market for the wines was gone, and their most-favored tax status was lost.

Eventually the French Crown repealed the taxes, and Bordeaux grew fat again. The Wars of Religion saw little conflict in the city, and the biggest news of the 17th century was the creation of the Médoc wine growing area. The Revolution and the Napoleons' misadventures (Nelson's blockade was a disaster for the city) were pivotal in starting a decline in Bordeaux's fortunes, one that lasted through World War II.

All that matters little today. Bordeaux is now France's fourth largest city, sixth largest port and exporter of the finest wines in the world. To the north of the city lies an ever-expanding industrial region with factories, dry docks and ship-building yards, chemical plants and oil refineries.

The southern riverfront is a parade of

Many cities still have their old gates.

elegant 18th-century houses. **Place de la Bourse** contains the **Stock Exchange**, **Customs House**, **Musée de la Marine**, and the **Fountain of the Three Graces**. The **Esplanade des Quinconces**, laid out in the 1820s, is, at 29 acres (11 hectares), the largest square in Europe. The heart of Bordeaux, the wine merchants, is based along **Quai des Chartrons**.

A stop at the **Maison du Vin** on Cours du 30 Juillet is mandatory for those wishing to visit the local wine cellars; it can also arrange private visits or public tours to the region's wine châteaux.

The **Grand Théâtre** faces onto **Place de la Comédie**. Built in 1780, its size, (285 by 143 ft/88 by 44 meters) matches its name and the neo-Classical facade is graced with grand Corinthian columns. The theater stands at one corner of a triangle of streets (**Allées de Tourney**, **Cours Georgs Clemenceau** and **Cours l'Intendence**) which enclose the core of classical Bordeaux 18th-century architecture.

North of **Place de Tourney** is the

Jardin Public and the **Musée d'Historie Naturelle**. At the final corner of this triangle is the **Place Gambetta** and an old entrance to the city, **Porte de Dijeaux**, still serving that function for the city as it leads to a street lined with fashionable shops.

The **Cathédrale de St André** faces the **Hôtel de Ville**; begun in the 11th century, its dimensions almost equal Paris' Notre Dame. The five centuries of construction and extensive restorations have, unfortunately, left no distinct architectural style.

A three-tiered 13th-century tympanum representing the Last Supper, the Ascension and the Triumph of Christ is on the **Porte Royale**. The 15th-century belfry is named after the archbishop who had it erected, Per Beyland, and the ornately carved and decorated spire is set apart from the church.

On the streets near the cathedral are the **Musée des Arts Décoratifs**, **Musée des Beaux Arts**, **Musée d'Aquitaine**, and **Musée Bonie**.

The 14th-century **Basilica St Michel** is close to the river just south of Pont de Pierre on Place Canteloup. Badly damaged by bombs during World War II, repairs were made to the facade, but many of the old stained-glass windows were replaced with modern ones created by Max Ingrand. Like St André, St Michel's belfry is separate from the church, and its 370-ft (114-meter) high spire is the tallest in southern France. The tower's **crypt** offers a number of macabre exhibits; climbing the 228 steps to the tower's viewing platform brings a breath of air and magnificent vistas over the sprawling city.

Two other churches interest: **St Seurin**, begun in the 11th-century with a 15th-century facade, has 6th-century tombs in the crypt. **St Croix** is classic Romanesque with the tympanum elaborately designed and carved.

Veteran car enthusiasts will enjoy the **Musée Bonnal-Renaulac** a taxi-ride away in the suburb of Begles.

Beyond Bordeaux is the **Gironde**, a seaway beyond the scope and ability (and rental agreement) of the average vacationer.

Left, wild iris decorate the waterway from sea to sea. **Right**, fishing boats head for work.

LA CHARENTE

"The most beautiful river of the realm" was how Henri IV (1589–1610) described the waterway which meanders 223 miles (360 km) from its source in Haute Vienne to the Atlantic Ocean. Henri's comments are still apt: the **Charente** courses slowly, snaking through wooded fields and lush pastureland, its banks dotted with farmhouses, villages and châteaux. In the spring and summer, flowers create colorful patches and fall brings gold and red to the overhanging trees.

Rich also in history, the river has been a route for defender and foe. Early in the ninth century, Saints and Angoulême were destroyed by the Norsemen, and during the 11th and 12th centuries when southwestern France was ruled by the Counts of Poitiers and Angoulême, the area was a center of commerce and learning.

The Charente was also a pathway for trade development: as early as the Gallo-Roman era, records indicate vessels were already carrying cargo. By the Middle Ages the river was the main commercial "road" on which the local products were exported to the Low Countries, Denmark and England. From Angoulême, cargoes included paper and stone, from Ruelle cannon and munitions were loaded, and at Jarnac, cognac. Agricultural products such as corn and meat formed the balance of the downstream produce.

In the 13th century, Philip the Bold and Louis X made improvements to the waterway. The creation of a military garrison at Rochefort in 1666 created more traffic, but excessively high tolls almost caused the death of commercial traffic. These were abolished in 1737; but by then, the proposed canal which was to link the Loire and Vienne rivers was no longer economically feasible.

At the zenith of Charente commercial traffic in the early 19th century, 66 barges were in service, and a round trip between Rochefort and Angoulême took about two weeks. In 1822, the first trip up the river by steam vessel was made by *Hirondelle*, and four decades later there was regular passenger service between Saints and Angoulême.

The arrival of the railroad in 1867 did not immediately affect freight haulage but by the end of World War I, traffic had dramatically declined and in 1926 the river was closed for commercial navigation between Montignac (13 miles/21 km above Angoulême) and Cognac. In 1957 the Charente was struck off the official list of waterways, but in the late 1970s, when pleasure boating became popular, lock repairs and dredging commenced, making it a charming river to cruise.

Today 80 miles (130 km) of non-tidal waterway between Angoulême and Tonnay, and a tidal stretch of 25 miles (40 km) from Tonnay to the mouth of the river, are navigable. No lock-keepers are present to help from Ecluse 1 in Angoulême through Ecluse 19, Crouin (hire firms give lessons in lock passage), but the final two, Blaine and Savinien, are manned.

Left, Angoulême sits high above the river. Right, setting off for some serious work.

On the Charente, there's a major hazard: water skiers and the wake they produce. They are allowed on 13 designated stretches, each well marked, but on busy weekends, the speeders tend to overshoot their areas. Check before confidently cruising into a seemingly deserted stretch of river.

There is a peace and tranquility about **Angoulême**. From miles away, buildings seem to form a huge pyramid, culminating in a city perched high (250 ft/ 76 meters) above the river. This tranquility continues in the perfect proportions of the Cathedral of St Pierre, the pedestrian shopping streets, and the proliferation of shops bearing well-known French designers' names. Unfortunately, it's a 10–20 minute uphill slog on foot from the **port area** of **l'Houmeau** to this haven (taxis sometimes available).

The city, known as Iculisma under the Romans, was capital of the Princes of Blood hereditary province, "Angoumois", during the Middle Ages. Papermaking was once the largest source of revenue; by the 17th century, more than 100 mills were in operation, sending the bulk of their produce to Holland. Revocation of the Edict of Nantes had a devastating effect: Huguenots were the primary artisans, and their departure from France after 1685 left an unfillable hole. The industry is still alive, but not with the same force it once was.

The views from the well-landscaped **ramparts** encompass more than 180 degrees; benches, *boules*-playing areas, and children's playgrounds add to the ambiance. The **Cathedral of St Pierre** (built between 1105 and 1128 with restorations in 1650 and 1875, the latter by Paul Abadie, architect of Sacré Coeur in Paris) combines Romanesque and Byzantine architecture. The west front has a beautifully sculpted facade containing over 70 figures; one of the most prominent is the Last Judgement.

Many 18th-century buildings, some built by the prosperous paper merchants, are on the **Citadel**. One is the **Hôtel de Ville** (also Abadie-designed), and its construction incorporated the 13th-century keep and 15th-century tower of an old château which stood on this site. The château was home of one of the illustrious figures of the Renaissance, Marguerite d'Angoulême, niece of Louis XII and François I's sister. Other outstanding period houses include the **Hôtel Dieu** and several on **Rue de la Cloche Verte**.

The **Musée Municipal** is in the former Bishop's Palace, and a pedestrian shopping area features an array of restaurants ranging from Vietnamese to Brazilian cuisines.

Even on Sundays, the best place to get fresh produce, meat and cheese is at **Les Halles** on the Citadel just above the port. Below, there's a fair selection of shops just off the bridge that's nearest the lock, but most of the restaurants of l'Homeau lack appeal. Opposite the port is a municipal campground and swimming pool; a miniature golf course completes the well-executed city entertainment area.

Leaving Angoulême, the river becomes rural almost immediately, twist-

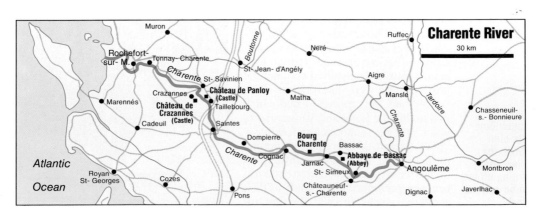

ing and turning through its tree-shaded course. **St Michel** is little over a mile from the river; to visit its early 12th-century church, moor at **Le Pont de Basseau**. The **Museum of Paper and Stationery** is located here in an old windmill. Unfortunately, the **Château de Fleurac** isn't open.

Just north of the river near **Ecluse 5**, **La Motte**, **Trois-Palais** is known for its Romanesque **Notre Dame church**, and a **chocolate factory**. A haven for choco-holics, there are tours (with samples) on irregular hours and days. At **Rochecorail** (right bank after the railroad bridge) John Calvin, the 16th-century Protestant reformer, wrote one of his books whilst living in one of the many caves in this area.

St Simeux boasts a watermill; with its hillside location, it's one of the most charming towns on the Charente and there are panoramic views of the river. A hire boat firm is located here; transients may use their facilities. Eel fishing is most popular on this reach; several islands created between the naviga-tion channel and the town offer a quiet refuge. More hidden backwaters surround the next lock, **Malvit** and its islands; mooring under the banks of willow trees allows much privacy.

The 15th-century spire of **St Pierre** marks the approach to **Châteauneuf-sur-Charente**; its facade is older, Romanesque. The river has narrowed to little more than a meandering stream with trees engulfing the banks of this attractive town. The Romanesque church in **St Surin** is a short walk off the river; the **Logis de Tillet** has a 15th-century chapel.

Moor at the **Pont de Vibrac**, and walk the half mile to the Auberge les Ombrages; set on a quiet road, the food matches the ambience.

The horse-chestnut trees bordering the river give **St Simon** much charm. Clustered stone houses and narrow streets complete the country village atmosphere. It was a leading barge building center in the 19th century; the only industry today seems to be catering to the tourist boats.

A hotel barge on the Charente.

The **Bassac Abbey**, constructed around AD 1000, is reached from **Pont de Viande**. Devastated and rebuilt during the Hundred Years War and disestablished during the Revolution, it is now the house of the Missionary Brothers of St Thérèse et l'Enfant Jésu. Inside, the carved choir stalls and the lectern are most interesting. Women in search of husbands should note the statue of St Nicholas; legend says that kissing its feet is sure to bring a mate most quickly. After seeing the religious, the secular is available at a small distillery near **Viande**.

On the run into **Jarnac**, delightful châteaux are scattered through the wooded fields; nearing town, the air thickens with the sweet smell of brandy, and one can almost become inebriated on the aroma. This comes from the estimated 20 million-plus bottles a year, or 2 percent of the entire production, that evaporates into the air. Described as the "angels' share", more often than not it is the visitor whose nostrils enjoy the bouquet. Jarnac, along with Cognac, some 7 miles (12 km) down the Charente, produces most of the world's finest *eau de vie*.

People who believe brandy to be a purely French concoction should know that Mr Martell, who produced the first cognac in 1715, was English, and its name comes from the Dutch word *brandwijn* (burnt wine). Brandy was first produced in large quantities in the early 17th century, and is made by mixing old and new wines together, distilling the resulting white wine several times, then ageing the beverage in oak casks made from trees from the Limousin. Courvoisier and Biscuit are headquartered in Jarnac; each conducts daily tours of its *chais* (cellars).

Jarnac gives the appearance of great comfort. There are shops, restaurants, and a swimming pool near the weir stream. Along with brandy, the town is known for a 1547 duel between the Count of Jarnac, Guy Chabot and François de Vienne. Henri II watched and the Count didn't lose.

From a narrow meandering stream, the Charente broadens as it heads towards **Bourg-Charente**. There are more exquisite châteaux, all privately owned, and all looking deserted; but on a bright sunny day, their sedate dignity bring memories of another era.

The imposing (and privately-owned) **Château de St Brice** has a look of occupation about it. Once visited by Catherine de Medici, Queen of Henri II, there are manicured gardens, bronze statuary of animals on the lawn, and slate-roofed turrets.

This is a gentle run; graceful farmhouses and the utility buildings associated with the work side of farming are interspersed among leafy glades. The stillness does not come with a noonday break, but with the feeling that time has stopped. Even the current is slow, and it is hard to realize that less than 100 years ago this was an enormously busy waterway with over 100,000 passengers annually carried between Angoulême and Rochefort.

Entering **Cognac**, the once prevalent navigation markers seem to disappear, giving the impression that Cognac does not especially welcome tourists. This suspicion is reinforced in the rather abrupt way outsiders are treated in the town's shops, and by the almost mechanical, by-the-numbers tours of the brandy firms, a far cry from the informality of Jarnac.

For all its unfriendliness, Cognac is the heart of the Charente vineyards. Like its up-river Jarnac cousins, the Cognac giants of Hennessey and Martell (daily tours are conducted) located their original factories next to the Charente for easy shipping.

The first Duc d'Angoulême, later François I, was born in 1494 in the Château de Valois, and spent much of his early life here (look for an equestrian statue of him in town). The château has seen a different life since 1795 when it became a *chais* for a local distillery.

There is the usual cluster of timbered houses in the **old quarter**, but any charm is missing. The uninspiring **St Léger** church is 12th-century, but the rose window is 15th-century. Of all the cities on the Charente, Cognac is the least appealing. Even the tourist office is hard to find. The **Port St Jacques** (its tower is 16th-century) does, however, offer convenient mooring and all facilities, including loading ramps for small, trailer-carried boats.

Port du Lys marks the boundary between Charente and Charente-Maritime and at **Dompierre-sur-Charente**, the hand-operated chain ferry for cars should be avoided.

At **Chaniers** the 12th-century church of **St Pierre** has a slightly lop-sided interior with the arch over the altar area appearing about five degrees off. This, however, does not distract from the austere lines and the beautiful simplicity of the church. Do note the inlaid seats on the chairs. On a practical note, the marina is a good one and local shops are fully stocked.

Approaching **Saintes-Savinien-sur-Charente** (or Saintes as it is more commonly known), one passes a proliferation of neat gardens. They are good omens; Saintes is more than pleasant. Marine facilities are excellent, and the carefully landscaped riverbanks are mirrored throughout the well-tended city. Sightseeing on either side of the river is within an easy walk; choose the right or left bank to moor, but water points are to be found on the right near the foot-bridge.

Capital of the former province of Saintonge, the Roman Mediolanum Santonum boasted major construction after Caesar's invasion of Gaul in 58 BC. The most obvious survivor of Roman occupation is the **Arch of Germanicus** relocated on the right bank and the center-piece of a riverside park; other remains are in the adjacent **Archaeology Museum**. The city was also sufficiently important to warrant an **amphitheater** measuring more than 400 ft by 325 ft (125 by 100 meters); make a point of looking for the well-preserved ruins west of the old part of town.

Saintes' historical position was further enhanced because it was on the Pilgrimage route to Compostella during the Middle Ages. The **Abbaye aux Dames** dates from this period; the portico and bell tower are superb.

The salon of Château de Panloy.

Once the home of *patagux* (freshwater pearl mussels), the industry was abandoned in the mid-1700s when it became a money-losing proposition due to the extreme difficulty of getting the mussels to pearl. One citizen, Dr. J.I. Guillotin, inventor of the infamous guillotine, was born here in 1738. The town was one of the major barge centers of the 17th, 18th and 19th centuries, and at one point, traffic was heavy enough to add *Le Port* to the town's name.

The old town is clustered around the old **Cathedral**, and several streets are filled with 17th and 18th-century houses. **St Pierre**, no longer a cathedral, is still given the courtesy title. Building starting in the 12th-century, was completed in the 15th. The Calvinists wreaked havoc with it in 1568, but undaunted Catholics rebuilt.

The 12th-century **St Eutrope** church has a checkered past: the relics of its saint were lost not once, but twice. Rediscovered for the second time in 1843, they rest in a crypt that has been described as being almost as beautiful as that at Chartres. Louis XI added the tower in the 15th century after a visit to the church cured an illness.

Culture is well represented: **Musée des Beaux Arts** is on Rue Victor Hugo, and filled with European paitings. **Musée Dupuy-Mestreau** exhibits local costumes and furniture; find it on Rue Monconsieil. Learn about prehistoric life at the right bank **Musée Educatif de Préhistorie**.

At **Port Bertau**, such 19th-century painters as Courbet, Gauguin and Pradelles sought refuge. According to Dangibeaud, it was an excellent area for landscape painters. Refuge seekers of another kind discovered a haven in **Bussac**; the Huguenots, fleeing religious persecution, found solace in the small town located half a mile from the river.

A string of small châteaux, none rivaling their grander cousins of the Loire valley, but pleasant to observe are on this reach. The **Château de Bussac** is one such, and on the eve of the battle of **Taillebourg**, Blanche de Castille, spent the night here. At that town, her son, Louis IX defeated Henry III of England in 1242, but only the ruins of a 15th-century château mark the battle site. Modern visitors will appreciate the mooring area with its general feeling of welcome. All supplies are available, but the restaurant situation isn't as promising as other towns along the river.

Grazing cattle populate the fields approaching **Port d'Envaux** and shaded country homes make appealing landscape pictures. The town welcomes children: near the pontoons is a playground with swings and a slide, all nicely set in sand.

Crazannes appears very reserved and very sure of itself, not welcoming tourists as readily as other places along the river. The **Château de Crazannes,** not visible from the river, is semi-surrounded by a moat, and is best known for its flamboyant doorway. It's easily reached from an anchorage in town. From there it's a bicycle ride of less than 2 miles (3 km).

The **Château de Panloy's** dovecote (three miles/five km from Crazannes) was built in 1620; an unusual feature is

River meets sea in Rochefort.

the ladder which turns on one axis, giving direct access to all the nests. The fact that there are more than 3,000 nests gives some idea of the size of the estate. It was the custom to allow only three nests per *arpent* (approximately 1½ acres) per estate; therefore, 3,000 nests meant an estate of about 1,500 acres (600 hectares).

The estate was bought in 1683 by Monsieur Labréthon de Faye, Councillor to the Parliament of Bordeaux and an ancestor of the present owner. The château was built in 1770, and tours visit the public rooms. In the living room hang five Beauvais tapestries from the cartoons of J.B. Huet, showing what 18th-century Parisians thought of country life. (Peasants seemed to work in silks and high heels). There are only three seasonal paintings in the living room instead of four. Winter is not represented because there is virtually none in this part of France.

St Savinien offers extensive pleasure-craft moorings and supply shops abound in this very agreeable town. To visit, take the right fork; to the left is the last lock and weir on the river; beyond is the tidal Charente. Until the 1850s, the construction of freight barges was the town's major industry.

Passing through the lock, another river emerges: the tideway rolls through marshland and muddy banks, fishing nets are suspended above the water, and clusters of typical Saintonge farmhouses with red-tiled roofs are scattered hither and yon. The landscape is singularly unattractive, with flat fields and power lines; negotiating a sometimes tricky tide can keep even that from being observed.

Tonnay is fighting a losing battle to make the town appealing to visiting boatpeople. The moorings are difficult: because the water is tidal, its level fluctuates approximately 7 to 10 ft (2–3 meters) below the concrete roadway and the walls are slanted. Sets of stairs are built into the quayside walls, but anchorage rings seem placed for cargo barges rather than houseboats. On the plus side, all services including repairs

Man's best friend stands guard.

are available, the service people are friendly and prices fair.

The only thing of note in Tonnay is the enormous suspension bridge which towers above the town. Built in 1885, it is 660-ft (204-meters) long, and was constructed to allow ocean-going vessels to sail upriver.

The river, as it approaches **Rochefort**, (3 miles/5 km from Tonnay) is like any other industrial riverfront: ugly. Spikey marshes populate one side, and warehouses the other. Chemical fumes spew into the air and the Charente has indeed lost its charm.

Approached by a well-marked series of buoys, the entrance to Rochefort's small boat harbor is easy to find, and sailing craft generally outnumber power. As befitting a naval town (even though it's 9 miles/15 km from the sea) the marina is one to treasure, and convenient for sight-seeing.

This cradle of the French navy lies in a large loop of the Charente. It was a sleepy village until Jean Baptiste Colbert, Louis XIV's canny finance minister, decided to build a safe port for French ships. Working nonstop, it was created between 1666 and 1668, and the town was laid out in a typical 17th-century new town design, a pattern of geometric grids.

At its height, Rochefort (Rock Fort) rivaled Toulon in power, but changing fortunes and ways of waging war led to a gradual decline. Today, fishing and tourism generate the most income, and in trying to attract the latter, many old buildings are being restored.

Near the Pleasure Boat Harbor is one of them, **La Cordérie Royale** (Royal Rope Factory). New inhabitants include a luxury hotel, an **International Naval Center** and **Bookstore** (a goldmine if one reads in French), and a **Museum of Rope**. Close by, Colbert's old **dry docks** are still visible although choked with weeds.

The **Naval Museum** is in the **Hôtel de Cheusses** near the Porte du Soleil; enjoy models of the boats launched from the yards. Look for the **Musée Municipal** on Avenue Général de Gaulle; one of its odder bits is a selection of Polynesian masks.

Rochefort's **Place Colbert** celebrates the marriage of river and sea with an enormous 18th-century stone fountain; on top Neptune (sea) and a female figure (river) gaze devotedly into one another's eyes. A museum celebrating the life of Naval writer and poet **Pierre Loti** (1850–1923) is located here. (Although he was born and died here, Loti's grave is on Ile d'Oléron where he's buried in the standing position.)

The estuary gradually widens as it nears the sea, eventually meeting the Atlantic opposite Ile Madam. The Ile d'Oléron, France's largest off-shore island after Corsica looms behind Madam. The cruise to **Portes des Barques** may be uninspiring, but the village is interesting. Fishing boats are pulled up on the flats at low tide, and one or two restaurants offer the local speciality, oysters. There are several full-service marinas and a wide range of shops. And for those who wish to visit the sea without venturing in it, this is as close as one can get.

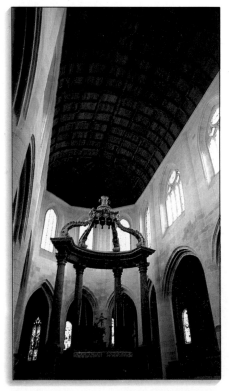

Left, interior of St Pierre in Saintes. **Right**, Roman ruins on Saintes' riverfront.

ALSACE-LORRAINE

Sauerkraut and sausages, half-timbered houses with storks nesting in the chimneys, plates of steaming quiche; Alsace-Lorraine is one of the most distinctive regions of France.

Once part of the Holy Roman Empire, both Alsace and Lorraine were acquired by France during the 17th and 18th centuries, but as a result of the 1870–71 Franco-Prussian war, much of the land was annexed to Germany. After World War I, the area returned to French rule, but again became part of Germany during World War II.

Since 1945 both Alsace and Lorraine have been decidedly French, but the region's checkered history has given it a sense of independence and individuality unlike any place else in France. Many of the people speak German as well as French, and the Alemanic influence is evident in the food, the wines, and even the architecture.

Principal canals serving Alsace and Lorraine are the Canal du Rhône au Rhin and the Canal de la Marne au Rhin. Most of the Canal du Rhône au Rhin was built between 1821 and 1833, although it was not until 1921 that the entire route was navigable. Constructed between 1838 and 1853, the Canal de la Marne au Rhin was built to connect Paris with the Alsace and the Rhine, and improvements made during the 1960s have made this canal one of the most efficient in the country.

Because of the rekindled popularity of transporting freight via barge, many of the waterways in this section of France are being enlarged and modernized to accommodate the increasing international barge traffic, and almost any type of cargo from bulk grain to fuel oil is carried along these canals.

Canal de La Marne au Rhin: Through a series of locks, tunnels and other devices, the 195-mile (314-km) long canal traverses Lorraine, climbs and burrows through the Vosges Mountains, then descends into the Alsace. The waterway begins at Vitry-le-François, in Champagne country, where it connects with Le Canal Latéral à la Marne.

Vitry-le-François is also a junction for the Canal de la Marne à la Saône. Set at a crossroads where these important north-south and east-west waterways meet, the town is an important barging center and has abundant marine supplies and barging services. Built as a fortified town in 1545 by François I to replace Vitry-en-Perthois which had been razed by Charles V the previous year, it was largely destroyed in World War II. Still standing however, is the magnificent town church built in the 17th and 18th centuries.

Continuing east, the canal runs through rolling plains and fields of grain to **Bar-le-Duc**, scene of local market fairs. An independent state from the 10th to the 14th century, Bar-le-Duc was absorbed into Lorraine in the late 16th century. Interesting sights include the church of **Notre Dame**, built in the 16th century, and the **Barrois Museum** which has artifacts dating from prehistoric times as well as local painting and

Left, the *Esprit* locks through. Right, strolling through town.

sculpture. The 14th-century church of **St Etienne** has a famous statue called *Le Squelette*, by Ligier Richier: when the 16th-century military hero René de Chalon, Prince of Orange, asked to be depicted as he would look three years after his death, the sculptor obliged. Bar-le-Duc is also famous for redcurrant jam. Several white and red wines are produced locally (and only sold in this region) and are worth trying.

From here, the canal climbs the hilly Lorraine countryside through a series of locks, culminating in a summit where barges must pass through the 16,320-ft (4,975-meter) **Mauvages Tunnel**. Traffic through the tunnel is one-way only, and boats hook up, 10 at a time, behind a chain tug which was built in 1912. Pleasure barges are positioned behind commercial craft, and the passage is slow and dark.

Emerging at **Mauvages**, boats then descend, through a series of 12 locks, into the valley of the **Meuse River** and the small city of **Toul**. An important Bishop's See in the Middle Ages, Toul was incorporated into France in 1648 by the Treaty of Westphalia.

Like many of the towns encountered on the canals of Alsace-Lorraine, Toul was fortified in the 17th century by the great French genius of military architecture, the Marquis Sebastien de Vauban who built fortresses throughout the country that were nearly impregnable. The massive stone walls and ramparts designed for Toul are still largely intact, and the canal actually runs through part of the old moat. Also worth

seeing here is the **St Etienne Cathedral**, built between the 13th and 14th centuries, with two octagonal towers 210 ft (65 meters) high, and a 14th-century cloister.

The nearby **Church of St Gengoult**, built between the 13th and 16th centuries, has some of the original stained-glass windows in the choir. *Le Dauphin* is a popular restaurant, and a small café here would be a good place to sample a *madeleine*, that light concoction of sugar, butter, eggs, flour and lemon that was invented in nearby **Commercy**.

Beyond **Frouard**, a short branch leads to the city of **Nancy**, founded in the 12th century to serve as the capital of the Duchy of Lorraine. The last of the influential Dukes of Lorraine was Stanislas Leszcynski, an exiled king of Poland who had the good fortune to have his daughter marry Louis XV. Louis granted the Duchy to Stanislas after the Polish king lost his crown in the 1733–38 War of Polish Succession.

Stanislas left behind a tremendous architectural heritage; try to see the grandiloquent **Place Stanislas**, located in the center of the city. With its gilded wrought iron gates, baroque fountains, and hanging lanterns, it is arguably the most beautiful square found in France. At the end of the 19th century, Nancy became the birthplace of *art nouveau*, and the **Ecole de Nancy Museum**, contains a collection of *art nouveau* objects ranging from individual items to a whole dining-room set complete with embossed leather ceilings. The **Museum of Fine Arts**, on the west side of Place

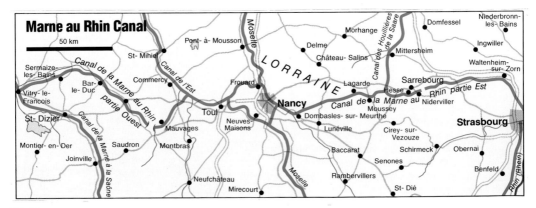

Stanislas, has European paintings dating from the 14th to the 20th centuries, and the **Lorraine History Museum**, in the old Ducal Palace, records 2,000 years of local history.

Reflecting Nancy's heritage as a mining town is the **History of Iron Museum**. Quiche Lorraine is a speciality at the Oxebon restaurant, and the Capucin Gourmand offers luxurious dining. The town has a population of around 100,000.

Outside Nancy, the canal goes through an industrial area marked by mines, wrought iron works, and massive foundries, and crosses the **Meurthe River** via a small aqueduct. **St-Nicolas de Port**, on the banks of the river, has been a center of industry and commerce since the Middle Ages. The town's 16th-century **Gothic Basilica** was built on the ruins of an earlier sanctuary that housed a finger of St Nicholas, brought from the Holy Land by the Knights of Lorraine. This is where Joan of Arc is said to have knelt before going off to fight the English.

Slightly farther on, at **Dombasle-sur-Meurthe**, the canal goes through the center of the **Solvay soda works**, where salt, chlorine, and bicarbonate of soda are produced. It may not be the most picturesque scene, but it is nevertheless fascinating to see. Barges are continually loading and unloading, and minirailway trains run overhead on little bridges. This massive factory has the largest furnaces in the world and its own fleet of 100 working barges.

The scenery becomes rural once again beyond Dombasle, and the small town of **Einville** is a good place for laying in supplies. About 6 miles (9 km) away is **Lunéville**, where, in the 18th century, Duke Léopold commissioned an architect to build a mini-Versailles.

Once home to the Dukes of Lorraine, the **Château of Lunéville** now houses a fire station, police station, and tax office, in addition to a **museum**. There are formal gardens, and during the summer, *son et lumière* shows are held in the chapel.

Beyond Einville, the **Fôret de Parroy** stretches to the south, and the **Sânon**

A warm Alsatian welcome.

river runs alongside the canal. At the village of **Lagarde**, the area's history comes graphically into focus with a German military cemetery at one end of town and a French cemetery at the other, both relics of World War I. Soldiers have stormed through this region in every European war in recent history. During World War II, the Germans came through twice, once on their way to Paris and again on the way out, and many houses still have bullet holes in the walls.

Farther on, boats pass through the **Etang de Réchicourt**, an old feeder lake for the canal. At the east end of the lake, there's a lock with a rise of 50 ft (15 meters). Six small locks were eliminated when the **Réchicourt-le-Château** lock was built in the early 1960s, cutting two hours off the transit.

At this point, the canal cuts through the **Fôret de Réchicourt** and then traverses more feeder lakes, including the vast 1,160-acre (470-hectare) **Etang de Gondrexange** reservoir, a popular spot for sailing and windsurfing. At some places, the reservoir, behind an embankment, is on a higher level than the canal, so it's possible to look up and see windsurfers whizzing by just a few feet above the waterway.

Branching off at the eastern end of the reservoir is the Canal des Houilleres de la Sarre (the Sarre Coalfields Canal), a forbiddingly named, but pretty waterway that passes through **Lorraine National Park**. It was built in the 1860s to link Lorraine with the coal-mining districts of the Sarre.

Farther along the Marne au Rhin, the canal crosses the Sarre River by means of a 146-ft (45-meter) aqueduct. In this area, the German influence becomes increasingly evident in such place names as **Hesse** and **Schneckenbusch**. The former has ruins of a **Benedictine Abbey** founded by the family of Pope Léon, who was from the Alsace. The **Hartzviller Glassworks** are a short bicycle trip away, and visitors can tour the factory and watch master glass-blowers in action.

Another good excursion from Hesse

is the town of **Sarrebourg**, at the edge of the Vosges Mountains, which form the geographical division between Lorraine and the Alsace. The 13th-century **Franciscan Chapelle des Cordeliers** has a modern stained glass window, titled *La Paix* (Peace) by Marc Chagall, which at 39 by 24 ft (12 by 7.5 meters) is the largest in Europe.

The **Sarrebourg Museum** houses artifacts dating from prehistoric and Roman times as well as modern local ceramics, and the sobering **Jardin de la Liberté** has 13,000 graves from World War I.

Just beyond Hesse, the canal passes the towns of **Schneckenbusch** and **Niderviller**, famous for its earthenware (the factory dates from 1735), before entering the two tunnels that cut through the Vosges. Both were built between 1850 and 1853 and have alternating one-way traffic. The first, the **Niderviller Tunnel**, is just 1,476 ft (450 meters), but the **Arzviller Tunnel** is 8,530 ft (2,600 meters) long.

Upon emerging from the second tunnel, visitors are in the **Alsace**, and stretched out below are the forests of the **Zorn Valley**. Just ahead lies one of the marvels of modern waterway technology, the **St Louis-Arzviller Inclined Plane**. It's a kind of giant bathtub on rails. A barge or boat enters the huge water-filled tank, which is then lowered (or raised) 350 ft (108 meters) down a 41 degree slope. When it was built in 1969, the inclined plane replaced 17 locks which used to take eight hours to traverse. Today's trip in the giant tub takes about 25 minutes, and the procedure may be one of the most photographed events on the canal. Serious photographers should try for a shot that looks down on the boat-filled Inclined Plane.

The canal then follows the course of the Zorn river where hills rise on either side of it. The charming village of **Lutzelbourg** actually lies at the junction of five valleys and water, food, and fuel are available, as well as exquisite cut crystal by master artisan Jean Wurm. Looming above the town on a 985-ft

Typical Alsace-Lorraine architecture.

(300-meter) cliff, are the ruins of a 12th-century château.

About 2½ miles (4 km) away is **Phalsbourg**, created in the 16th century by Count Palatin and fortified in the 17th by Marquis Vauban. It was the home town of Emile Erckman, who, with Alexandre Chatrian wrote popular novels about the Alsace; visit also the **Erckman-Chatrian Museum**.

Past Lutzelbourg, the canal cuts through the **Fôret Domaniale** to **Saverne**, a busy market town with tradition-al Alsatian half-timbered houses and lovely rose gardens. From 1417 to 1789, Saverne was the seat of the Strasbourg Bishopric, and the red sandstone **Rohan Château**, summer palace of the bishops of the powerful Rohan family, is an impressive sight.

No fewer than five ruined medieval castles dot the hillsides surrounding Saverne, all dating from the 11th and 12th centuries, when the perils of the times prompted the building of protec-tive fortresses. Walks from the canal to these castles take one or two hours, but the views from them encompass the entire Alsatian plain, and on clear days, it's possible to see the magnificent spire of Strasbourg Cathedral, some 18 miles (30 km) away.

Most famous of the ruins around Saverne, the **Château de Haut-Barr** sits on a 1,476-ft (450-meter) crest. One of the owners, Jean de Manderscheidt, a bishop of Strasbourg, founded a drink-ing club here. To qualify, potential mem-bers had to down in one gulp an onyx-horn filled with 5 pints (almost 3 liters) of white wine.

Beyond Saverne, the canal passes through the plain of Alsace and past such typical Alsatian farming villages as **Lupstein**, **Ingenheim** and **Walten heim-sur-Zorn**. Narrow, crooked streets wind past half-timbered houses with steep roofs and little windows, and large front doors open to reveal court-yards bordered by farm buildings. All around is heard Alsatian, a Germanic dialect even the Germans can't under-stand. Storks can often be seen nesting in the chimneys, and Alsatian tradition

Candles light the gloom of Strasbourg's Cathedral.

says that that brings good luck to the household for a year.

Ahead are the outskirts of **Strasbourg**, capital of the Alsace, and one of the most cosmopolitan cities in France. The canal runs past the **Palais de l'Europe**, which houses the Council of Europe and the European Parliament.

Founded by the Romans in AD 16 as a fortified stronghold called Argentoratum, the city was later conquered by the Franks and christened Strateburgum (crossroads). Louis XIV occupied the city in 1681 after the Holy Roman Empire could no longer hold onto it. To fortify it, Louis had Vauban build massive walls. Until the Revolution, Strasbourg remained fairly autonomous; then the Republicans asserted their authority over the city. After the 1871 Prussian War the city and province were transferred to German control.

Located on the banks of both the Rhine and Ill rivers, and near the borders of France, Germany, Switzerland, Belgium, and Luxembourg, it remains a crossroads to this day and is rich with history. Johann Gutenberg lived here from 1434 to 1444 while perfecting the printing press, and Roger de Lisle wrote *La Marseillaise* in 1772.

Strasbourg seems made for visiting by barge. Bordered by the **Ill** and a small canal called **Fosse du Faux**, the oldest and most interesting part of the city is essentially an island. Barges can moor at **Quai de Pêcheurs**, just steps away from the old town, and boats that are small enough can navigate the narrow canals of **Le Petit France**, the old Quartier des Tanneurs, (Tanners' Quarter) which today is a charming district of restaurants, cafés, and half-timbered Alsatian houses with flowering window boxes.

The most famous of the city's attractions is surely the **Cathedral of Notre Dame**, built of rose-hued sandstone from the Vosges Mountains. Its construction spanned five centuries from 1015 to 1439, and its design reflects a range of styles from Romanesque to late Gothic. The *horloge astronomique* (**astronomical clock**), made by Swiss clock makers in the 16th century, features a parade of

the Apostles, and a cock's crow greets the appearance of St Peter. Inexplicably, the clock chimes not at 12 noon, but 15 minutes past.

Food is nearly an obsession in Alsace-Lorraine. There is *foie gras* from Strasbourg, blue trout from Mulhouse and, of course, Quiche Lorraine. Liqueurs such as Kirsch, Mirabelle, and fruit brandies are produced locally, and the *charcuteries* produce a bewildering variety of sausages, *pâtés* and *terrines*. Strasbourg has many good restaurants where visitors can sample such local dishes as *tarte a l'oignon* (onion tart) or *choucroute* (sauerkraut, sausages, bacon, pork and potatoes). Good restaurants include Au Crocodile, which is formal and expensive, and L'Ami Schutz more casual and friendly.

Alsatian wines are ranked among the great vintages of France. They are characterized by rich bouquets, fruity tastes and a freshness that makes them a delight to drink. Also to be sampled are the local Reislings, Traminers, and perhaps some of the less well-known wines such

Altar of the Anointer in Colmar.

as the Gentil, Klevner and Gries varieties (which may be sold only here). Alsatian wines are classified by grape varieties, rather than by region, and the wine must be bottled where it is grown.

Le Canal du Rhône au Rhin: While Strasbourg marks the terminus of the Canal de la Marne au Rhin, it is also the beginning of another important waterway. The idea of joining the Rhine and Rhône rivers by a navigable waterway was first proposed in 1744, but the full length of the canal was not opened until 1834.

The canal flows south from Strasbourg, roughly parallelling the **Rhine**, and since most commercial traffic is on the Rhine, this is usually quite a peaceful run, past small French villages with such improbable names as **Gerstheim**, **Obenheim**, and **Boofzheim**. At **Friesenheim** the canal joins the swiftly running Rhine, where small barges rub shoulders with large freighters and cruise ships. This busy commercial waterway, where huge 2,000-ton barges go thundering past, makes a sharp contrast to the placid waters of the canal. These are now international waters, with France on one side and Germany on the other.

Breisach-am-Rhein, a town on the German side of the river, was once French. One winter the Rhine changed course, and almost overnight Breisach became German. Because of customs regulations, it's best to moor on the French side of the river at **Neuf-Breisach** and simply walk or bicycle across the bridge for a glimpse of Germany.

From Neuf-Breisach, several excursions into the Alsatian countryside are possible. At **Haut-Koenigsbourg**, there is a 15th-century castle that was restored for Kaiser Wilhelm II during the German occupation. The **Humanist Library** at **Selestat** contains a letter proposing to name the Americas after Italian navigator Amerigo Vespucci, and **Kayserburg** is the birthplace of Albert Schweitzer.

Two of the best-known Alsace wine villages are also close, in the foothills of the Vosges. **Riquewihr** is a little medieval town with stone walls, cobblestone streets, and vineyards all around.

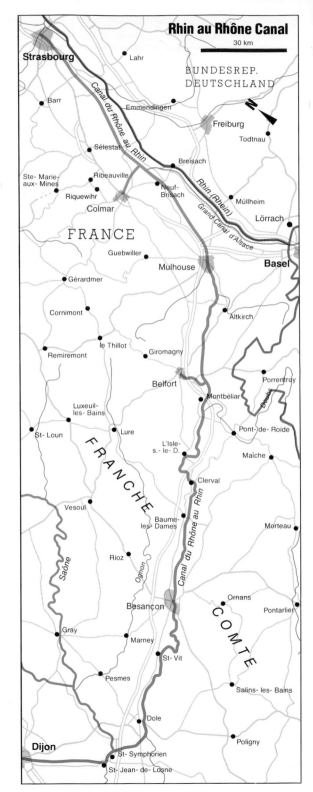

Rhin au Rhône Canal

30 km

Ribeauville is slightly larger, but also charming, with a Renaissance fountain and the ruins of three medieval castles.

Just below **Breisach-am-Rhein**, smaller craft can exit the Rhine and head northwest on the **Colmar Canal** to **Colmar**, or south on the **Grand Canal d'Alsace**, built after World War I as a lateral canal along the Rhine.

Once a Free City of the Holy Roman Empire, the modern industrial city of Colmar retains remnants of its eventful past. Burghers' houses from the 16th and 17th centuries line many of the streets, and the 13th-century **Dominican Church** has an altarpiece by 15th-century Colmar artist Martin Schongauer. The **Unterlinden Museum**, in the old **Dominican Convent of Unterlinden**, houses the Isenheim Altar, a masterpiece of German painting which was executed around 1515 by Matthias Grunewald. Colmar was also the birthplace of Frederic Auguste Bartholdi, designer of the Statue of Liberty, and the **Musée Bartholdi** houses historical artifacts from Colmar as well as remnants of the artist's work, such as a model of Ms Liberty's ear. The Schillinger is considered to be the town's most elegant restaurant.

The Grand Canal d'Alsace continues south from Breisach and meets the lower portion of the Canal du Rhône au Rhin, which branches off north and west through the **Fôret de Harth** to **Mulhouse**. An old textile town, Mulhouse has several interesting museums, including the **Musée National de L'Automobile**, containing the largest collection of Bugattis anywhere in the world. It was started by the Schlumpf brothers of Switzerland who bankrupted their textile company by funnelling off funds to their private collection. After the brothers fled the country, angry workers broke into a factory thought to be empty and discovered the cars.

There's also a **Railway Museum** housing Général de Gaulle's personal carriage as well as a collection of old steam engines, and a **Fabrics Museum**, where visitors can watch textile printing machines in action. The **Moulin du**

Mulhouse's Automobile Museum offers vintage racers.

Kaegy serves good food, and offers a pleasant atmosphere.

Further along the canal, the small town of **Dannemarie** has barge services and is a good base for an excursion to **Belfort**, another town fortified in the 17th century by Vauban. Strategically positioned to overlook the **Belfort Corridor**, a gap between the **Vosges** and the **Jura mountains**, Belfort has served as a vital defensive outpost since 1226. The fortress that Vauban created withstood three different sieges, the last in 1871, when the fortifications were over 200 years old. The **Lion of Belfort**, a giant red sandstone statue 72 ft (22 meters) long and 36 ft (11 meters) high was created by Bartholdi to honor those who withstood that year-long siege.

Just beyond Dannemarie, at **Valdieu**, the canal climbs the hillside via a flight of 16 locks in the space of about a mile, a trip that typically takes several hours unless there are a number of commercial barges which always go first.

At this point, the canal is traversing an area known as the **Franche-Comté**, literally "free-county", a region that was more or less independent for many years. Through a series of political marriages it became, during the 16th and 17th centuries, a territory of Spain. For two centuries it was French speaking, but titularly under Spanish dominion, so it became fairly autonomous. Under Louis XV the French eventually took the region back, but a certain sense of independence has remained to this day, and a definite Spanish influence on the architecture can be seen.

In **Montreux-Château**, just beyond Valdieu, this influence can be seen in the wrought iron grille-work on the windows and in pleasant little court-yards. All that's left of the château here is a pile of stones in a field, but this is a good base for an excursion to **Ronchamp** to see the **Chapel de Notre Dame du Haut**, the striking steel and reinforced concrete masterpiece designed in 1955 by Le Corbusier.

Montbeliard is the commercial and industrial center that is home to the Peugeot automobile factory (visits here

Alsace grapes are grown...

are possible). Capital of a duchy for 400 years, Montbeliard has a 15th-century château built by Henrietta of Wurtemberg.

The canal begins to follow the course of the **Doubs River**, and the region is dotted with pretty villages with stone houses and flower gardens. **Colombier-Fontaine** and **Colombier Chatelot** are both pleasant and offer good services. At **l'Isle-sur-le-Doubs** the canal actually merges with the river. The town itself, divided by the river into three different sections, is lovely, and diesel fuel is available on the quay.

Beyond l'Isle, the river proceeds to wind into the hilly countryside. **Clerval**, located at the bend of the river, is an old Roman settlement and has an 18th-century church with a lovely 16th-century *Pietà*. It's also a good place for provisioning as well as a base for a visit to the 12th-century **Château de Belvoir**. Once a bishop's residence, the castle has been restored, and its kitchens, bedrooms, chapel and armory are open to the public.

...and harvested near Riqueville.

Baume-les-Dames is a town of small houses built of beige and blueish limestone. It was here that, in 1776, the Marquis Claude-François-Dorothée de Jouffroy d'Abbans built and tested the world's first experimental steamboat. The vessel was 98 ft (30 meters) long with a beam of over six ft (two meters), and was powered by a Watt engine. Although the craft made several successful runs between Besançon and Montbeliard, the Marquis and his boat faded from the pages of history. A monument near the bridge was erected in 1884, however, to mark his efforts.

Below Baume is one of the most beautiful river runs in France. Sheer white limestone cliffs rise from the banks of the Doubs, and at **Besançon**, the river does a 2-mile (3-km) horseshoe loop around the city. Barges and boats, however, can take a short cut through a tunnel in the rock.

Founded in Roman times as the town of Vesontio, Besançon was later an important cultural and commercial center of the Franche-Comté, and is the birth-

place of Victor Hugo. Nearly 400 ft (120 meters) above the city is the **Citadel**, built in 1674 by Vauban on the site of an old Roman fort. Today the Citadel houses a variety of museums, including the **Musée Populaire Comtois**, a folklore museum that has an old nail-making machine and lace-making equipment, the **Musée d'Histoire Naturelle**, and the **Musée de la Résistance et de la Déportation**, a moving tribute to heroes of the French Resistance.

The waterway beyond Besançon shifts back and forth between the river and stretches of canal. At the small village of **Routelle**, an excursion can be made to **Arc et Senans**, the Royal Salt Works built in the 18th century by noted French architect Claude Nicholas Ledoux. In an early attempt to create a planned community, Ledoux built a total environment for salt workers. Success was mixed, however, since an absence of chimneys created a hot and smoky work area, and salt motifs in the design constantly reminded the employees of their work. The salt works were eventually taken over by the State, and today are the headquarters for the **Center for Reflections on the Future**, a group that does, among other things, research into alternative energy sources. Farther along, the waterway passes the town of **Orchamps**, birthplace of Gustav Courbet, and just downstream from Dole, the canal finally splits off from the river for good.

The capital of Franche-Comté until the end of the 17th century, **Dole** was robbed of its title by Louis XIV who moved the capital to Besançon to punish Dole for its independent spirit. Dole still has the largest church in the Franche-Comté, the 16th-century **Eglise Notre-Dame**, with vivid stained glass windows. The 242-ft (74-meter) steeple was actually built as a look-out tower. Dole was the birthplace of Louis Pasteur, and his home is a museum.

Beyond Dole, the waterway continues on to the small town of **St-Symphorien-sur-Saône**, where the canal meets the **Saône** river.

Right, a peaceful punt.

THE CANALS OF BURGUNDY

Food, wine, history and scenery are the principal characteristics of the region that for 500 years was the home of the powerful Dukes of Burgundy. Located at the heart of France, Burgundy is also situated in the valleys of the Seine, Loire and Rhône rivers. This unique geography has allowed the building of canals throughout the region, and for cruising, there are over 1,200 miles (1,900 km) of waterways.

Today the Yonne, Nivernais, Bourgogne and the Central form the nucleus of some of the most popular cruising waterways in France. Although there is commercial traffic on some, most are tranquil havens for relaxing on private boats or hotel barges. And since this is Burgundy, there is never far to go for good wine or food.

Burgundy produces over 40 million bottles of wine a year and the wine areas welcome visitors. Chablis, Vougeot, Chambertin, Nuits, Pouilly-Fuissé are all here for the tasting. During September and October the harvest is in full swing and festivals can be found. Kir is a classic Burgundian drink: one part Cassis de Dijon (blackcurrant liqueur) to two parts aligoté (a dry white wine from the Hautes-Côtes).

Then there is the food. Burgundian cuisine is rich, flavorful and draws heavily on the wines and local ingredients for flavour. *Boeuf bourguignon, coq au vin* and *escargot bourguignon* are all local specialities. *Moutardes de Dijon* are known as the finest mustards in France, perhaps even the world.

Food is a part of the culture. After every rain, visitors are often startled to find villagers literally beating the bushes to find the increasingly scarce *escargots* (snails). To make the traditional Burgundian dish, they are cooked with garlic and butter, but visitors will find many other variations as well.

And Burgundy's history: crusades began here, kings waged war, and Caesar won the three parts of Gaul near Vercingetorix. In the 13th and 14th centuries, the Dukes of Burgundy were more powerful than the kings of France. Their wealth and influence are reflected in the myriad châteaux that dot the region. There are churches dating from the 9th century and before, Roman and Merovingian ruins, and even artifacts from Mesolithic man. Clearly, Burgundy has been a popular destination for thousands of years.

Le Canal de Bourgogne: Most likely it was the Romans who first dreamed of linking the Saône and Seine river valleys as a convenient trade route between the Mediterranean and Northern Europe. But it took the French in the 18th and 19th centuries to make the dream a reality by creating the Burgundy Canal. Today only a few commercial craft ply its quiet waters, most of them carrying bulk cement and grain. But the lack of commercial traffic has been supplanted by a boom in pleasure boats, making this one of the most popular routes for pleasure boats in the region and perhaps France too.

The canal follows the Armançon, a

Left, balloon to bicycle communication. Right, Adam and Eve in St Florentin.

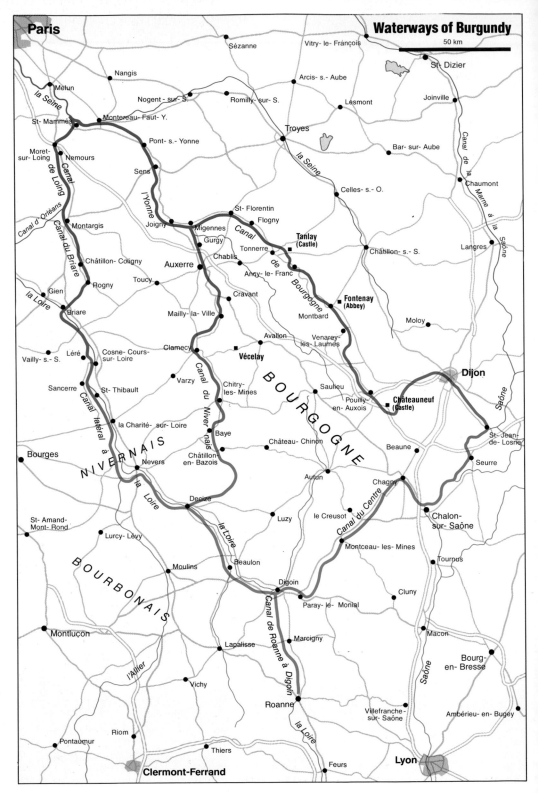

Paris

Waterways of Burgundy

50 km

Sézanne · Vitry- le- François · St- Dizier

Nangis · Arcis- s.- Aube · Joinville

Melun · Nogent - sur- S. · Romilly- sur- S. · Lésmont

la Seine · Bar- sur- Aube

St- Mammès · Montereau- Faut- Y. · Troyes

Moret- sur- Loing · Nemours · Pont- s.- Yonne · Celles- s.- O. · Langres

Canal de Loing · Sens · la Seine · Châtillon- s.- S. · Canal de la Chaumont

Canal d'Orléans · Montargis · l'Yonne · St- Florentin · Tanlay (Castle) · Canal de la Marne à la Saône

Canal du Briare · Joigny · Flogny · Tonnerre

Châtillon- Coligny · Migennes · Gurgy · Canal · Ancy- le- Franc · Fontenay (Abbey)

Rogny · Auxerre · Chablis · de · Montbard · Moloy

Gien · Toucy · Cravant · Bourgogne

la Loire · Briare · Mailly- la- Ville · Venarey- les- Laumes

Léré · Cosne- Cours- sur- Loire · Clamecy · Avallon

Vailly- s.- S. · Varzy · Vécelay · Saulieu · Dijon

Sancerre · Chitry- les- Mines · BOURGOGNE · Pouilly- en- Auxois · Châteauneuf (Castle) · Saône

St- Thibault · Canal du Nivernais · Beaune · St- Jean- de- Losne

Canal latéral à · la Charité- sur- Loire · Baye · Château- Chinon · Seurre

Bourges · NIVERNAIS · Nevers · Châtillon- en- Bazois · Chagny · Chalon- sur- Saône

St- Amand- Mont- Rond · Decize · Autun · le Creusot · Canal du Centre

Lurcy- Lèvy · la Loire · Luzy · Montceau- les- Mines · Tournus

BOURBONAIS · Moulins · Beaulon · Digoin · Cluny

Montluçon · Lapalisse · Marcigny · Paray- le- Monial · Macon

l'Allier · Vichy · Canal de Roanne à Digoin · Bourg- en- Bresse

Riom · Roanne · Villefranche- sur- Saône · Ambérieu- en- Bugey

Pontaumur · Thiers · la Loire · Feurs · Lyon

Clermont-Ferrand

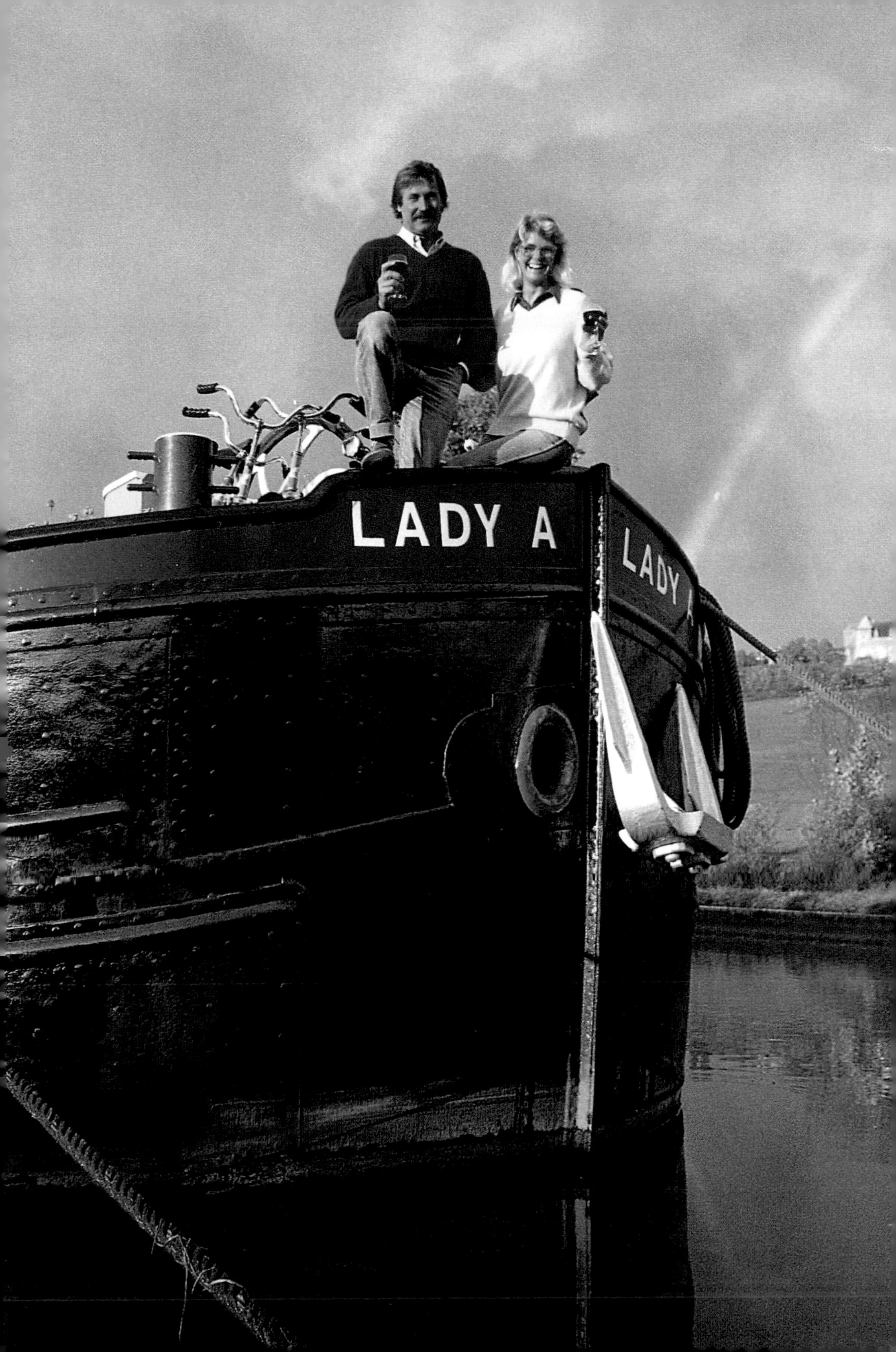
LADY A
LADY

tributary of the river Yonne, and the Ouche, a tributary of the river Saône, on its course across the rolling countryside of Burgundy. However, in order to cross the mountains near Pouilly-en-Auxois, a very long tunnel had to be constructed and a series of reservoirs built to ensure adequate water flow on the route. On the Burgundy Canal, the engineering is remarkable; the scenery, atmospheric villages and interesting historical sites make the canal one of the most pleasurable in France.

Officially the canal begins at the town of **Laroche Migennes** where the Yonne Canal branches off to Auxerre, but **Brienon** marks the first town on it, offering good shops and services from which to start a journey. In addition to a 13th-century church and an interesting 18th-century washery, this is also a trading town. Below Brienon, look for a railroad bridge where the super-fast Trains à Grande Vitesse (TGVs) cross, a good place to reflect on the advances in transportation in the last 150 years.

High on a hill above the canal **St Florentin** has a lovely church dating from the 14th century. Remains of the fortifications that made this a formidable stronghold can still be seen in the town. Notice also an old fountain in the center of town; Adam and Eve, *au naturel*, are two of the statues carved on it. Two of France's greatest cheeses, St Florentin and Soumaintrain, are produced near here.

Flogny, some distance away on the canal, is the next town for good provisions along a stretch of the canal that passes many small farming villages.

The countryside is beautiful, studded with rolling hills and patches of woods. **Tonnerre** is a sizeable town and canal port, and a center of trading since Roman times. In the middle of town is the **Fosse Dionne**, a circular stone laundry basin dating from the time of Caesar and still filled with ultra-blue water from a natural spring.

Examples of typical Burgundian architecture can be found, and red roof tiles indicate older buildings. The Ancien Hôpital or **Notre-Dame des Fon-**

Preceding page: "bon voyage". Below, the Round Tower of Château de Tanlay.

tenilles, a 13th-century hospital, was begun by Marguerite de Bourgogne. The grand hall, over 260 ft (80 meters) in length, where the beds for the sick lined the walls, is worth seeing.

There is another famous, or infamous, resident of Tonnerre who should be remembered. Charles Geneviève Louis Auguste César Andrée Timothée Deon de Beaumont lived from 1728 to 1810, changing roles from male to female (at one time he posed as a female spy) as it suited him. He was honored for his exploits as both man and woman, and only when he finally died was it definitely proved that he was male.

In a country filled with châteaux, the example at **Tanlay** is usually pointed out as the finest. Hot-air balloon launchings are sometimes held in the old stable areas and if available offer a fine view of the château after lift-off.

Tanlay has been in the same family since 1704 and tours of the two buildings that comprise the edifice are offered. A curious octagonal room in the château, the **Tower of the League**, once was the site of secret meetings of the Huguenots. Of further interest is the painting on the room's domed ceiling of historical people dressed (or undressed) as mythological figures.

An easy walk from the port at **Ancy-le-Franc** is another fine château. Here, the buildings are more fanciful and have been likened to the Fontainebleau school of architecture. Many fine old stone houses and other buildings are found in **Cry-sur-Armançon.**

The canal winds among hills and rolling farmland with white Charolais cattle everywhere. The canal banks have been planted with plane trees and poplars which open up to offer views of the hills and an occasional marble quarry. Just outside **Buffon** are the remains of a large 18th-century forge that attests to the considerable industrial activity in the area that provided much of the impetus for 18th and 19th-century canal construction. Tours of the restored buildings can be arranged.

Less than 4 miles (6 km) east of Montbard is the **Abbeye de Fonteney**, foun-

Cruising past Tanlay.

ded in the 12th century by St Bernard. Carefully maintained for centuries and finally restored by the Montgolfier brothers (of hot-air balloon fame), it stands as a rare example of a perfectly preserved Cistercian abbey. The scriptorium, dormitories, church, kitchens and other buildings are all in order, as if the monks were about to move back in.

Montbard is a large industrial town that offers good barging services and a large market, but no charm. This was the birthplace of the great French industrialist-turned-naturalist Comte de Buffon. He built a garden on the site of a ruined fortress built by the Dukes of Burgundy. Only two towers now remain but exploring the overgrown park makes an interesting walk.

Venarey-les-Laumes is the last town before the climb to the summit begins in earnest. There are good services here and an interesting side trip: 2½ miles (4 km) to the east is the village of **Alise-Sainte-Reine**, site of the battle where Caesar besieged Vercingetorix in 52 BC and where Gaul finally fell to the Ro-

mans – look for a massive statue to the Gallic leader.

Fortified for the journey uphill, keep one cheerful thought in mind: there are only 56 back-breaking, thirst-producing locks between here and Pouilly, then there's the tunnel to negotiate, and finally, almost the same number of descending locks to Dijon!

If all this is too daunting for one go, take a break at **Pouillenay** (nine locks cleared, 47 to go) and hire a taxi for the 6-mile (10-km) trip to **Semur-en-Auxois**, perhaps one of the best small Burgundian cities in the area. Everywhere, small houses crowd onto narrow streets and the 14th-century towers stand guard over everything.

Notre-Dame de Semur is a beautiful example of the Gothic church in Burgundy. The museum and library contain some beautiful 10th-century manuscripts as well as geological and paleontological works. Sports fans will want to visit on 31 May when France's oldest horserace is held here.

The canal continues to rise through

Left, looking over Dijon. **Below,** a cluster of Burgundian roofs.

the seemingly endless series of locks, as it threads through a rather narrow cut on its way to Pouilly-en-Auxois and the summit. Once reached, there are very good boat services here and shops for provisioning. But the real attraction (beside the waterside cafés) is the **Pouilly tunnel**. The 1,088-ft (3,350-meter) mole hole can take two hours or more to traverse, and making the passage in the dark, low tunnel is a memorable, if not totally enjoyable, part of cruising the canal.

The descent offers more of the same: lock after lock has to be tackled. The canal offers views of the dense forest and lovely small villages. But watch very carefully because after **Ecluse 8**, from **Vandenesse**, there is a breathtaking view of **Châteauneuf** perched on its hilltop just east of the canal. This is one of those picture postcard views, and the reality is no less than the expectation, the 12th-century structure having survived in good shape. The turreted castle, which is open for inspection, was begun by Guy de Chaudeney and ex-

pansion continued until at least the 15th century. The village within the fortified walls contains several houses built for rich merchants and a variety of interesting shops; a restaurant offers fine dining amid the splendors of one of the most interesting places in Burgundy.

Between here and Dijon the waterway passes through thick forests and more small villages. Several have good shops and are located right on the canal. Because of the variety of trees that are to be found in the forests here, a cruise along this reach of the canal is especially popular in fall, when the foliage is blazing with color.

As the countryside changes to suburbs, it is evident that the waterway is nearing **Dijon**. The canal locks in the center of the city lead to a special mooring basin reserved for pleasure boats, and this is perfectly situated for exploring the city on foot. There is a well-tended public garden next to the mooring, and the commercial shopping center is only a five-minute walk away.

Once the capital of Burgundy, this

The Burgundy Canal at Vandenesse.

town, dating from pre-Roman times, when it was known as Dibio, rose to prominence in the 13th century, and for the next 500 years was the seat of a power in the heartland of France. Destroyed and rebuilt several times after the Romans, the greatest devastation came from a fire in 1137. Rebuilding was completed by Duke Hugues II who enclosed the city with thick stone walls and fortified gates.

In the 14th century, one family was responsible for the ultimate rise to greatness: Philippe the Bold, his son Jean Sans Peur (*without fear*), and grandson, Philippe Le Bon (*the good*). By the middle of the next century, the Kingdom of Burgundy ruled an area that ran northward from the Loire River and Jura mountains as far as the Low Countries. Always at odds with the Kings of France, and sometimes even allied against them with England (Joan of Arc was captured by the Burgundians and given to the British), Burgundy did not become a part of France until 1477 when Charles the Bold died.

Dijon reflects that era of power in its public buildings. **Place de la Libération** is the spiritual, if not actual, center of the city and was laid out in 1682, the same year the the **Palace of the Dukes of Burgundy** was built. Behind the Palace, up 316 steps, **Tour Philippe Le Bon** offers magnificent views of the city. While in the vicinity, don't miss the **Musée des Beaux Arts** in one wing of the Palace. It's a treasure-house of modern art and remnants from Burgundy's glorious past.

The clock tower of the 13th-century **Church of Notre Dame** originally had only one mechanical man who paraded when the hour was struck; now there are three figures, a woman and two children, the last added in 1881. Inside, look for the Black Virgin: dating to the 11th century, it is one of France's oldest wooden sculptures. The modern tapestry details two important events in the city's history: liberation in 1513 and 1944. The 14th-century **Cathedral of St Bénigne** was built on the site of an earlier church. Although Gothic, the

Kayaking on the canal.

120

architect incorporated the Romanesque doorway into the building.

Outside, the richly varied Burgundian roof tiles can be seen in the older buildings throughout the town. Beside the Musée des Beaux Arts, several other museums offer glimpses into Dijon's past, including archaeology, which is housed in an old Benedectine abbey next to St Bénigne.

Of course, no visit to Dijon would be complete if one didn't buy a few jars of the local mustard. Shops carry a wide variety of styles and types, more than 150 at the last count, including ones flavored with herbs, the ancient style with whole grains, and the more familiar smooth and hot mustard.

From Dijon the canal heads south in a nearly straight line across the wide plain between the city and the river Saône. But, as if to compensate for the plainness of the terrain, there are impressive châteaux along the way and some charming lock houses. There is a particularly lovely château at **Longecourt-en-Plaine**, and mooring in front of it in this small town makes one feel a part of the past, when carriages rolled through the countryside on the way to Paris. Finally the town of **St-Jean-de-Losne**, a major port on the Saône, signals the end of the Canal du Burgogne.

L'Yonne: From its junction with the Seine at Montereau until it ends at Auxerre 67 miles (108 km) later, the river offers 26 locks, a variety of weirs, many bridges, and some tricky boat handling. Many of its locks have widely sloping sides and some skill is needed to manage them, though lock-keepers are generally helpful. However, a voyage along this canal is well worth the small effort.

The canal along the Yonne was begun in 1740 by the Duc d'Orléans who sought to tame the rocky and shallow Yonne River. However, for the next 200 years the project remained uncompleted, with grain barges and log rafts from the Morvan the chief users. Real construction on the present-day canal began in 1840 with the construction of the sloping-sided locks and other improvements

Fields of rape cover Burgundy's hills in springtime.

to the channel. Today, the canal is chiefly used by pleasure craft, although in summer and fall there is some commercial traffic with grain barges carrying the local harvest.

Montereau is a large commercial barging center because of the Seine barge traffic. From here there is not much to see but grassy fields and the occasional gravel pit. The small village of **Misy-sur-Yonne** has several shops and at **Pont-sur-Yonne** there are more shops, and a 13th-century church.

Sens can't be missed, part of the town is situated on an island in the center of the river. A visit to **St Etienne's Cathedral** and the adjoining palace is a must. Begun in 1140, it was the first Gothic cathedral built in France. Richly decorated both inside and out, the Cathedral has an impressive collection of stained glass and statuary. Its treasure, along with that of the church of St Foy at Conques, is one of the richest and finest in France, and includes the vestments of Thomas à Becket, the legendary Archbishop of Canterbury. For provisions, the town market offers good produce and is worth a visit to see its wrought-iron architecture and the nearby half-timbered houses.

Villeneuve was begun by Louis VII in the 12th century. A red-brick tower and some remains of walls along the river are part of the original fortifications. There is also the dungeon of a 12th-century royal castle, and it's easy to think of Eleanor of Aquitaine looking out on these very same sights.

From here, the Yonne takes on more character with small villages and lovely countryside to cruise. At **Villevallier** a bridge spans the canal, connecting the town with **St Julien-du-Sault**. It's worth taking a walk to this small village to see the 13th-century church's stained glass and an example of a 16th-century wooden house.

From the **Chapelle de Vauguillain** above St Julien there are fine views of the countryside.

Several pretty locks are sited on this section, and the canal and river wind together through gently rolling farm- **Boat ahead!**

land and woods until they reach **Joigny**. A large part of Joigny dates from the 15th and 16th centuries, and the half-timbered homes, small squares and winding streets are great fun to explore even though it means a long walk uphill. The oldest houses in the town can be found around **St Thibaut's** and **St John's** churches. The former, built in 1529, has a Nativity of the school of Pays-Bas as well as a Crucifixion from the school of Anvers. The latter contains woodwork and furniture from the Abbey at Vézélay.

Beyond **Laroche-St-Cydroine**, vessels can turn left for Laroche Migennes and the Canal de Bourgogne or continue to the right to Auxerre and the Canal du Nivernais. On the path to Auxerre, the first village is **Bassou** with several shops for provisioning. From here the canal returns to its rural feeling with several very lovely locks and a path that reveals wooded hillsides and small farms. The security fencing and watchtowers along the route are jarring, but they belong to a military facility. **Gurgy**, has an inter-esting old church and small shops for provisioning.

Auxerre emerges along the curving river in very dramatic fashion. Dominated by the spires of St Etienne's Cathedral, the Church of St Pierre en Vallée and the Abbey of St Germain, the town, where both Napoleon and Joan of Arc traveled the cobbled streets, spans both sides of the Yonne. Tour boats, commercial craft and pleasure barges moor along both banks, and there are several full-service marinas which also offer repair services.

Almost any climb up the hill leads to something interesting in this old town, but be sure not to miss **St Etienne**. A Gothic structure built on the site of a much earlier Romanesque church, the cathedral contains a unique fresco, of *Christ on Horseback*, in the lower vault, and there are also some remarkably preserved illuminated manuscripts.

The **Abbey of St Germain** is famous for its 9th-century frescoes, among the oldest in France, and a walk reveals streets of half-timbered houses dating

Below, every French town has its war memorial. **Right**, overlooking Sens.

from the 15th century. Along the waterfront are many shops and open-air cafés; a tourist information office is near the river.

The region around Auxerre is noted for its fine wines and there is a tasting cellar near the tourist office where local vintages are also sold.

Le Canal du Nivernais: From Auxerre, the waterway rolls southward toward **Decize**. The canal was designed to link Paris to the Loire River. It stretches 108 miles (174 km) amid forests and farmlands of the Yonne, Cure, Aron and Loire river valleys.

The canal carries almost no commercial traffic but is a favorite of pleasure barges because of the scenery, the food that can be had in some exceptionally fine local restaurants along the route and, of course, the Burgundy wines. Much of the canal's banks have been planted with fruit trees, and the forests of the Morvan provide further interest. Continuing south, the canal remains part of the Yonne River for some miles before finally taking its own route.

The rolling hillsides south of Auxerre provide tantalizing glimpses of vineyards, and just below the small town of **Champs-sur-Yonne** the village of **Bailly** is a good stopping point to visit some of them. **Saint-Bris-le-Vineaux** is 2 miles (3 km) away and wine tastings are offered here by the Société d'Intérêt Collectif Agricole du Vignoble de l'Auxerrois.

The region is well known for its wines, which include a *Crémant de Bourgogne*, a sparkling wine found throughout the region. Vineyards here also produce good reds and whites from vines that date back to the Middle Ages, having escaped some of the phylloxera that destroyed so many vines in the 19th century. These *appellation* controlled wines are excellent buys and little known outside Burgundy. Medieval cellars are located under much of the town and tours can be arranged. Elsewhere, there are some fine 16th-century buildings and a small 13th-century church. This stretch of the canal reveals several fine châteaux and the home of the famous sculptor Pierre Merlier.

The canal curves around **Vincelles**, where wines were once loaded onto barges and shipped to Paris. The old village washhouse has been converted into a **museum** that preserves a variety of documents and artefacts concerning the canal and the Yonne River. Across the river, a small nightclub is located in the vaulted cellar of a 13th-century monastery.

This is a good place to tie up and visit **Irancy**, a beautiful and not-to-be missed village about 2 miles (3 km) from the canal. Hills planted with vineyards and orchards frame the village and its 12th-century church. The vineyards produce wines that are bold and full of tannin, wines that are suitable for long ageing. With this in mind, it's best to buy older years of the local vintages. There are also some fine rosé wines made and sold here.

Vineyards are everywhere now, as the rocky hills rise from the valley. After **Cravant**, watch for a short side canal that is navigable as far as the villages of **Accolay** and **Vermenton**. **Provisioning a hotel barge...**

Returning to the Nivernais, make a sidetrip to **La Grande Grotte d'Arcy-sur-Cure**, a huge underground cavern.

Mailly-le-Château sits high above the canal which makes a 180-degree bend beneath the town. It is a steep but worthwhile climb to the town to see the view from the castle and visit **Eglise St Adrien**, a 13th-century church that has a belfry topped with gargoyles in early Gothic style. The cliffs that offer the view from Mailly begin to rise in earnest, and at the **Rochers du Saussois** they offer enough height to provide rock climbers with good ascents. For the more cautious, several paths lead to the top and provide more lovely views of the canal and the countryside.

Chatel-Censoir occupies a curve in the canal and can be recognized by the **Church of St Potentian** which dates from the 15th century. Surrounded by 17th and 18th-century houses, the church, whose crypt is believed to date from the 9th century, is built on an even older Roman site. It's well worth a visit for the varying architectural styles and periods it represents. Just below Châtel-Censoir, at **Ecluse 56**, **La Place** is certainly one of the most beautiful locks and houses along the entire Nivernais.

The village of **Coulanges-sur-Yonne** has several shops for provisioning but the main reason for stopping here is to hire a taxi to visit the superb, hilltop town of **Vézéley**, about 12 miles (20 km) away. Traces of Mesolithic civilization can be found here, dating from 10,000 BC. There are remains of Roman baths to explore and other early sites. But the most important reason to visit is the **Basilica of St Madeleine**, considered one of the finest examples of Romanesque architecture in the world. The basilica is constructed on the site of a 9th-century monastery; its nave is nearly 200 ft (62 meters) long, with a series of columns decorated with religious motifs. The view from here over the Cure River Valley is splendid; it was from this hill-side in 1146 that St Bernard read the Papal Bull which launched the Second Crusade.

In the village of **St Père-sous-**

...and enjoying its comforts.

Vézéley, which lies near the foot of the hill where the basilica stands, is one of the great restaurants in France, Marc Meneau's L'Espérance.

Located at the joining of the Yonne and Beuvron rivers, the market town of **Clamency** is the perfect place to moor a day or so. (Vézéley is reachable from here, too.) Guided tours of the half-timbered houses are available during the season. The tourist information bureau can supply maps and suggestions for exploring this charming town that is crowned by the 13th-century flamboyantly Gothic **church of St Martin**. Logs, cut from the forests of the Morvan, were floated downriver from this point and a statue commemorates the gallant men who made the journey on the log rafts. Be sure to walk along the quay for some good views of the town and its wall.

From Clamency, the canal has several drawbridges that can make the passage interesting. All have keepers; slow down on approaching, blow horn and hope the keeper is at home!

At **Villiers-sur-Yonne**, there is an interesting display of Merovingian artifacts that can be seen in a small museum. A short walk from the canal, **Monceaux-le-Comte** is a small market town with ruins of a 13th-century château. **Chitry-les-Mines** was an important silver mining town and has a 14th-century château that featured in the resistance during World War II. Tours can sometimes be arranged through the owners, so it is best to inquire locally. About 2 miles (3 km) away, the market town of **Corbigny** has good shopping.

The canal from here takes on a whole new character as it climbs toward the summit. From **Ecluse 16**, **Sardy**, there are some 16 locks within a space of 2 miles (3 km), and three short tunnels after the last one at **Port Brûlé**. These are approached through narrow cuts in the rock and are quite picturesque. Once beyond the tunnels, it's all downhill.

At **Baye**, a little way past the tunnels, is the **Etang de Baye**, a large lake reserved for fishing and sailing. The canal here passes many small villages and **The Nivernaise countryside.**

farms, and boaters will encounter some double locks at **Chavance** and **Marré**.

Pleasure boats often tie up at the very charming **Chatillon-en-Bazois** across from the towers of the château. The canal makes a sharp 180-degree turn here and continues on a very winding course that passes another château and some very well-kept farms.

Cercy-la-Tour rises above the banks of the canal; visit the 12th-century Romanesque church with its fine steeple. The ruins of an ancient fortress offer views of the countryside. There are good shops and provisions, and the town is a great place for walking. Approaching Decize, there is much to see.

Decize has been known since Roman times, when Julius Caesar wrote of *Decetia* in his Commentaries. The small manufacturing town, the birthplace of the 18th-century revolutionary Louis-Antoine de Saint-Just, occupies a rocky spit of land that divides the Loire River from the Nivernais Canal. Here, the **Canal Latéral à la Loire** can be joined. **St Are's church** has a Merovingian crypt and there is a Roman chancel in the **Chapelle St-Pierre** in the former Couvent des Minimes. There is a lovely park in Decize and a long shaded walk that stretches for over half a mile (900 meters) through the city.

Les Canaux du Centre: A cruise on these waterways offer bargees five for the price of one. The Loing, Briare, Latéral à la Loire, Centre, and Roanne à Digoin canals are also some of the most interesting to cruise because they still carry a lot of commercial traffic. Frequently a laden barge will pass in the other direction, and the towns along the canals have rich histories tied to the days when barging was a prime means of transporting goods to market.

The earliest to be constructed was the Canal de Briare, between Briare and Montargis. Originally planned in 1604 by the Duc de Sully and King Henry IV, its purpose was to link the Seine and Loire river valleys. The king's assassination and other problems delayed completion until 1642, when the Briare became the first canal of its kind in Eu-

Choose your own means of transport.

rope. The portion of the journey from Montargis to the Seine was traversed on the precarious and frequently flooded River Loing, until the Canal du Loing was completed in 1723.

First conceived in the 16th century under François I, the Canal du Centre, which links Digoin with Châlon-sur-Saône, was not begun until 1784. Finally finished in 1794 after the Revolution, the canal ascends the hills separating the Loire and Saône valleys by way of 80 locks. When travel on the Loire River became difficult because of winter flooding and summer water shortages, the Canal Latéral à la Loire was built to connect the Canal de Briare and the Canal du Centre, and opened in 1838. Also opened in 1838, the Canal de Roanne à Digoin was conceived to join the steel, cotton and textile mills of Roanne with markets along the Loing and the Center Canals.

The **Canal du Loing** veers south from the River Seine at **St Mammes**, a large commercial barging center, and follows the path of the **River Loing** as it winds south and east. Calm and serene, the canal contrasts starkly with the crowded Seine. And although the number of coal barges has declined there is still a good deal of commercial traffic since the canal forms part of a main French trade route.

Just beyond a railroad viaduct is **Moret-sur-Loing**, an enchanting medieval town with stone gateways, the lovely **Church of Notre Dame**, ancient doorways along the Rue Grande, and one of the oldest bridges in France. Impressionist painter Alfred Sisley lived at 19 Rue Montmartre. On Saturday evenings during the summer, a *son et lumière*, a sound and light show, tracing the town's 900-year history is presented on the banks of the Loing.

Across the canal in the village of **Bourgogne**, is Clemenceau House, called **La Grange Batelière** (bargehouse). Dedicated to the Tiger of France, Georges Clemenceau, the tiny museum displays memorabilia from the life of the man who was premier during World War I.

Outdoor cafés are a perfect place to sample Burgundy's wines.

The Loing River is close on the right, and beyond the river, the forest of **Fontainbleau**, as the canal continues south. Just before the town of **Nemours**, the canal joins the river for a brief *racle* (joining), then branches off again. From here, the river is on the left, at some points separated from the canal by only narrow spits of land.

Nemours, with just under 12,000 inhabitants, has a 12th-century castle and the 16th-century **Church of St John the Baptist**, built to house relics of the prophet brought back from the Second Crusade. Fantastically shaped rocks decorate a park called the **Rochers Greau**, or Greans Rocks.

Sycamores, called plane trees in France, line the canal as it approaches **Nargis**. From here, it's a short excursion to **Château-Landon**, which has a Romanesque church. The **Abbey of St Severin**, with magnificent frescoes, was founded by the 6th-century Frankish king, Clovis.

Where the now defunct Canal d'Orléans enters from the right, the Canal de Loing becomes the **Canal de Briare**. Just beyond is **Montargis**, capital of the Gatinais area. The canal goes right through the city center, and often the townspeople come and stand on the bridge to greet passing barges. Smaller canals branch off to the side, earning the town its nickname the "Venice of the Gâtinais." Small dinghies are filled with flowers and strategically placed along the streams.

The town has a big open-air market, the charming **Church of the Madeleine**, and the **Girodet Museum**, which displays local artifacts from prehistoric times to the present. *Praslines* (pralines) were invented here by the chef of the Duc de Plessis-Praslin, in the time of Louis XIII, and are on sale everywhere.

Just before **Montbuoy**, the remains of a Roman amphitheater can be seen to the right, and in **Châtillon-Coligny** is a 12th-century castle built by the Count of Sancerre. The grounds may be visited during the summer.

At **Rogny** , the now disused seven-rise staircase of locks stand. They were

Spring
weeding-out
in Sancerre.

in use from 1642 until 1887, when they were replaced by six separate locks. The old arrangement is preserved as a monument and is floodlit at night.

Below **Ouzouer-sur-Trezée** the Briare Canal takes an offshoot to the Loire River and the **Canal Latéral à la Loire** continues on, actually crossing the Loire at the town of **Briare** by means of a spectacular aqueduct built in 1890 by Alexandre Gustav Eiffel. At 2,150-ft (662-meters) long, the **Pont-Canal St Firmin-sur-Loire** is the longest canal bridge in the world.

From here, the canal follows along to the west of the Loire and continues south to **Châtillon-sur-Loire**, a charming town with an old church and 15th-century houses. As the canal then passes through an area of flat plains and small villages, it approaches **Le Sancerrois**, the land of goat cheese and wine.

Barges can anchor at **St Thibault**, an old boatmen's village that overlooks a navigation between the canal and the river. The Boating Club here welcomes people from visiting barges. **St Satur**, across the canal has camping and shower facilities.

On a hilltop west of the canal, **Sancerre** is a village of narrow, winding streets and remnants of history. It was a Protestant Huguenot stronghold during the Hundred Years' War; the **Tower of Feifs** is all that remains of the 14th-century fortress built by the Count of Sancerre. Walking up to the town on the **Promenade de la Porte César** reveals views of the Loire countryside.

The vineyards surrounding Sancerre are famous for their dry wine from Sauvignon grapes. And at nearby **Chavignol**, one of France's most famous goat cheeses is made, *crottin de Chavignol* (literally "horse dung", after the small, round shapes), a rich creamy cheese sold in various stages from soft to aged and very dry. The château at **Les Garennes** has cheese tastings, and visitors can watch the goats being milked between 4.30 and 5pm. For a light meal and a sample of a local Sancerre wine, try the Auberge Alphonse Mellot.

South of St Satur, vineyards can be

The museum at Marcigny.

seen from the barge, and **Ménétréol** is a convenient stop for food. When anchored in the basin at **La Chapelle Montlinard**, it's easy to walk or bicycle across a 16th-century stone bridge to **La Charité-sur-Loire**, on the east bank of the river. The **Basilica of Notre Dame** was founded here in the eighth century; present buildings date from 1107. At one time it was one of the largest churches in France, second only to Cluny. Once a great port city, La Charité was the scene of one of Joan of Arc's defeats in 1429.

A variety of food stores and bars cater to barges at the commercial port of **Marseilles-les-Aubigny**, where the Loire seems inches away and is dotted with islands. At **Le Guétin** the canal crosses over the **Allier River** via a 1,115-ft (343-meter) long aqueduct. From here it's easy to bicycle to an old round lock, no longer in use, on the Allier.

Farther down, a branch veers off to **Nevers**, perched above the Loire. Capital of the Nivernais, this city has historic sights such as the **Ducal Palace**, now

used as a court of justice, and the **Cathedral of St Cyr and Ste Julitte**, built in a variety of architectural styles from the 10th-to-16th-centuries. Ste Bernadette of Lourdes died here in 1879, and her body is kept in a glass casket in the chapel of the **Convent of St Gildard**.

In the 16th century, Nevers became famous for its *faïence*, (hand painted enamelled earthenware), and visitors can tour the workshops of Bout-du-Monde, the city's oldest pottery factory.

Returning to the main canal, barges pass farmland and picturesque villages. Near the lock at **St Maurice**, another branch leads to the Loire, Decize and the Nivernais Canal.

Farther south on the Latéral, **Dompierre-sur-Besbre** lies at the end of another short canal branch and has a docking basin, showers, and a swimming pool. Just below this offshoot, the canal crosses the tiny **River Besbre** via a small aqueduct, then continues south, and again crosses the Loire via the 780-ft (240-meter) long **Digoin Aqueduct**.

The **Canal de Roanne à Digoin**, which branches off south at this point, is less traveled than the other central canals, but offers some nice surprises for the boating enthusiast with a little extra time. The town of **Marcigny**, an easy bicycle ride from the canal port of **Chambilly** has 11th-century timbered houses, the 15th-century **Tour du Moulin** and Muscadine chocolates.

The port of **Roanne** dates from the 1st century BC, and is also home to the legendary Hôtel des Frères Troisgros restaurant, reason to make that 35-mile (55-km) detour.

At **Digoin**, the Canal Latéral merges with the Canal du Centre and continues south and east to **Paray-le-Monial**, where 17th-century visions of Ste Margeurite-Marie Alacoque gave rise to the cult of the Sacred Heart, and made the town a pilgrimage site. Visitors can see the 12th-century **Sacred Heart Basilica** and the old mansion of the Cardinal de Bouillon's Pages, where items from Ste Margeurite's life are displayed.

Beyond **Paray**, the canal turns north-east and continues through the industrial center of **Montceau-les-Mines**, and past the iron and tile-making town of **Montchanin**. **St Léger-sur-Dheune** has a 16th-century church with an octagonal tower. Near the town of **St Gilles**, is the 13th-century **Château de Rully**. The canal then flows past the wine-making region near **Santenay**, and at **Chagny**, another small industrial town is Lameloise, one of the finest restaurants in Burgundy.

Set at the junction of the Canal du Centre and the River Saône, **Châlon-sur-Saône** was founded by Julius Caesar as a supply base during his first campaign into Gaul. Now a thriving commercial center of 50,000, the town has preserved an old section of paving-stone streets and timbered houses near the river. The **Denon Museum**, in a former Ursuline convent, has art and artifacts dating from Gallo-Roman times, and the **Museum of Photography** is near the market area.

From here, barges and boats can travel up or downstream on the River Saône. North and east of Châlon, the town of **Seurre** has narrow medieval streets and a 13th-century cathedral. **Beaune**, capital of the Dukes of Burgundy in the 13th and 14th centuries, is a taxi ride away away. Today this town of 20,000 people is the center of the **Côte d'Or**, the famed Burgundy wine-producing area.

Constructed in 1443 as a hospital for the poor, the **Hôtel Dieu** is a dazzling example of Flemish Gothic art and architecture. Colorful tile-roofed gables surround the courtyard of the complex, which was built by Nicholas Rolin, Chancellor of Burgundy, who also commissioned *The Last Judgment*, a polyptych by Roger van der Weyden, and is on display in the museum.

The **Musée du Vin**, in the **Hôtel des Duc de Bourgogne** has exhibits on winemaking and tapestry weaving, and many of the underground *caves* are open for wine tasting. In the **Notre Dame Basilica** are Flemish tapestries from the 15th century.

Beyond Seurre, the Saône continues north and east and meets the Burgundy Canal at **St Jean de Losne**.

Left, firing up a balloon. **Right,** the roof of Beaune's Hôpital.

THE MAYENNE AND THE SARTHE

The Mayenne and Sarthe might be called the "step" rivers of the Loire. They are considered part of it, yet are not of it: they flow into the Maine River which empties into the Loire. There is no string of memorable châteaux to visit; the ones here were not built by royalty or their mistresses, but by merchants and industrialists, men who made money rather than inherited it.

Yet history is alive along these banks: Henry II of England was born in Le Mans, many battles of the Vendéen Revolt were fought between the two rivers, and the château of Angers, seat of the Anjou family, was the focal point for a brilliant period in French history.

Angers, on the 5-mile (8-km) long **Maine River**, is the start of any journey up the Mayenne or Sarthe. Moorings are on the left bank opposite the château. A wide variety of shops are near, the marina offers repairs, water points and fuel.

Originally a Gaelic settlement, Angers became the Roman Juliomagus. 867 saw the start of a six-year submission to the Normans; they were finally driven out by Charles the Bald and Salomon, Duke of Brittany.

In the Middle Ages, Angers rose to importance as the capital of Anjou and residence of the Plantagenets. (Although the Plantagenets were English kings, they originated with a French count; even their name is derived from a French word which began when Prince Geoffroi of Anjou started wearing a piece of broome, *genêt*, in his hat. Plantagenet became his name and that of his descendants. Remember, too, that Henry, and other English kings of this period, spent more time in France than in the country whose crown they wore.)

The Anjous were an ambitious lot, and in the Middle Ages, one way to power was through marriage. Two of their unions were particularly brilliant. The first took place in 1129 when Foulques, Comte d'Anjou, married his 16-year-old son Geoffroi to Matilde,

the 29-year-old grand-daughter of William the Conqueror. The second occurred when their son, Henry Plantagenet, wed Eleanor of Aquitaine in 1152. Eleanor, recently divorced from Louis VII of France, brought to the new marriage her French lands.

When the newlyweds combined their possessions (his: Anjou, Maine, Touraine and Normandy; hers: Poitou, Périgord, Limousin, Angoumois, Saintonge, Gascony, Auvergne and Toulouse), their acreage was greater than those held by her ex-husband.

After Henry became King of England in 1154, most of western France became English territory. The power generated by the English connections and its strategic river location made Angers a logical center.

English domination was not to last. The separatist whispers in the annexed lands became a shout and in 1205, the French, under the leadership of Philippe Auguste, took Anjou and Angers. (The French and English continued their struggle for supremacy, one that only

Left, lazy afternoon on the Mayenne. *Right*, 16th-century carving in Angers.

ended with the conclusion of the Hundred Years War in 1453 when England lost all French lands except Calais.) In 1246, Louis IX (St Louis) gave Anjou to his brother, Charles, and in 1360 it was declared a Duchy.

Charles continued the Anjou tradition of power-grabbing, heading to Italy at the behest of the Pope, adding the Kingdom of Naples, and the title, King of Sicily to Duke of Anjou. Charles, however, had outreached himself: on Easter Sunday in 1282, the downtrodden Sicilians, angry at a slur cast upon a local woman, butchered over 6,000 French troops.

During the Revolution, Angers was pro-change and the Cathedral became a Temple of Reform. Taken by the Vendéen royalists, the city was recaptured by the Republicans, and held by them through several attacks until the Revolt died a violent death.

Today, Angers is best-known as the center for Anjou wine, still the city's most notable export. Two universities founded by various Dukes of Anjou still flourish, and while agriculture is the area's primary source of income, industry is slowly making its mark. "Civilized" easily comes to mind when describing the city.

Sometimes called Black Angers because of the color of its roofs (which were produced from a slate found in the nearby quarry of Trelaze) the city is dominated by the immense **Château de Foulques** sitting above the main river. Erected between 1228 and 1338, construction began under Louis IX and ended during Philip the Bold's reign.

One of the best examples of French siege architecture, the walls extend for more than half a mile, connecting 17 towers. Each of the towers, 130–160 ft (40–50 meters) high, wears a black dunce-cap roof. A drawbridge allows one entrance, and a few defensive slits are the only break in an otherwise solid wall of stone. The moat is empty; looking into its grassy bottom, grazing deer and bright flower beds contrast and dilute the harsh, forbidding expanse.

The **Apocalypse of St John** tapestry

Country chapels abound in "Pays de La Loire".

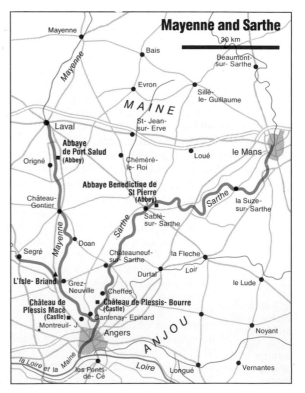

has its own, purpose-built and specially lighted exhibition room in the château. Commissioned by a Duke of Anjou, it was drawn by the Bruges artist Hennequin after some miniature paintings, then woven in Paris between 1375 and 1380 by Nicholas Bataille.

Only 350 ft (107 meters) of the original 545-ft (168-meters) long tapestry remain, but each panel is a gem, showing John in a Gothic setting, writing down his musings of the mind as that muse plays out about him. Some of the brilliantly executed panels detail everyday life, others, scenes from the Bible, but the most vivid ones look like the result of a major drug trip.

Although the Apocalypse hung in the cathedral for many years, it was taken down after the Revolution and left to rot. In 1843 it was bought for the paltry sum of 300 francs by the then Bishop of Angers who had it restored; now the value of the oldest surviving medieval tapestry is incalculable.

Inside the château's early 15th-century **Ste Geneviève chapel** (built by the protectress of Joan of Arc, Yolande d'Aragon), the magnificent 16th-century Flemish tapestry, *Passion and Ressurection*, is on display.

The old city lies between the château and the **St Maurice Cathedral** (steps lead directly up from the river to it). Two of its three towers are over 240-ft (75-meters) tall; the center one, an addition in the 16th century, is much smaller and is topped by a belfry and lantern tower.

The cathedral was built in the late 12th century with a nave 290-ft (90-meters) long and 55-ft (17-meters) wide, its vaulting is in the Angevian style. At the time of construction most cathedrals had vaultings no more than 30 to 40 ft (9–12 meters) wide; this one was the largest ever attempted, and was only accomplished by making the key of the ogives 10 ft (3 meters) higher than the side and cross arches. St Maurice was restored in the 16th and 18th centuries, but the windows are 12th-century and original.

The damage to the main doorway

Angers' Château presents a stern facade.

took place during the Wars of Religion and the Revolution. Note the tympanum of Christ surrounded by symbols of the four Evangelists; on the third level of the facade, St Maurice stands in the middle of figures dressed in 16th-century military uniforms.

When wandering along the **Rue Beaurepaire**, notice the 15th-century courtyards. **Place de la Laiterie** is very characteristic of old Angers and **Maison d'Adam** on Place Ste Croix boasts beautiful half-timbering. The 15th-century **Logis Barrault** is on Rue Toussaints and houses the **Musée des Beaux Arts**. The **Turpin de Crissé** collection is in the **Hôtel Pincé**, a Renaissance building of the late 1520s carelessly restored in the 19th century; its range of art and archaeology includes an Iron Age griffin's head discovered in the Loire. **St Serge** also has Angevian vaulting; note, too, its choir and 12th-century monochrome glass windows.

Among the parks and gardens of the city, one stands out: the **Jardin des Plantes** near **St Samson** was founded more than 150 years ago and is filled with a wide variety of plants, especially the magnolia and camellia trees for which the city is known.

On the north side of the river, the **Musée de Jean Lurçat** is located in the **Hôpital St Jean** which owes its existence to Henry II's wish to atone for the execution of Thomas à Becket in 1170. Here the works of Jean Lurçat, who lived between 1892 and 1966 and helped to revive the art of tapestry, are on display. Also note the Angevin vaulting in the great Salle de Malades.

The Maine divides into two rivers upstream of the railroad bridge near Angers: the Mayenne going to the left, the Sarthe straight ahead. For the most part, the Mayenne cuts a narrow swathe through steep valleys until its upper reaches; the Sarthe's path is through generally flatter land, its course a series of loops and bends. Both rivers flow through similar-looking countryside: rolling fields, some in pastureland with shady meadows, others under cultivation and here, agriculture is king, tranquility his queen.

Villages are the norm, large towns rare and many miles can pass with no habitation. History awaits at many a mooring, but the lasting memories will be of agreeable lock-keepers, picturesque watermills with hidden backwaters, a restaurant appearing from nowhere, and meeting the locals.

La Mayenne: The river was used for commercial transport as early as 1492, but it probably was not until 1536, when the inhabitants of Laval petitioned the king to make the route suitable for large craft, that it became a money-making venture. During the 17th century the upper areas became profitable when Cardinal Mazarin (governor of France during the boyhood of Louis XIV) widened the locks from Laval to Mayenne. Between 1859 and 1864 the river was canalized, and although railroad competition had arrived, a steady traffic of chalk, stone, wood, coal, grain, fruit and vegetables was carried on the river.

Records of 1899 indicate there were over 1,200 movements through lock 34 at Château-Gontier. Not too much should

The Mayenne's calm waters are great for children to enjoy.

be made of the 1936 record amount of 218,000 tons: it was mostly slate from the great quarries near Angers. Traffic gradually declined and eventually the middle and upper river reaches couldn't be navigated.

Fortunately, the upsurge in pleasure boating resulted in a rescue of the river. Today 60 miles (98 km) with 25 locks between Angers and Lavel can be enjoyed. A further 20 locks north to Mayenne are in the process of restoration, and should be opened by the early 1990s giving another 21 miles (35 km) of navigation. Cruising is a pleasure: a keeper mans every lock and enough marinas make quartermastering easy.

Entering the Mayenne, the change from city to country is dramatic: flat marshes, often in flood tide, emit an almost eerie quality, even in bright sunlight. **Cantenay-Epinard** has all facilities and is a pleasant village. **Montreuil-Belfroy** marks the end of the bleek, deserted landscape. The town is about half a mile uphill walk from the lock; river valley panoramas are the reward.

Three miles (five km) away is the **Château de Plessis-Macé**, a superb Medieval/Renaissance complex. Originally built in the 12th century, extensive renovation took place in the 15th. The moat adds an air of mystery, and in the chapel note the 15th-century paneling.

At the bridge at **Juigné-Béné** is a restaurant and garage. Approaching **Sautré** note the broad weir and mill; to its right is one of the many châteaux along this river. At **Ecluse 43**, **La Roussière**, one of the millhouses has been converted into a charming residence. Look for **Pruillé** sitting high above the river's left bank.

Grez-Neuville spreads to both sides of the river. It has a 12th-century church, 17th and 18th-century houses built of grey stone, and a 21st-century mechanical lock. Le Cheval Blanc is a good place for dinner, but for dedicated do-it-yourselfers, basic food shops are on the right bank.

After the long lock cut, the **Oudon River** is almost immediately on the left. This short but charming navigation can

Newly-ploughed field.

be explored to Segré and back in a day or two *(see page 142)*.

Remaining in the main channel, **l'Isle-Briand** is best known for its **horse stud farm** (Haras Nationaux de l'Isle-Briand). To visit, prior permission is required. Like many other villages on the Mayenne, **Montreuil-sur-Maine** is located on a hillside. A watermill erected in 1858 is near the lock, but think before mooring overnight: a church clock chimes frequently.

Chenillé-Changé has one of the prettiest lockhouses on the river, and the millhouse near the weir is still in operation. Mooring at one of the nearby jetties which cater for visitors, it makes a pleasant background noise. A small marina is here, along with two small restaurants, but no shops.

Still a wide band of water, the river continues in its own meandering way past tree-shaded slopes. Climb the hills to **La Jaille Yvon** for magnificent views of the surrounding countryside. It was this vista that attracted the 19th-century *nouveaux riches* and caused the con-

struction of so many châteaux throughout the valley. One is just after Jaille, another on the right bank at **Le Port Joulain**. None are open to the public, but looking at them brings thoughts of forgotten splendor.

Daon is a small city but with a danger: water skiing. The town has all facilities, a fair selection of restaurants, and is a pleasant place for overnight moorings. From Daon to **Ménil**, the river travels through an absolutely gorgeous reach. The occasional farmhouse is surrounded by patches of multi-hued greens, cattle are black and white dots on the green, and fishermen are everywhere. Except for the occasional glimpse of a car, or a plane above, one could be in another century.

Ménil makes another good stop; there are several restaurants and *crêperies* near the quay. For more elegant dining, continue upriver to **Ecluse 38**, **La Petite Bavouze**, and sample the lockside restaurant.

The 11th-century **St Saturnin** church is in **Azé**; its frescoes are from the 12th, and the rather fussy-looking altar is a 17th-century addition. (To visit, moor on the right bank near the slipway before the railway bridge; the church is a 10-minute walk inland.)

Château-Gontier was in the heart of Royalist *Chouan* country during the 1793 Vendéen Revolt. Once a leading river port, modern boaters will appreciate the superb facilities of the local marina. The town is the busiest veal market in France, selling more than 5,000 calves each market day. In the 11th century, the Comte d'Anjou, Foulques Nerra, built a château here, but nothing remains except its **church of St Jean**.

The **museum** (Rue Jean-Dourre) has a collection of Greco-Roman and medieval art. A climb to the **Promenade du Bout du Monde** near the old **Priory**, gives pleasant river views. The energetic can bicycle the 2 miles (3 km) to **Bazouges** and visit the **St Martin church** which has a 17th-century altar.

Ecluse 33, **Mirwault**, is visually rewarding: mills decorate either side of the river, a château sits in solitary ele- **Locking through is easy...**

gance in the midst of large trees, and a cozy restaurant beckons.

Water-skiers are allowed on the reach to **Ecluse 32**, **La Roche**. Just beyond **Ecluse 30**, **La Rongère**, note the château high above the left bank. The **Château of Morière** comes into view after **Ecluse 26, Persigand**.

Moor by the bridge at **Port Rhingeard** to visit the **Trappist Abbey of Port-Salud**, home of that rather pungent cheese. Created by the Trappist monks, who founded their abbey in the 13th century, the cheese was made entirely by the monks until the late 1950s when they sold the licence to a commercial company. Visits to the abbey church are possible and the cheese is for sale in the gift shop.

The river widens as it continues toward Laval. Rolling hills replace steep banks, and the rural atmosphere remains until **Ecluse 23**, **Cumont**.

...when it's all automatic.

Laval straddles both sides of the river with most of the historic area on the upper ground to the left. The **château**, built by the Counts of Laval but taken over by the state during the Revolution, is not one but two: the Renaissance **Château Neuf** faces **Place de la Tremoille** and houses the **Palais de Justice**; the **Vieux** consists of two right-angled wings (one 13th-century, the other 15th) with an oak-roofed medieval keep between them. The 11th-century **crypt** was once used as a chapel. In the older portion, the **Hall of Honor** is over 95-ft (30-meters) long.

Two museums are in the building: one is devoted to locally-found artefacts, the other to pririmitive paintings. Pride of the latter is *Le Douanier* by locally-born artist, Henri Rousseau. (He's buried in the **Jardin de la Perrine**.) The ramparts have mostly disappeared, but some fragments may be found in **Porte Beucheresse** (Rousseau was born in one of its twin towers).

La Trinité was declared a Cathedral in 1855; orginally 11th-century Romanesque, its style today could charitably be called "hodge-podge". The interior, except for the tomb of a 14th-century bishop, and some Aubusson tapestries,

is equally devoid of distinction. Around the cathedral area are 16th-century houses, the ground floors are now shops, and the overhanging upper-storey windows all seemed to be filled with lace curtains.

There are some fine Renaissance stained-glass windows in the 15th-century church of **St Vénérand**; one of the Passion should be noted. In **Notre Dame d'Avénières**, the polychrome statue of *Christ on Tiptoe* is an unusual piece of art. The triptych of the Pietà is 15th-century, but the stained-glass windows are modern, designed by Max Ingrand.

Two old *bâteaux lavoirs* (laundry boats) have been restored; one houses a nautical club and the other, the St Julien, is a museum. Laundry boats were introduced on the Mayenne in the 1850s; by the mid-1870s there were more than 25 in service, and as late as the early 1960s five were still working.

These barges were, in essence, floating sweatshops; the dirty laundry would be collected from private houses and taken to the boat. There, washerwomen would work up to 14 hours a day in hot, muggy conditions. The owner, who lived on the upper deck, could keep an eye on the lower one where the women toiled. The *St. Julien,* commissioned in 1904, was in service until 1970, and given to the city in 1971. Artifacts include photographs and an ancient example of one of the first electrically driven spin-dryers.

With the restoration of the river, Laval has created good mooring facilities with a full-service marina. The most convenient shops are on the river's right bank, and the tourist office is in the middle of a riverside park on the left.

L'Oudon: The 11-mile (18-km) three-lock journey to the head of the navigation makes a charming one or two day sidetrip. Similar to the Mayenne in landscape, it also followed the Mayenne's development. Locks were constructed in the mid-19th century, and, although as recently as the late 1960s commercial barging was still a viable presence, only pleasure boats ply the river today.

At **Le Lion d'Angers**, the first town

Laval reflected.

after leaving the Mayenne, moorings and water points are on the left immediately above the bridge. If visiting the National Stud Farm, this is the best place from which to start. Restoraton of **St Martin church** in the 1850s uncovered a series of 11th-century frescoes.

The upstream run is peaceful and quiet with few human intrusions except near the tiny hamlet of **La Roselle** and its dozen or so houses. **Ecluse 3** (the first) arrives at **Himbeaudière**; there's a 4-mile (6-km) run to the second.

The lock at **La Chapelle sur Oudon** is graced by a mill converted into a home. The village is a 10- to 15-minute walk at the top of a hill, a place a Disney director might choose to make a movie set in quintessential French countryside. Look for the church with an inverted hare bell spire.

The third lock, **Maingue**, is less than half a mile from Segré, the uppermost halt in the Oudon valley. Dock near the bridge just before the lock to visit the 18th-century **Château de la Lorie**; it's about a mile away.

Approaching **Segré**, the non-navigable **Verzée River** flows in from the left; moor just before that on the left bank of the Oudon. Excellent facilities (fuel, water points, repairs) are operated by a local boating club.

The town is pretty and the city fathers welcome tourists with landscaped walks along the riverside walks, and a good selection of attractive shops and restaurants. For determined sightseers, there are some remains of an 11th-century **castle**. Look for old houses on Rue Pasteur, the exterior of the 17th-century Château de la Loge may be admired, and finally, a domed church looking like a scaled-down version of Paris's Sacré Coeur.

La Sarthe: A first cousin to the Mayenne in looks and demeanor, the **Sarthe** meanders from its source in the Fôret d'Encouves upstream of Alençon through an area known as Angevin Maine. An easy river to negotiate, the Sarthe plows a busier row than the Mayenne, but is still rural enough for hours of solitary cruising along its 81-

Cruising and grazing.

mile (131-km), 20-lock run between Angers and Le Mans.

Although the Sarthe was used for many centuries as a "road", it was not until the 14th century that commercial development of the river began. Early in the 17th a large barge fleet plied the river, but because of shifting water depths and silting, navigation was uncertain and extensive restoration was needed between 1744 and 175l. By the late 1770s, craft, aided by flash locks, could travel upriver to Malicorn, (25 miles, 40 km downstream of Le Mans).

Plans were drawn to canalize the Sarthe to Alençon and then to the headwaters of the river Orne, creating a waterway between Brittany and the Normandy coast via Caen. The cost, and falling commercial traffic were the final obstacles to completion. By the end of World War II commercial carriers had disappeared and after that, the Sarthe's near-death and resurrection parallels the Mayenne's.

Less than an hour's cruise from Angers and it's a different world: the banks are marshy, reedy, and low. **Escouflant** offers the **Abbey of Perray** with a 12th-century tower and 17th-century convent. Nearby is **Les Sablières**, a leisure park created from a worked-out gravel pit, offering children a day's entertainment.

The **Loir River** (not to be confused with the Loire) enters from the right several hundred feet before **Briollay** which the Celts called Briara-Ledus. The river here is very narrow, probably less than 50 ft (15 meters), and is a haven for birds.

One of the most outstanding châteaux in the area, **Le Plessis-Bourré**, is within cycling distance (about three miles/five kms) from either Briollay (moor on the left bank near the bridge) or via the road opposite **Vérigné**. The castle is approached behind a large meadow and is flanked by a copse of trees.

Erected in the 15th century by Jean Bourré, a financial secretary to Louis XI, in a style inspired by the château at Langeais, the white building carries the traditional dark grey slate roof, and is moated. The outbuildings are later, 17th century, and the interior matches the outside in charm.

The guided tour takes visitors through the Hall of Justice, the library (note the collection of fans), several salons, the Guardroom, (its 15th-century ceiling painted with allegorical figures; Chastity as a Unicorn is particularly appealing, as are other humorous and moral scenes), and the beautifully austere St Anne's chapel.

After 11 miles (18 km) of lock-free cruising from Angers, the first one arrives at **Cheffes**. Scores of fishing punts line the island here, and the prudent navigator will tread carefully through the channel markings. A commercial harbor in the 18th and 19th centuries, agriculture and tourism are Cheffes' main source of income today. To dock for supplies, first transit the lock and approach from upriver.(It's even possible to visit Plessis-Bourré from here, too.)

Moulin d'Ivray sits on a backwater of the river; take the right fork near **Porte Bise**. Several large islands and

Local hero Robert Le Fort stands guard in Châteauneuf.

inlets offer an afternoon or evening's haven. In town is a 16th-century chapel.

The house gardens of **Juvardeil** reach the water's edge, and each has its own dock and small punt. There's a mixture of architectural styles, 16th-century abutting 1930s modern. One of the leaders of the Vendéen Revolt, Bonchamps-Charette, was born here.

This Revolt had its genesis in March 1793 when peasants of the Vendé, *Les Chouans*, a naturally conservative and deeply religious group, were sufficiently angered by Republican excesses to start agitating for a return of the Crown. Joining forces with the old nobility, they became known as the Whites (as opposed to the Blues of the Republican Army). The Rebels' initial forays were successful: Thouars fell in May, Saumur and Angers in June.

A major defeat occured at Nantes a few weeks later. Underarmed and badly organized, the movement deteriorated, and the Blue army pursued the Royalists relentlessly. October brought a devastating rout in Cholet; the *Chouans*

fled and more than 80,000 people found themselves at St-Florent-le-Vieil, a small town on the Loire, downstream of Angers. Several thousand Republican prisoners happened to be imprisoned in the local church, and the Vendéans, using "eye for an eye" reasoning, planned a revenge killing.

The mortally-wounded Bonchamps begged a favor from his compatriots: to spare the prisoners' lives. This they did, and visitors to St Florent can visit the church, and see Bonchamps' tomb, but no plaque is in the town of his birth.

A statue of local hero Robert le Fort looks over the town square of **Châteauneuf-sur-Sarthe**, which also has an excellent selection of riverside restaurants. **Brissarthe** welcomes boats with a riverside sign reading, "*2 épicers* (groceries), *1 boulanger* (baker), *2 restaurants, 1 camping, 1 bois* (woods), *1 église 15th XVeme*".

The **15th-century church** is beautiful, and many of the surrounding houses are built in typical gray stone Anjou style. Le Fort, a warrior of the Carolig-

Le Fort died in front of this church in Brissarthe.

ian king, Charles the Bald, died in front of the church in 886 after a battle with the Normans. Inside the church, look for a statue of Le Fort and some 10th-century low-relief sculptures.

The moorings for **Chemire** are a little over a mile from the town center; the trip's reward is a church whose choir and transept date to the 12th-century; the **St Sérène chapel**, often called Chapel of the Frogs, is 17th. The Hôtel de Ville was a parsonage in the 16th-century when it was built. If supplies only are wanted, however, the much-closer-to-the-river **Morannes** might be a better place to shop.

From here to Sablé-sur-Sarthe (10 miles/17 km), no towns intrude, only a few houses at **Pincé** and the nearby **Le Moulin de Beffes**. The latter is a dream: gardens brighten the green lawns and the water's edge, a restaurant serves good food, and several former weirs help form very private moorings at the islands opposite the lock.

High above the river's left bank an 18th-century **château** is the most vis-ible landmark when approaching **Sablé**. Constructed in 1711 by Colbert de Torcy, nephew of Colbert (one of Louis XIV's ministers), it's now a National Library and opened only for special exhibits. Sablé does lots to make the visitor feel welcome. Signs in three languages are at the marina (two boat hire firms, full services); flower beds line the attractive river-walks, and a pedestrian mall makes shopping easy.

The non-navigable **Erve River** wanders through town, and enters the Sarthe near the bridge.

Opposite the château sits the 19th-century neo-Gothic **Notre Dame church**; inside, look for the 15th-century windows which survived the massive renovation. On weekends, water-skiers and local sculling and kayak clubs are a particular hazard.

The Benedictine **Abbey of St Pierre** looms like a massive black shadow over the river at **Solesmes**. The stone is a marble quarried at the nearby Port Etroit which also supplied stone for Versailles. Originally founded in the early 11th

Left, the spire of Juvardeil. Below, saying thank-you to the lockkeeper.

century by monks from Marmoutier, the current building is 19th-century neo-Gothic without any redeeming architectural qualities.

The abbey church, however, has a 15th-century nave, but centerpiece is Solesmes Saints, a 16th-century set of sculptures. Visitors may attend the Gregorian Mass on Sundays. (Dock at **Port de Juigné**, cross the bridge.)

Cruising past the same bridge, turn around for another look at the abbey. Ahead, the river begins one of its most exquisite runs: the course is gentle with no sharp bends or hidden curves as far as Malicorn-sur-Sarthe. There is a series of small villages with houses neat and tidy. Colorful gardens, willows and poplars line the bank, a large château or three stands in stately readiness, and the rolling hills are checkered with fields of cereal grasses or grazing cows. The camping sites along this stretch also add a brightly-colored distraction.

Juigné-sur-Sarthe arrives first and sits high on a hill, its Romanesque church looking more like a medieval fort. At **Avoise**, it's worth noting *La Perrine de Cry*, a 13th-century manor house. On top of the hill at **Parcé**, 16th- and 17th-century buildings are found, and the Roman tower used to be part of the ancient **St Pierre Church**. To visit Parcé, ignore the lock and head toward the right side of the river; moor just beyond the bridge.

After **Ecluse 10**, **Ignères**, a 6-mile (10-km) lock-free run makes for lazy cruising. The Auberge d'Acras is on the river at Dureil, and an enchanting place to spend a lazy afternoon. The **Château de Pêcheseul** is owned by the Champaigne family who played an important role in the the Wars of Religion. It is closed to the public, but the view of it from the river is lovely.

Reality in the form of **Malicorne-sur-Sarthe** arrives sudddenly and jarringly. The tree-hidden **château** (visits possible), was built in the 17th century and was frequently visited by Madame Sévigné. Malicorne was once a Chapelain's benefit, and a further bit of history includes a massacre of the *Ch-*

Below, picnic by the Sarthe and, **right**, swans in the river.

ouans. The **pottery workshops** can be visited; the permanent exhibition contains an excellent collection. Docking here is on the right bank beyond the lock, and everything is within walking distance, including the château.

Continuing upstream, the **Château de Rive Sarthe** is almost immediately on the left, then **Château Monadon** appears on the right. **Noyen** is a pretty little town with a riverside park. **Farcé-sur-Sarthe**, up the hill from the river, offers a pleasing vista; look for the grocer, restaurant, and a Gothic church.

The 15th-century château in **La Suze sur Sarthe** was built on the site of 10th-century fort. Quartermasters will appreciate the "Hyper Market" that's open seven days a week, 12 hours a day. It is a busy city; many restaurants and bollard moorings make the town a pleasant overnight stop.

Roëzé-sur-Sarthe is a pretty village; to visit, tie up at the bridge. **Ecluse 5, Roëzé** marks the beginning of the man-made cut by-passing some very twisting turns of the river. The river returns at **Fillé** a charming village with the usual assortment of shops, churches and cobbled streets. Another cut is created at **Ecluse 4, Spay**, built to avoid the river's constant silting. The end of this run begins another water-skiing area beyond **Prélandon**.

This also marks the end of the rural atmosphere as the suburbs of Le Mans begin to emerge. Beyond **Arnages** waterskiers again intrude.

By **Ecluse 2, Raterie**, there's no mistaking the industrial might of Le Mans, and its a boring, but fortunately short, run toward **Ecluse 1, Le Mans**, (The waterway coming in from the right is the non-navigable **Husine**) and berthing facilities in the heart of the city. After cruising through the ugly outskirts, it comes as something of a surprise to see carefully tended riverside parks, well-signed marinas offering water points, repairs and fuel, and sightseeing a 10-minute walk away.

The city is best-known for the annual 24-hour endurance automobile race, but history climbs the east bank of the Sarthe

One of the many private châteaux along the Mayenne and Sarthe.

to an **Old Town** brimming with the echoes of victor and vanquished.

The Gauls called Le Mans "Oppidum Suindinum", and the Romans built the first walls, so massive and strong that they still rise in a sheer height from the Sarthe. Industry is no stranger to the city: in the 8th century Charlemagne noted that it was one of the most industrious in his realm. Nor has Le Mans avoided warfare: William the Conqueror took it (and Maine) in the 11th century; in 1793, the *Chouan* faction of the Vendéen Revolt suffered one of its worst defeats here, and 1871 the Prussian victory over the city almost guaranteed the final outcome of the Franco-Prussian War.

Roman Le Mans also boasted an **amphitheater**, of which nothing remains today. Traces of the three aqueducts which carried the city's water supply can, however, be found in some Old Town basements.

Focal point of the medieval area is **St Julien Cathedral**, dedicated to the man who brought Christianity to Le Mans in the fourth century. Around this Romanesque-Gothic creation are clustered beautiful 15th-century houses in an area mostly off-limits to cars.

The **Place des Jacobins** is on a much lower level than the cathedral. Looking up at the powerful display of flying buttresses which support the choir, one appreciates the construction difficulties a 13th-century architect must have faced. (On Sunday mornings, a large market is held in the square.)

Taking the steps beside the cathedral toward **Place St Michel**, notice the line of **Canons' homes**. (The 17th-century poet Paul Serron resided at No 1.) Look right and up at the 205-ft (64-meter) tower and toward the richly ornamented 12th-century south porch (often compared to Chartres). The west face of the Cathedral looks onto **Place Cardinal Grent**, its Romanesque facade contrasting with the Place's Renaissance houses and buildings.

The interior inspires flights of fancy and flights of horror. The **choir** is of the former persuasion and breathtakingly

Strolling through Le Mans' Old Town.

size, Nantes is surprisingly easy to sightsee, especially when berthed in the midcity Pleasure Boat Harbor. Despite severe bombing during World War II that destroyed much of Nantes, most historical monuments have been reconstructed or restored.

Because of its strategic position on the Loire River, Nantes has been involved in major and minor wars since its founding during the Gallo-Roman era. The most prolonged was the 14th-century War of Succession, revolving around the Breton aristocracy who wished an independent country, and the French kings who felt Brittany should be part of a greater whole.

In 843 the Normans devastated the city, killing first the bishop, who was celebrating mass, and all his congregation. Havoc followed for almost 100 years until Brittany was released from its bondage by Alain Barbe-Torte. The famous "Cookbeard" returned from exile in England and led his ragtag army of rebellious citizens against the barbarians. To the victor belong the spoils, or in

his case, the capital, and Barbe-Torte, who also took the title of Duke, choose Nantes as his.

For the next several hundred years, depending upon which faction was ruling Brittany, the capital seesawed between Nantes and Rennes (which finally won in 1213). When Duke François II and later, his daughter, Duchess Anne ruled in the mid-to-late 1400s, Nantes became the undisputed center of power, learning and art, if not the capital.

In 1598 Nantes gave its name to the treaty that assured Protestants in France the freedom to worship as they chose; Louis XIV's repudiation of it 87 years later caused the Huguenots to flee.

One of the more unsavory bits of Nantes' history was its connection with slave trade in the 18th century. Not that slaves were actually brought into the city, but many ships carrying them from Africa to America were Nantes-based. After dropping the human cargo in the Antilles, the ships loaded raw sugar (paid for with profits made from the sale of humans), which was refined in Nan-

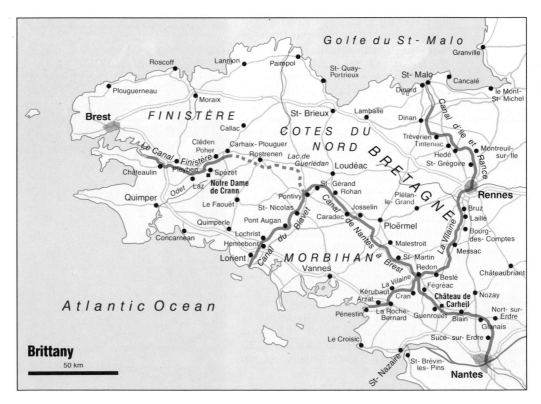

tes and sold throughout the Continent.

Another blot occurred after the Revolution when Royalist citizens were filling the jails to overflowing, and room was needed for new arrivals, Carrièr (local enforcer for the Paris leadership), whose mission was "to purge the body politic of all the rotten matter it contained" plotted upon a novel, if gruesome, means of creating more space: he decided to drown those already imprisoned. Over 4,000 men, women and children were put on boats in the center of the Loire; when those were scuttled, the inevitable happened. Receiving the news in Paris, the Convention belatedly realized that this was not the way to win the public's hearts and minds, and reacted swiftly: Carrièr was executed.

One of the better resolutions of the Revolution, the severing of all connections with the slave trade, led to a decline in Nantes' fortunes. The decision may not have been totally altruistic: French farmers were beginning to realize the cash-crop value of sugar beet, (still true today) and West Indian sugar represented an economic threat. No slaves to transport and no sugar to import meant a dramatic loss of revenue, and the city suffered.

Not for long. Nantes looked toward industry and industry looked back. Today, the city is considered one of the industrial powerhouses of France; there are numerous foundries, boilermaking and engineering works. In the agricultural sector, canneries, biscuit and sugar refineries lead the list, and the Nantes shipyards together with those in St-Nazaire do most of the work for the French navy.

Nantes' premier attraction is the massive **Château des Ducs**. Duke François II commenced building it in 1466, but Anne finished it. During the League, the Duke of Mericoeor added battlements and in the 18th century the château passed to military control.

Henry IV signed the Edict of Nantes within the walls, and among the better-known prisoners were Comte de Chalais (a conspirator against Richelieu), Duchess du Berry (she thought Louis-

Nantes'
**Château des
Ducs.**

Philippe not worthy of his job), and Gilles des Rais (better known as the pirate, Bluebeard). Today, the imposing fortress contains three museums, the **Maritime Museum** (which has interesting exhibits featuring the town's old trading days), the **Museum of Decorative Arts** and the **Museum of Local Popular Art**.

The Gothic Cathedral of **St Pierre et St Paul** is prettier inside than it looks from out. The interior sweeps a breathtakingly high 113 ft (35 meters), and is light and airy, unlike other cathedrals of the same vintage. The tomb of Duke François II is in the south transept; commissioned by his daughter Anne after his death in 1488; the design is by Michel-Colombe, a Breton artist, and it's regarded as one of the most outstanding works of its day.

The **Fine Arts Museum** located on La Rue Gambetta has one of the best collections outside Paris, with works by Ingres, Georges de la Tour, Courbet and Perigini. Other good displays can be found in **Palais Dobrée** and **Manoir de**

la Touche just off Rue Voltaire, and the **Museum of Natural History** on it. The **Jules Verne Museum**, at 3 Rue de l'Hermitage, celebrates the Nantes-born author.

No visit to Nantes would be complete without a walk through its old town; look for 18th-century houses on **Places Graslin** and **Royale**, **Rue Crébillion** and **Cours Cambronne**. Walk to **Quai des Fosses** for a good view of the port; Nantes may be 30 miles (50 km) from the sea, but one could not tell this from looking at the 3 miles (5 km) of harbor facilities.

Before cruising off, browse at the **Boating Library and Bookstore**, housed in a converted barge near the Pleasure Boat Marina.

The 12 miles (21 km) up the **Erdre** from Nantes to the canal entrance are lockless and free of historical monuments. After the concrete and steel of Nantes, enjoy the steeply wooded and house-dotted hillsides. This river/lake was created in the 6th century when St Felix, then Bishop of Nantes, looked for a way to rid the city of the disease-bearing insects that lurked in the marshlands north of the city. He had a dam constructed which created a lake whose deep waters denied the pests a breeding ground. Once the area was safe, it became a weekend retreat, a position it still occupies.

It is hard to go for more than a mile without encountering a boating facility, water-skiing run or wind-surfing club. Except for the bridge at **Sucé** where the river narrows and turns sharply right, navigation is simple. Beyond the bridge, a stretch of water 3 miles (5 km) long and 1,600 ft (500 meters) wide ensures enough space for every sort of water sport. The hills of the lower river have disappeared giving way to low-lying reed-filled ground, and in the migration season it's a haven for birds.

As the river narrows again, the route for **Redon** and **Pontivy** appears to the left. If the journey up the Erdre has been a doddle, head north four miles (seven km) to **Nort-sur-Erdre**. It's a pretty trip to **Pont St George**, where river navigation ends, and the small port has

Windsurfing on the Erdre.

facilities, shops and restaurants, making it a most pleasant overnight stop.

At the end of the Erdre, the lockkeeper at the canal's first lock, **Quiheix**, is a friendly man with several dogs and a wife who takes obvious pleasure in her home. After the busy Erdre, one feels a sense of isolation: there are few houses until **Blain**. The summit is reached at **Ecluse 7, le Pas d'Héric**, with a 5-mile (8-km) cruise until the next bit of lockwork, when the descent to Redon begins.

Approaching Blain, the ruins of a 15th-century château can be seen on the left, and the town offers all facilities to the tired, hungry and thirsty sailor.

The **River Isac** winds in and out of the canal, creating a series of calm backwaters; one can anchor in them, spend a lazy afternoon or swim. Some trees line the banks, but except for occasional patches, are thinly spread.

Rejoice: the stretch between **Ecluses 16**, **Melneuf**, and **17**, **Bellions**, is one of the longest reaches on the canal, offering 14 miles (23 km) of lock-free cruising and several places to visit. After the second river loop, **Château Carheil** can be spotted on the right bank. Built in 1659, it sits in the middle of a 200-acre (80-hectare) park. There are tours March through September during the day and by candlelight on Wednesdays and Saturdays. The church in **Guenrouet** (a few minutes walk from the next bridge) has magnificent examples of post-war stained glass windows.

From **Pont-Miny**, fourth bridge from lock 16, **Fégréac** is less than two miles away. Attractions include old houses and a 15th-century calvary.

These ecclesiastical monuments are peculiar to Brittany, and many were built in the late 16th century to ward off the plague or, later, to give thanks for not having contracted the illness. Although many are large and executed by well-known artists, the form is the same: the Virgin and Her life and the life of Christ, starting with the Annunciation and Visitation through the Resurrection, and Ascent to Heaven are depicted. Before the advent of literacy, priests

Windmills today are just decorative.

would use the calvaries as a teaching method, standing in the pulpit pointing to scenes that would illustrate a point being made or a story told.

Immediately after the next bridge, a non-navigable waterway swings in from the right, **Ecluse 17** is straight ahead and, beyond it, the **Vilaine** *(see page 178)* enters the canal. Redon is four miles (seven km) north; follow the markers into the Grand Basin to overnight. If transiting, take the left fork for Josselin and Pontivy, the right leads toward Rennes. Redon is a charming town *(see page 180)* with all facilities and excellent sight-seeing.

Leaving Redon after a very straight rock-lined cut, the **Oust** makes its first appearance, flowing in from the left. Like the Isac before it, the river meanders in and out of the canal, creating private coves and sheltered lees.

Before proceeding through **Ecluse 19, la Maclais ou Painfaut**, consider a side excursion some five miles (nine km) up the **Aff River** to **La Gacilly**. There are no locks and the entire excursion can be made in a pleasant half-day's cruise. Follow closely the marker buoys: the Aff's start is rather marshy, the river is lined with reed beds.

On the left, just beyond the **Sourdéac Bridge**, is a small château; then the waterway begins to narrow substantially and the trees, unlike most other portions of the canal, come down to the water's edge and envelop it. La Gacilly arrives unexpectedly and appears awash in geranium pots. From the stark modern bridge which marks the end of navigation to the smallest cottage, all buildings near the bridge have red and pink flowers perched in every niche. Perhaps the flowers are explained by La Gacilly's newly-arrived status as an artistic center.

Leather workers, glass blowers, potters, jewellers working with semi-precious stones, and iron sculptors create a variety of crafts in a variety of qualities, and all are for sale in a surprisingly untouristy town.

Returning to the canal, it's a pretty straight stretch of cruising for about 4 miles (6 km) when the river makes a

Left, headless in Carhaix-Plougher and, below, contortions in Malestroit.

sharp right. **St-Martin-sur-Oust** and sustenance are about a mile from the eight-arched bridge which is beyond **Ecluse 21, Gueslin**.

Rochefort-en-Terre is a little over 5 miles (9 km) from the bridge (if there are no taxis available, resort to bicycles). The **castle** is open daily in June and July; only sections of the wall, ruined towers, and some underground passages remain, but the **museum** is interesting as are the views of **Gueuzon Valley** from the terrace.

Several streets have 16th and 17th-century houses, and the **Notre Dame de la Tronchaye** dates from the 12th century with further additions in the 15th and 16th. Interior highlights include a wrought-iron grill and a Renaissance altarpiece adorned with painted wood statues. A statue of the Lady of La Tronchaye is venerated because it was found in a hollow tree where it supposedly had been hidden centuries earlier from the invading Normans. On the first Sunday after 15 August it's the object of an annual *pardon*.

The *pardon*, or pilgrimage, is another Breton tradition, and with few exceptions, these take place from May until the end of September. Religious in nature, and dedicated to a specific saint or religious figure, the faithful use the occasion to seek forgiveness for their sins, fulfill a promise, or simply give thanks for a good year. Everyone wears their best, the day is spent in prayer, and a parade with the venerated object at the fore is the climax of the day. During the procession, candles, banners and a statue of the venerated one are carried while other pilgrims sing hymns and priests scatter Holy Water over the attending crowd.

Today, religion is relegated to the early morning hours, with secular fun (and commercialism) filling the balance of the day. For those anxious to see traditional Breton dress, a *pardon* may be the place to do so, since the wearing of "Sunday best" still applies.

Malestroit is the base for a hire-boat company; its marina offers all services to the passing cruiser. There is a **market**

Replacing the typical grey slate Breton roofs.

every Thursday, and, a good selection of Gothic and Renaissance houses survive. One on the **Place Bouffay** has an unnerving carving: a citizen in his nightshirt beating his wife. These fanciful carvings continue at the church of **St Giles**; one depicts an acrobat in full flight and several animals whose origins leave much to the imagination.

The **Musée de la Résistance** is dedicated to Brittany's part in World War II and is 4 miles (7 km) from Malestroit. It has a wide range of exhibits, including newspapers, ration books, clothing, uniforms from both sides and an excellent film covering the war from beginning to end.

After a sharp right turn after the bridge near **le Roc St-André**, **Château Crevy** appears at the head of the next bend. **Montertelot** has a faded look to it, although there are many well-preserved, half-timbered houses in it, and the dockside church has portions dating from the 12th century.

Ploërmel, once seat of the Dukes of Brittany, is 4 miles (7 km) up the road. The town was founded in the 6th century by **St Armel**. (A statue in the church that bears his name shows the saint taming a dragon.) The ornately carved 16th-century west portal is one of the church's outstanding features. Unfortunately, field glasses are needed to fully appreciate the humor of many scenes. The reset stained-glass windows are of the 16th and 17th centuries; in the chapel are white marble statues of Johns II and III, Dukes of Brittany during the 14th century. Look for half-timbered houses on **Rue Beaumanoir**.

Those with a taste for modern history will enjoy the statue of Dr Guerin, creator of lint surgical dressings; first used in the Franco-Prussian war of 1870, the bandages led to the saving of lives.

One of Brittany's better-known sorties, the Battle of the Thirty, occurred in 1351 on a heath mid-way between Ploërmel and Josselin (bicycle the 2 miles/3 km from the bridge near **St-Gobrien**; look for a stone marker on the NR24). By the middle of the 14th century, when the War of Succession was at its peak, the Royal French forces held

Josselin. Their foes, the de Monforts, were in strength at Ploëmel.

After a long series of battles that decided nothing and left the countryside ravaged, the leaders realized something had to be done. That something was a battle pitting 30 of the best fighters on each side against one another in hand-to-hand combat; the last man standing would decide which side won. At the end of a long March day, Josselin was declared victor.

The canal continues on its semi-deserted route until arriving at the most unforgettable piece of architecture on the entire waterway: the **Château of Josselin**. Photographs don't do it justice, and it's one of the few examples where reality is as good as anticipation.

Approaching by water, at first only the conical towers jutting above the trees are visible. Nearer, the massive Breton grey-stone walls appear, seeming to form a barrier against all intruders, and the much smaller and more insignificant town buildings peep from behind the castle as a child glances at the world from behind the safety of its mother's skirts.

The first fortress on this site was started around the year 1000 by Guthenoc de Porhort, but it was his son Josselin who completed it, and gave the Castle and town its name. Since then, the Castle has been razed and rebuilt innumerable times, lastly and most notably in the 1490s.

One of the more flamboyant owners of the castle was Olivier de Clisson, whose mentor and idol was his mother. De Clisson's father was beheaded for betraying the French during the War of Succession. When his head was displayed on the walls of the castle at Nantes, this remarkable woman took her children there to view it, and said, in effect, "Let's get the bastards who did this". They probably did.

Before the final battle was waged, she had sunk every ship that got in her way, and destroyed six castles unfortunate enough to favor the French side. In the process, Jeanne de Belleville turned her son Olivier into one tough person.

He served with distinction in the English army and later, with the French under Charles V. The great Bertrand du Guesclin became a close friend; when he died, de Clisson succeeded him as Constable of France. In 1370, on marrying Marguerite de Rohan, de Clisson took possession of Josselin Castle which he strengthened and fortified (nine towers were built), making it one of the most important inland strongholds of Brittany. Unfortunately, his patron, Charles VI went mad, and the old warrior was banished by his War of Succession rivals to the fortress on the river, where he died in 1407.

Less than 100 years later, the reigning Duke of Brittany, François II, seized and destroyed Josselin to punish John II de Rohan for his loyalty to the King of France. When François II's daughter, Anne, became Queen of France, she gave money to John II as an act of reconciliation, enabling him to rebuild.

John was smart enough to show gratitude: look for the embellished letter "A" (standing for you-know-who) placed in every conceivable (obvious) part of the building. When finished, the castle more than matched the family motto, "*Roi ne puis, Prince ne daigne, Rohan suis*" (I cannot be King, I scorn to be a Prince, I am a Rohan.)

Alas, this gentrification program suffered another defeat in 1629 when five towers were destroyed. Richelieu was the leveller because, once again, another Rohan (Henri) was leading the Huguenots, a cause most unpopular with Louis XIII's Prime Minister.

Since de Clisson's death, through revolution and war, death and taxes, the Rohan family has maintained ownership of the castle. Their last major renovation was in the latter part of the 19th century, and today, tourists can see some of this splendor.

The **Basilica of Notre Dame du Roncier** (Our Lady of the Bramble Bush) is famous for its *pardon* held every 8 September. The church gets its name from an incident in the 9th century when a peasant working in the fields, found a statue of the Virgin. Wanting to properly honor it, he took it into his home

A Breton farmhouse.

and set up a small shrine. The statue, obviously not happy there, returned to its original spot in the fields.

The farmer repeated this process several times, and each time the statue ended up where it started. Finally, after several hundred years, someone deduced that the Virgin wished a church built where it had been found, and in the 11th century one was raised. For some unrecorded reason, the statue was burnt in 1793 (possibly a consequence of the Revolution) and only a fragment remains, displayed in a reliquary in the Sanctuary. Olivier de Clisson and his wife Marguerite de Rohan are also buried inside; photography enthusiasts should make an ascent of the tower for unusual views of the castle.

As befitting any major tourist attraction, there is a plethora of souvenir shops filled with goods of varying taste and quality. Just down the street from the castle is the **Puppet Museum**, located in one of the town's many half-timbered houses. Transient moorings are next to the castle, with water points but no fuel. The town has several restaurants, shops, and a generally pleasant ambience. The dining room of the **Château Hotel** overlooks canal and castle, the food is good and no tie is required for dinner.

From Josselin, the waterway continues to climb, locks begin to arrive more frequently than before – a preparation, perhaps, for the great onslaught after Rohan. From **Ecluse 50**, **Kermalin**, a **Trappist Monastery** founded in 1841 is within walking distance; the cloister is closed, but a slide show can be seen at the Gate House. On Sundays from Easter to September, visitors are permitted to attend the Gregorian Mass.

Rohan, named after the family who own Josselin Castle, is without grandeur. But it is a pleasant town and the place to turn around if you don't want to tackle the locks to Pontivy.

Between Rohan and **Pontivy's Marina** are 55 locks within 15 miles (24 km) separated into three flights. Once committed to a flight, it is almost impossible to take a breather because the **Before...**

lock-keepers usually man two and three locks each, and expect boaters to maintain a certain schedule.

From locks 56 to 78 it's a miserable slog to the summit reach: 23 in less than 3 miles (5 km). But after the last lock, aptly named Bel Air, there are a further three glorious, magnificent, restful miles (5 km). But don't rejoice too quickly; the next locks (79 to 87) are more like an escalator than a waterway, with nine in half a mile.

Those wanting (or needing) a breather can dock at the bridge below 87, **le Couëdic**. After laboring through the previous torture chambers, the last 4 miles (6 km) and l9 locks into **Pontivy** are a breeze. Congratulations! The greatest concentration of locks in France has now been covered.

Exhausted, dripping with sweat, and cursing the brain that first contemplated the idea of a boating holiday, be happily advised that Pontivy is an enjoyable town with plenty to do. There's a castle to explore, a large selection of restaurants, a full service marina, lots of shops and some of the friendliest local townsfolk along the canal.

In 1807 Napoleon turned the sleepy village into a military base, then ordered it redesigned; the result was a grid of streets, giving Pontivy the orderly look it enjoys today. (A few half-timbered houses around the **Place du Martray** remain, but most were destroyed when the new city was built.) Canal construction was the next bit of urban renewal, and the grateful citizens, so pleased at the revenues and jobs brought by cargo boats, changed the town's name to Napoléonville. With the fall of the first Empire, Napoléonville reverted to its original name. In the second Empire, guess what happened? Some time later, however, once and for all, Pontivy became and remained Pontivy.

The **Château** predates the first name-change; Jean II de Rohan, (he of Josselin ownership) built the rather squat-looking building in the 1480s. Heavily fortified, the ramparts were 64 ft (20 meters) high. Defensive no longer, the moat has been lined with grass and the

...and after.

inside is barren, except for an ethnographical exhibit.

Le Blavet: From Pontivy, the western leg of the canal is closed, and so the intrepid boatman must turn left into the river which ends at Hennebont, 37 miles (59 km) and 28 locks later. (The tidal waterway to Lorient for experienced boaters covers a further 7 miles/13 km).

The name "canal", when applied to the Blavet, is a misnomer; it's an ordinary river with locks, but one look at a map of Brittany and it's understandable why the canal was connected to the Blavet in 1825. Cargo ships could then sail from St-Malo through the province (instead of around it) giving the ships safe passage to a variety of destinations.

Cargo ships are no more; isolation, peace, beauty, and visions of wide valleys and well-maintained farms and lock houses will be pictures in the mind after the journey has finished. Many keepers work two locks; there may be some delays, but smiles and good nature are the rule rather than the exception on this waterway.

From **Ecluse 8**, **Guern** (10 miles/16 km from Pontivy), it's less than 2 miles inland to **Chapelle St Nicomède**. The 16th-century Gothic church is deserted and locked; peering in the windows does not help; all is dark and dim, but the carvings outside on the Gothic fountain are superb.

St-Nicholas-des-Eaux is delightful. In an area with few boating facilities and marinas, this comes as a welcome surprise. There are several restaurants, and for the very energetic, a walk up the hill (30 to 60 minutes along the road) brings the site of ancient **Castennec**. Not much of that remains, but the view of the Blavet and St-Nic is lovely; not as grand as advertised (it's impossible to see the entire loop the river makes) but as an overall picture, worth the exercise.

After St-Nic, don't expect any watering holes until **Pont Augan**. The scenery more than compensates, with the river cutting a narrow swathe through tree-shaded cliffs. The narrow valley gives the feeling of being at the end of the earth, and only the sight of an occa-

Along the Blavet at St Nic des Eaux.

sional track or railroad track intrudes. Leaving Pont Augan and its amenities, (including a small boatyard where fuel and repairs are available), the river once again returns to its solitary character.

Between **Ecluses 19** and **20**, **Minazen and Manérued**, is a sign saying, "Visit the 16th-century Breton Village". Moor at the small dock, cross the road and begin a seemingly unending uphill climb through bramble and bush until a cluster of Breton farm houses comes into view. Plans are afoot to turn this into a living museum, but at present, there is only a rather meagre display about life on the canal during the past two centuries and a small café.

Gardens growing to the river's edge announce **Lochrist** and its **Municipal Park and Boating Center**. **Ecluse 28**, **Polhuern**, is just beyond the town and signals the end of the non-tidal river.

Fortunately, **Hennebont** is a cycle ride away. The city has a long history, one inexorably intertwined with the War of Succession which began with the death of Duke Jean III, and the subse-

quent fight between his niece, Jeanne de Penthièvre, and her brother, Jean of Montfort, for the Duchy of Brittany. (Read carefully now, the Js are many and inter-related.)

Jeanne, wife of Charles de Blois was supported by the French, her brother by the English. During the conflict, Jean's wife, Jeanne of Flanders, came under siege at Hennebont by Charles de Blois and the French. Despite an heroic defense, the walls were breached and defeat seemed imminent. A wily negotiator, as well as an admirable fighter, Jeanne contrived to have it both ways: even if reinforcements did not arrive by a certain date, she would still leave the castle with honor intact. If they did, she would fight on. And in a fairy-tale ending, the English fleet sailed up the Blavet before the appointed date, and rescued the town.

Only the 13th-century **Broërec Gate** and some ramparts are reminders of that long ago war; the rest of the castle disappeared in the blaze of Allied bombing over Lorient during World War II.

Happy cruising!

Notre Dame du Paradis looks more impressive from afar; the 230-ft (72-meter) spire makes it so. The *pardon* is celebrated every year on the last Sunday in September.

Near Hennebont is the famed **Brittany Stud Farm** which has over 150 stallions in residence. Not confined to thoroughbreds, it also breeds draught horses, Breton Post-horses, and other locally needed breeds.

There's a frequent train service into Lorient; but, if you must travel the river, check with the lock-keeper at Polhuen about tides. It is essential to pay strict attention to the channel markings; at low tide it is extremely shallow, and rocks are everywhere. Private craft must moor in the **Pleasure Boat Harbor**. A modern structure there houses a **Museum**, **Tourist Information Center** and several restaurants of varying price and quality.

With the destruction of 85 percent of **Lorient** during World War II, few pre-1940 buildings still stand. The nearby commercial **Fishing Port** was purpose-built in 1920 and is one of the most efficient in Europe. There are two unloading areas, the **Bassin Long** and **Grand Bassin**, each with jetties, processing and loading sheds, and all other accoutrements necessary to take seafood from ship to supermarket. The **Auction Hall** and **Warehouses** are open to the public; best to visit early in the morning.

Le Canal Finistère: Perhaps the most under-used, beautiful and isolated waterway in France is the 39-mile (74-km) long western branch of the Nantes à Brest Canal. Cities are non-existent and towns rare. Wild iris blaze in the springtime, trees droop to the water's edge, others form a tunnel through which a boat can travel. Cows graze in the few open fields, there are glimpses of migratory birds resting between journeys, and old lock-keepers' cottages, turned into weekend retreats, are charmingly decorated.

Locks come at intervals far enough apart to allow pleasant cruising without the feeling of being a slave to the wind-

The Finistère Canal.

lass, and the towpath is weeded and walkable. Even in high tourist season, one can putter aimlessly and alone, floating through whatever time warp one prefers from lock to lock lost in the reverie of the warm sun and light breezes of western Brittany.

Once part of an extensive network, the waterway was cut in two when the Guerlédan lake and dam opened in 1928. The Finistère branch fell into disrepair, was officially closed to traffic in 1957, and total ruin seemed imminent. In 1972 it came under the auspices of the Department of Finistère who recognized the growing attraction of inland cruising and its economic importance. They ordered the renovation of the locks, making it possible now for small boats to cruise the canalized Aulne and Hyères rivers from Port de Carhaix to Port Luanay. (Although the tidal Aulne Maritime is navigable for a further 20 miles/ 30 km, it's not recommended for the novice boater, and most rental agreements forbid it.)

All 33 locks except for Guily-Glaz

Port Launay, end of the Finistère.

(opened by Napoleon III in 1858) are unmanned, but beginners need not fret: hire firms give lessons, and a windlass goes with every charter boat. (Owners must rent one from the lock-keeper at Guily-Glaz or in Châteauneuf-du-Faou from the navigation office.)

It's 4 miles (6 km) from the **Port** up to **Carhaix-Plouguer**, and the town gives little evidence of its importance during the Roman era when it was the hub of seven roads. The spires towering over the town belong to the church of **St Trémeur**, and over the door is a statue of the saint whose life story makes for grim recounting.

The father of this man was the Count of Cormorre who, when a seer forecast one of his sons would kill him, slew his first four wives as soon as they became pregnant – not even waiting to see if the child might be a girl. The fifth, through some ruse, did give birth, and secreted her son with a religious order.

Many years later, Cormorre met Trémeur, was struck by the man's resemblance to his late wife, and had him

beheaded. Not one to be deterred, St Trémeur picked up his head, put it under his arm, walked to his father's house, and threw some dirt on the building. Then, according to legend, the castle dramatically collapsed, burying the evil Count, alias the Bluebeard of Cornouaille, thus fulfilling the prophecy. Every statue of St Trémeur takes care to depict him with his head under his arm, and so it is here.

La Tour d'Auvergne (1743–1800), the town's most famous son, was both a scholar and a soldier. He spearheaded the fight for the preservation of the Celtic language (even to the point of trying to prove that Adam and Eve spoke in Celtic), and the independence and sovereignty of France.

At the age of 54, La Tour (real name, Théophile Malo-Corret) re-enlisted in the army and won many honors: Bonaparte even offered the man a seat on the Legislative Council. It was refused, but La Tour did accept a sword of honor and the title First Grenadier of the Republic. The city pays homage to its most cele-

brated son on his nameday, the last Sunday in June.

Other sights are few: the Renaissance house of the *Seneschal* (governor) is now a tourist information center; note the fine faces carved on the upper storey. Shopping, however, is good, and a number of restaurants can relieve the cook's burden.

Just beyond **Ecluse 203**, **Kergout**, note a beautiful house on the right which has a backwater next to it. That's the **Hyères River** entering the canal; navigation on it isn't possible, but it provides a quiet mooring.

Cleden-Poher is 2 miles (3 km) uphill from the canal. Moor at the bridge beyond **Ecluse 206**, **Stervallen**, and take the road to the right (the not so interesting **St-Hernin** is the same distance left). Cleden offers a butcher, a baker and a bar; it's a friendly town, and the church calvary worth the trek.

The **Aulne River** and civilization intrude at **Pont-Triffen**; three miles (five km) up the road and beyond the town of **Spézet** is **Notre Dame du Crann Chapel**. (If the church is locked, get the key from the presbytery.)

The exterior of the building, built in 1532, is unremarkable; but the stained glass windows, installed 100 years later, are magnificent. Even on a gray day, the light streaming in through the windows gives them a luminosity of their own. St Ligius, the patron saint of farriers, is represented in the south aisle. The Passion, the Last Judgement and the Triumph of Christ are in the chancel with other Biblical scene. For those sailing the waterway on Trinity Sunday, the *pardon* here should not be missed.

Spézet is a prosperous town with several restaurants, and many stores to reprovision if more supplies are needed than are available at Pont-Triffen.

Unlike earlier locks, the approach to **Ecluse 210**, **Penity**, and its weir, is dangerously open. Fortunately, it and similar ones all the way to Châteaulin are marked with yellow buoys. To the right, civilization appears very briefly in the form of a major highway and one or two prosperous looking farms.

Châteauneuf du Faou, the first town

Part of a calvary.

of any note, sits about 300 ft (100 meters) above the canal, and a well-signed (four languages) path to it lets one avoid the busy highway. There's a friendly pub/café near the mooring facilities where thirst can be slaked before and after the trek!

Ponder, however, before exerting: Châteauneuf may not be worth the climb. Aside from the church which is architecturally boring and historically uninteresting, there's really not much to see unless it's the second Sunday in August when the annual *pardon* is held.

Just beyond Châteauneuf's bridge is a full-service marina, and the adjacent sports center has tennis courts. Since the Aulne is noted for its salmon fishing, it and other places along the river also cater to fishermen. Many of the locks also have small gates in the weirs that open during the spawning season to help the fish travel upstream.

Pleyben's calvary and parish close.

At **Pont Pol**, the *Auberge du Saumon* serves that fish as its speciality, and offers overnight moorings. On a clear day, exercise enthusiasts may want to bicycle the 4 miles (7 km) up to **Laz**. One cautionary note: it's necessary to carry one's own sustenance. Except for the sweeping views, there is little else in the town to sustain the sweating and thirsty traveller.

It's a 3-mile (5-km) trip from **Pont Coblant** to see one of Brittany's largest and best-preserved parish closes. **Pleyben's calvary** was first built in 1555, and since then other figures have been added. (The Last Supper and Washing of the Disciples' Feet in 1650; the last images were carved in 1743.) The life of Christ is displayed on all four sides; to start from the Nativity, look for the statue of the Virgin holding Elizabeth's hand, and continue from there in an anti-clockwise direction.

Two belfries dominate the church: the tower on the right is Renaissance, the other Gothic. On each side of the porch leading to the church entrance are beautifully carved statues of saints and other religious figures. Inside, three large stained glass windows depict the Passion, and the 16th-century carved panel-

ling is decorated with a series of mytho-logical and religious scenes.

The church is the focus of the town; shops and restaurants surround its wide close, and aromas emit from several *crêperies* and bakeries. The marina at Pont Coblant offers all services, and a restaurant there produces good meals. From here, the Aulne begins a series of twists and turns that more than triples the direct line to **Châteaulin**.

The first indication that the waterway is not going to continue in its isolated mode arrives at **Ecluse 235**, **Coati-grac'h**, in the form of a low modern building on the right with a modern factory behind the old lockhouse. Tall apartment buildings are the next im-pediment to the view. On the left, houses begin dotting the riverside, each with a garden and a small dock, an air of smug prosperity about them.

So begins Châteaulin. Rounding a sharp right bend the town fully impacts: plane trees line both sides of the river, attractive buildings behind them. The side street are filled with shops and restaurants, and hills surround the town, creating a green bowl.

Since salmon fishing is so important on the Aulne, it's only natural that that fish should be included on the city's coat of arms; look for it on official buildings. The **Hôtel de Ville**'s clock tower and the **Chapel of Notre Dame** are the only obvious things to see but there's a tourist office near the bridge.

Because it is cozier, **Port Launay** appears more charming than Châteaulin. Houses stand eave to eave, their facades mirrored in the water, and the pastures across the river give a wonderful open-ness. There are ramps for small boats as well as moorings for deep-water craft, and several swans seem to prefer here to anywhere else.

For those going all the way (at least to the last lock), a giant aqueduct signals **Guily-Graz**. That's the end of the non-tidal road and the end of the line for the rental boat skipper. (If attempting a jour-ney down the **Aulne Maritime**, check with the lock-keeper for tides and sail-ing times.)

Many old mills line the Ille.

Le Canal d'Ille et Rance: Originally conceived as a means of avoiding the difficult passage around the Finistère headland, today, the 152-mile (244-km) 64-lock Canal d'Ille et Rance et la Vilaine from St-Malo to the Vilaine estuary gives an opportunity for discovering the heartland of Brittany.

There is great diversity of scenery and water, and the journey can be divided into four stages: the tidal Rance from St-Malo to Le Chatelier (14 miles/22 km and two locks), the Canal d'Ille et Rance to Rennes (53 miles/85 km, 47 locks (or one almost every mile); the canalized Vilaine flows from Rennes to the barrage at Arzal (81 miles/131 km, 15 locks); the last four miles (seven km) are the tidal Vilaine. The first and last stages should be undertaken only by experienced sailors who are familiar with tidal navigation.

Records indicate the Vilaine was one of the first waterways in Europe equipped with pound locks, and by the 1550s was navigable from the Bay of Biscay to Rennes. In the mid-1700s,

plans were drawn to cut a canal from Rennes to Dinan, but these were sidelined by the French Revolution, and it was 100 years later, in 1890, when passage between the English Channel and the Atlantic became possible.

The 1879 Freycinet Act authorizing the enlargement and modernization of canals did not help the Breton canals: they had no connections with the rest of France and were ignored. Even so, the Vilaine was such an inexpensive and efficient way to move freight that from a high of over 170,000 tons in 1886, the figures for 1936 were only slightly less, 163,000. By the 1960s, however, commercial traffic was no longer viable, and thought was given to filling in the canal, and allowing the Vilaine to suffer from benign neglect.

Fortunately, the barrage and dam at Arzal and the boom in canal boating arrived about the same time, the late 1960s and early 1970s. The result of the former was a much longer stretch of non-tidal waterway. As to the latter, the tourist department established a com-

The port of Dinan.

mittee to rebuild the canals, to improve and add to existing facilities, and to get locals involved. And they got it right: despite unpredictable weather, the Breton canals are some of the most enjoyable and well-maintained to traverse anywhere in Europe.

All the locks on the stretch to Rennes have keepers, the towpaths are in good shape, and the landscape is lush and verdant with a series of very pretty lockhouses alongside the water.

The massive lock and barrage at **La Chatelier** commences the non-tidal Rance; there's a large, full-service marina, lots of room to berth, and a hire cruise firm. The waterway is lake-like until the approach to Dinan, when it narrows abruptly. The banks are high along this stretch of water, wooded, and only the occasional dot of a house or small château indicate that this is one of the most populated areas of Brittany.

At the port of **Dinan**, mooring on the left bank is forbidden, and unlike most inland ports, an anchorage fee is levied. The full-service marina also has a crane

to step masts. Buildings line one side of the port and there's a pretty Gothic bridge upstream.

The **Old Town** is at the top of a very steep (240 ft/75 meters) hill overlooking the port (taxis available). At the top, the **English Garden** offers magnificent river views; other good ones are from the **Petits-Fosse Promenade** located outside the ramparts.

The medieval town has tortuous, twisting, cobbled streets, 15th and 16th-century half-timbered houses with Breton slate roofs. There are also various craft workshops in weaving, pottery, canework and glass-blowing for the visitor to explore. Sidewalk cafés and restaurants abound, and Thursday is market day. One of the nicest times to stroll this city is early in the morning before others are about. Walking quietly through the streets the shadows seem to turn time back two or three hundred years.

The 14th-century tower of the **Castle**, known as the **Duchess Anne Dungeon** is over 100 ft (34 meters) high, and contains a **Museum of Breton History** along with numerous ethnographical objects from the Rance area.

The **Place du Champ Clos** was the site of a famous duel. In 1359 Dinan was under a siege led by the English Duke of Lancaster; its defense was directed by Bertrand du Guesclin. The future Constable of France, needing a breather, asked for a truce of 40 days; then, if the town had not been relieved, the English would be declared victors.

Bertrand's brother, Olivier, left Dinan unarmed, and in violation of the truce was taken prisoner by an English knight named Canterbury, and a ransom of 1,000 florins was demanded. Bertrand challenged Canterbury to a one-to-one duel, and defeated the English knight. Olivier was released, and Canterbury, true to his word paid du Guesclin 1,000 florins. In the final twist, Canterbury not only lost the contest and the money but also, because of his dishonorable behaviour in violating the truce, Lancaster stripped the Knight of his commission in the English army.

In death du Guesclin was treated more royally than the kings of France: they

Signs indicate available services at each port.

only had three burial places (one each for the heart, head and entrails), but he was honored with four. Why? Du Guesclin always wanted a burial at Dinan; when he died at Châteauneuf-de-Randon in 1380 the body was first embalmed at Le Puy, and the Church of St Lawrence received the entrails.

Unfortunately, embalming had not quite attained the scientific standards that it has today, and shortly thereafter an unpleasant odor arose from the corpse. The flesh was quickly removed from the skeleton and buried in the Franciscan church at Montferrand (destroyed in 1793 during the Revolution), and the remains were boiled. By the time the funeral cortège reached Le Mans, an order was received to take the body to the Cathedral of St Denis in Paris, so off the skeleton went. Only the heart arrived at Dinan, where it lies in the church of **St Sauveurs** behind a heart-shaped cenotaph in the north transept. (Look for a statue of du Guesclin on the square named after him.)

In St Sauveur, notice a modern-stained glass image of Anne of Brittany; it's one of several windows depicting Breton and French heros. The church is a mixture of Gothic and Renaissance, constructed between the 12th and 16th centuries with an 18th-century altarpiece, and a steeple built to replace one destroyed in a fire.

Old houses abound on **Rue du Jerzual**, the **Place des Merciers** and **Rue de la Lainerie**. The **Tour de l'Horloge** (Clock Tower) houses a small museum. The **Governor's House** is on a road leading to the river, and the **Church of St-Malo** has a 15th-century chancel and apse.

If feeling especially energetic, walk along the towpath to **Léhon**. It's shaded, the river is exceedingly narrow and follows a winding course. Or, moor at a small landing above a little stone bridge. Léhon has few shops, but it does have a splendid open-air swimming pool and there's the partly-ruined priory church of **St Magloir** and a 17th-century cloister to explore.

A rule prohibits overnight mooring

Five wheels.

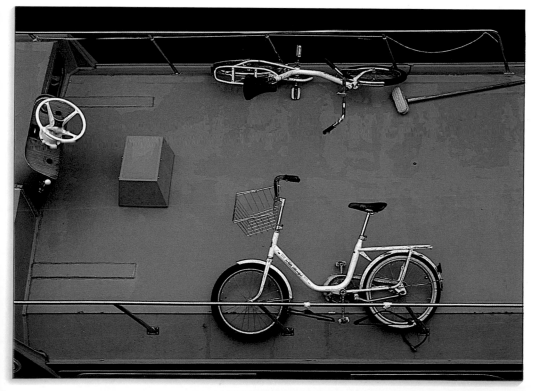

between **Ecluse 47** and **Ecluse 43**, **La Roche**, because of flash floods, (in the summer and fall the rule is regularly ignored). Just before **Ecluse 46**, **Pont Perrin**, is a beautiful château; at **Ecluse 45**, **Boutron**, there's a working water wheel and at the next, **Mottay**, an old mill, **Le Moulin**. The many derelict farm buildings indicate the number of people who are leaving the agricultural sector. Despite European Economic Community farm subsidies, earning power has declined and the sons and daughters of Breton farmers are leaving the land. For hunters of real estate bargains, Brittany is a paradise and no more so than along the canals.

Note that some of the lock gates here are operated with a capstan. Elsewhere, wooden balance beams are in use, although some have been taken off and more modern winding devices installed. **Ecluse 43** marks **Evran** (moorings and all supplies available); a plaque on the lock cottage records a record drought that caused the closure of the canal from June 1921 to February 1922. **Trévérien**

is another charming town; there's a canal-side church with a square tower and spire, and a wharf and shopping facilities.

There's a winding hole (a wide part of the canal where boats can turn around) in **St-Domineuc**. An exercise course runs on both sides of the canal bank with timber obstacles, parallel bars and an instruction board illustrating other blood-pulsing movements.

Tinténiac, the largest town between Dinan and Rennes, comes complete with a full range of shops and restaurants and a full service marina, but not much more. It is, however, handy for excursions. **Montmuran** where du Guesclin, whose second wife, Jean de Lavel was a Montmuran, was knighted in 1354 is 3 miles (5 km) away (take the road to Les Iffs). Not much remains of the 12th to 14th-century castle except a large tower and flamboyantly styled chapel. From the top of the towers are views of Hédé and Dinan.

Combourg is 8 miles (13 km) from Tinténiac. Built in the 11th century and enlarged in the 14th and 15th, it's been owned by the du Guesclin family and the Count of Châteaubriand. **Château Lanrigan** is another three miles (five km) to the east, and is open in the summer. Built of granite, its balanced proportions recall many of the Loire valley châteaux.

Passage between **Ecluses 29**, **Petite Madeleine**, and **15**, **Ille**, is regulated to conserve water; to avoid waiting time, check with the first lock-keeper for timings. **Ecluse 31**, **Dialais**, marks the start of the 11-lock **Hédé** flight, and if passing straight through, it should take about two hours. If not, notify the first keeper who will inform his colleagues up the line. Every keeper looks after two locks, and breaking the chain means extra work and time lost for all.

When stopping to visit Hédé town, moor just north of **Ecluse 28**, **La Madeleine**. It's little more than a mile up a steep hill; at the outskirts is a large 19th-century Gothic château. The town consists of a broad square, the usual Romanesque church, a post office, and several restaurants. Beyond the **Théatre** **Sketching the canal.**

de Poche (Pocket Theater) are the ruins of an ivy-covered 11th-century château with views over the valley.

The summit cut is about 7 miles (11 km) long and the water sources for the canal, the **Basin de Bazouges**, and **Basin de Partage des Eaux** are located here, the latter at **Ecluse 20**, **Ville Morin**. The descent to the River Vilaine begins here, and so does one of the prettiest stretches of the waterway. The lock-keeper's house at **Ecluse 19**, **Courgalais**, has flower boxes in the window, and at the 17th, its name, Lengager is spelt out in shrubbery.

The shopkeepers of **Montreuil-sur-Iles** appear distinctly unfriendly and serve with a grudge rather than a grin. The lockkeeper at **Ecluse 16**, **Haute Rouche**, has a wonderland of flowers and ceramic figures. **St-Médard-sur-Ile** is very boat-orientated town: although the town is at the top of a hill, shops and facilities lie next to the canal.

At **Ecluse 11**, **St-Germaine**, flowerpots are secured around the entire lock area making everything awash with blooms. The town is up a steep hill with vistas of the area. **Betton** has a very nice marina with a post office near the dock. There's an absolutely gorgeous weir at **Ecluse 3**, **St-Grégoire**; gardens come down to the water's edge, willows overhang the banks, and the ubiquitous fishermen are everywhere.

By **Ecluse 2**, **St-Martin**, Rennes and the Vilaine River have arrived. This lock is different from the previous ones: hoot to get the lock-keeper's attention, and a green light indicates when it's safe to proceed. Moorings within a five-minute walk of all sightseeing are just beyond **Ecluse 1**, **Mail**. The **city marina** is pleasantly landscaped and offers water points.

Rennes is a pleasure: pedestrian malls ensure easy walking, restaurants abound (in one square near the Cathedral, Vietnamese, Italian and French sit beam to beam), and fresh meat, vegetables and cheese are available at the indoor market on the **Rue de Nemours**.

Rennes also has a long history: the Celts built the first houses, the Romans

The lock at St-Germaine-sur-Ille.

put walls around them; in 1213 it became the capital of Brittany; a fire in 1720 devastated most of Rennes, but the city rebuilt, then survived most of the Revolution's excesses. Modern Rennes bears no resemblance to it's sleepy past. Although many buildings are classical 18th-century architecture, the city is home to two modern universities, and is a vital contributor to France's electronic and communications industry.

A long rivalry with Nantes ended when Rennes, with its more defendable interior position, was declared the capital of Brittany. And though the Dukes may have preferred to live in their fortress at Nantes, they came to Rennes for their inauguration. The marriage of Duchess Anne and Charles VIII of France in 1491 did more than unite two people: it plighted the troth of Brittany and France as well. Losing independence did not mean losing privilege: Parliament was established here in 1561, and except for a short period in the 17th century, it remained free to set its own laws until the Revolution.

RESTAURANT
Du Chalit

It was in Rennes that Bertrand du Guesclin first made his name. Although born into a good family, his manner did not match his heritage, and made him the black sheep of the family. In 1337, however, there was a tournament in Rennes. Du Guesclin wanted to compete but his family stopped him. Finally, bullying one of his Rennes cousins into loaning him armor and a horse, du Guesclin competed anonymously, unseating several of his opponents. Realizing a winner when he saw one, father and son were reunited, and the young man went on to fame and fortune and died a hero.

Ménage-à-trois may be a French phrase, but Anne of Brittany and her marriages took it one step farther. Anne, the heir of François II, was only 12 when he died in 1489, but that didn't stop her from having a proxy marriage to Maximilian of Austria the next year. However, Charles VIII who adored land, decided he had to have Brittany and the easiest way to get it was to marry young Anne.

Charles was, unfortunately, currently married to Marguerite of Austria, daughter of the same Maximilian who had just married the Duchess. That little fact didn't deter Charles. He proposed, Anne said "No", preferring the *status quo*; Charles didn't and deciding "no" was a word he didn't like, laid siege to Rennes in August 1491. Hunger is a great incentive to changing one's mind; thus Anne agreed to meet Charles.

From statues and portraits (usually flattering in those days) neither one, except for their positions, could be considered a great catch. She was homely and had a limp; he was short and ugly with large eyes and a mouth that gave him a slightly stupid look. Rather peculiarly, Anne and Charles took to each other, but there remained the leftovers, father and daughter who liked their *status quo*! After some royal wrangling, the Court of Rome agreed the proxy and unconsummated marriages didn't count, and Brittany and France were wed in December 1491.

The fire of 1720 gusted through Rennes for over a week, and the damage **Signs point the way to...**

was so extensive and the cost of rebuilding so great that Louis XV guaranteed the funds for rebuilding. The architect, Jacques Gabriel was commissioned, and gave the city the 18th-century face it shows the world today.

One part of old Rennes did survive the great fire; a few of the 15th and 16th-century half-timbered houses can be found in the streets around the Cathedral. Peek in the courtyard of the **Hôtel du Blossac** in the **Rue de Chapitre**; there's a lovely curving staircase leading off it. One of the most beautiful houses is at **3 Rue St-Guillaume**; the **Place de la Lices** was site of the tournament where du Guesclin triumphed. The famous mayor, Leperdit, who had the courage to resist Paris's demands for the mass genocide of Rennes' population during the Revolution, resided at **19 Place Ste-Anne**. This is a typical French town square, being given over to a tree-bordered car park with good sidewalk cafés from which to watch the world stroll by.

The **Cathédral St Pierre**, finished in 1844, is the third one on this site. The altar is most impressive, but is almost overshadowed by the rest of the rich interior. The 16th-century stained glass windows of **St Germain** depict the Virgin's life. **St Sauveur's Chapel of Our Lady of Miracles** is dedicated to the Saint who delivered Rennes from the English in 1357.

From the outside, the former **Parliament House** of Brittany is not impressive; the interior tells a different story. The architect of the Luxembourg Palace in Paris, Salomon de Brosse, was commissioned, and the building, now housing the **Law Courts**, was constructed between 1618 and 1655. Over 100 representatives from the noble Breton families governed the Province from here, and despite the fact that seats were for sale (for a little less than $1,000 in today's money), great respect was accorded the office holders. Although damaged in the Great Fire, it escaped destruction, and Gabriel restored it.

The colonnaded **Salle de Grosse Pilliers** is followed by **Salle des Pas Per-**

...Rennes' variety of cuisines.

dus. Its wooden vaulted ceiling is painted in blue and gold with the coat of arms of Brittany and France at the center. There's a double staircase sweeping up to the first floor, and the walls are filled with paintings by some of the finest artists of Louis XV's day.

None of this prepares the visitor for the most impressive room, the **Grande Chambre**, the former parliamentary debating area. Over 66 ft long, 33 wide and 23 high (20 meters by 10 by 7), the panelled ceiling and woodwork are stunning. There are 10 Gobelin tapestries on the walls; representing scenes in the history of Brittany, they took 24 years to weave. The loggias, or boxes, which enabled visitors to watch the debates below, saw many illustrious visitors including Madame Sévigné, writer of the famous letters.

In contrast, the **Banqueting room** of the baroque **Town Hall** seems almost plain. That and its great clock "**Le Gros**" were also Gabriel's work. All that remains of the 15th-century ramparts is **La Porte Mordelaise**.

The **Breton Museum** tells of the province's history. Every room details a particular period from pre-historic to the present. There is also a superb ethnological section in the last gallery with artifacts from 1789 to 1914. The **Musée des Beaux Arts** has a varied collection, and the **Breton Car Museum** is less than two miles from the city center.

La Vilaine: The river does not deserve its name, "ugly" or "nasty". It is a delightful waterway, filled with long and pleasant reaches. Perhaps the name originally came from the tricky tides, shallow waters and rock-strewn river-bed that caused the sinking of many a ship before the channel was cleared and locks built. Despite the clearings, the Vilaine is still a river, and navigation markers should be carefully followed.

Leave behind the industrial area of Rennes as quickly as possible It's a jumble of tower blocks, factories, electric pylons, and other messes. Beyond **Ecluse 3**, **Apigné**, make a sharp right turn and there's a tree-shaded, quiet backwater. Below **Ecluse 4**, **Cicé**, is a

Redon's harbor.

turning area for large barges. Above **Le Pont Réan** are several islands to be avoided, and navigation through the eight-arch stone bridge is a little tricky. (There's a boat hire firm/marina here that offers all facilities.)

The **Parc Naturel de Boël** starts one of the most spectacular stretches on the entire river. It's a deep cut with cliffs high above the river, undergrowth and trees covering it. Poplars and willows also overhang the water, and on weekends it's flooded with visitors. Because of this, many excellent restaurants have opened between **Ecluses 7**, **Boël**, and **8**, **Bouëxière**, among them Le Vieu Moulin de Boël, where an afternoon's kir can be one pleasure on a lazy summer's day, Au Fil de l'Eau, and Le Moulin de Bouëxière.

Several châteaux dot the hillside of the next few reaches. There are basic facilities at **Pont de Macaire**, and up a steep hill, the church at **Saint Malo de Phily** is interesting and there are lovely views over the valley.

More happy cruising.

There's another hire cruiser firm in Messac with a new, purpose-built marina, and a wide range of boating facilities including a crane, slipway, fuel (diesel and regular) and repair yard. For shopping, dock at the stone quay near the bridge below **Ecluse 12**, **Guipry**.

Before the canalization of the Vilaine it was only possible to navigate upriver as far as Guipry. Because of that, and the salt trade, Guipry became an important town in the 17th century. The salt was collected in an area near St-Nazaire and brought by barge to Guipry where a tax called the *gabelle* was levied. Since every subject was required to buy a certain amount of salt every year, the taxes were substantial and the men who collected the tax were called *Gabelous*.

Near the lock on the Messac side is the tiny **Chapel of Notre Dame de Bon-Port**. The Lord of Tréguilly, whose vast stores of sea salt were threatened by an unusually high river tide, built the church in 1644 in gratitude for not losing his valuable commodity. Every July, on the next to last Sunday, the church's *fête* takes place.

Malon marks the final lock before Arzal; this allows over 30 miles (50 km) of lazy cruising. Another beautiful area of the Vilaine also begins. Known as **Corbinières**, it's typical of "*la Bretagne Sauvage*" (wild Brittany). On either side are forests, **le Bois de Boeuvre** and **le Bois de Baron**. There are rocky cliffs covered with pine trees, chestnuts and oaks; anglers on the bank and in punts attest to the popularity of fishing. The towns tend to be further away from the river and even fewer houses are along the banks.

At **Beslé**, the Hotel du Port is attractive and offers good food at a reasonable price; uphill are the town and shops. The scenery changes again: the cliffs and forests are no more, and in their place sparse, flat, and deserted countryside appears. It is a great relief to enter Redon and its busy harbor.

Redon is the junction with the Canal de Nantes à Brest, west to Josselin and Pontivy, or southeast to Nantes. The town is divided into the newer section, north of the Nantes canal, and the older,

located on the small island formed between the Vilaine and the port (all facilities). Here are cobble-stoned streets, older buildings, and the more interesting restaurants and *crêperies*.

Originally founded in the 9th century as a Benedictine abbey, the town flourished, and by the 14th was walled (some of the remains can be seen around the **Quay St-Jacques**). The abbey church of **St Sauveur** looks weird: the 13th-century Gothic tower is separate from the church, the result of a fire in 1782. Located on the **Place de l'Hôtel de Ville**, Cardinal Richelieu erected the elaborate high altar when he was Commendatory Abbot, and it looks out of place in the Gothic chancel. The Tourist Office is across the square from the church, the staff speak English and German, and are most helpful.

Heading south, the river cuts through a wide valley with gently-sloping hills as it gradually increases in width. Four miles (7 km) down it is the left-hand turnoff to Nantes. At **Cran**, note the swing bridge that opens for large craft and sailing vessels. Several day-tripping boats ply this stretch from Redon or **La Roche Bernard**, but in general, the Vilaine is not heavily traveled.

A large suspension bridge soaring over the river at a height of over 160 ft (50 meters) is the first indication of La Roche Bernard. Built in the 17th century, the town was a large shipbuilding center, now it's an equally important marina. The river is extraordinarily wide, and not only are power boats berthed at the floating jettys, but so are numerous sailing craft.

Although situated high above the water, the town is delightful to wander through. From the lookout (marked with an old cannon) there are views up and down the river. Places to eat and shop abound, and one souvenir might be a pair of locally made clogs.

Only 6 miles (9 km) of waterway remain until the barrage of **Arzal**. Beyond it, the 4 miles (7 km) to the sea is best left to the experienced yachtsman. From La Roche Bernard several beaches are nearby and **Vannes** is 24 miles (39 km) away by road.

Left, cafés are near most marinas. **Right**, Rennes' Old Quarter.

A CRUISE THROUGH ILE DE FRANCE

Not a single waterway, but five constitute a circular trip through one of the most historic and beautiful regions of France. The anti-clockwise journey from Paris encompasses Champagne country, the land of Joan of Arc, some of France's oldest and most elegant châteaux, ancient cathedrals, its richest and most fertile farmlands, and bloodiest battlefields.

The Ile de France is the land where French kings were crowned, and where they were buried. Clovis was the first; although Soissons was his capital, he journeyed to Reims for anointing, beginning a tradition that lasted for more than 1,300 years. St Denis, near Paris is home to royal bodies, if not their *actual* bodies, as violence has also struck the heart of France. During the Revolution, Republicans carried off the remains and only the elaborate tombs bear witness to the regal past of France.

And painters have found inspiration along these waterways. Cézanne and Gauguin, were struck by the light at Auvers, and their impressions are on display in museums throughout the world. And Van Gogh is buried above the waters of the Oise River.

Cruising is generally hassle-free. All the locks are automatic and usually manned, and locking-through lessons are given before a rental boat ventures from the yard. On most locks, instructions for operating them are clearly written in four languages. Commercial traffic has a very definite right of way, and small craft are only permitted in locks after the big boys have been accommodated. If there's no room in the "inn", then pleasure boats wait until the money-makers pass through.

La Marne: The river flows from its source in the plains of Langes into the Seine near the ugly Parisienne exurb of Alfortville (just over 3 miles/5 km from the back-end of Ile St-Louis). Navigation is possible on the Marne and its Latéral Canal for 153 miles (245 km) through 33 locks and two tunnels, one near St Maur, 1,950 ft (600 meters) long, the other at Chalifert, 940 ft (290 meters) to Vitry-le-François. In this chapter, however, we are concerned only with the 122 miles (196 km) to Condé-sur-Marne and the Canal de l'Aisne à la Marne.

Although the Marne has been navigable for centuries, the river was not canalized until 1865. The Latéral was completed in 1845, as a means of providing a safe and constant navigation to the Rhine and Saône rivers. Then, as now, agricultural products (mainly wheat) were the primary cargoes followed by coal and slate.

The Marne scenery doesn't improve until Nogent-sur-Marne, but it's not until Lagny that all urban blemishes are left behind. Once free of the cities, concrete docks and sides give way to overgrown riverbanks abounding with weeping-willow trees. Prim modern bungalows sit next to houses looking as if they have not had a coat of paint since the day they were built, and all climb the steep hillside in neat, orderly rows. Where there

Left, spoilt for choice. **Right**, Bacchus smiles over the champagne.

are fields, corn appears a major crop, so are potatoes.

The major development in the area has been the huge **Euro Disney** resort at **Marne-la-Vallée**, southeast of Lagny-sur-Marne. One-fifth the size of Paris, it encompasses such Disney staples as Main Street USA, Frontierland, Fantasyland and Sleeping Beauty's Castle. Two things distinguish it from its California and Florida precursors: the comparative lack of reliable sunshine and the fact that, being in France, it serves alcohol.

Lagny has a museum, and a wide variety of shops; beyond town, the Touring Club of France operates a full- service marina.

Above the river at **Chalifert** the turret of an old fort/castle looms, reminiscent of an earlier conflict. Just before the tunnel a restaurant sits beside the yacht-basin. Emerging from the blackness, climb the banks to **Coupvray**, home of Louis Braille the inventor of the world's major system of reading for the blind. His parents' home is a museum open ine summer.

St Feron Cathedral's spire leads

boaters toward **Meaux**, capital of Brie, and its first-rate marina at Le Marlin. The city became a See in the 4th century, yet the Cathedral is a late addition, constructed between the 12th and 16th in a style best described as Gloomy Gothic. Inside is the tomb of Bossuet (the Eagle of Meaux), once bishop of the city. He lived between 1627 and 1704, and tutored the Grand Dauphin.

Although the city has been walled since the Gallo-Roman period, the walls standing today were constructed by Monsieur de Ligny in 1660. The gardens, designed by Le Nôtre, are a treat for weary eyes. Unfortunately the building that forms one of the park's boundaries has graffiti marring its walls and some of the expressions date to the mid-1950s. **Musée Boussuet** is in the old Episcopal Palace and contains a fine collection of prehistoric relics, art of the Middle Ages, and information relating to the Prelate.

The recently-landscaped Boulevard Jean Rose follows the walls and ends at **Place Doumar**; at its center, the inevi-

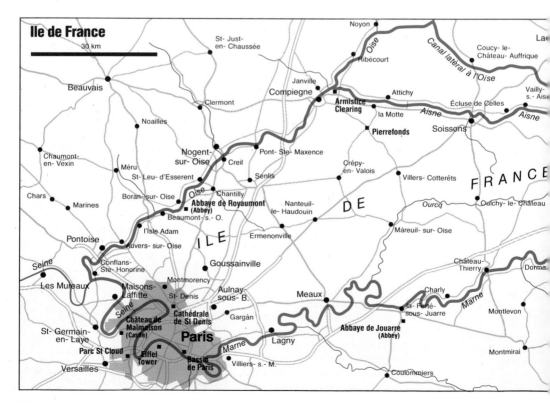

table monument to France's war dead. One of the most memorable events of World War I, the reinforcement of the Marne by Parisien taxicabs, is celebrated each September. In 1914, when the Germans seemed to be on the verge of breaking through, men and munitions were carried by taxi from the capital to Meaux, thus stemming the invasion. A plaque on the road to Soissons commemorates the farthest point that the German High Command reached during World War I.

Trilport is a pleasant little town with small market gardens. Modern versions of old timbered houses are indistinguishable from the real things at **St Jean les Deux Jumeaux**. Shops and services are not available in great quantity; but there are some nice moorings if a quiet overnight stop is desired.

Just beyond the railway bridge at **Poincy**, a full-service, pleasure-boat harbor sits on the left bank. The river rolls through a wide valley; there are cultivated fields, mostly of wheat, and little if any woodland.

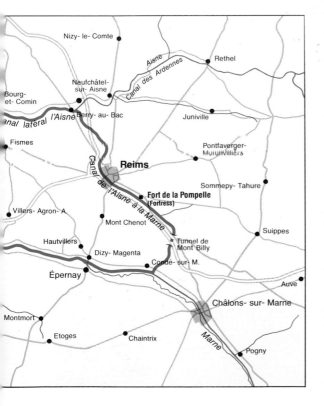

A succession of grain silos announces the arrival of **La-Ferté-sous-Jouarre**, the aroma of commercial bakeries add more evidence to its agricultural importance. Larger than it looks, there's a good selection of restaurants and shops. Along the river is a municipal sports and equestrian center, complete with tennis courts.

Less than 2 miles south of La Ferité is the Benedictine **Abbey of Jouarre**. Founded in the 7th century, the current buildings are 17th. Visit the Carolingian and Merovingian tombs, then climb to the top of the Tower.

Gliding along the river is almost like being inside a person's home; most curtains are open as if the residents forgot that a passing stranger might be able to peer inside. Families eat, laugh, talk, children play and fight.

The loops the Marne makes along this stretch would do justice to any amusement park ride. There are more curves and twists than the greatest thriller.

Vineyards begin to appear at **Charly-sur-Marne**, but the great Champagne region does not begin until after Château-Thierry. From here to the Canal de l'Ainse à la Marne most towns have one or more vintners who offer tastings of varying quality. Some of the more enterprising owners provide small docks and a path to the tasting room; others put signs at town docks.

Château-Thierry can't be missed: the town's name is spelled out in flowers along the bank of the river. Because of its geography, the town has been the victim of numerous sackings over the course of its history. Named after an 8th-century Merovingian king, Thierry IV, the city is overlooked by the ramparts of an old fortress. Charles Martel built them in the 8th century, and they offer good views of the valley. **St Crépin Church** is of the 16th century with modifications throughout the years (note the bullet holes on the front).

A local boy made good, Jean de la Fontaine, was born here in 1621; the poet's home is a museum detailing his life and his Fables. Joan of Arc passed through the **Porte St-Pierre** in 1429.

About 3 miles (5 km) west of town on what is now called **Hill 204**, a decisive battle in 1918 pitted the Second Division of the American army and the French 39th Division against the Germans. The battle raged for five weeks with the Allies finally victorious. The people who died in that conflict and other battles of the Marne are somberly remembered in white marble.

Six miles (10 km) northwest from here along Rte D-9 is **Belleau** and its famous **woods**. Look for abandoned guns marking the place where the American Marines' Fourth Brigade engaged the Germans in 1918. The cemetery with its 2,000 tombstones brings a nerve-tingling experience to some, but for many others, tears.

Beyond Château-Thierry, no roads run close to the canal; neither do houses, and most towns are not on the river, but perched on top of the vine-covered hills. For the sailor who prefers solitude, this stretch of water is sheer delight. Even the occasional passing commercial barge is not intrusive.

The Champagne-producing vineyard area has arrived in force, and the grapes growing on the undulating hills are a glorious sight for any bubbly-lover's eyes. Planted almost entirely on the northern bank to take maximum advantage of the sunshine, the fields seem to go on forever. Appropriately, the road that wends through them is called **La Route du Champagne**.

To call itself "champagne" the wine must be produced from specified grapes grown in a well-defined area. This district is not large, approximately 94 miles (150 km) long with a width that fluctuates between 1,000 and 6,500 ft (300 to 2,000 meters) with the best growths in the chalky soil that lies between Epernay and Reims and along the banks of the Marne River.

Still wines have been a product of this region since the Gallo-Roman era, but it was not until the 17th century that an obscure monk, Dom Pérignon, discovered the formula for champagne. He realized that if certain wines were re-fermented in the spring, they fizzed (the result of a build-up of carbon dioxide in the bottle). The earliest champagnes

Left, Château-Thierry's War Memorial on Hill 204. Below, Belleau Wood's peaceful look belies its bloody history.

tended to explode from their bottles, and were given the names *sauté bouchon* (cork popper) and *vin diable* (devil's wine). When stronger bottles and better corks were developed, the wine became transportable, and the rest of the world could enjoy this exuberant drink.

Principally a white sparkling wine, some rosé and red champagnes are also produced; made with a combination of red and white grapes, *Méthode Champenoise* is strictly observed. After harvesting, the grapes are pressed and the liquid put in casks. These are then taken to the vintner who will complete the fermentation and blending process.

In December, the wine has the first of three *rackings* where the best is drawn from the barrel, and impurities are left behind. The January *racking* begins the real *coupage* or blending, when other grapes which have been fermenting separately will be added, giving the champagne its distinctive taste. Those mixed with wines from a single town are called *vins de cru*, a multi-area blending results in *vins de cuvée*.

In the springtime, the champagne is bottled after its last *racking*. A *liqueur de tirage* (sugar dissolved in old champagne) is added to aid in fermentation and help create the bubbles.

During the next step, the bottles are turned frequently to remove any sediment buildup. After the ripening period (the length depends upon the vintner) *remuage* (shaking) and *dégorgement* (shooting out the sediment) takes place. The former is the very gradual turning of each bottle from the prone position to one totally upside down. The latter process is what it sounds like, a tricky procedure if done by hand.

Finally comes the *dosage* or sweetening of the champagne. The *liqueur d'expédient* does that, and *brut* (raw or driest), *sec* (dry), or *demi-sec* (semi-dry) should be on every label, telling the consumer what to expect. A new cork (the best are made from Portugese or Spanish trees) is put in the original bottle, and depending upon the quality desired, the wine will continue to ferment for up to seven years.

United States Military Cemetery in Belleau.

Then comes the most magical time. Chilled flutes stand ready for the chilled wine. The tin-foil wrapper is removed, followed by the cork's wire casing. Gentle pressure of thumb against cork, slowly circling the bottle. There's a hollow pop, a wisp of smoke, and then the foamy, pale-gold liquid tumbles out of the bottle. Only a confirmed Philistine would fail to derive any pleasure from the sight of tiny bubbles floating upward through the glass, bringing a tickle to the nose and a festive air to the most mundane occasion.

Barzy-sur-Marne has a squat Norman church and a big château surrounded by glorious, glorious vineyards. Across the fields at **Rosay** a fortress-style church sits in isolated splendor amid its own vineyard; the town is a short distance away.

Dormans is not charming. It sprawls up the south side of the valley in an untidy mess of buildings with a waterfront lacking any style. Historically, it's somewhat better: the large château was built by Louis XIII, and the Battle of the Marne is memorialized at **Chapelle de la Reconnaissance**.

"Scarface" is a nickname most associated with an American gangster of the 1930s, but another earned the name in the 16th century. During the Wars of Religion, the Catholic Duke du Guise who was fighting Henri III near Dormans, was severely wounded, resulting in the sobriquet, *le Balafré*.

At **Port-à-Binson**, the Sailing Club offers good overnight moorings. **Châtillon-sur-Marne** is a little over a mile up the hill; note the statue of Urban III, Pope between 1088 and 1099. A local man, Eudes de Châtillon (his real name), is known for mounting the First Crusade in 1095.

Damery is on the river and a most pretty place. From here, walk across the Marne and through the long avenue of trees to *Auberge de la Chaussée* for a delightful country meal.

To champagne lovers, Epernay is the center of the world, but mention **Hautvilliers** (moor at **Cumières**; it's about a mile uphill), and the true connoisseur

The Marne countryside.

188

grins. For this was the home of Dom Pérignon, father of the original bubbly, and where some of the finest champagne grapes are grown today. The priest who lived between 1638 and 1715 was cellarmaster at the Benedictine Abbey (visits possible) for 47 years, and also gained a reputation as a master blender. Note, too, the many small shrines dedicated to the good Dom which decorate the walls, roof and sides of many houses and municipal buildings in town.

Where else except in the town where champagne was created would you find the hands on the town clock represented by a bunch of grapes and vines. The sundial at the **Hôtel de Ville** also has each hour embellished with a cluster of grapes. Houses, too, are adorned, with wrought-iron signs hanging from them, each representing some part of Champagne production.

Walking or bicycling around the hill of Hautvilliers, one sees many famous names, Dom Pérignon, Moët et Chandon, Tattinger, Pol Roget. Each section of vineyard is carefully delineated, and

the nose twitches at the thought of so much pleasure to come

There are two ways of travelling to **Epernay**. One is to cruise 3 miles (5 km) up the Marne from **Ecluse 15, Dizy**. (Navigation forward from Epernay is not possible; one must return to the lock.) Or, moor at Dizy and bicycle. Of course, this can cause problems when returning to the boat laden with several cases of champagne. If the cruise into town is made, moorings are at the Sailing Club, and all sightseeing (and Champagne tasting and buying) is a short walk away.

Three of the world's most famous champagne vintners are headquartered in Epernay: Moët et Chandon, Mercier, and De Castellane. If touring those three establishments isn't enough to slake your thirst, stop by the **Museum of Champagne and Pre-history**, which is in a 19th-century château.

At the Dizy lock, the Marne ceases to be navigable, and the very straight **Canal Latéral à la Marne** takes over. The canal passes under shade trees; beyond

Champagne vineyards.

them are flat open fields and grain elevators. It's a let-down after the rolling Champagne hills, and although **Ay** is another stop along the Champagne trail, and Laurent Perrier is headquartered in **Tours-sur-Marne**, the vineyards are, unfortunately, no longer visible from the canal.

Le Canal de l'Aisne à la Marne: Arriving in **Condé-sur-Marne**, a very abrupt left turn by the grain elevator brings the north/south waterway. The Latéral continues eastward to Vitry-le-François, where it joins the Canal de la Marne au Rhin for a journey into Alsace-Lorraine *(see page 99)*.

The only reason for this purpose-built waterway was to link two very busy rivers, the Marne and Aisne. Completed in 1866, it made possible continuous navigation from Belgium and Holland into France's heartland. The connector runs for 36 miles (58 km) to Berry-au-Bac where it meets the Canal Latéral à l'Aisne.

In between, there are 24 locks (all radar operated) and one tunnel, the 7,474-ft (2,300-meter) Billy-le-Grand which forms the summit reach. (One-way traffic; entrance is controlled by lights.) Trees line most of the banks – a welcome relief from the sunbaked Marne. It's a raised waterway, and the vistas of rolling fields appeal.

Two warnings: stock up on all supplies; until Reims, shops and marinas are in very short supply. On public holidays, it's forbidden to moor between **Ecluses 24 and 17, Condé and Vaudemange**; the day before, these locks shut down three-and-a-half hours before normal closing. Bad timing can result in an unwanted overnight mooring.

Coming out of the tunnel through **Mont-de-Billy**, a restaurant, the Auberge de la Voute, sits on the right side. Still not hungry, wait until **Sept-Saulx** and try Le Cheval Blanc.

At **Sillery**, smoke-belching factories pollute both sides of the canal; the cemetery across from the boat basin contains the bodies of many Frenchmen killed during World War I.

Visible from the canal, but about 2 miles (3 km) from it (moor in Sillery) is

The name says it all.

190

bleak, wind-swept **Fort de la Pompelle**. Now a museum filled with evocative memorabilia, the fort, built in 1800, stands as it was at the end of World War I, a pile of sand-bagged rubble. Inside are mementoes, uniforms, photographs of Reims' destruction, medals, and armaments. A stone marker with a dozen or so crosses behind it commemorates those people who died here between 1914 and 1918.

From Sillery, the **Cathedral of Notre Dame**, 7 miles (11 km) to the north, is clearly visible on a good day. Looking at today's vital city, it's hard to realise that during World War I **Reims** was a battleground, and over three-quarters of the town was obliterated. The cathedral was severely damaged, but survived.

The city also had its famous moments during World War II: Eisenhower was headquartered here, and in 1945 he took the German surrender in the **Salle de Guerre** (War Room) of a local college. The room has been left as it was at the end of the war, and can be visited.

Reims takes it's name from a Belgic tribe, the Remi, and when Paris was still only a minor river crossing, Reims was an important Gallic city. Known as Durocortorum under the Romans, over half a dozen trade routes passed through the city, and Hadrian called Reims his "Athens of the north" because of its rich and varied cultural life.

Reims was one of the first cities in northern France to forsake paganism. In 406 the city was razed by the Franks, and its bishop, Nicasius, slaughtered in the first cathedral (which the undeterred citizens quickly rebuilt). Clovis was converted by St Remi, then bishop, and in 498 when Clovis became the first king of France, he was crowned in the cathedral, starting a tradition that lasted through 37 monarchs, ending with Charles X in 1825.

In 1210, the 5th-century cathedral was completely destroyed by fire. The present building was started almost immediately and finished less than 100 years later. Built at a time when Gothic style was at its zenith, the cathedral is one of the greatest structures of its kind.

Window on a working barge.

At 450-ft long by 120-ft high, (138 meters by 37m) it is longer and taller than Notre Dame in Paris. The width is less, 98 ft (30 meters), but the twin towers soar 267 ft (82 meters).

The **Rose Window** is 39 ft (12 meters) across, and the earliest stained-glass windows date from the 13th-century. Unfortunately, most were destroyed during the many bombardments. Braque and Chagall have had their modern designs transferred into stained glass windows in two of the small side chapels.

There are more than 2,300 statues on the facade and one of the most famous is on the left door, the **Smiling Angel**, the *Sourire de Reims* who, it is said, protects the city.

Despite another serious fire in 1481, vandalism during the Revolution, and the damage suffered during the two world wars, the cathedral is still very much like the building where Joan of Arc crowned Charles VIII in 1429. (A statue of her on horseback is in front of the Palais de Justice.)

Champagne is the number-one industry, but it is not the oldest; textiles get that honor. Mumm and Pommery have the largest **cellars** in the city, with over 10 miles (18 km) each. Arrange visits at the Tourist Office.

The **Port de Mars** is the only surviving artifact from the Roman era; it's on Place de la République. An equestrian statue of Louis XIV sits on Place Royale surrounded by 18th-century buildings.

The **Basilica of St Remi** is two centuries older than the cathedral; although damaged during World War I, it's been restored. Built in the 11th-century, it is Roman in style with two square towers 182 ft (56 meters) high. The tomb of St Remi is behind the altar. Its 12th-century abbey is a **museum** devoted to medieval art and archaeology; in summer, attend a *Musique et Lumière*.

Other museums to enjoy include **Musée des Beaux Arts** with, among other things, a superb collection of tapestries; the **Palais du Tau**, a former Royal residence, displays originals of statues that once graced the cathedral, and other religious items; and **Musée** Statuary on Reims' Cathedral.

192

du Vieux Reims has displays of costumes, furniture and other antiques.

Leaving Reims is prettier than entering it; passing under the bridge near **La Neuvillette** comes peace and tranquility with nary a village or house until **Loivre**. The canal seems to float above its surroundings, giving good views of the countryside for the 12 miles(20 km) of its life beyond Reims.

L'Aisne et son Canal Latéral: At Berry-au-Bac a right turn takes one to Neuf-châtel-sur-Aisne and Belgium; a left continues the Ile de France exploration. The canal/river forms a navigable waterway 57-miles (92-km) long from here to its junction with the River Oise just north of Compiègne.

Canal du Champagne was the name given to the proposed waterway that would link the Aisne and Meuse rivers via the River Bar. By 1841 when the canal was completed, it took a different route, was longer, and somehow lost its original name.

Although lots of cargo traffic is encountered, this is a pretty cruise that passes through working farmland. The novice boatman need not worry about the locks; there are only 13, all are mechanised, and keepers are present to help in case of any trouble.

Berry-au-Bac is fun. It's a major mooring for the large cargo barges and it's not unusual to see 10 or 12 packed along the quay. Watching these 123-ft (38-meter) black rectangles negotiate the sharp turn from canal to canal makes parallel parking seem easy. The marina offers all services, and there are shops and restaurants.

The waterway branching right before **Ecluse 4, la Cendrière**, is the **Canal de l'Oise à l'Aisne**. (Those wanting a longer journey can cruise north on it for 30 miles/48 km to Abbécourt; then turn south on to the Canal Latéral à l'Oise and travel an additional 21 miles,/33 km to rejoin this journey a few miles below Janville.)

Vailly-sur-Aisne has great moorings (all services), and it's the last easily-reached provisioning stop before Soissons. A discothèque and bar are next to the quay, and two restaurants in town,

the Cheval Blanc and Cheval d'Or offer regional food.

Ecluses 7 and 8, Celles, mark the division betweeen canal and river, and with it the banks are more overgrown and wilder-looking.

The tall spires which announce the arrival of **Soissons** belong to the abbey church of **St-Jean-des-Vignes**. Soaring 240 ft (80 meters) into the air, only they and the facade of the 13th-century building are intact, although parts of the cloisters, refectory, and cellar remain.

Soissons' history is more ancient than St Jean: Clovis defeated the Romans near here, and his son, Clotaire, made it his capital. The town is also noted for the "vase story." Clovis, newly converted to Christianity, decided that loot plundered by his troops should be returned to the people from whom it had been stolen. Unfortunately, some of his men still believed in the traditional, "To the victor belongs the spoils," and there was considerable reluctance to comply with the King's order. So one particular warrior who had taken a liking to an especially fine vase, smashed it rather than give it up.

Adopting the age-old principle, "Don't get mad, get even," Clovis waited patiently. Years later, the King recognized the offender. With a thrust of his sword, Clovis cut the warrior in two, supposedly saying, "I do to you what you did to the vase."

During two world wars, the town sustained an enormous amount of destruction, consequently, most of the buildings are less than 50 years old. The **Cathedral St-Gervais-et-St-Protais**, Gothic in style, has been restored since its virtual destruction in 1918. Inside, look for Rubens' *Adoration of the Shepherds* in the north transept. The stained-glass windows above the choir are from the 13th and 14th centuries. Observe also the bullet marks on the cathedral's exterior.

The 12th-century abbey of **St-Léger**, devastated by the Protestants during the Wars of Religion, is opposite the cathedral. Inside is a memorial to the victims of the Nazi atrocities. Near it is a World

Left, sculling on Canal de l'Aisne à Marne. **Below**, prow of a péniche.

War I memorial. Look for Musée Municipal on Rue de la Congrégation.

Pleasure boats should dock in Soissons on the left bank between **Pont du Mail** and **Ecluse 10, Vauxrot**. On the east side of the cathedral square is a daily-except-Sunday market; since most upcoming villages are off the river, stock up on needed supplies here for the journey ahead .

Leaving Soissons, one is very quickly in flat, open countryside with the never-ending corn and sugarbeet fields spreading over the wide valley. Clusters of post-war houses, decorate the hills; occasionally, a survivor of the carnages that have swept through the region stands among its newer neighbors.

Pont Fontenoy, just beyond Ecluse 11, offers Du Bord de l'Eau Auberge; overnight moorings are available for those dining in the restaurant. Feeling like some exercise? Make short excursions to **Courtieux** to see its 12th-century church, and then **Jaulzy**'s, which was built between the 12th and 16th centuries. **Attichy** holds a Sunday market selling a little bit of everything; its swimming pool and other recreational facilities will delight children.

Six miles (10 km) up Rte D-335 from the bridge of La Motte, sits **Pierrefonds**, one answer to Disney's Fantasyland castle. (Photographers will note it's an afternoon excursion).

Nothing can prepare the eye for the sight of this massive, granite extravagance that looms over the small town sitting on the eastern edge of the Forêt of Compiègne. There are eight massive towers topped with black slate connected by massive battlements which form an uneven rectangle. A guided tour of it includes the Emperor's Apartment, Knight's Hall, Guard's Room, and the Chapel.

The original château on this site was built in the 1390 by Louis, Duke of Orléans, a brother of Charles VI. Alas, the Duke did not have much time to enjoy it: in 1407 he was killed, a deed which further divided the Orléans and Burgundian factions in their fight for control of the French monarchy.

During the Hundred Years War,

Going from one waterway to another can be a tight squeeze.

Pierrefonds was occupied by both the English and French, and in 1413 was burned while the then current Duke of Orléans was captured at the battle of Agincourt. Taken to England, the Duke spent 25 years in the Tower of London, not returning to France until 1440.

In 1616, during the Prince of Condé's rebellion against Louis VII, the Julius Caesar tower was bombarded, and despite the wall's bulk, collapsed. As a final measure of his power, Cardinal Richelieu had all the towers dismantled, and after the Revolution, the castle was allowed to disintegrate even further.

For some reason, Napoleon fell in love with the place, and in 1848, Pierrefonds was declared a national monument. By 1861 Viollet-Le-Duc was commissioned to renovate, but it became not so much a restoration as a total redesign. Work stopped in 1870 when the Franco-Prussian War was declared, but Le-Duc was not to be deterred. In 1873, he issued a call for work to recommence; his death in 1879 prevented his finishing it. That was left to his nephew, the architect Ouradour, who took over and in 1885 completed this romanticized version of a Gothic fortress.

La Motte also marks a change in the river. Gone are all traces of agriculture, heavy forestation takes its place. **Forêt de Laigues** begins on the right, to the left, **Forêt de Compiègne**.

Moor by the bridge at Le Francport to make the half a mile walk to **Clairière de l'Armistice** (Armistice Clearing) where the German Army surrendered to Marshall Foch on 11 November 1918. The railcar on view is not the original one; that was destroyed by Allied bombing of Berlin. How did the present one come to be where it is? Never known for his kind nature, Hitler played a game of revenge.

As a measure of one-upmanship for the earlier humiliation of his country, Hitler insisted that the 1940 French surrender take place in the same railway carriage on the same siding. The carriage then went to Berlin and became a monument. At the end of the war, the French found a similar railway car and

Aisne landscapes range from wooded hillsides...

completely refurbished it to match the original car.

Touring the car brings poignant memories. The brass of the wooden coach gleams as that of no other railway coach has every gleamed. Every detail is perfect, down to the last piece of paper and inkwell. At the far end of the building is an eternal flame, and stereographs present views of different World War I battlefields.

There are two monuments situated close to the car: the first is a statue of Marshal Foch, and the second depicts the fallen eagle of Germany. A riverside restaurant offers pleasant dining, the forest has picnic tables. The Aisne continues its gentle flow, bordered by the gardens and weekend homes of city dwellers until Choisy-au-Bac arrives in a few miles.

L'Oise: The river rises in Belgium's Forêt d'Ardennes, and wends its way in a snaking path southwest to Vadencourt where it passes under the Canal de la Sambre à l'Oise. From there, it more or less runs parallel to that waterway as far

as la Frette where its own Latéral Canal takes over. The river, for navigation doesn't appear until Janville; from there the journey south and west to a confluence with the Seine at Conflans covers about 60 miles (100 km) and seven, radar-controlled locks .

Linked with several other waterways, the Oise forms one of the major north-south waterways. Most of the traffic is commercial: over 30,000 boats a year travel the river/ canal, (an average daily rate of 60 to 70). This should not cause panic; the river is wide, and there are many pleasant stretches and enjoyable ports of call.

Compiègne is well worth a visit. It is the first port of call after leaving the Aisne, and boats can moor along the quay or in the small city marina (all services) on the left bank. A favorite retreat of French kings, Compiègne was also where Joan of Arc was captured in 1430 by the Burgundians before her subsequent handover to the English and execution at Rouen.

The first château here was begun in

...to sloping farmland.

the 14th century by Charles V. Louis XV began enlarging this building, but died in 1774 before it was finished. Louis XVI finally completed it in 1785, four years before the Revolution.

Romance also reared its lovely head within the walls: Louis XVI and Marie Antoinette met here for the first time. But it was Napoleon III and Empress Eugénie, another pair of star-crossed lovers, who made Compiègne the epitome of social life. 1870 and the Franco-Prussian War brought that to a halt.

The **Palace**, which was once the third most important in the nation after Versailles and Fontainebleau, is now a **museum**. Most notable are the Imperial and Royal apartments where Empire furniture, tapestries and other *objets d'art* are on display. Also in the Palace grounds, the **Musée de la Voiture** contains both motorised and animal-powered vehicles.

An equestrian statue of Joan of Arc graces the courtyard of the **Hôtel de Ville**. A similar one of Louis XII is one of many figures on the front of the late Gothic edifice. From its belfry, uniformed figures appear to mark the hour. In the same building the **Musée de la Figurine Historique** contains a collection of miniature soldiers along with diaoramas of various battles. Antiquities are in **Musée Vivenel**; the **Beauregard Tower** is believed to have been Joan of Arc's prison.

Soon after leaving Compiègne most traces of city life disappear as the river courses through a low, wide valley. At **Verberie** ask permission to moor at the local sailing club. It's a charming place with a few old houses and the 19th-century **Château Aramont**.

At **Pont Ste Maxence**, moor on the left bank below the bridge. The **Eglise de Pont Ste Maxence** is 15th/16th century, and the next-door **Eglise de Sarron** is Romanesque. Philippe le Bel founded the **Abbaye Royale du Moncel** in the 14th century. The highlights here include the Abbesses' refectory, cloister, charter room, and the Fécamp Tower.

The smokestacks of **Nogent-sur-Oise**

Pierrefonds' castle.

and across-the-river **Creil**, do not bode well for sightseeing. Before hurrying onward, give the two a chance. The most convenient place to moor is by the bridge which spans the head of **St Maurice Island**, although public docks are further downriver on the left bank. Creil offers **Maison Gallé-Juillet** and its collection of furniture and *faïence* (earthenware). Other attractions include the 14th-century church of **St Medard**, and the **Jardin Publique**. In Nogent, look for the facade of the 15th-century **Sarcus Château** that's been re-erected in **Parc Houbigant**.

St-Leu-d'Esserent's 12th-century **abbey church** was made from stone taken from the same quarry that supplied Chartres and Versailles. The stained-glass windows are modern, but do not detract from the church's beauty.

From here, it's 3 miles (5 km) along Rte D-44 to **Chantilly** with another 6 miles (10 km) through Forêt Chantilly to Senlis. (Taxis are available if bicycling does not appeal.)

Known throughout the world for its lace and *crème Chantilly* (whipped cream), the French consider the Château and its race course and stables of more importance. During the racing season, when world-class meets are held, appearance is a social must. (Tourists should avoid this time since all buildings are closed.) Set in the middle of Le Nôtre-designed gardens the present château was preceded by five; the first was built by Cantilius, a Roman general, from whom the city's name is taken.

One of France's most graceful châteaux, the domed turrets and dark slate roofs are surrounded by, and reflected in, one of Le Nôtre's lakes. The château is actually two. The **Condé Museum**, a magnificent collection of stained glass, tapestries, paintings, and other artifacts, is housed in the 19th-century **Grand Château**. (The Condé Rose Diamond is only exhibited at weekends.) The older **Petit Château** is now a library.

Note the equestrian statue of one owner, Baron de Montmorency, adviser

Below, the forest of Compiègne offers picnic grounds and quiet walks. Right, Marshall Foch stands over the Armistice Clearing.

to six consecutive kings, Louis XII through Charles IX. This remarkable man, also known as Le Grand Connétable, was the second most important man in the country. Another famous owner was the Great Condé; his descendant, the Duke of Bourbon, regained possession after the Revolution, but in 1897 the château became the possession of the State.

Senlis still has some 2,730 ft (840 meters) and 16 towers of its Roman wall. Hugh Capet, founder of the French royal dynasty was declared King of France here (then only a small area of the modern country) in 987. Parts of his castle still stand, and most of his descendants lived in it during their reigns. An 18th-century priory is now a **Museum of Hunting**.

Cathedral of Notre Dame is the center for a rabbit warren of old houses and narrow, crooked streets. The spire thrusts 260 ft (80 meters) into the air; the Romanesque west front contains a carved doorway recounting scenes from the Virgin's life.

Beware speed boats and water-skiers at **Boran-sur-Oise**. One positive note: visiting boats can use the yacht club facilities. There's also a swimming pool children will enjoy.

Less than 3 miles (5 km) from Boran is **Royaumont Abbey**; founded by St Louis in the 13th century, the Cistercian abbey is one of the most beautiful Gothic structures in France. During the Revolution, the church was burnt, but the carefully restored abbey buildings remain. In private hands since the late 19th century, tours include the refectory, cloisters, and chapel.

L'Isle-Adam gets its name from a Lord of Villiers called Adam who, in the 11th century, built a castle on the larger of the two islands here. But the town's history goes farther back when it was Roman Novigentum. Louis the Pious fortified L'Isle in 825, but that fort was destroyed 61 years later. Another Pius, this one Robert, rebuilt in 1014. **St Martin Church**, was started in the 16th century and finished in the 19th, and is worth a visit.

Commercial barges at work.

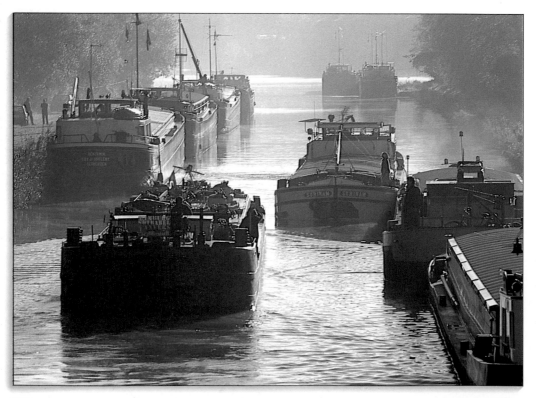

None of the impressionists who painted here, (Cézanne, Pissaro, and Gaugin among others) would recognize the "light" of **Auvers-sur-Oise** anymore. That which attracted them has gone as industrial smog and fumes arrived. The Café Ravoux, where Vincent Van Gogh killed himself, is now called **Café à Van Gogh**. He and his brother Théo are buried in the local cemetery; look for a monument to the artist in **Parc Van Gogh**.

In 1652, 1720 and 1753, Parliament was exiled to the city of **Pontoise**. There are some ruins of the ancient walls, but it is the narrow streets clogging traffic which most remind one of the town's ancient past. **Notre Dame Church** is older than it looks; much damage was done during the 16th- century siege of the city. Inside note the 12th-century tomb of St Gautier and the 13th-century statue of the Virgin. Take the steps up through the **Jardin Publique** to **St Maclou Church**, a Gothic structure renovated in a variety of styles.

From Pontoise, the Oise makes a large loop and soon after passing Neuville-sur-Oise, a right turn brings Rouen and the sea; a left turn, Paris.

La Seine: Entering the river at **Conflans-Ste-Honorine**, one is greeted with the sight of hundreds of barges parked four and five deep along the river. Laundry hangs to dry, potted plants stand in lace-curtained windows, and neighbors talk to one another. A typical domestic scene? Yes, only these take place on 123-ft (38-meter) long *péniches* (French commercial barges).

Reinforcing barging traditions, look for one named *Je Sers*; it serves as a chapel for the barge-residing locals. The last weekend in June many river people gather for a waterborne festival, *Pardon Nationale de la Batellerie* (National Pilgrimage of the Barges). Up the hill, a **Museum of Canal History** is in Château du Prieuré. It has exhibits tracing the life of bargemen, models, and other marine equipment.

Quartermasters should visit **Maison G. Piednoël** on Place Fouillère; it's in the manner of an an American delica-

No prizes here for Best-kept Barge.

tessen. Transient moorings are here with marine supplies available. For great views up and down the Seine climb to the footbridge that's next to the one for traffic.

Forty-five more miles (72 km) and the tip of Ile de la Cité will be dead ahead of the boat's prow. If going in a straight line, the distance would be about a third; but the Seine starts a series of three gigantic loops as it weaves between history and industry on its way to the City of Light.

The cruise into Paris passes a number of historical places. All of these can easily be visited by public transport from the Port de Paris Marina, but for those who wish to stop on the voyage in, public moorings at many bridges and locks make this possible.

The scenery swerves from miserable to magnificent; for example, the sewage works opposite La Frette-sur-Seine are almost next to Maison Lafitte Racecourse. In general, it's a pleasant cruise, and although much industrial ugliness does intrude close to Paris, the journey is an interesting one. For the most part, the left bank takes the high ground, the right the low. New apartment buildings mesh with houses that have been on the river for a century or more and many of the homes have individual boat docks. There are yacht clubs, some welcome visiting boatmen; towns offer municipal swimming pools, tennis courts and public moorings.

At **St-Germain-en-Laye**, moor at **Pont de Pecq** and walk uphill to visit the **Château de St Germain** and its Museum of National Antiquities. The nearby **Saint Chapelle** was built in 1230, 10 years before its namesake in Paris; admire Le Nôtre's splendid **Grand Terrasse**, but observe Paris from the **Petit**.

Port Marly sits at the head of a long chain of islands which bisect the Seine for the next 6 miles (10 km). **Château de Malmaison** where Empress Joséphine died, is reached by taking the right channel around Ile de Chiard, and mooring near Pont de Ruiel. Napoleon spent the days between his Waterloo defeat and his St Helena exile here; now it's a

<u>Left</u>, a miniature Statue of Liberty greets boaters to Paris. <u>Below</u>, La Défense reflected.

museum devoted to Napoleon Bonaparte and Josephine.

Ugliness arrives in force with **Port de Gennevilliers** and its plethora of oil refineries, grain silos, warehouses and other accoutrements of a busy harbor.

Ile St Denis is more than four miles (seven km) long. To visit the **Cathedral**, take the left-hand channel. The Canal St Denis enters from the left just before Pont de l'Ile St Denis; moor on the river just beyond that bridge.

St Denis has something in common with St Trémur, the Breton saint: after decapitation both walked with their heads in their hands. Where St Denis supposedly stopped, his church stands. The original one was constructed in the 5th century by Ste Geneviève, patron saint of Paris, but was replaced by the present 12th-century Gothic Basilica.

Dagobert, king between 629 and 639, was the first French monarch buried here, and during the next 12 centuries, most French monarchs were also interred here. Unfortunately, during the Revolution the fanatics dug the bodies up and destroyed them. Fortunately, the tombs were saved, and are on view.

The **Dogs' Cemetery** of Asnières is on the right below Pont de Clichy. Since it opened in 1899, over 100,000 pets have been buried within its gates. One of the saddest deaths concerns a St Bernard named Berry who met his end when a rescuee mistook the poor dog for a bear come to kill. Look also for the grave of a movie hero, Rin Tin Tin.

The towers in the right foreground are those of **Défense**. Begun in 1958, it's one of the most extensive new cities ever created. Covering almost 2,000 acres (800 hectares) the glass and chrome skyscrapers have rapidly changed the face of western Paris.

From here it's a long loop until the heart of Paris; the back of the **Bois de Boulogne** is on the left with **Longchamps Race Course** hidden behind the trees. Once a royal hunting forest, the 22,225 acres (900 hectares) were given to the people by Napoleon III.

Near Pontelle de l'Avre and Pont St-Cloud is the St-Cloud City Marina, **Parc**

The Eiffel Tower seen with the eyes of a turtle.

de St Cloud covers over 1,100 hilly acres (450 hectares), all landscaped by Le Nôtre. Look for **Musée Historic** in The Lodge. The **Grand Jet** spurts 138 ft (42 meters) into the air; next to it is the Lepautre-designed **Grand Cascade**. From the terrace of the **Rond Point de la Bulustrade** you can view Paris.

The **National Porcelain Museum** is a short walk from Pont de Sèvres; chinaware from all over the world is on display; there's an audio visual show, and on the first and third Thursdays (except July and August), porcelain-making is demonstrated.

Iles Seguin and **St Germain**, unpleasant industries and highrise apartment buildings follow. After passing underneath Pont Mirabeau, the **Statue of Liberty**, a pint-size version of the lady in New York Harbor, appears at the head of **Allée des Cygnes**; to the left is Radio France House.

The **Eiffel Tower** arrives, and so does the Paris of posters and travel guides. Pont d'Iéna divides the Trocadero Gardens from the Tower, and on the skyline straight ahead is **Sacré Coeur**. The Tokyo Palace Museum looms just beyond Pont Ile Debilly, then the Grand and Petit Palais are on the left with Musée Gare d'Orsay on the right. The Obelisk in Place de la Concorde is barely visible above the tops of the trees. Jardin des Tuileries appears as a row of trees, then the Louvre, as an expanse of marble.

Ahead now is **Ile de la Cité**. Pont Neuf, the oldest bridge in Paris becomes a shadow above, then the spires and gargoyles of Notre Dame are seen as if with the eye of a turtle. Booksellers are above on the right, below them a string of permanently-moored houseboats and the Marine Police.

Ile St Louis slips by, and the end of the journey and the **Bassin du Canal St Martin** arrive on the left. The Basin and the Port de Paris Arsenal Marina are reached via a lock situated under **Pont Henri IV**; (entrance is controlled by lights). The marina is well equipped. Métro stations, Bastille and Quai de la Rapée, are at either end.

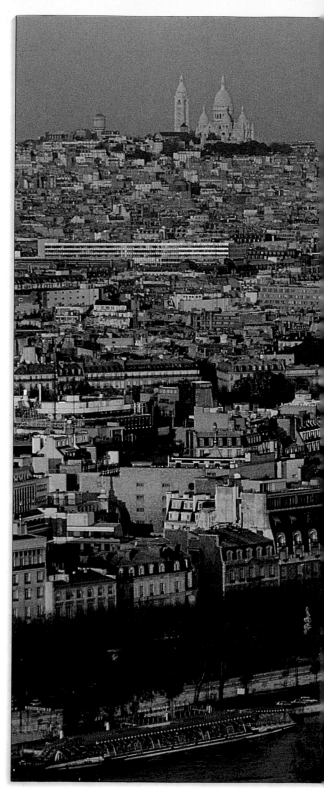

<u>Right</u>, Paris, the City of Light.

LA SOMME

It is usual for mention of the Somme to conjure up images of stinking death in squelching mud. Of dead hands caught in the cruel rust of barbed wire, and long lines of young men, each with his hand on the shoulder of the one in front, all newly and painfully blinded. Of others choking in the savage vapors of poisonous gas. About a million men were killed or wounded in the appalling horror of the Battle of the Somme, a million lives ended or wrecked in a mere four months in 1916.

So it comes as a shock, almost, to discover that the Somme is, in the main, a charming and tranquil river to travel, carrying less commercial traffic than other waterways in Northern France. It is also user-friendly, and for those wishing to transport a boat from the Channel to the Mediterranean, the Somme affords a delightful alternative to the more commercial and heavily traveled Calais and Dunkerque routes.

Although the river rises almost 155 miles (250 km) from the sea in Fonsommes, the navigation only covers 97 miles (156 km) and 25 locks from St-Valéry-sur-Somme on the Channel to Ecluse St Simon where it ends in a T-Junction with the Canal de St Quentin.

St-Valéry-sur-Somme is a quiet resort with excellent beaches and a thriving fishing industry. Its main claim to fame is that it was from here that William the Conqueror sailed to change the course of English history in 1066. Some of the old ramparts still stand above the seafront promenade; in the old town, two churches are of interest: **St Martin** perched at the edge of the ramparts, and **Chapel of the Mariners** where the body of St Valéry is entombed.

During the summer, a **tourist railway** operates around the bay. Taking in the towns of **Cayeau-sur-Mer**, **Noyelles** and **Le Crotoy** (Joan of Arc was imprisoned here in 1430), the 1887-opened line offers 17 miles (27 km) of easy sightseeing. **Rue** is 5 miles (8 km) north of Le Crotoy. Once a thriving medieval

port, it's now very much inland. On arrival, observe the miles of sand dunes, and visit the Flamboyant Gothic chapel.

As befits a port, St Valéry's marina is filled with sailing vessels, and colorful fishing boats. All services are offered, including mast stepping. The tidal estuary on which the town sits can only be entered or left during high water; contact the lock-keeper, or follow a larger boat. (For those not wishing to enter the tidal waters, berthings are available just before the lock; the town is within easy walking distance.)

Abbeville, ancient capital of Ponthieu, was an English possession from 1272 to 1477, apart from a short period when it was ruled by the Dukes of Burgundy. It passed firmly into French hands in 1514 when 53-year-old Louis XII married Mary Tudor, aged 16. Although he died three months later, their marriage, and the union of France and England is symbolised by a stone lion rampant with a royal coat of arms in the **Church of St Vulfran**, where the wedding ceremony took place.

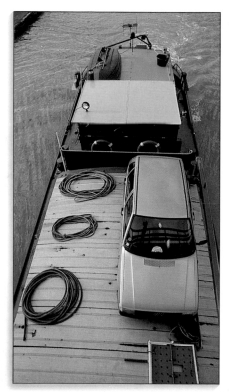

Left, cargo barges where the Somme meets the Canal du Nord. **Right**, many barge owners carry their car.

The English returned during World War I when the town was their army's headquarters. During World War II, the area suffered extensive bombing and over half the city was destroyed. The **Musée Boucher de Perthes** contains about 3,000 engravings and has sections dealing with archaeology and natural history.

Those with time and energy might make an excursion to **St Riquier** (five miles/eight km from Abbeville) and **Crécy-en-Ponthieu**, another eight miles (14 km) up Rte D-12. At the former, the Flamboyant Gothic abbey church has a nave 300 feet (95 meters) long. In 1346, Edward III won a battle near Crécy which started the Hundred Years War.

Abbeville is easy on boaters. The river's banks are well tended and moorings are handy for shops and restaurants. Beyond Abbeville, other attractive villages and towns follow, with châteaux at **Epagne**, **Pont-Rémy** and **Long**. At the latter, notice, also, the Hôtel de Ville with its splendid 19th-century Gothic tower.

Neither **Longpré Les Corps Saints** nor **Condé-Folie** is on the river; to visit either, moor near the bridge at **Etoile**. The ruins of the 12th-century **Abbaye du Gard** appear on the right a mile or so beyond Hangest-sur-Somme.

The Somme dreams on, passing **Picquigny**, where the Hundred Years War was brought to a close with Edward IV of England and Louis IX signing a treaty on the bridge. The monarchs were so suspicious of each other that they could only shake hands on the deal through an iron railing The ruins of a château rise above the town; part of it can be visited. Look for British graves of World War I in the cemetery near the **Pavillion Sévigné**.

With a population of 125,000, **Amiens** is a busy industrial city. Once capital of Picardy, the town has had a lively history, and has seen a few armies marching backwards and forwards across its stage. The Celts called it Samarobriva (Bridge on the Somme), the Romans, Ambiani. The Norsemen roared through in the ninth century, and the plague in the late 1660s. In this century, two world wars have added to Amiens' turbulent history.

Water plays an important role in the life of Amiens: the St Lew Quarter is divided by canals and streams, and nearby are the **Hortillonages**, 720 acres (300 hectares) of market gardens and orchards irrigated by a network of tiny canals, along which high-bowed punts take produce to market. The canals are ancient, formed by past diggings in the Middle Ages. It's also possible to hire one of these special punts which are called *les bâteaux à Comet* (the comet boats) for a private cruise through the area's waterways.

Much of the old part of the city was destroyed in World War II. The **Cathedral of Notre Dame**, which has the largest area of any church (69,000 sq ft/ 7,700 sq meters) in France, was started in 1220 on the site of its burned-out predecessor. The nave is 470-ft (145-meters) long, and the 135-ft (42-meters) high vaulted ceiling is supported by 28

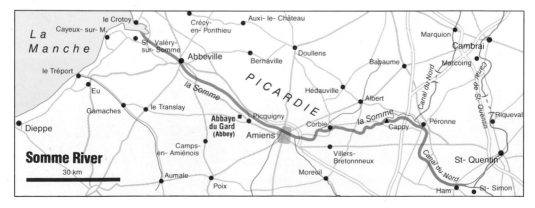

Somme River

pillars. The transepts are decorated with rose windows, and the 367-ft (112-meter) spire dates from 1529. The 16th-century choir is noted for the 3,000-plus carvings of Biblical scenes which decorate its stalls. During World War I, the placing of sandbags saved the building from serious damage.

The **Musée de Picardie** has archaeological collections, medieval sculptures and furniture, and a collection of paintings which include works by Frans Hals and El Greco. Nearby is the **Library**, which holds about 1,200 manuscripts dating from the 9th to 16th centuries. Local history is explored at the **Musée d'Art Local et Historie Régionale** on Rue Victor Hugo. Jules Verne lived in the city after 1871; his museum-home is on Rue Charles Dubois.

Viewed from the map, the distance between Amiens and Péronne looks much less than the distance between Amiens and St Valéry. But this leg is padded out considerably, to about 37 miles (60 km), by the Somme's meandering course.

This is a great area for fishing folk. A profusion of lakes and pools, many formed by the river's original course, and all rich in aquatic wildlife, has attracted generations of anglers and encouraged the development of a quiet tourism industry, which means there is no shortage of restaurants.

Less than 13 miles (20 km) out of Amiens, **Corbie**, a lively town with good boating facilities, stands at the confluence of the Somme and the Ancre rivers. Nothing remains of the 7th-century Benedictine abbey founded by Clovis II's queen, St Bathilde, but several other ecclesiastical buildings hold much interest: the Romanesque-Gothic door on the **Church of St Stephen** is now the entrance to a nunnery.

St Peter's Church was once much bigger; restorers in the 19th century decided that it was too long, and shortened it by a third. Among the religious articles on display inside, notice a scale model of the church as it originally looked.

About 2 miles south of Corbie, near

Velliers-Brentonneux, the Canadians have erected a memorial to the more than 10,000 men who died during World War I. From **Ecluse 11, Foissey**, more World War I battlefields are to be found not far away. **Albert**, 6 miles (10 km) north of the river forms one leg of the sad triangle.

The British are represented at **Thiepval** 4 miles (6 km) up the D-151 with another Canadian Memorial less than 2 miles away at **Beaumont-Hamel**.

At **Cappy**, a little over 12 miles (20 km) before Péronne, it's possible to board a small-gauge steam train, a relic of World War I when it hauled munitions between Froissy and Dompierre.

A little beyond **Ecluse 7, Sormont**, and just before Péronne, **the Canal du Nord** is encountered; a left turn leads toward Douai, the Grand Gabarit Canal System, and Belgium. Going right, the Somme and Canal du Nord flow south as one waterway for 10 miles (16 km) until Rouy-le-Petit.

(The Nord then continues south as a solitary waterway for 20 miles/32 km, five locks and one 3,445-ft/1,060-meter tunnel until it joins the Canal Latéral à l'Oise near Pont l'Evêque. From here, the waterways of the Ile de France *(see page 183)* are not too far away. But left to Arleux and the road to Belgium there's 39 miles/63 km, 12 locks and another, much longer, 14,135-ft/4,350-meter tunnel to negotiate. In both tunnels, vessels travel under their own steam, and traffic is controlled by lights and closed-circuit television. Opened in 1965, the Canal du Nord is characterless, but it was designed for speed and efficiency rather than leisure boating.)

From the boating point of view, **Péronne** is ideal. It has a small but modern marina with all facilities, and rental cruisers are available. There is a freight port, too, but much of the traffic heads along the Canal du Nord towards La Liaison au Grand Gabarit.

Located at the confluence of the rivers Somme and Cologne, Péronne traces its past to the seventh century when an abbey for Scottish monks was founded by St Fursy. The city was largely de-

The Somme flows near Ham.

stroyed in World War I and badly damaged in the 1939–45 conflict, but it still has a 13th-century château, the **Porte de Bretagne** (a gateway dating from the 17th century), and an **Hôtel de Ville** of the Renaissance period. **Musée Danicourt**, in the reconstructed Mairie, houses collections of jewelry and coins, among other things.

Péronne is famous for its eels, grown in local ponds and smoked or served as a pâté, and also for its vegetables, which are produced in canalside market gardens with the Spanish-sounding appellation, *hardines*.

Offay offers the **Domaine des Iles**, an attractive leisure center and amusement park, and a restored Romanesque church with modern windows designed by Max Ingrand.

Ham is a pleasant place noted mainly for its 15th-century fortress which the Germans destroyed in 1917. Over the centuries, the fortress had been used to hold political prisoners, and they were meant to stay there, for the walls were 36 ft (11 meters) thick. But they were not thick enough to hold Louis Napoleon Bonaparte, later to become Napoleon III. In 1846, after six years of confinement, he managed to escape disguised as a workman and safely made his way to England.

Four miles (7 km) beyond Ham, and the Somme comes to an end; a turn into the **Canal de St Quentin** brings the possibility of eastern France and the Ardennes (right) or northern France and Belgium (left).

Southbound, the St Quentin covers just 16 miles/26 km with 10 locks to Chauny where it links into the Canal de l'Oise à l'Aisne. Going north to Belgium, there are 41 miles (66 km), 25 locks and two tunnels – one 3,565 ft (1,098 meters) long, the other 18,425 ft (5,670 meters) – to traverse on the way to Cambrai. Going through the tunnels costs money and is a bore: a string of mixed vessels are joined together and towed the length of it. The whole process takes about eight hours and towing takes places twice in each direction every 24 hours.

Sunset near the river.

The Low Countries

75 km

Borkum

Emden

Terschelling
Ameland
Dokkum
Delfzijl

Vlieland
Leeuwarden
Groningen

Harlingen
Winschoten

Texel
FRIESLAND
Assen

Den Helder
Heerenveen

Lemmer
Emmen

North Sea
Hoogeveen

HOLLAND
Ijssel - meer
OVERIJSSEL

Alkmaar
Zwolle
Almelo

Zaanstad
NEDERLAND

Haarlem
Amsterdam
Enschede

GELDERLAND

Aalsmeer
Hilversum

Leiden
Apeldoorn
Amersfoort

Boskoop

's- Gravenhage
Delft
Gouda
Utrecht

(Den Haag)
Arnheim

Europoort
Rotterdam

Nijmegen

Dordrecht
BUNDESREPUBLIK

HOLLAND
Hertogenbosch
Boxmeer

Haamstede
Willemstad
Duisburg

Breda
Mühlheim

Middelburg
Tilburg
Eindhoven

Bergen op Zoom
Venlo

Blankenberge
Turnhout
Roermont

Oostende
Herentals
Bree
Düsseldorf

Brugge
Antwerpen

de Panne
DEUTSCHLAND

Roeselarde
Gent
BELGIË
Leuven
Hasselt
Köln

Kortrijk
St.- Truiden
Maastricht
Düren

Oudenaarde
Brussel/ Bruxelles
Aachen

Lille
Tournai
Liège

HAINAUT

Béthune
Namur
Huy
Spa

Mons
NAMUR

Arras
Charleroi

Cambrai
Dinant
BELGIQUE
Prüm

Chimay
Givet
la- Roche- en- A.

FRANCE
Bastogn

St. Quentin
Vervins
Bouillon
LUXEMBOURG
Trier

Charleville- Mézières
Arlon
Luxembourg

Laon
Longwy

212

THE LOW COUNTRIES

Appearances, like reputations, are frequently unearned or incorrect. And that is never so true as when people think about Holland and Belgium, those two small countries which have been inexorably intertwined through earlier centuries, and often known collectively as The Low Countries.

Belgium, it is said, is staid and dull, and of course, "it always rains there". Holland, on the other hand, is not thought dull, but its windmills, tulips and wooden shoes conjure up stereotype images that make the country seem a "little too cute".

And boating? Does Belgium even have inland waterways? Holland? What if there's a leak in the dike, and no little boy to plug it with his finger? Today's floating tourist need not imagine such nautical nightmares: the waterways of Holland are too important to be allowed to depend upon the fingers of little boys. The same is true for Belgium (although it has no legendary little boy). Busy with commerce today as in yesteryear, the Netherlands' and Belgium's canals and rivers are a vital part of both country's lives.

Much of Holland has been reclaimed from the sea. Students of history will know that it is a nation of the sea, its former empire extending to every ocean. At home, the life of the Dutch is as close to water as is the life of its sailors. What better way, then, to come to know the country and its people than to share their waterways.

"It's Tuesday, it must be Belgium..." Too many tourists approach the country with hazy visions and a hurried visit. Home of the European Union bureaucracy, Manneken Pis, and pommes frites, it has much to offer; but the visitor too often pauses at Brussels' Grand Place, then hurries through Bruges or Ghent before hastening on to other countries.

However, for the thoughtful traveler, this means that there are many touristically untouched places to tarry. As with its neighbor, The Netherlands, there is no better way to explore the "off-beat" than to follow the paths that built both nations, to wend along the waterways of the Walloon and the Flemish, and to make an exploration of the byways of Holland, a nation literally built upon water.

Travel the waters of the Low Countries, and you will find all the well-known visions – and much more.

BELGIUM

What makes a country? History? Geography? Earthquakes? Biology? What became "Belgium" was a natural borderline between the extremely flat countries in the north, and the outlets of a far more rocky and hilly country in the south. Also relevant is the theoretical border between the fancy lifestyle and lively Latin world, and the far more rational and stolid way of living of the Anglo-German part of Europe which is illustrated by the language border between the Flemish and Walloons.

Belgium has also known many occupiers, and although Julius Caesar wrote that the Belgians were the bravest of all Gauls, several countries considered Belgium their own. Among them were the Romans, Germans, French, Austrians, Spanish and finally the Dutch. Those who came and stayed introduced their rules, habits, ways of work and play. Belgium today might be compared to a child who has had a number of nursemaids, and absorbed a lot of their habits, both good and bad. Today's nursemaids are the bureaucrats of the European Union since Brussels has become the EU's principal administrative hub.

Culturally, one can enjoy an almost unlimited variety. For example, Belgium is Rubens in Antwerp, the Van Dyke brothers in Bruges, Breughel in Brussels, and Ensor in Ostend. Also belying the country's stuffy atmosphere, cafés are open from 10am until late in the evening. And for the hungry, every city and town boasts a wide scale of restaurants, and even the French admit that dining in Belgium is as good as eating "at home".

Belgium has almost 1,200 miles (2,000 km) of navigable waterways, making it the densest waterway system found in Europe, and quite possibly the world. One of the major routes links the North Sea with the Maas (Meuse) river and the industrial region beyond it. Others join the Dutch delta with Ghent, Antwerp and Brussels and with the rest of Europe. Except for the two major

rivers, the Meuse and Schelde (Scheldt), and a few small streams, most of the Belgium waterways were developed for trade transport.

The first traces of organized navigation are to be found in the 5th century when archival information notes the collection of taxes by feudal landlords for the passage of vessels through their territory. It was not until the 10th century, however, that existing rivers were adapted for better navigation and purpose-built canals were dug.

Although some form of tide control was in place beforehand, the first true sea locks did not appear until the 15th century. The earliest viable commercial routes appeared in the coastal plains near Zeebruge and major dredging took place to keep the River Zwin free from silt, creating what became Belgium's primary harbor, Bruges.

By the end of the 15th century, a network of canals had been dug enabling navigation during high tide on the upper Schelde, Haine and Scarpe Rivers. The connection between Brussels and the

Schelde, the Brussels to Rupel Canal was completed in 1561. The closing of the Schelde by the Dutch in the 18th century led to the execution of large-scale works in the interior of the country, but it was the 19th century's Industrial Revolution that led to the remarkable boom in waterway construction and improvement. During the Dutch occupation, and the reign of William I, king of the Netherlands, several works were started, and after the Belgium Revolution of 1830, the Belgium government took over the completion of these projects.

With the advent of steam power at the beginning of the 20th century, the waterways needed to be adapted and enlarged to accommodate the larger vessels that steam could propel.

It is only in the past few decades that trucks and planes have taken over from barges as the primary means of freight haulage. The struggle for an ultra-efficient waterway network isn't over yet, though faster-moving methods of transport mean ever-increasing rivalry and price competition. Yet the government continues to invest in the waterway network, enlarging canals, bridges and locks.

Unfortunately, this modernization in the name of progress has caused the closure or elimination of some of the more picturesque stretches of waterway to make way for the income-producing "big boys". Consequently, pleasure cruising is more difficult and unattractive in many parts of the country. Contrary to what has happened in France and Holland, where older, narrower waterways have been saved for tourists to enjoy, the Belgium government has undertaken only minor initiatives to make its waterways more attractive to the visitor (and local yachtsmen) in spite of the growing intensity of demands from the yacht clubs and tourist organizations.

But for the adventurer who enjoys cruising in company with vessels five times larger, a voyage through Belgium can be a fascinating experience. The country is rich in history, art, fine restaurants and museums. There are cas-

Ostend harbor.

tles to explore, and stretches of beautiful and deserted countryside still exist in the eastern regions.

A ring around the country: On a waterways map of Belgium, the system forms a neat and tidy circle around the country. From Antwerp, three major radial axes give passage to the major parts of the country. Two transversal axes were also created linking the coastal harbors of Ostend and Zeebrugge with Ghent, Antwerp and Liège; a southern one connects Liège, Namur, and Mons with Lille and Dunkirk in France. But for the traveler who wants to explore only Belgium, it's easily possible to make a circle, seeing the major cities, and ending up where one started.

If coming from the North Sea, the easiest way to enter the inland waterway system is through **Ostend Sea Harbor** following the **Plassenael Canal** towards Bruges. (Coming via the Ghent-Terneuzen Canal, should be avoided since it is a waterway filled with intensive commercial traffic and surrounded by ugly industrial scenery.)

Boat owners should note two items. First there is a fee (the most expensive water use tariff in Belgium) for entering the inland waterway system through Ostend's **Demysluis**, 400 Bfr. Second, because Ostend is filled with commercial and military shipping, it has become extremely crowded, and small boats should pay particular care to lights and marker buoys.

Picturesque **Ostend** has three **yacht harbors** for visiting boaters. Two, Montgomery and Mercator (the much preferred one) are near the town center. (Avoid the third, located near the very noisy merchant ship and navy dockyard.) Named after a century-old schoolship which is permanently moored at the dock (when not out on training sails), the Mercator is a delightful harbor with all marine facilities.

Ostend is an old fishing harbor which has evolved during the past hundred years into a more luxurious seaside resort. Leopold, the first King of the Belgians, had great influence in the development of the city, and the grateful

townspeople have named statues, monuments, restaurants and pubs after their king.

An important German submarine base during both world wars, the city suffered from extensive Allied bombing. Another disaster, this time a natural one, occurred in 1953 when a huge tidal wave broke the sea dikes. But the city quickly responded to both setbacks, and is today considered the most important seaside resort in the country.

Although the temptation may be to cruise onward, the city offers the visitor a few reasons to linger. The **beaches** are extensive, clean and well-maintained. Beyond them lies the **Zeedijk**, a 9-mile (15-km) long dike which is 100-ft (30-meters) wide and ranges in height from 25 to 33 ft (8–10 meters). Built to protect the low-lying land and the city from the pounding sea, the promenade on top offers lovely walks.

One stroll might be to the **Staketsel**, two piers that were built to protect the harbor. The pier that lies closest to town has a café on it, and an afternoon watching the ships enter and leave Ostend gives an idea of the harbor's importance. A trip to the **fishing harbor** makes an interesting early-morning excursion. The boats arrive in the pre-dawn hours, with an auction of their catch taking place soon afterward. These same boats are blessed every year amid much pomp and procession on the first Sunday after 28 June.

The first Queen of the Belgians, Louise-Marie, who died in Ostend in 1850, is buried in the **Church of Sts Peter and Paul**. The neo-gothic building is a turn-of-the-century replacement for a 14th-century structure that was destroyed by fire. Those wishing to try a thermal bath should look no further than the **Palais des Thermes**. There are numerous treatments available, ranging from a mud soak to electro-therapy.

It's 10 miles (17 km) from Ostend to Bruges. In a little less than 2 miles (4 km), a right turn on the Plassendaele Canal takes the boater south to Nieuwport and Dunkirk. The landscape is typically *polder*, that is, land reclaimed from the sea, and very flat. Astern, the buildings of Ostend form a flat line against the horizon.

Many of the bridges on the Belgian canal system are fixed, but some, like the upcoming Nieuwege, need to be opened to allow craft through. Three sharp blasts of the boat's horn is usually enough to attract the keeper's attention, but sometimes, especially on the smaller canals, patience, and more than three toots is required. The bridge negotiated, **Bruges** is beyond the highway.

It may be tempting to moor at the pontoons directly ahead on the left. Don't. They belong to the Bruges Roeiklub (Bruges Rowing Club), and docking is prohibited for all but members. Take care also that the boat's wake doesn't damage the rowboats, sculls and skiffs which are berthed here.

The canal makes a three-quarter ring around Bruges, one of Belgium's most historic and beautiful cities which deserves its title, "Venice of the North". The traject is cut into smaller pieces by means of six turning or swing bridges, and one lock complex. While taking a

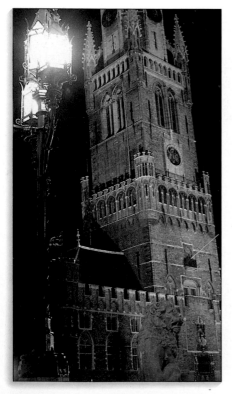

Bruges by night.

small boat through these busy waters, try to ignore the fact that these are the most polluted in Flanders, that the barges (called *Lichters*) are some of the biggest on any waterway, and concentrate on getting safely to the quiet oasis that is Bruges.

There are overnight moorings just beyond the **Dammeportsluis**, but better ones (except for the nightly ringing of the church bells) are in the **Coupure**, the area where the canals which intersect the city begin. From here, all Bruges is available on foot. For those who cannot abide this kind of noise, more modern and quiet docks, although much further from the city center are found in the southern reaches beyond Gentpoortbrug and St Katalijnepoortbrug near the city's by-pass highway.

In the 7th century, the old capital of Flanders was known as Monicipium Brugense, but Bruges' modern name comes from the Norsemen who called it Bruggia (mooring place). A major trading center from its earliest days, the city reached the zenith of its power in the 12th and 13th centuries when it controlled most of the English trade. Bruges came about this monopoly because it was the "Flemish Hanse in London"; the city's power did not wane until the 16th century when the city finally lost its centuries-long struggle against an enemy it could not conquer: silt. The Zwin became clogged, the shoreline changed, and no longer could Bruges call itself a port city. This also ended Bruges' long fight with Ghent and Antwerp when each claimed to be the most important in Flanders.

When this happened in the late 1700s, Bruges began its decline. Amsterdam, and later, Antwerp took over the role of primary port, but the tradesmen of Bruges did not give up. Their modern idea: Zeebrugge, less than 8 miles (12 km) away is fast becoming an international port, and while not conferring great status on Bruges, its creation meant that some of the money which would normally go into Antwerp's coffers, now stays closer to home.

Now the capital of West Flanders,

An early morning cruise.

and a center for commercial activity. The Old City, despite destruction of the city gates due to traffic needs (only four remain), is a warren of gabled buildings and streets intersected by canals. The **Markt** is the start for all sightseeing; its **Halle** was built in the 13th and 14th centuries. The adjacent belfry (272 ft/ 83 meters) has 366 steps to climb for superb views over the city, and its 1743 Carillion contains 47 bells. After returning to earth, head next door to the **Folk Lore Museum**.

Leaving the Markt, the **Burg** is almost around the corner. Located here are the **Landhuis**, built in 1622, the 14th-century **Town Hall**, and the 16th-century **Recorder's House** which is now part of the Law Courts (Their main buildings are on the next street). The **Chapel of the Holy Blood** received its name from a supposed gift to the city in 1150 of a few drops of Christ's blood.

As befits a city of culture, there are many museums. The **Groeninge** has an excellent collection of Flemish paintings; **Gruuthuse Palace** offers antiqui-

ties and applied arts; **Memmling** displays art by that painter; at the **Begijnhof** (still inhabited by Benedictine sisters), the museum inside takes the viewer through the history of lace-making; the 1276-founded **Hospice de Potterie's** museum contains copious ecclesiastical art and jewels.

Sightseeing boats offering tours of Bruges leave from the **Rei**. At night, the flood-lit buildings are a spectacular sight from land or from a boat gliding through them. From **Steenhauserdijk** and **Groene Rei** observe the old buildings with their picturesque gables.

Before leaving Bruges, consider two side trips. The **Damsevaart**, a charming but now-closed waterway leading to **Damme**, can now be explored via a public sightseeing boat that plies these waters daily in season. **Ooidonk Castle** is also not far away, and a guided tour through the house and grounds is a lovely way to spend an afternoon.

Leaving Bruges for Ghent (30 miles/ 41 km from the Dammeportsluis to Ringvaart Ghent), the landscape is an improvement over the stretch from Ostend. Those with a VHF radio can tune it to Channel 20, and call the bridgekeeper at Moerbrugge to have it opened before arrival. If needing fuel or repairs, the **Beernan Yacht Club** offers all facilities to passing boats. From here, the scenery changes; major waterworks emerge, and after Aalterburg, are buildings totally devoted to industry.

Just after **Bruggewyk**, another diversion is also possible. Turning right into the **Afleidingskalaal Leie** leads to the River Leye (Lys) to Roeselare, Kortrijk and France. Following the Leie also brings an incredible amount of industrial archaeology along the bank. Once, the Lys contained the most ideal water in which to *ret* (soak) the flax from which linen was then woven. That industry died out years ago when the river not only lost it's quality, but became extremely polluted from the French factories just over the border. The deserted factories attest to the decline in the local industrial base and the loss of jobs that went with it.

But back to happier times on the road

Two views of the Belgian countryside.

to **Ghent**. Less than 2 miles (3 km) from the city proper, the **Ringvaart** is reached. This waterway circles Ghent, allowing vessels which do not wish to transit the city a faster passage around it. Ignore the Evergem Lock which gives access to the industrial port of Ghent, and the Schelde. Instead, cruise straight ahead – although getting into Ghent can be a little confusing. The most direct route is not open since the wealthy residents who have houses along the Leie River want to preserve their privacy and intrusions from the boating "Peeping Toms". So, head along the Ringvaart in either direction, following signs into town.

Look for mooring facilities along the **Verloren Kost Brug**. A new marina is being built near the Court of Justice. Its completion should double current boat capacity. Another municipal project is the renovation of the swing bridges; making them moveable once more would allow more pleasure boats into the city. As of now, the bridges only open at night for an hour because pleasure cannot interfere with tram traffic!

Ghent has much to offer, and the history of Flanders is intertwined with this remarkable city. Here one finds relics of a continual struggle against several occupiers which is reflected in the buildings, city squares, museums and churches. Like Bruges and Amsterdam, smaller canals weave a network between the ever-winding streets and lanes from the center, allowing smaller barges to moor next to impressive warehouses and early factories.

Arriving from the west, one is greeted with the silhouette of a few skyscrapers, but more with the elegant towers of the **City Hall**, **St Michael's Cathedral** and its **Belfry**. Pay also a visit to the ancient **Bijlok Hospital** and **Gravensteen Castle** (centered in the middle of a warren of streets).

Ghent is where the "ring around Belgium" truly begins. Whether one heads first eastward for Antwerp and Brussels or south to Tournai, Mons and Charleroi, each can end in Ghent. For this voyage, we start with the latter; unfortunately, marinas are scarce along this

route until Peronnes, so cruise away from Ghent prepared.

The **Upper Schelde** branches off the Ringvaart, and for the first seven miles (13 km) the waterway is large enough to accommodate vessels up to 2,000 tons (1,818,000 kgs). A small boat is perfectly safe, but one must constantly be on the lookout for the behemoths: they have (and take) the right of way. But the biggest dangers come from their wash, and the disregard their captains sometimes have for the posted speed limit.

The scenery is mostly rural except for one or two towns and some factories. **Oudenaarde** is the first town of any real consequence, 14 miles (26 km) from Ghent. Look for moorings behind the locks named for the town, once known for its textiles and tapestry weaving. Today, the city has no working mills, but in the **Cloth Hall** (Lakenhalle), the industry's evolution from hand weaving in the Middle Ages through the eventual decline and termination of the local trade is traced. Also on display is the most famous tapestry to be created in the town, the *Verdures*.

The beer connoisseur should try the locally-brewed beverage. It's slightly sour with its own distinct taste, and is one of the 350-plus brands brewed in Belgium. In every city and town, and even small villages, each tavern or bar will have an extremely wide variety to choose from, and some must even be served in a specially shaped glass.

Leaving Oudenaarde, once past the last bridge (B1) the river makes a sharp turn to the right. An old, dead-end branch enters the navigable waterway from the right. This causes heavy cross currents, so beware while on this stretch. Seven miles (13 km) later and the **Berchem Kerkove Lock** appears.

The first records of shipping on this part of the river go back to the 10th century when goods were shipped between Ghent and the French city of Cambrai. The Upper Scheldt was always navigable, but it's depth and width were not great, and as the need for bigger boats to carry more produce increased, so did the need for a deeper and

Mons, as seen from its belfry.

wider river. A dam, the Belvedere, was constructed to collect the water; when enough had built up behind the barrier, the gates were opened, and craft could proceed up river. These were known as *Drijfdagen* (floating days), and the wooden *lichters* took four or five days to reach Ghent.

Although some locks were built from the 14th century onward, it was not until the 19th before major works were undertaken. The river bends were straightened, five dams with larger locks were constructed, permitting the modern barges to work the waterway. Almost all these structures were destroyed during World War I, but the Ministry of Public Works rebuilt bigger and better, and it is not unusual to see long strings of 123-ft (38-meter) barges easily passing through the locks.

Behind the **Bercham-Kerkove locks** are the chimneys of the Ruien Power Station. After the next three bridges, the canal from Kortrijk (Courtrai) appears on the right. At this point, if you feel a slight bump in the water, it's because the boat is passing a border – not a geographic one, but one of languages. For here, the Flemish-speaking area of Belgium ends, and the French one begins. This also means that all signs and ensigns and boat terms will be in that language. So don't think you've gone crazy if the word seems a little different for the same function.

Just beyond the **Espierres Lock** is the canal of the same name. Turning south onto it, one ends up in France. But our route takes the Haut (high) Escaut River to the city that is called **Doornik** in Flemish, but is better known by its French title, **Tournai**.

One of Belgium's oldest cities, Tournai was known as Turris Nerviorum during the Roman period, and by the 4th century it had become heavily fortified. The Salien Franks made it their seat of government, but when Clovis became King of France in 486, he moved the capital to Soissons, Tournai lost its importance. In 1188, the city became part of France, only to have Charles V cede it to the Netherlands in the 1520s. After that, it followed the fortunes of the Neth-

erlands until 1830 when Tournai became part of the newly-created Belgian nation.

The **Cathedral of Notre Dame**, possibly the most beautiful Gothic church in all Belgium, is the city's crowning glory. Construction took place in the 11th and 12th centuries, with restorations in the 19th. The central tower soars 272 ft (83 meters) into the sky, and inside, the three-aisled interior is 440 ft (134 meters) long, 216 ft (66 meters) wide and varies in height between 79 and 198 ft (24 to 60 meters). The north and south doors are elaborately sculpted, and in the transept, note the stained glass windows which illustrate the See's history. The treasury, which contains many religous artifacts and tapestries, shouldn't be missed.

Also worth a visit are the Renaissance-style **Cloth Hall**, the recently renovated **Market Square** and the 12th and 13th-century **Belfry**. There are also clusters of houses from the Middle Ages throughout Tournai, and an old bridge, the **Pont des Trous** (Bridge of Holes)

which has very narrow openings between the piers. (Pay strict attention to the traffic lights when passing through them.)

Antoing and **Peronnes** come and go, but before entering the Peronnes lock, another option arrives: the Schelde branches south and soon flows into France. Those staying on the "road" to Mons can enjoy the comforts of the **Peronnes Yacht Club** which is located on an artificial lake created between the first two locks on the **Peronnes-Nimy Canal**. Upon departure from the club's comforts, leaving the lake can cause great surprise. The fall in the water level at the next lock is 39 ft (12 meters) – quite a daunting experience for a small boat. Beyond it, the ADEPS Marina and slightly farther along is the RCAT Yacht Club. Both offer visitors use of their facilities.

After the railway bridge another hazard is encountered: water skiers and power boats are allowed on weekends and holidays so take care to avoid these madmen and their wash. And smile happily at the second railway bridge for this is where their empire ends.

There are many comfortable moorings on the route into Mons. Several private boating clubs open their docks to transients, and municipal facilities are usually adequate. **Hautrage** offers fuel as well. Although the canal is bordered by greenery, the influence of 19th-century industrial works is inevitably visible. Several modern cement plants are here and the reminders of a once-flourishing coalpit industry create further blemishes. The Ath-Blaton Canal, offering another route to Ghent and Antwerp, is the next waterway branching off, but the waterway has been closed to private boats by the short-sighted Belgian Authorities.

Transient moorings at **Mons** are found on the artificially created **Lake Grand Large** where three yacht clubs are situated: Atlanta II which uses an old, renovated barge for the clubhouse, Le Club Nautique de Mons Borinage and ADEPS, which belongs to the national sports organization.

The city can only be fully appreciated by walking through the narrow and winding streets near the **Market Square** (Grand Place). This is built as a half-circular design around the Baroque **Belfry**. (Take an elevator to the top of the 276-ft/84-meter structure for great views over the city). To ensure good luck and to make sure that all your wishes will come true, don't forget to caress the head of the little bronze monkey which sits on the Place.

Don't miss the **Municipal Museum** with its collection of World War I and II memorabilia, ceramics and coins. Nearby is the **British and Canadian Memorial** designed by Lutyens, the British architect responsible for many of the government buildings built by the British Raj in India. Nearby are the ruins of the **castle** of the Counts of Hainault (Henegauwen), which can be visited.

Beyond Mons, the journey takes the boat along one of the most remarkable canals in Belgium: **Le Canal du Centre** (The Central Canal). Less than 12 miles (20 km) in length, its main claim

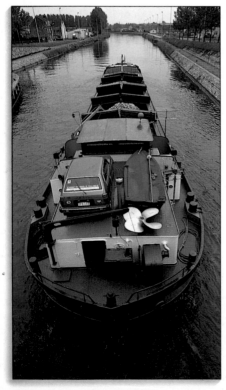

One of the "Big Boys".

to fame is the terrain it flows through. Linking the River Maas (Meuse) with the western waterway network, it falls almost 308 ft (95 meters) from Mons to Houdeng.

It took many years to construct the canal, but it was finally opened in 1888 when King Leopold II cut the tricolored ribbon signaling that the revolutionary new link was operational. The drop in height is accomplished with the aid of four hydraulic boat lifts, soon, unfortunately, to be one elevator when the construction at Strepy-Thieu is finished. While the elimination of the four narrow locks is bad for the pleasure traveler, the commercial user of the waterways will be able to send barges of up to 1,350 tons (615 metric tons) on the Canal du Centre. After going down the last elevator, there are two marinas a short distance away.

Sipping your next drink, consider the next stage of the cruise. Will it be a left turn and Brussels, or a journey straight ahead where the Meuse awaits beyond Charleroi and Namur?

Capital of the Black Country, the number of industries – coal mines, glass and iron works around the city attest that **Charleroi** received its title honestly. It is a pleasant place, but offers no reason to remain.

Namurs, 34 miles (55 km) up the Sambre River, is better. Located at the confluence of the Sambre and Meuse Rivers, when the Romans arrived it was already a fortified town. Because of its strategic position, Namurs has been subjected to many seiges and bombardments throughout the centuries. In this one, it was twice a key element in the Belgian defence line, and each time, in 1914 and 1940, the Germans easily rolled across it.

Looming over the city is the **Citadelle**, and without a car the easiest way to reach it is by cable car. The **Château of Namurs** is here; also the **Museum of Arms and Armaments**, located in two medieval buildings.

The **Old Town** is centered around the classically-styled **Cathedral St Aubin**. Inside, note statues by Delacroix, and

A blowable horn.

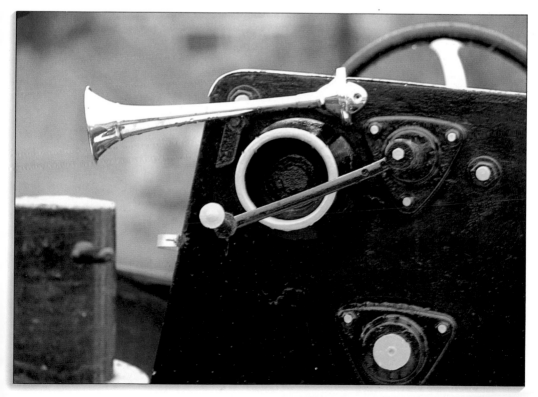

visit the **Treasury**. The only surviving Gothic building in Namurs is the **Church of St Jean**; built in the 15th century, its interior is intensly Baroque.

The **Stock Exchange** is on **Place d'Armes** along with a **Belfry**. Nearby is the **Convent of Notre Dame** and its Treasury. The **Archaeology Museum** is located in the 1560-built **Ancienne Boucherie** (Butcher's Hall).

The run along the Meuse River to Liège (38 miles/ 60 km) is one of the prettiest in Belgium, lined with wooded slopes, small villages, and ruined castles. At **Marche-les-Dames**, five miles (eight km) from Namur, the river is overlooked by massive rock formations. A cross at the top marks the spot where, in 1934, King Albert I fell to his death. **Andenne** is a pretty town with a Romanesque church and two decorative fountains, the 16th-century **Bear** and the 17th-century **St Begge**.

In 1095, Peter the Hermit preached about the First Crusade in the hills near **Huy**. But the town's pride is the **Collegiate Church of Notre Dame**. Begun in 1322 and completed in 1377, it is the most important Gothic structure in Belgium. Note especially the carved west portal and the **Rose Window**.

On the **Grand Place**, the **Bassilia**, is the only Gothic fountain still standing in Belgium. Inside the nearby **Town Hall**, built in 1766, is a museum containing a good collection of paintings. Other exhibits are in the **Municipal Museum** located in a former Franciscan Monastery. For an overall view of the town, take the 2-mile **cable car** that travels from its beginning on the left bank of the Meuse up and over the Citadelle to **La Sarthe**.

Leaving Huy, half the distance to Liège has been covered, and the towns of Ampsin, Ombret-Rause and Ramet are quickly passed.

The Flemish **Luick** (but the French **Liège**) was founded in the 7th century; today, its the fourth largest city in Belgium, and one of its most important industrial areas. Sitting at the confluence of the Meuse and Ourthe rivers, its port is large enough to accommodate

Grand Place, Brussels.

the largest commercial barges which bring in supplies of iron ore. Small boats can feel lost but transients are offered moorings and the facilities of the Yacht Club of Liège, located conveniently along the Quai de Rome.

Sightseeing is confined to the west (left) bank; the heart of the city is shaped by three squares, the **St Lambert**, **de Maréchal** and **de la Républic**, and around, or near them are most of the places to visit. **Basilique St Martin** has a tower that can be climbed; built in the 13th century, it was burnt in the next, and was rebuilt in the 16th. The feast of Corpus Christi was first celebrated here in 1246, and plaques on the wall commemorate that event. The **Treasury** is the most note-worthy part of the **Church of the Holy Cross**. At **Musée des Beaux Arts**, a portrait of Napoleon by Ingres is one of the featured exhibits. If overnighting, *Au Vieux Liège,* offers dining with a river view, and on every Sunday morning, a **Flea Market** operates on Quai de la Batte.

From Liège, a right takes the boat to Maastricht and Holland *(see page 247)* or left to Antwerp. The purpose-built **Albert Kanaal** to Antwerp is not very attractive, and is filled with monster cargo boats, but it's the most direct route to Antwerp. Because the waterway was built for speed, it's easy to travel. Only six locks break up the 85-mile (136-km) journey, and although commercial barges have the right of way everywhere, especially in lock passage, delays are uncommon. Numerous towns along the route offer marine facilities, but they are not totally geared up for private boats. This lack of interest is shown most graphically in the distance between mooring rings: they are placed for 123-ft (38-meter) barges, not boats one-fifth that size.

Less than a mile from Liège stands the statue of King Albert on **Ile de Monsin**, which marks the official beginning of the canal that bears his name. (For those who desire a more rural, slower and lock-filled journey to Antwerp, take the Zuidwillemsvaart Canal that is a sharp right opposite Briegden. The canal forms

The city's flea market.

the top of a heart, (with Dessel as the inward point), as it wends its way through Northern Belgium, linking up with the Albert Kanaal near Wetschote).But remaining on the Albert, **Hasselt**, the capital of Limbourg, was an important market town by the early Middle Ages. That importance continues today and is further reinforced by the number of industrial buildings in the town. The 11th-century **St Quentins Cathedral** is attractive, but the reason to stop here is not the town or its Yacht Club (visitors welcome), but the **Bokrijk Estate**.

Located about 12 miles (20 km) from Hasselt on road No. 22, the 1,334-acre (540-hectare) park has a château to tour, a Museum of Natural History and an Open Air Museum featuring windmills, farmhouses and other buildings.

At **Kwaadmechelen**, the waterway to the right flows to Dessel. **Olen** and its industry are fast left behind, but **Herentals** (where another right leads to Dessel) is more charming. The 14th-century **Town Hall** has a Carillon in its tower, and in the **Fraikin Museum** are the

works of that sculptor. The carved 16th-century altar in the **Church of St Waldetrudis** is by Borremans.

The **Canal Nète**, at **Grobbendonk**, offers a short-cut to Brussels which eliminates the need to travel there via Antwerp. Still soldiering through on the Albert, at **Viersel**, take a look at the 14th century Hovorost Castle.

Massenhoven is the butt of malicious gossip which alleges that flies instead of raisins, were put into the Christmas pudding several centuries ago. This supposed act gave the local inhabitants the unhappy nick-name of *Vliegen-stovers* (fly stewers).

Although one of Belgium's oldest cities, **Wijnegem** has lost most of its charm as its industry developed. Some of the 17th-century Kijkuit Castle remains, as does the Renaissance Pulhof Castle, but that's about it. A little less than 2 miles up the canal is **Wetschot;** then comes **Antwerp**.

The city acquired its name through one of history's more gruesome legends. In Roman times, an ogre named Druon Antigonus, inhabited a castle where the city now stands. As travelers sailed up and down the river, Druon would ask for money. If someone refused to pay it, the loss of a hand, "*hand-werpen*", was the result. (In the middle of the city's **Grote Markte**, look for the late 19th-century **Brabo Fountain** depicting the Roman Governor ridding the city of the ogre by throwing the giant's own hand into the river!)

There are references to Antwerp as early as the 7th century, and by the 11th it was an important harbor. In 1313, the city became the headquarters for the Hanseatic League, and when Bruges' harbor was no longer viable, Antwerp became the principal city of the region. By the mid-1500s, over 100 ships a day visited the city, whose population exceeded 100,000.

Prosperity began to wane in the late 1570s when the Spaniards sacked the city. Further blows were dealt when trade was transferred to Amsterdam and Rotterdam (because the city had been captured by Duke Alexander Farnsee), and when the 1648 Treaty of Westph- **According to an early engraving...**

230

alia was signed and the Schelde was closed, all seemed lost. Napoleon however, turned the tide: in 1803 he ordered new docks built and the river dredged. Despite some economic setbacks, and the bombings of two world wars, Antwerp's fortunes have remained on the prosperous side.

Today, although it's not on the sea (Antwerp is 55 miles/88 km from the Schelde's estuary), shipping and ships are the most important industry, followed by banking, diamonds and petrochemicals. The commercial docks are enormous and forbidding, but the private owner can take heart and head for the non-tidal **Imalso Yacht Harbor**. Situated across the river from the Willemdock, it's the perfect place to stay (a pedestrian tunnel to the main part of the city is about half a mile from it).

The first order of sightseeing should be a cruise of the **commercial harbor** and a walk along the **waterfront**. There are over 3 miles (5 km) of riverfront quays that are 325-ft (100-meters) wide, and they form the basis for delightful promenades. Elevated pedestrian terraces overlooking the river are at the **Ernest van Dijckkaai** and **Jordaenskaai**; cafés along them offer places to rest and enjoy the view. Sightseeing boats leave from near the **Steen** (part of the former castle of Antwerp). Also near the Steen is the **National Maritime Museum**, with a wonderful collection of ships from all over the world, nautical instruments and maps.

Standing a few blocks off the river, the **Cathedral of Notre Dame** is Belgium's largest Gothic building. Construction started in 1352, and was not finished until late in the 16th century. It stands 384 ft (117 meters) long, 180 ft (55 meters) wide, and 131 ft (40 meters) high with its largest tower 404 ft (123 meters) tall. Damaged during the French Revolution by Republicans who sought to export their ideas, it was renovated in the 19th century, and all the exterior statuary is from that period. Inside, some of Rubens' masterpieces are hung in the transept and choir.

Located on **Grote Markte**, the 16th-

...**Gaasbeck Castle hasn't changed over the years.**

century **Town Hall** displays the history of Antwerp in the form of tapestries. Other old buildings on the square were built to house various guilds such as coopers and grocers.

The Museum for Applied Arts and Local History is in the old Butchers' house. Works of the printer Christoph Morteus are in the museum named after him. **Rubens House** is a museum to that famous painter. The **Academy of Arts** is away from the old part of the city, but worth a visit; the same is true for the **Royal Museum of Fine Arts**.

Those interested in ethnic history should venture into the **Jewish Quarter**. The largest such community in Europe, it runs north from Koning-Albert Park to the Central Station. Most of the inhabitants are Orthodox Jews, and aside from the **Diamond Stock Exchange** there are several old synagogues that can sometimes be visited.

Special **markets** include the Sunday-morning **Flea Market** on Blauwtoren-plein, and the Easter-to-September **Antiques Market** which runs all-day Saturday on Hendrik Conscienceplein.

Out of Antwerp, Brussels, capital of Belgium, is 36 miles (57 km) and three locks away. It's not a pretty cruise; factories and other plants line most of the banks, and private boats can feel threatened by the endless parade of commercial barges. At **Niel** (a town known for brick-making) the man-made **Canal de Bruxelles à Rupel** arrives. (From here, a direct return to Ghent is 41 miles/ 67 km down the rivers Durme, Dendre and Schelde.)

Boom has also been creating bricks since 1235 when the monks of Abbey St Bernard started making them to sell. If you're interested, tours of the brick-yards can be arranged. A sad memory of World War I and the famine it brought is remembered in the town's nickname, *hondefetters*, "dog eaters". On another hand, if trying horse-meat steak is a life's desire, restaurants in **Vilvoorde** specialize in them.

Brussels arrives and with it moorings at the **Royal Yacht Club** which allots 100 berths for visiting boats. Its ameni-

Church statuary.

ties, besides a full range of marine services, includes a bar and restaurant which is open until 11pm.

St Géry, the man who brought Christianity to Belgium, is supposed to have founded Brussels in the late 500s. By 970, a stronghold had been built by Charles, Duke of Lower Lotharingia, and in that same century, because of its position mid-way between Bruges and Cologne, Brussels grew into a prosperous trading center. The fortifications, not torn down until the 19th century were constructed in 1530.

French became the fashionable language when the Dukes of Burgundy held luxurious court in the city; later rulers provided even more glittering displays: Charles V's was especially rich. The Dutch first rebelled against the Spanish in Brussels, but the defenders held the day. The wars and revolutions of France also adversely affected the city, and it was not until Belgium was an identity of its own, with Brussels its capital, that the city flourished.

The touristic heart of Brussels is the **Grand Place**. Surrounded by the Town Hall and the buildings of former guilds, it is 360 ft (110 meters) long and 223 ft (68 meters) wide. A renovation undertaken in 1695 left most of the Romanesque and Gothic buildings with Baroque features; but enough traces of their former lives remain, and the small square is one of the most gracious and harmonious anywhere. It is to be especially admired in the evening when the buildings are illuminated.

Think of Brussels and of course, **Manneken Pis** (a fountain depicting a little boy relieving himself), immediately comes to mind. It is possibly the best-known tourist site in Belgium, he stands on a crowded street just minutes from the Grand Place, and locals grumble good-naturedly as tourists move this way and that trying to catch a glimpse or a photograph of the fountain. His history is obscure: one legend says he was a little boy taking revenge against a hated Spanish occupier. The statue has been stolen by both the English (1745) and French (1747), and it was this latter

Smoking isn't outlawed everywhere.

theft that started the custom of giving "him" clothes: Louis XV donated elaborate costumes as a means of French atonement.

Brussels is noted for its museums and other cultural events. **The Royal Museum of Art and History** is the city's best and best-known; the collections range from ancient Egypt to modern automobiles. The Flemish primitive paintings in the **Museum of Ancient Arts** are superb; *art nouveau* is featured at **Horta Museum**; and in the **Museum of the City of Brussels**, its history is traced through a variety of exhibits (here, too, is the wardrobe of "Pis"). For a change of pace, the **Brewery Museum** is concerned with the nation's favorite drink. **The Royal Museum of Central Africa** houses a collection of artifacts from Belgium's former colonies. And children will love the "hands-on" museum that's been created for them on Rue de Bourgemestre.

No-one should miss the **Atomium**. Built for the World's Fair of 1958, this replica of a molecule of iron strikes a

pose against the city's skyline and is visible from most parts of it. The permanent exhibit contains one on the peaceful uses of atomic energy, and a traveling one relates to other energy sources.

After dark, most theaters offer productions only in the French language, but the National Opera and Ballet Béjart are universally understood. Jazz lovers should head for the **Brussels Jazz Club** which has shows almost every evening. Puppetry, once a prime source of entertainment for Belgians and for which the country was renowned, is making a comeback. The **Théâtre Toon VII**, operating out of a small building off Petite Rue des Bouchers, offers nightly performances by one of Belgium's puppet masters, José Géal.

For dining, there is a wealth of fine restaurants. Some even suggest this is why Brussels was chosen as headquarters of the European Community. Three which deserve mention are Villa Lorraine, Comme Chez Soi, and Barbizon.

While Brussels-based, several excursions are easily undertaken. The **Castle of Gaasbeek** is 10 miles (16 km) to the southwest; this medieval building contains a fine collection of antiques and paintings. Nearby, **Beersel Castle** contains little more than the moated three towers and a wall of the original 14th-century building.

No visit to Belgium would be complete without visiting the site of **Waterloo** (11 miles/18 km south from Brussels). The famous battle that pitted Napoleon's army against the one commanded by Wellington took place on 18 June 1815; the French defeat led to Napoleon's eventual downfall and a restructuring of Europe. Also on view is the **Lion's Mound**, an artificially-created 130-ft (40-meter) hill built by the Dutch; the lion on top was a gift of France, and 260 steps lead up to it. There is also a **museum** and the usual assortment of trashy souvenir stands.

And so, back to Ghent, the Belgian circle's beginning. The waterway that brought Brussels is retraced to Rupelmonde; a left turn is made, and in less than a day's non-stop cruise, the journey is completed.

Left, a ceremony to remember Belgium's war veterans. **Right**, Tournai Cathedral.

FROM DEN HELDER TO MAASTRICHT

As legend would have it, the best, sometimes only, way to build a road in a low, marshy land like the Netherlands, almost two thirds of which lies below sea level, is to dig a canal. Removing soft layers of peat in this way allows sound foundations to be introduced for the hard road on top. The base often penetrates 50 ft (15 meters) into the soft layers, explaining why some Dutch roads were the most costly to build per mile in the entire world.

Expense aside, however, the idea of filling-in canals for use as roads was spurred by the rising prosperity of the Netherlands where car ownership accelerated and never slowed down. But before the advent of highways and railways, relative latecomers to the Netherlands, the building of canals, dams and dikes was a core activity of the maritime-minded Dutch who took the lifesaving technology of water control as seriously as they do life itself.

Building canals, which complemented the reclamation by dikes of what would otherwise have remained seabed, entailed the introduction of draconian laws prohibiting feuds, or sometimes even disagreements, when dikes needed repairs. Those breaking the dike peace were sentenced to execution, a fate second only to flooding. Even the legend of the little boy plugging the dike with his finger was realized when the so-called "Law of the Spade" decreed that those unable to repair breaks should place their spades there until help arrived and the dike could be repaired.

The fearsome rigor with which the Dutch approached dike and canal building was born of countless struggles to keep the waters at bay, struggles that saw the submergence and recapture, perhaps half a dozen times, of highly prized patches of land. Indeed, delve into the ancient records and one encounters countless phantom villages which disappeared virtually overnight after a massive storm.

A cruise from north to south: Ruler straight and immaculately trimmed at the edges, the hand-dug **North Holland Canal**, along which traders used to be pulled by horse on their way to the East Indies, was Amsterdam's first, although far from last, attempt to counteract the relentless silting up of the Zuiderzee, the great sea arm that once engulfed the north.

The canal was completed in 1825, a year after the founding of a new company, the *Nederlandsche Handelsmaatschappij*, to revive the Dutch trade with the East Indies which had been nearly obliterated during the Napoleonic wars. To finance the improvement of such internal communications as new roads and canals, customs duties were raised and taxes slapped on everything.

Thanks to the trusty North Holland Canal, barges, steamers and even smallish ships can get from the wholesome cheese-market town of Alkmaar in the north to Amsterdam, some 20 miles (33 km) south. The canal is a classic example of the more than 5,000 miles (8,000 km) of navigable canals and riv-

Preceding pages: what big feet you have. **Left,** Holland's national flower, and **right,** a favorite son, Rembrandt.

ers, about 50 times the average width of the country, which have provided the means by which cities, such as Amsterdam, could spring forth and blossom like the myriad tulips.

Alkmaar, where our barge journey begins, is a well-preserved example of a small and ancient Dutch town which fortunately never disappeared. Despite a busy town center, which bustles with local villagers on weekdays, it retains an air of tranquility due largely to the surrounding canal along which boaters, bargers and even the odd canoeist glide peacefully.

The **cheese market**, to which visitors flock *en masse* on Friday mornings between May and September, is presided over by the architecturally eclectic weigh-house comprising several older buildings joined together in 1599. The cheese-tasting and weighing ritual, when tight-fisted buyers have been known to get hand-fisted with tenacious sellers, is as colorful to observe as the carriers' brightly-lined costumes.

The tiny, quaint-looking facade of the **Town Hall**, dating from 1509, stands as an anachronism, rubbing shoulders with modern steel and glass buildings lining the brick street. It is a favorite with German tourists, for whom the itinerant barrel organs grind out oomp-pah at every corner. Swarms of Germans invade Little Holland, as they see it, to escape the smoggy Ruhr Valley.

Before cruising south, consider a 26-mile (42-km) detour north to **Den Helder**. A major naval base and fishing port, the town is situated on the tip of Northern Holland Province with Texel Island lying between it and the North Sea. Napoleon changed centuries of obscurity when his fortifications bestowed upon Den Helder the title, "Gibraltar of the North."

Over a century earlier, a naval battle in 1673 pitted the locals against the combined English and French fleets. The Dutch, under Admiral de Ruyter won. The English were again unlucky in 1799 when, joined by the Russians, they lost to the French. Today, bulb growing is important; so is the naval port. Pho-

Sailing on the Nord Kanaal...

tography enthusiasts are advised not to point their cameras in its direction.

There's a nature park, **De Donkeree Duinen** and a 4-mile (6-km) stretch of dunes to explore. In the nearby village of **Huisduinen**, climb the 225-ft (69-meter) high **lighthouse** for a 360 degree view.

A trip to **Texel** offers good birding and tastings of a local delicacy, ewe cheese; ferrys leave from the harbor near the monument to Dutch sailors who lost their lives in both World Wars. The 15-mile (24 km) long island is 6 miles (10 km) at its widest. A **Museum of Antiquities** is located at **Den Burg**, and the **Museum of Texel** is near **De Koog**. The nature reserve is in the northern end of the island (make advance bookings during the breeding season).

Returning to Alkmaar, sail down the North Holland Canal past the boating lake of Alkmaardermer, along the narrow Markervaart, and into the old sea arm called Zaan, where more than a thousand whirling windmills used to supply villagers' with their only means

of power. The small wooden houses of the carefully reconstructed old village of **Zaanse Schans** bear witness to the long gone pioneering days of the area. The Schermer nearby is a *polder* (reclaimed land) drained in 1530 with the help of 52 windmills.

Sail past the numerous small bridges approaching **Zaandam**, through the historic locks known as **Wilhelmina Sluizen** and, looming majestically ahead is the towering silhouette of **Amsterdam's Westertoren**, the highest church tower in the city, and certainly one of the most impressive.

On reaching the Dutch capital, the North Holland Canal joins the North Sea Canal which stretches across the narrow strip of land to **Ijmuiden** (11 miles/19 km west of the junction; the locks here are some of the largest in the world, and seeing them in operation is an experience). The canal allows ships to reach Amsterdam directly from the North Sea instead of having to travel north up the coast to approach through the Zuidersee, much of which is now

...and on the sea near Amsterdam.

poldered though it once formed a Rhine estuary. It eventually became a shallow inland sea which, in 1932, the Dutch divided between the outer Waddenzee and the inland Ijsselmeer.

The Dutch capital began as a tiny fishing village called *Amstelvedam* where the River Amstel met the IJ, a tidal section of the Zuidersee. To the minds of some, mostly those living far from the city, Amsterdam retains its village mentality through its essential closedness toward interlopers, even though the foreign population maintains the capital's cosmopolitan flavor.

The Dutch in general, and the country-folks in particular, have not forgiven the Amsterdam merchants, who placed profits before patriotism, for having supplied the Spanish forces during the Eighty Years War with Spain. For this, and for supporting Dunkirk privateers who preyed on other Dutch shippers, Amsterdammers remain forever damned.

Mooring at the adjacent docks, take a stroll along the notorious **Zeedijk** canals where drug addicts share the streets, and not infrequently their needles with the prostitutes. Tourists never cease to wonder at who scrubs and polishes the spotless windows behind which the scantily-clad ladies of the night, and often day, display their nubile wares. The fact is, with few exceptions, they do the scrubbing in between knitting and serving customers.

Not that this is all Amsterdam has to offer. The cultural life is vibrant and lively enough to rank it fourth after London, Paris and Rome as a European center of cultural excellence. The Dutch National Ballet and the Netherlands Dance Theater are worth leaving the barge to visit, as is the Concertgebouw Orchestra housed in the equally unpronounceable building of the same name. Despite the paucity of good Dutch theater, there is a wealth of farce from **English Speaking Theater of Amsterdam**, a long-established group of amateurs whose ability on stage fortunately matches their zeal for performing.

Painting is, of course, the Dutch forte,

The tray's empty after Alkmaar's market.

and the **Van Gogh collection**, housed in its own museum adjacent to the Amsterdam **Municipal Museum** on Paulus Potterstraat, boasts a fabulous variety of the master's works. More *avant garde* creations are to be found in the nearby **Stedlijk Museum** which, along with frequent exhibitions of local works, is home to several Mondriaans, Appels and Constants, whose freedom of expression and use of color inspire visitor and painter alike. For lovers of the traditional, the **Rijksmuseum** is a must; it has a superb collection of Rembrandts along with other Dutch *genre* painters. More of Rembrandt's work is in his home on Jodenbreestraat.

Learn about Holland's seafaring tradition at the **Maritime Museum** on Kattenburgerplein. The **Tobacco Museum** on Amstel details one of the Netherland's major imports from the East Indies. To see what a 19th-century shipyard might have looked like, visit the **'t Kromhout** on Hoge Kadijk.

Anne Frank's House on Prinengracht remembers the two years she and her family hid from the Nazis. The **Jewish History Museum** on Nieumarket offers further evidence of World War II atrocities. Climb the towers of **Westerkerk** (Prinsengracht) and **Old Church** (Oudekerksplein) for bird's-eye views of Amsterdam.

Drool over the gems at the **Amsterdam Diamond Center**. It is one of the leading gem markets in the world, an industry that began in the 16th century. Get tiddly at the **Brandy and Liqueur Tasting** at C.V. Winjnand Fockink on Pijlsteeg. This is not as easy: hands cannot be used while drinking. Amsterdam is also a city of **markets**; the Flea Market operates daily except Sunday on Waterlooplein; so does the Flower Market on Single. The Antiques, Stamps, and Rare Books Markets are open on irregular days; check locally.

Before returning to one's own barge, consider the tourist barge service which offers an Amsterdam dinner cruise by candlelight. It's worth the investment if for no other reason than it frees one from the worry of determining which bridges open and which do not.

A cheese-maker at work.

Tucking into the *pâté d'agneau avec crudités* is the tastiest way to view, in glass-enclosed comfort, the capital's 160 canals and 1,000 bridges, the sameness of which seems irrelevant after the second bottle of *Côtes du Rhônes*. This is how to view the squatter's haunts and the merchant's mansions where Amsterdam's regents once lived prosperous, secure lives. By night, the tall, gabled townhouses are transformed into a fairy-tale wonderland of twinkling lights reflected in the water. Night-time also helps one to forget the brackish green canal water which serves as a dumping ground for anything from refuse to unwanted bar guests.

Hard as it is to believe, the city rests on millions of piles; the town hall, now the **Royal Palace** of Amsterdam, rests on no less than 13,659 sturdy piles. (The Dutch count everything from their monuments and money to the seemingly countless dog droppings which litter the capital's streets.)

The city's restaurants reflect the great gastronomic legacy from the Nether-

lands' former colonies. Indonesian or Indo-Chinese restaurants, where peanut butter is poured over meat with the relish reserved by Americans for ketsup, serve gluttonous portions of *rijsttafel*, or rice tables, which provide fuel for the most ravenous of bargees.

From Amsterdam, head southwest for the Bishop's city of **Utrecht**, taking the 45 miles (72 km) Amsterdam-Rhine Canal which connects Amsterdam to the River Rhine. Built a decade ago to compensate for the decline of Amsterdam following the loss of Dutch colonial trade, the canal, which restored much north European commerce, involved the enlargement of the existing Merwede Canal between Amsterdam and Utrecht and the construction of a new canal from the Merwede at Utrecht to the River Waal at Tiel, with a branch to the Lower Rhine at Vreeswijk.

Reducing by 25 miles (40 km) the shipping route to Germany, the canal opened up the Rhine hinterland to waterway traffic. You should not be surprised, therefore, to see pusher barge convoys making their way to the German border.

Pause at Utrecht, the religious and scholarly center of the Netherlands where medieval churches, abbeys and university buildings provide uplift of a kind quite different to that in Amsterdam. Utrecht began as a Roman fort called Trajectum ad Rhenum, guarding a ford over the Old Rhine. Still surrounded by a moat with two narrow canals (the Oude and Nieuwe Gracht) floating through it, the city was home to St Willibroad, the English monk responsible for converting many Dutch to Christianity.

Equestrian statues of the Saint, which pop up in the most unlikely of places throughout the city, provide appropriate setting for the endless chiming of the 50-bell carillon, the country's largest, housed in the aptly named **Dom Tower**. A 364-ft (112-meter) tribute to Gothic architecture, the tower dominates the city physically now as it did religiously before. Topped by a weather vane representing St Martin cutting off part of

An evening "Roundvaarten" cruise in Amsterdam.

his coat to warm a beggar, the Dom is as entwined in Utrecht's history as it is in the city's architecture.

The **Cathedral of St Michael** to which the Dom is attached, was begun in 1254 and finished in 1517, and is on the site where the Romanesque St Martin Church once stood. Unfortunately, a fire in 1674 destroyed all but the choir and transept of the original Cathedral.

The **Cloisters** link the Cathedral to the University, and the **Museum of Gold**, **Silver and Clocks** is next door. The **Central Museum** displays a superb collection of Dutch ecclesiatical art. The history of Christianity in Holland is presented at **Het Catharijne-convent**. Utrecht's wealth of churches and cloisters attracted merchant wealth in the Middle Ages when the canals, with quiet quayside cellars, sometimes extending deep under the houses, were built. As the level of the surrounding land rose with soil and waste, quays appeared which, when linked, formed new streets, resulting in the phenomenon, unique to Europe of two-level streets. Strolling along the lower quayside level is reminiscent of Venice, but for the distinctly un-Italian waiters who are quicker at billing than service.

Following the war, Utrecht's 19th-century innards appeared obsolete to the ever-modernizing Dutch. The railway station was integrated into a new city plan incorporating the enormous **Hoog Catharijne** shopping center, a glass and concrete complex of 200 brightly-lit shops.

Leaving Utrecht, continue along the Amsterdam-Rhine Canal until the complex lock system at Tiel where the canal meets the River Waal, a branch of the Rhine flowing through fertile lowlands lying in the protective shadow of dikes. The rich past of this province, **Gelderland**, for centuries an autonomous duchy, can be seen in the small historical towns and imposing castles lining the riverbanks.

During the Ice Age, glaciers forced their way from the North Pole as far as Gelderland. The ice-cap, hundreds of feet thick and constantly moving, forced

Reflected houses in the Prinzen-kanaal.

back the earth to form hills. When the ice melted, the water formed deep valleys. To the south of these, in a wide valley, the rivers wound their way inexorably toward the North Sea.

Just over 10 miles (16 km) from here, in September 1944, Gelderland became involved in one of the most significant military operations of the war: Operation Market Garden. American and Canadian troops reached this area from Belgium and, within a few days, secured the bridge of the River Waal. To seize another bridge, further up, over the Rhine, a ten-thousand strong British airborne group landed on the moorlands near **Arnhem**. The operation failed and, after a week, just 3,000 survivors limped in retreat over the Rhine (the incident was recounted in the film *A Bridge Too Far*).

Coninuing along the lush banks of the Waal, one soon arrives at **Nijmegen**, the country's oldest city, granted city rights 1,900 years ago by the Roman emperor, Trajan. Discoveries unearthed from Roman times are so numerous that the **Rijksmuseum Kam** was founded

to house them. But the multi-cultural influences on Nijmegen go further than that. In the Middle Ages when it belonged to the Franconian empire, Emperor Charlemagne had a palace built built on the Valkof which was later destroyed by the Normans. The many imposing medieval buildings that remain bear witness to the city's former wealth and power.

Built on seven hills and providing panoramic views across the River Waal, Nijmegen gives the impression of a cheerful and colorful city, one more in keeping with the *bonhomie* of the Catholic South than the stern asceticism of the Calvinist North.

The **Grote Markt** marks the city's center; the 1612-built **Waag** was the Municipal Weighing House, today it's only opened for exhibits. Buried in the tomb of nearby **St Stevenskerk** is Catherine of Bourbon. **The Municipal Museum** is in the Commnderie van St Jean.

Walk to the **Valkhof**; once a fortress originally built in 786; Henry VI, the son of Frederick Barbarossa and Bea-

A lock on the Waal near Nijmegen.

trix of Burgundy was born in it in 1165. The **Carolingian Chapel**, consecrated by Leo III in 799, is all that remains of the once vast complex. The **Belvedere**, a 16th-century tower, offers views of the city while dining in its restaurant.

Several smaller old towns are within easy reach of Nijmegen. For example, there is **Zaltbommel** where the composer Franz List, once drawn by the tones of the carillon, ventured on land to meet the carillon player's daughter who also happened to be a gifted pianist. List arranged for the girl to study in Paris where she met the Impressionist painter Edouard Monet, whom she later married in the Zaltbommel City Hall.

Karl Marx, the revolutionary historian, is also reputed to have stayed in Zaltbommel as guest of relatives when he wrote his seminal work analyzing the downfall of capitalism, *Das Kapital*. Sometime after he left, it was the turn of the Philips brothers to seek inspiration of an altogether different sort. Their work on the design of the first electric light bulbs laid the foundation for to-day's giant electronics multinationals.

The town of **Buren**, a few miles away, is quite different in character. Its crumbling town walls and gates mirrors its appearance in the Middle Ages. Look out for the **Royal Orphanage**, a revealing sign of the times, and the enchanting mill, one of whose walls bears the name of the Prince of Orange who once reigned supreme.

Leaving Nijmegen, follow the River Maas (Meuse) which meanders south through the Netherlands' hilliest province of **Limburg**. Flowing through rolling green hills, on which are perched a surprising number of castles and manor houses for a nation that claims to be non-Royalist, the Maas connects with the **Julianacanal** that takes one direct to Holland's southern-most city, **Maastricht**, known as the Paris of the Benelux for its charm and elegance.

Founded in the dawn of Christianity by Roman legions in search of a place to bridge the river, the city's fortifications, churches, châteaux, canals and refineries trace its long march of progress from

Along the Oudegracht Canal in Utrecht.

its belligerent emergence in the 11th century as a vital buffer state to the 19th century when Maastricht led the country into the Industrial Revolution. Ironically now, however, the area has one of the highest unemployment rates, due in part to the closure about 20 years ago of the Limburg coalmines.

Like Utrecht, Maastricht, dates from its time as an Episcopal residence. Two remarkably preserved Romanesque churches, **St Servaas** and **Onze Lieve Vrouw**, along with 1,400 cultural monuments, remind us that it was here that pilgrims used to flock, as indeed they continue to do every seven years when the gilt-copper chest containing the bones of St Severaas is carried aloft through the city center.

South of Onze Lieve Vrouw, the 750-year old **Helpoort**, the country's oldest surviving town gate, leads out to part of the old market ramparts. North of the wall, a labyrinth of narrow, winding streets, with cobble-bricks instead of stones, heads toward the **Vrijthof Square**, shielded from the midday sun by the shadow of St Servaas.

Not surprisingly, considering its location at the junction of the Dutch, German and Belgian borders, Maastricht is a popular holiday district with the Dutch who dash south in relief from the zealots up north. This is in spite of the love-hate relationships between the Belgians, which is what the southern Dutch basically are, and their northern neighbors whose king, William, decreed in the distant past that French should be replaced by Dutch as the official language of northern Belgium.

William's autocratic rule encouraged the incipient Belgium nationalism, which can still be felt in Maastricht now. And in 1828, this brought the Belgium Liberals and Catholics together in an official union of opposition. Two years later, in August 1830, the Belgium Revolution broke out. But that is another story, providing sufficient food for thought as the barge chugs on across the border.

Right, windmills are a distinctive part of the Dutch landscape.

A DUTCH CIRCLE

Before leaving Holland however, consider a run around the **Randstad**. Just 45 miles (72 km) long and 40 miles (64 km) at its widest point, the Randstad is a horseshoe-shaped chain of towns containing only a tenth of the Dutch land mass, yet almost half its population, and most of its major cities and historic sites. The region is also perfect for marine sightseeing since all the cities are connected by Holland's vast waterway network.

The **Amstel-Drechtkanaal** leads south from the capital. The towns pass quickly: Ouderkerk, Uithorn and the first lock where Kromme Mijdrecht enters on the left. The Drecht Kanaal flows off right, the Aarkanaal continues straight ahead. Beyond Papenveer, the Leidsch Vaart is the waterway to the right, and when the Oude Rijn bisects the canal, the Aar is left behind and the Gouwe takes over. All this may seem confusing with so many short waterways within the larger one, but directional signs are frequent.

Which came first, the town or the apple? **Boskoop** is a tasty Dutch version; in the town are acres of nurseries specializing in flowering shrubs and trees. Spring brings a pastel rainbow.

Gouda sits at the confluence of the Gouwe and IJssel rivers. Granted a charter by Count Floris V in the 13th century, the market town perches in the middle of a large fertile *polder*, and is best known for its cheese, *Gouda Kas* which can weigh up to 22 pounds (10 kg); the **Cheese Market** is a summer attraction each Thursday at the Weighing-House which was built by Pieter Post in 1668.

Clay pipes are another famous Gouda product and **Pijpenmuseum de Moriaan** is filled with hundreds.

The once-moated Gothic **Town Hall** is the oldest in Holland. Its Renaissance tower dates from 1603; the astronomical clock has moving figures chiming the hour with the obligatory carillon.

St Janskerk is near **Markt Square**;

at 377 ft (115 meters) long and 148 ft (45 meters) wide, it's the largest church in Holland. Inside, the stained-glass windows display a wide variety of artistic styles. An old hospital dispensary is an exhibit at the **Municipal Museum**.

From Gouda, **Rotterdam** offers two routes: long and easy, or short and difficult. The former runs along the Rotte River, it finally curls into the north side of Rotterdam. A direct link with the Delftsche Schie to Delft eliminates any need for a small boat to thread its way through Europe's largest port. Latterly, if "challange" is your middle name, the more direct IJssel to the tidal Niewue Maas leads to an adventure among boats that dwarf.

Whatever the previous choice, a cruise around Rotterdam's **harbor** is a must. Consider, however, joining an **Haven-rondvaarten**, and letting its captain do the driving; frequent departures leave from the dock at **Willensplein**. (A statue here, **De Boeg**, stands as a monument to Dutch seamen who perished during both world wars.)

Left, a Dutch treat: bicycles and steep-pitched roofs. **Right**, a canal in Delft.

Construction of the purpose-built **Europort** in 1966 made it the largest in the world in respect of volume of goods handled. Consider the statistics: over 500 tugs nudge a daily average of 600 ships of all sizes to or from the 375 miles (600 km) of available mooring space. About 450 dock and container cranes handle in excess of 616 million tons (280 million metric tons) of cargo annually using 15 roll-on/roll-off ramps and 87 oil ramps. Tank storage capacity tops 1,130 million cubic ft (32 million cubic meters), and 250 miles (400 km) of railroad tracks carry the cargo away. If a ship needs repair, there are 35 floating and dry docks to do the job. If one needs building, this is the largest yard on the Continent.

To service the port and its attendent industries, almost 200,000 people work directly in the port including a third of all Dutch customs officers.

Although a modern looking city, Rotterdam's history is medieval. (That look is a result of the Allies' 1940 bombing which devastated the city; Ossip Zadline's 1953 rememberance of that is his massive **Monument for a Destroyed City** on the **Blaak**.) In the 13th century, the River Rotte was dammed where it joined the Maas, hence the city's name.

A fire in 1585 destroyed most of Rotterdam; before rebuilding was completed, the city was inundated with waves of refugees from the Spanish Netherlands (Belgium). A port since the early 1600s, Rotterdam was never considered an important one until the 1830-closing of the Schelde Estuary began an upturn in the city's fortune. In 1866 the Maas was dredged and deepened, and in 1872 when the Nieuwe Waterweg was constructed, the city began its period of spectacular growth.

Most sightseeing is within walking distance of the **Euromast**. For an eagle's-eye view, take an elevator to the top. There's a small (30 person capacity) viewing platform at 600 ft (184 meters), but more space and restaurants are at the 340 ft (104 meters) level. On the ground, the **Park** offers a green interlude and numerous cafés along the

Left, an 18th-century canal barge figurehead.

The Randstad Cities

Parkkade give rest to the feet and views of the river.

Pride of the city is **Museum Boymans-Van Beunin** and its collection of Dutch *genre* paintings. The **Museum of Geography and Ethnography** is at the end of Willemskade, and the **Taxation Museum** isn't as boring as it might sound; tools of the smuggler's trade show the lengths people will go to avoid paying taxes.

Navigation buffs should visit **Prins Hendrik Maritime Museum**. Next to it is the oldest surviving ship of the Royal Dutch Navy; the **Museum Ship Buffel** displays many examples of shipbuilding, and that craft's history.

Nearby is newly-restored **Delfshaven**, built in the 15th century to serve as port for the then very important Delft. After the pilgrims left England due to religous persecution, they lived here before their 1620 voyage to the New World; look for a bronze tablet in the **Oude Kerk** commemorating that journey. The **Museum of Local History** is on Voorhaven; the House of the Grain Carriers sits on Voorstraat and holds the **Museum of Pewter**.

Less than 7 miles (11 km) west along the waterway from the Euromast is **Schiedam**, once the greatest gin producing city in Europe. It's still producing, but only 50 of the 300 distilleries remain. Dutch gin is called *genever*, and the seven years it ages in peat-buried vats give it its distinctive bite; Bols and Melchers are the best-known makers (visits possible); and the **Museum of Wine and Spirits** is a must.

Quiet and serene **Delft** comes as welcome relief, and it's hard to believe it once dwarfed Rotterdam in importance. A small city of tree-lined canals, picturesque bridges and houses, carpet making and brewing gave the city prosperity long before the distinctive blue and white pottery made it famous. Granted a charter in the 13th century, the construction of Delfshaven in the 15th enabled the city to compete with other towns for shipping trade. Porcelain production started in the 17th century, and is still a leading export.

Rotterdam harbor from the TV Tower.

The **Oostpoort** may be the mariner's first view of Delft. Built in the 14th century, it's the city's only remaining Medieval city gate. Another landmark is the 354-ft (108-meter) high tower of **Nieuwe Kerk** (great views from it, and the carillon plays on Tuesday, Thursday and Saturday mornings). Begun in the late 1390s, construction was completed a hundred years later. The Baroque tomb of William the Silent is an artistic masterpiece. Also entombed here are 41 members of the House of Orange, including Queen Wilhelmina, grandmother of Beatrix, Holland's present monarch.

At the opposite end of the **Markt** is the **Town Hall** which dates from 1620. The **Flower Market**, held every Thursday, is a short walk away on Hippolytusbuurt, near the **Oude Kerk**. In the leaning tower of that 13th-century building, a bell, cast in 1570, hangs. Its circumference is 23 ft (7 meters), it weighs almost 20,000 pounds (9,000 kgs), and was last rung at Queen Wilhelmina's funeral in 1962. Inside the wooden-vaulted church are the tombs of several military heroes, and on the streets nearby are old houses.

The **Prinsenhof** was for many years home to the House of Orange; in 1584, William I was murdered in front of it by a Catholic extremist and mementos from the Eighty Years War with Spain form one section of the museum. In one part of the building which was originally the Monastery of St Agatha, look for the double-galleried ambulatory, the only one in Holland. Jan Vermeer is the city's most famous son, and **Museum Paul Tétar van Elven**, displays, among other things, a 17th-century artist's studio like one in which the artist would have worked.

No visit to Delft would be complete without a visit to a pottery firm. Several offer tours; the most famous is **De Porceleyne Fles**. The **Museum Huis Lambert van Meerton** houses a superb collection of pottery as well as other applied arts. Those wanting a true Delftware souvenir should note the trademark before parting with money;

Walking
through
Madurodam.

many imitations abound in the city's shops.

The Hague seems only several revolutions of the boat's propeller from Delft. In actual fact, the run is a little over 6 miles (10 km). Seat of the Dutch Parliament and home to foreign embassies, but not the country's capital, confusion sometimes also arises over its name. The Dutch have two for it; *Den Haag* or "The Hedge" came first, and somehow evolved into *Gravenhage*, meaning "Count's Hedge."

As befits its status, The Hague is a neat and orderly city with a network of small canals cutting through attractive parks. An obscure backwater until the then King of Holland, Louis Bonaparte, granted its charter in the late 18th century, Louis took as he gave: removing his residence to Amsterdam also removing the city's newly-found status.

The **Binnenhof** (tours possible) forms the core of the Old Town; the original building was a castle built by Count William II of Holland in 1250. Now, it is venue for both houses of the Dutch Parliament. A statue of the same William graces the plaza in front of the **Buitenhop**, and the **Gevangenpoort Museum** contains a gruesome collection of medieval torture instruments. The **Museum of Costumes** also has a collection of furniture, and the buildings are reflected in the **Vijiver**, an ornamental lake.

The **Picture Gallery** and its superb collection of 17th-century Dutch masters is in the **Mauritshuis**, designed by Pieter Post between 1630 and 1640.

The **Old Town Hall** is 16th-century with later additions. **Grote Kerk** is across the square from it; note the finely vaulted ceiling and carved pulpit. The 315-ft (96-meter) tower is open in July and August.

Slightly away from the confines of the Old Town, **Spinoza's House** is on Paviloensgracht, and at the end of the street is a statue of the philosopher who lived in The Hague from 1671 until he died six years later (look for his tomb in **Nieuwe Kerk**).

Further outside the center is the **Vre-**

Courtyard fountain of the Binnehof.

despalais (Peace Palace) which houses the International Court of Justice. Tours available; note especially the Great Hall of Justice. On one side of **Scheveningse Bosjes**, a few miles from The Hague, is **Madurodam**. A miniature reproduction of all things Dutch, the football-sized park is a delight for children.

The university town of **Leiden** is another 7 miles (12 km) and four locks up the waterway. Upon arrival, the Oude Rijn divides and several tributaries twist through the city, making for enjoyable waterborne sightseeing. Best overnight docking is in **De Haven** (harbor) near **Zijlpoort**, a former city gate.

Afoot, the streets form a labyrinth in which the unwary can soon get lost. To get a bearing, climb the ramparts of the **Burcht**, an old fort located at the confluence of the Oude and Nieuwe Rijns. From the top, all of Leiden is visible.

The **University** was a gift in 1575 from King William (the Silent) who was impressed by the locals' fortitude during the Spanish seige of the city between 1573–74. But the city was founded long before the university: its charter was granted in 1266, and by the 14th century was known for the quality of its woven products. This city of intelectuals did not forget those less well-off, and a series of *Hofjes* (Almshouses) were built. Today, these 16th and 17th-century buildings fill a variety of roles including student dormitories. One of the largest, 1681-built **Meermansburg**, is open; note the portraits in its **Regents' Room**.

The 16th-century **Town Hall** was devastated by a 1929 fire, and only its facade has been restored. The **Blue Stone** marked the site of two important municipal responsibilities: the execution of criminals, and the burning of inferior cloth so it could not be sold.

The **Museum De Lakenhal**, once the Clothmakers' Guild Hall, serves up a collection of fine art (local boys Rembrandt and Jan Steen, among others), period rooms and applied arts. **Rijksmuseum Boerhaave** goes scientific with historic instruments of the applied sciences. **The Museum of Clay Pipes**

A quiet waterway.

has uncountable numbers of them; rock enthusiasts should wander through **Rijksmuseum van Geologie**.

The **Museum of Ethnography**, specializing in Indonesian artifacts, is near the 1700-built **Morspoort**, another of Leiden's fortress gates.

Americans will want to head for the **Pilgrim Fathers Documentation Center**. Many of those fleeing persecution in England stayed in Leiden before sailing to America. Their spiritual father, John Robinson, lived on Kloksteeg from 1611 to 1625. His tomb is in **Pieterskerk**, and a plaque on the wall recalls the 1620 *Mayflower* voyage.

Rembrandt was born near the university in the **Weddelsteeg** (his studio was on Muskadelsteeg), and a bronze bust of him is on **Witte Single**. Also in the vicinity is the **Botanical Garden**; founded in the 1587, it's one of the oldest in Europe.

Before sailing onward, consider two short side-trips. One is a five mile (nine km) trip west on the Oude Rijn toward the sea. It brings the resort of **Katwijk**, miles of dunes, and the **European Space Center** (visits possible).

The other journey is longer, a triangle that sails through some of the oldest Dutch canal architecture. Cruise the Oude Rijn eastward until the Heimenswetering; left on that brings a T-Junction with the Does River which returns to Leiden. In **Koudererk**, see the windmill where Rembrandt's father lived. Visit **Alphen a/d Rijn's Avifuauna Bird Sanctuary**.

Travelling to Amsterdam, two routes beckon: the more direct cuts diagonally across the Haarlemmermeer Polder on the northeastern branch of the Ringvaart. It passes through **Alsmeer** which has the largest **flower market** in the world. Morning tours are available; one fascinating part is the **Auction Room** where, in contrast to most sales, bidding starts high and continues downward. A form of Blind Man's Bluff, the trick is to figure out how low the price will go before another buys.

Heading north, in springtime, color blazes from both sides of the waterway as the canal cuts a path through the heart

Flowers are shipped from the Alsmeer Market by the jumbo jet load.

of tulip growing country. During those weeks in April and May, first port of call is **Lisse**; from there the famed **Keukenhof Garden** is half a mile away. Within the 70-acre (28-hectare) park over 700 varieties of tulips are grown in magnificently landscaped grounds.

Back on the canal, **Bennebroek** offers flower lovers **Linnaeushof Garden**. For a better understanding of how the Dutch reclaimed land from the sea, the **Cruquius Museum** is devoted to the history of *polder* making. The round building was an 1840s pumping station that helped to drain the land, and its 12-ft (three-meter) diameter steam engine is the largest ever made.

Lying on the Spaarne River, and surrounded by a series of canals, **Haarlem** got its name from the German *harulahem,* or settlement. Famous for the growing of tulip bulbs, the city became infamous in 1573 when, during the Eighty Years War, all of its Protestant citizens, the clergy and the army were put to death by the victorious Spanish.

Radiating from **Grote Markte** are

ten streets which form the **Old Town's** core. A statue in the square is of I.J. Costner, Gutenberg's contemporary, whom the Dutch credit with inventing printing. The tower of the 15th-century **Grote Kerk** rises 262 ft (80 meters) into the sky. More outstanding than the interior is the church's organ. Designed by C. Muller in the 1730s, it has 5,000 pipes, 68 stops and three manuals. Mozart played on it, and concerts are regular events today. Look also for the tomb of Frans Hals, and admire the early 16th-century choir screen.

The 1598-built **Waag**, or Weighing House, remembers the days when bulk goods were weighed and taxed before being sold to the public in smaller lots. Next to it is **Teyler's Museum**, founded by a wealthy cloth manufacturer who bequeathed the funds to start the Netherland's first museum. Opened in the 1780s, its collection is eclectic: paintings, drawings, scientific instruments, geological specimens.

From the **Gravenstenenbrug**, a picturesque lifting bridge, enjoy views of boats on the river and gabled houses lining the banks. Frans Hals is also celebrated at his name **museum**; the building was once a male hospice, now it showcases the artist who died in 1666.

Zandvoort, a few miles drive west of Haarlem, is on the North Sea, and site of the annual Dutch Formula 1 Grand Prix auto race. From here, make excursions into **De Kennemer Duinen**, a national park that seeks to preserve the sand dunes from erosion. Ride the elevator to the top of the 197-ft (60-meter) **Observation Tower** to see all.

Spaardam, halfway between Haarlem and the Nord Kanaal, is where the legendary little boy supposedly stuck his finger into the dike, and saved Holland from inundation. A statue identified as Hans Brinker says he did it, but Americans may find this confusing. Their Hans Brinker was connected with a story about silver skates. Never mind. The green and white gabled houses are pretty, the statue is cute, and Amsterdam is, almost, around the corner. The Nord Kanaal awaits just up the road, a right turn, a few more miles, *et voilà.*

Left, tulips under cultivation. Right, a model poses at Keukenhof Gardens.

258

FRIESLAND

Cruising through Friesland, one could be forgiven for feeling it's not part of Holland. The province has its own language and literature, and its people feel distinctly separate and superior to those who live in the southern climes of the country. This is the land of Holland's earliest settlers, of those who fought and conquered the sea, and who, through the centuries, have retained their own sense of identity.

One regional proverb seems to sum up the Frisian character: "With five weapons shall we keep our land, with sword and with shield, with spade and with fork and with the spear. Out with the ebb, up with the flood, to fight day and night against the North-king and against the wild Viking, that all Frisians may be free, the born and the unborn, so long as the wind from the clouds shall blow and the world shall stand."

When the Romans arrived in the 1st century, the area had been populated for several centuries by a race whose origin is lost to history. In their retention of customs and language (even the road signs are in both Dutch and Frisian), the Frisians resemble the Scots and Celts, but in coloring, the Swedes immediately come to mind.

Friesland was never regarded as a hospitable place. The Greeks called it the "land of eternal fog." From the beginning, the Frisians continually fought with equal fervor both the North Sea and their human enemies; until both were subdued, not much else mattered. With the formation of dikes, and stable living conditions, trade links were formed and several cities joined the Hanseatic League.

At one point, Friesland stretched from what is now northern Germany westward to today's North Holland province. The formation of the Zuiderzee and the breakup of land into small islands meant the decline of Frisian power. Yet even during Spanish dominance and the Eighty Years War with them, the Frieslanders remained staunchly themselves, fiercely Protestant, the majority severe Calvinists.

Towns were traditionally built on *terps*, high mounds that were safe from the ever-encroaching sea. That self-defensive measure is no longer needed; dikes are everywhere, acting as sea walls, surrounding towns and fields. Some form canal walls, raising the water so that a boat floats 10 ft (3 meters) above the ground around it.

Architecturally, traditional gabled townhouses contrast with Frisian farmhouses and their pyramid-shaped roofs. Town Halls and churches are five and six centuries old; several cities have watergates equally ancient. The church belfries are particular to this region; called *Klokkenstoelen*, they were built of wood at a time when cost prohibited anyone building anything higher, and of any other materials.

Geographically, the province is divided into two parts; along the Waddenzee, rolling dunes stand in front of reclaimed land which can be marshy and lake-like. Farming is popular here: sugar

Left, Hindeloopen painted furniture is mostly found in museums. Right, how to eat herring.

beet, potatoes, grain and flax the primary crops. Always a favorite with sailors because of the lakes, the rise in popularity of flat-bottom boating has brought an influx of tourists.

Inland, treeless pastureland feeds the cattle that produce most of Holland's dairy and meat products. The distinctive black and white Frisian cattle were first bred here as were the black horses, and herds of both can be spotted from a boat. In the southeast, some forestation exists, but that land is in the minority.

Friesland is bisected with hundreds of small canals and lakes making it difficult to plan a point-to-point journey, but giving the freedom to take a right or left as the mood or sightseeing inclines. For holiday makers, the region is a delight; locks are few, facilities many. Bridges are generally high enough to allow a small boat to pass through without the delay of opening it, and keepers are usually willing to lend the novice a hand. When the navigation passes through a large lake, marker bouys point the way.

As a rule, moorings run by a city operate on a fee-paying basis; the larger the boat, the more it costs, but all have fuel and water points. If a totally rural overnight is desired, it's always possible to anchor outside town.

Sneek, located in the middle of the Frisian lake district, is the province's largest boating center although not its capital. All facets of boating are possible here from renting to chandlering to joining in the conviviality that every yacht harbor brings.

The twin-towered **Watergate**, built in 1613, is the sailor's first view of Sneek; it's also the last of three gates that once guarded the city. The 15th-century **Town Hall** is noted for its richly ornate rococo facade.

The **Martinkerk**, also 16th-century, has a sacristy 100 years younger. The **Museum of Navigation and Antiquity** boasts a series of model ships and other marine objects.

Forming a wedge spreading south from Sneek, the Frisian *meers* (lakes) offer untold hours of unfettered cruising. Slotermeer, Fluessen, Koevorder-

Herring nets hanging out to dry.

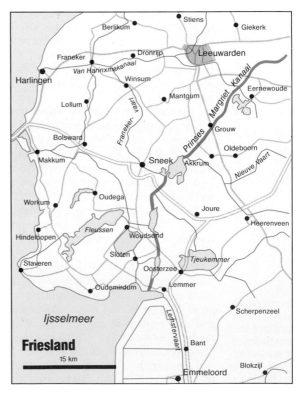

meer and Tjeukemeer are some of the biggest, but many, many others can be explored. Closest is **Sneekermeer** which, despite many facilities for water sports, has an abundant wildlife and bird population. The **Prinses Margriet Kanaal** runs northeast from here towards **Groningen**, and an exploration of that province.

Woudsend is on the route to **Slotermeer**, first of many old villages. **Sloten**, just off the lake, whose old town was created in the traditional Frisian star design. It's a charming place of well-kept houses and an enormous windmill.

Lemmer is the last (or the first) boating center in Friesland and can be reached through **Groote Breken**. Locks at this point allow passage from the canals into the IJsselmeer. The pumping station works effectively at keeping the *polder* dry; a fantastic 360,000 gallons (1,550,000 liters) of water goes through it in a minute.

Friesland is rich in sandy beaches.

Heeg sits at the northern end of Fleussen, largest of the *meers*; water sport facilities abound around its shores, and a canal at the south end leads to the best-missed port of Staveren.

Hindeloopen perches on a peninsula jutting into the IJsselmeer. Once a major Zuiderzee port, the town became a member of the Hanseatic League in the 14th century. Its sea locks protect old houses, wooden bridges, and a town of unique charm. The Swedish-inspired painted furniture made famous by the town is today mostly found in museums (many examples are in the **Netherland Open Air Museum** near **Arnhem**). Two museums here are worth a visit: **Hidde Nijland** displaying local antiquities and costumes in the Old Weigh House, and the **Lifeboat Museum** in an old lifeboat house.

Further north and inland **Workum** is an historic supplier of eels to discriminating palates, and is also known for its pottery. The center is especially attractive with its 17th-century **Waag** and 18th-century Town Hall; photograph also the many-gabled houses. At **De Hoop**, an old shipbuilding yard, watch the workmen build and restore boats using old-fashioned tools.

The detached tower of **St Gertrud-iskerk** was never finished, but its organ, installed in 1697 is one of Friesland's oldest. Note especially the hand-carved biers. Every guild made one on which its members could be carried to their final resting place. Each bier was painted in the colors of the guild and the emblem of the trade (doctor, shipbuilder, farmer, blacksmith, etc), plus appropriate quotations from the Psalms were carved on the sides. The exception to this colorful send-off was for suicide cases; their biers were painted a somber black.

On the coast due north lies **Makkum** (the most direct route goes through Gaast) within sight of the giant sea locks on the **Afsluitdijk**. The villagers do constant battle with Delft for supremacy in making the prettiest pottery. To watch the blue-and-white china under production, visit the 325-year-old **Royal Markkumer Potteries**; the town's Waag is a showcase for the very desirable product.

Within the area of the three previously mentioned towns lies a well sign

posted trail (bicycles necessary) called *Aldfaers Erf Route*, loosely translated as "The Heritage of Our Forefathers." Houses, farms, craft and workshops have been carefully restored and manned to show the modern visitor how the Frisians once lived. Among those towns on the trail are Exmorra, Ferwoude, Allingweir and Piaam.

Bolsward is less than a two hour cruise east of Makkum (via the Geeuw and Wijmerts Canals). A member of the Hanseatic League, the city's Renaissance **Town Hall** has been called one of the most beautiful in Friesland. The 15th-century **Martinkerk** has elaborately carved choir stalls and a pulpit created in the 1660s.

Harlinger sits about 12 miles (20 km) along its name canal from Bolsward. Once a major port for shipments to and from the East Indies, rows of old warehouses line the docks in memory. Its historic **Old Town** is preserved as a national monument; a city also of many fine houses, some of the best are on **Kliene Bredeplaats**.

The **Municipal Museum** has a collection of tiles, maps, silver and model ships. One place for a quiet walk is through the **English Gardens**. Planned and planted in the 18th century, they're atop the ramparts.

Franeker is a short, about five miles (eight km), cruise eastward on the Van Harinxma Kanaal. Astronomy enthusiasts will appreciate the perseverance of one Eise Eiseinga. He was a local wool merchant who had a passion for astronomy. Lacking any university or school facilities, he built his own **planetarium**. His home is open for visits; notice the attic machinery. The **Town Hall**, built in the 1590s is one of the province's oldest. Another lovely house is **Martinhuis**, built in the late 1490s.

The Coopmanhuis, now the **City Museum**, is actually two houses, one constructed in 1662, the other 80 years later. The exhibit concerns the years when the town had a leading university. (Napoleon burnt it in 1811.)

Travelling another 9 miles (15 km) straight east brings Friesland's capital, **Leeuwarden**. Located at the conflu-

Frisian pottery set for tea.

ence of the Ee and Vlie Rivers, Leeuwarden is the result of combining three *terps* in the 1430s. The enclosing of the Middelzee lost Leeuwarden its port, but the city recovered, becoming the region's commercial and agricultural hub. Still with the look of a fortified town, a canal rings the city, and several others wander through it. The **Old Town** is shaped like a star, a typical design of old Frisian towns.

Americans have special reason to enjoy Leeuwarden; it was here that the fledgling nation was first recognized in 1782. Look for a plaque in the **Provincial House** commemorating the event. Also on display is a letter from John Adams, dated in 1783, and sent from Paris, thanking Leeuwarden for helping the United States. American ties go even further: Peter Stuyvesant, founder of New York City, was born here under the name of Petrus Stuiffsandt.

Another local, Mata Hari, World War I's infamous spy arrived in 1876. Her statue stands near the house where she was born; it's now the **Frisian Literary Museum**. Resistance members of World War II are remembered with a monument on the rampart.

The **Frisian Museum**, with exhibits pertaining to local culture, has one of the best provincial collections in Holland. Two sections in it beckon: the Popta silver and the Hindeloopen furniture. Across from the museum sits the privately-owned 16th-century Kanselarij, once a court building. Another must is the **Princessehof** and its ceramic exhibition.

The Gothic **Oldehove** was supposed to be much taller. Unfortunately during its construction (1529–32) land subsidence showed up (or down), and the very-leaning tower was stopped at 130 ft (40 meters). The **Waag** was a project of 1598, and like **Over de Kelders Utrecth**, has double-decker streets.

Do not miss the huge statue of a Frisian cow called *Us Mem* (Our Mother) on Zuiderplein. Funny though it seems to tourists, the cow, a mainstay of the Frisian economy, is treated seriously and with due honor.

A canal near Sneek.

Whether puttering down the Thames in a cabin cruiser or luxury hotel barge, squeezing through the barely-passable width of a Midlands canal in a highly decorated, classic "narrowboat", exploring Scotland's Caledonian Canal or the Norfolk Broads aboard a sailing vessel, the waterways of England, Scotland and Wales offer a glimpse into their historic past and vibrant future.

England, wrinkled with rivers and canals to the seas which surround it, lures the traveler with journeys into its history as well as its countryside. On the English canals, the boater can also trace the birth of the Industrial Revolution.

Along the rivers lie the ancient lawns of Oxford and Cambridge. The Royal River, the Thames, gives its voyagers a panorama of regal history: William the Conqueror's Tower of London; Henry VIII's Hampton Court; and Windsor Castle, in residential and ceremonial use by today's Queen Elizabeth II.

But the splendors of Britain's navigable waterways are not confined to the regal. On those waters, the traveler passes parks and meadows, island pubs, and waterside plant and animal life to enchant the quiet viewer.

Great Britain's waterways are easy to explore. Those who seek a casual or occasional cruise will find many passenger boats from which to choose. For the charterer, there are scores of vessels available – punts, powerboats, canal boats and sailboats.

And what of your companions on these waterways? Loners, couples, families – all are afloat in Britain. The pace is yours to set, as is the atmosphere: picnics and parties; slow meandering or measured sightseeing. Just select your pleasure.

Preceding pages: Ellesmere Port, where large ships meet small barges; sculling on the River Thames. **Left**, autumn on the Grand Union Canal.

SOUTHEAST ENGLAND

Since Adam first bit the apple, an undercurrent of scandal has flowed beneath the tranquil waters of the **River Thames**. King Henry VIII frequently slipped by boat between Westminster, Hampton Court and Windsor, to conduct his clandestine, extra-marital affairs. In the 18th century the infamous Hellfire Club met in secret, at Medmenham Abbey near High Wycombe. To add spice to their orgies, young virgins, disguised as nuns, were smuggled in by boat to avoid arousing suspicion.

Naked bathing parties at Spring Cottage on the Thames, at Cliveden, brought infamy in 1963 to Christine Keeler, Mandy Rice Davies and the Minister of War, John Profumo, and ultimately led to Profumo's resignation from the Cabinet and a weakening of the Conservative government. (The 1989 movie *Scandal* was based on the events.)

For nonseekers of the infamous, the Thames carves a broad, friendly highway through southern Britain, opening up a picture book of English history, architecture, and culture. Even under leaden, rain filled skies or carpeted in early morning mist, the Thames exhibits its landscapes that have inspired such great artists as Turner and Whistler. Absorbing this rich diversity from a cruising boat, the visitor will quickly slow to the sedate pace of the river and succumb to the enchanting atmosphere of tranquility that exists so close to the bustle of major cities.

The navigable Thames stretches from Lechlade in Gloucestershire to Teddington Lock at the tideway; between the two lie 125 miles (200 km) and 44 locks, each administered by the Thames Water Authority. Below Teddington, where water levels are governed by tides, the river is controlled by the Port of London Authority, and rental craft are banned.

There are two reputed sources of the River Thames: **Thameshead** in Trewsbury Mead and **Seven Springs**, near Cheltenham, the acknowledged source of the Churn. Of these Thameshead, 3 miles (5 km) west of Cirencester in Gloucestershire lays the better claim. However, for most of the year the spring is not visible and in winter is little more than a bubbling brook. In contrast, Seven Springs and the Churn provide the embryo river, although the Churn is only a tributary of the Thames, which it joins at Cricklade.

From the old Roman town of **Cricklade**, the Thames, swelled by the tributaries of the Churn and the Ray, flows through the villages of **Castle Eaton** and **Kempsford** to **Inglesham**. At Inglesham, a round tower marks the junction with the disused Thames and Severn Canal, and also the upper limit for cruiser navigation.

Within a mile, the river reaches **Lechlade**, a quiet little town of wide streets and Cotswold stone buildings. The town is dominated by the graceful spire of the parish church of St Lawrence, inspiration for Shelley's meditation *Summer Evening*; the poet stayed here in 1815, after rowing up river from Windsor with friends.

Lechlade makes an ideal base for the

Left, family fun on a narrowboat. **Right**, a busy summer day on the Thames.

boater who wishes to explore the villages of the Cotswolds. For walkers, **Fairford**, an ancient market town on the river Coln is 4 miles (6 km) to the west. Here are many picturesque houses, an old mill on the river bank, and the overwhelming beauty of the 15th-century stained glass windows in the parish church. For those remaining in Lechlade, the town has several restaurants and good pubs.

Just below Lechlade the river runs down to **St John's Lock**, where the statue of **Old Father Thames** is found. Carved originally for the Crystal Palace, it was rescued from the burned-out ruins and placed at Thameshead. Years later it was moved to the present site.

Continuing below St John's bridge, the river passes the beer garden of the Trout Inn, a rightly famous 13th-century Cotswold stone pub whose interior boasts a collection of stuffed pike around its cosy, wood-panelled walls.

After a mile of meandering through lush meadows, **Buscott Lock** comes. For the river user, a stroll from the lock leads to **Buscott House** and **Park**. Built in 1780 in the Adam style, the house is set on high ground at the center of a landscaped park, with an Italianate water garden linking it to a large lake. Now administered by the National Trust, the house makes an ideal setting for the Farringdon collection.

After Buscott is a very rural stretch of river winding slowly through farmland. Here it is much easier for the boatman than the motorist to approach Kelmscott. Situated on the north bank, this tiny village is noted for **Kelmscott Manor**, the home of William Morris. Regarded as the father of the Arts and Crafts Movement, Morris lived at the manor until his death in 1896, and the house reflects his work as craftsman, artist, designer and printer, and with prior arrangement can be visited during the summer. Kelmscott is also known for the fine 16th-century pub, the **Plough Inn**, serving real ale, snacks and meals in its flagstone-floored bar.

The church at **Eaton Hastings**, provides interest on a quiet stretch of river

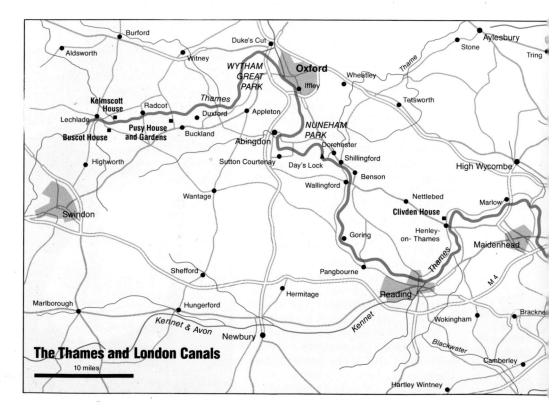

The Thames and London Canals

10 miles

before reaching **Grafton Lock**, another lonely outpost a further half mile beyond. Then follows four tranquil miles (6 km), broken by **Radcot Bridge** and **Radcot Lock**; the former is one of the oldest on the Thames and was the site of a fierce skirmish during the Civil War, when Royalist forces held it against Parliamentary cavalry. By the bridge now stands the comfortable **Swan Inn**.

The scenery changes at **Rushey Lock** and the weir pool is remarkably attractive. Next comes **Tadpole Bridge** where boaters can make another land excursion to **Pusey House Gardens**, considered to be among the greatest in England, with shrub roses, water garden and fine herbaceous borders. The walk, or bicycle ride, is about 4 miles (6 km) from the river, and afterwards weary returnees can find sustenance at the **Trout Inn**.

Curving sedately through remote, unspoiled countryside, the most beautiful stretch of river above Oxford is arguably that from Tadpole to **Shifford**: the navigation channel passes through a tree-lined cut to the lock, which was the last to be built on the Thames, in 1898.

The medieval bridge at **Newbridge** spans both the Thames and its tributary, the Windrush, and on the north bank stands an excellent pub, **The Rose Revived**. A short walk from the river leads to the straggling villages of **Longworth** and **Hinton Waldrist**. The old rectory at Longworth was the birthplace of Dr John Fell, instrumental in the foundation of the Oxford University Press in the mid-17th century.

Appleton has a moated manor house and attractive cottages can easily be reached from the track above **Northmoor Lock**. At **Bablock Hythe**, 4 miles (6 km) above Newbridge, a classic river port is reached. The *hythe* or ferry still runs during reasonable hours (in other words, when there's anyone operating it), carrying pedestrians across for a few pence. **The Ferry Inn**, on the left bank, offers basic marina services to boaters in addition to the usual refreshments.

Towards **Pinkhill Lock** the river meanders past **Farmoor reservoir**, the

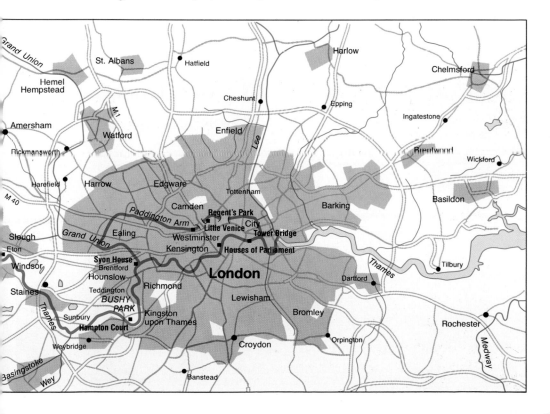

grassy banks of which reach down to the riverbank. After it, a further 4 mile (6 km) cruise leads to **Eynsham Lock** and thence to **King's Lock**, the lowest manually operated lock on the Thames. Between the two locks, on the right bank is **Wytham Great Wood**, owned by Oxford University. This huge wood is a haven for birds, including nightingales, warblers, teal and heron.

From King's Lock, the river swings south and distant views of Oxford's dreaming spires can be taken across the meadows. One mile further on, **Godstow** and its **Nunnery** arrives. Here is where Fair Rosamund, beloved mistress of King Henry II, was educated and died, reputedly poisoned by Queen Eleanor of Aquitaine. It was also at Godstow in 1862 during a trip on the river that Lewis Carroll told the story of *Alice in Wonderland*. Another Godstow landmark, the **Trout Inn**, should be included in any itinerary. A lovely, ivy-covered stone building, it was built in 1138 as a hospice for the nunnery.

Past Godstow, with Port Meadow on the left, the river approaches the outskirts of Oxford. The channel becomes narrow and tree lined, and the **Oxford Canal** *(see page 300)* branches off to the left, with terraced railway cottages lining the towpath.

The journey through Oxford begins at **Osney Bridge**. The lock at Osney is reached through a charming urban riverscape, popular with Oxford residents and tourists alike who flock down to the lock area and the Waterman's Arms.

From Osney to **Folly Bridge** there is a short stretch of industrial landscape and evidence of new development, but there are numerous access points to the towpath which lead the boater into Oxford itself. **The Head of the River**, a pub-restaurant complex, occupies an old warehouse building on the left bank below the bridge.

The terrace, which still sports the dockside crane, looks across to Salter Brothers, one of the river's passenger launch operators. Below Salter's and, opposite **Christ Church Meadows**, a line of public moorings follows the tow-

Near the Thames's source at Lechlade.

GLOUCESTER WATERWAYS MUSEUM

Although not on the Thames, Gloucester is a short train ride from Oxford. If time permits, a detour to this museum will enhance one's knowledge and understanding of the British waterways and their history.

In a little over 200 years, the British canal system was born, developed to a spectacular heyday and, with the advent of the railroad, slowly choked to an undignified decline. From the primitive "flash locks" that tamed the natural waterways in the 17th century the engineers Brindley, Telford and Dudley evolved the skills necessary to interconnect and expand the country's unique system of man-made navigation.

As industry bloomed people and bulk goods were quickly moved around the country, trade was brisk and vast fortunes were won and lost. With the canals came a boat culture of nomadic bargees who plied their trade throughout the industrial heartland, a people with their own lifestyle and rich customs and traditions.

Fast, modern transportation has largely reduced this colorful pageant to the realms of folklore and, with this in mind, the National Waterways Museum at Gloucester has been created.

Funded by the British Waterways Board, a government-sponsored organization responsible for 2,000 miles (3,000 km) of waterways, the museum is ideally sited in the historic Gloucester docks. A listed, seven-storey warehouse has been refurbished and converted to house a fascinating tribute to the pioneers of the canal age.

Visitors to the museum can relive this exciting period of history aided by working exhibits, live craft demonstrations, workable machinery and models, archive film and sound recordings. The museum both entertains and informs, entry is through a replica lock chamber giving an instant insight into the workings of a lock. Inside, the floor space is devoted to the exhibits; the building itself is a magnificent masterpiece of late 19th-century architecture.

The Llanthony warehouse is flanked on one side by the barge arm, where cargo was once transferred from seagoing vessels to barges. This waterside area is now the home for the museum's growing collection of historic craft. On the barge arm the visitor can see the largest floating exhibit, the impressive No. 4 steam dredger. The dredger has been fully restored and is a working display, when the museum is open she is steamed and the bucket chain turned.

Also part of the floating display, the lovingly renovated butty boat *Northwich* is a rare survivor from the canal age. The butty boat is an unpowered narrowboat and this fine example is unique in having very low freeboard and graceful lines. *Northwich* is painted traditionally in the livery of the pre-1920 Fellows Morton and Clayton.

At the other side of the museum a canal maintenance yard has been reconstructed, using the roof and columns of an abandoned pumphouse and parts of old canal buildings. In this series of structures, which clearly illustrate the simple harmony of canalside settlement, the visitor can wander through workshops where canal crafts are shown.

The featured attractions include displays of traditional narrowboat painting, smithing, ropework and carpentry. Additional entertainments, which may vary from week to week, offer horse-drawn bus rides around the docks, pulled by Peter, the museum's shire horse, and working engine demonstrations. The museum gives a visitor the unique chance to rediscover canals and their fascinating history, from the distinctive boat decorations to the mystique of the boat people and canal workers. Cut off from society, these romantic individuals evolved their own pattern of life.

On the narrow canals the colorful "roses and castles" decoration is just one of the great variety of canal traditions in art, dress, language and folklore that the museum brings vividly to life. The history of this almost forgotten society, boatmen, wharfhands, boat builders and navigators, is opened up, using an absorbing combination of artifacts, models, maps and wallcharts, film, photographs and demonstrations.

Gloucester docks stand at the northern end of the Gloucester and Sharpness canal, half a mile from the city center. ∎

path. A walk along the towpath leads back to **Folly Bridge**, and across the river. St Aldates draws the walker to Carfax, Oxford's city center. *(see page 304).*

The passage downstream leads slowly out of the city, the college boat houses are left behind and the boater approaches **Iffley Lock**. Gradually the city disappears astern, and a curious blend of woodland, industry and suburbs gives way to **Sandford Lock**. Sandford village typically centers around the church, which has many Norman features. The pub, the lockside **King's Arms**, has ceilings made from old barge timbers.

Two miles below Sandford on the right bank is **Radley College**. Founded in 1847, it was based around Radley Hall and is now famed as a rowing school. On the opposite side of the river lies **Nuneham Park** and **Nuneham House**, an 18th-century Palladian mansion owned by Oxford University.

A further 3 miles (5 km) and **Abingdon** is reached, through Abingdon Lock. The town dates from the foundation of

the Abbey in AD 675 was refounded, under Benedictine rule, in 995. Parts of the old buildings remain, and are administered by the town's Civic Society.

Interesting streets and buildings abound in Abingdon; many fine houses date from the 17th and 18th centuries, and there are also good examples of medieval and Tudor dwellings. Of particular note is the **Town Hall**, recognised as one of the finest in the country. Built in the late 17th century by Christopher Kempster, one of Wren's city masons, it has an open ground floor, once used as a market, and the upper floor, previously a courthouse, is now a museum of local life.

Below the 15th-century **Abingdon Bridge**, the River Ock enters the Thames beside the Old Anchor Inn. The bridge once marked the start of the now-disused Wiltshire and Berkshire canal. The river now heads for open country, entering **Culham Reach** before a sharp turn to the left signals the entrance to Culham cut which leads to **Culham Lock**, the only way to continue downstream. But, as its name implies, it cuts off a section of the river that is worth investigating.

To enter the cut, make a tight turn to the right just below the lock, doubling back under **Sutton Bridge** gives access to the severed, southward swinging river and **Sutton Pool**. This delightful spot, a truly quiet backwater of the Thames, is lagoon-like and has a mystical quality. A 7-ft (2-meter) waterfall prevents further progress upstream but it is a good place to stop and walk the village streets of **Sutton Courtney**, a charming village ranged around a wide road and central green. Two small pubs and a quaint little store grace the village High Street. The old church has a splendid timbered roof and interesting interior woodwork. In the churchyard are the graves of Lord Asquith, British Prime Minister from 1908–16, and Eric Blair, better known as George Orwell, author of *Nineteen Eighty-Four.*

After Culham, the river runs a more direct course to **Clifton Lock**. The weir stream below the lock is navigable upstream as far as The Plough Inn at **Long**   **A Thames waterman in ceremonial dress.**

Wittenham, a real ale pub with snack and restaurant facilities. Beyond Clifton Lock, the church and a cluster of thatched cottages at **Clifton Hampden** appear. Above the 19th-century brick bridge is the **Barley Mow**, a superb, old-fashioned riverside pub, built in 1350. Jerome K. Jerome, author of *Three Men in a Boat,* described it as having a storybook appearance.

Once past the village, the river curves gracefully to the east with **Burcot** on the left bank, then south towards **Day's Lock**, and then the **Thame** river joins from the left. This tributary, navigable by vessels up to 25 ft (8 meters), leads to moorings below Dorchester Bridge. **Dorchester**, a peaceful country town, was once a cathedral city and center of a see of six dioceses. Today it is noted for the magnificent **Abbey Church of St Peter and St Paul**. The earliest parts of the building are 12th-century, but most date from the 14th, including the shrine to St Birinius, the first bishop of Dorchester in 643.

Elsewhere, there are many fine ex-

amples of beautiful early English architecture, especially in the narrow High Street: among them, **The George** was built in 1499 as the Abbey brewhouse and now serves real ale and traditional English fare. **The White Hart** is a 17th-century coaching inn, and is open to non-residents.

Into open countryside once more, along a particularly scenic stretch where wild life abounds. In addition to common birds – mallards, coots and swans – the observant may spot the rarer kingfisher and grey heron. At **Shillingford** the river is overlooked by the Shillingford Bridge Hotel where there's mooring space at a nominal charge.

Below **Benson** the river heads for **Wallingford**, passing Howberry Park Institute of Hydrology, once the home of Jethro Tull (1674–1741), considered to be the father of mechanized farming techniques. From the river, Wallingford is dominated by the tall, open spire of **St Peter's Church**. One of the oldest royal boroughs, the town received its charter in 1155. Many parts of the original

"Swan upping" – counting all the Thames – swans, turns into a party.

Saxon defences still remain, although the castle was sacked by the Danes, and then completely destroyed by the Commonwealth forces in the Civil War. Today Wallingford is a busy agricultural center, its narrow 17th-century streets often choked with traffic.

Beyond Wallingford, the river is wide, scenic but otherwise unremarkable as it flows 5 miles (8 km) towards the next lock at **Cleeve**. Below Carmel College are the villages of **North** and **South Stoke**; but the prominent feature of this stretch is the sprawling Victorian redbrick expanse of **Fairmile Hospital for the Aged**.

After Fairmile, the river passes under the majestic **Moulsford Viaduct**, a tribute in brick to the architectural genius of Isambard Kingdom Brunel; its skewed arches have a unique herringbone effect in their brickwork.

Continuing, **Moulsford** and the historic riverside inn, the **Beetle and Wedge**, come into view. Formerly a manor house, this inn featured as Potwell Inn in H.G. Wells's *Mr Polly*; the author having stayed there while writing much of the book.

The navigator now approaches **Cleeve Lock**, having covered, since Benson, the longest distance (7 miles/11 km) between any two locks on the entire river. Passing through Cleeve there follows the shortest distance (just over half a mile) before the next, at **Goring**. From the lock, little can be seen of the town itself, but the riverside mill, quaint Victorian boathouses and the heavily restored 12th-century church mark the start of one of the more picturesque stretches.

At Goring, the steep sides of the Chiltern Hills and the Berkshire Downs crowd in on the river, creating a narrow channel with imposing, wooded sides. Goring itself is connected to the Berkshire bank, and the village of **Streatley** by a bridge which spans the lock and the rushing weir pool. On that pool, in Streatley, is the 18th-century Swan Inn. In front of the inn is the old Magdalen College barge, now much restored and put into good use by the hotel owners as a function room. There are a number of public moorings on the Goring side below the lock, making this popular river resort a pleasant place to visit or to overnight.

The railroad crosses the river once more, at **Gatehampton Bridge**, another Brunel construction. Then, following the line of the railroad, the river continues past the **Childe Beale Wildlife Trust Park**, which was set up to guarantee that the riverbank would remain undeveloped. Beyond the Trust land, a line of Victorian Houses, known locally as "the seven deadly sins", heralds the arrival of Pangbourne.

Pangbourne is an untidy collection of houses, stores and pubs, the product of many styles and periods. Nevertheless it makes an excellent base for exploration and the riverfront terrace of The Swan Inn, a perfect mooring from which to start.

It is a little over a mile to **Basildon Park** and the magnificent Palladian mansion, **Basildon House**. Built in 1776 by the architect John Carr of York for Sir Francis Sykes, an executive with the

An official at Henley Regatta...

East India Company, it was discovered in a state of disrepair by Lord and Lady Illife who lovingly restored it. Now administered by the National Trust, Basildon is a treasure trove of beautiful paintings, furniture and china.

Across the toll bridge from Pangbourne is **Whitchurch**, an unspoiled village with water mill, church, small cottages and two pubs.

Leaving Pangbourne, the river carves through the Berkshire farmland, passing **Hardwick House** and racehorse stud, and thence to Mapledurham Lock which has a large and attractive weir pool. Beyond it is **Mapledurham House** and **mill**, an Elizabethan manor house believed to have been the inspiration for the artist E.H. Shepherd when he drew Toad Hall in Kenneth Grahame's book, *Wind in the Willows*.

Below Mapledurham, river and railroad run side by side as the landscape changes and open land gives way to the urban sprawl of **Reading**. In the 1890s, Jerome K. Jerome described this county town as a blot on the river landscape, and little has changed since then. It's a business town surrounded by light industry. The playwright Oscar Wilde (1854–1900) was broken by two years' hard labour in the red-brick jail.

Very close to inundation by the outskirts of Reading, the little village of **Sonning** is the epitome of the English riverside community. Spoiled only by a very busy main road, it is an area of great charm and character. The little islands that rise in the river make the views especially pastoral. From moorings by the towpath, or outside the White Hart Hotel, a few steps take the visitor to the idyllic High Street. Here, in spring, the gardens are ablaze with color, the pastel-painted houses complementing the picture postcard scene. But for an elegant evening and excellent food, return to the river and The French Horn restaurant.

Between the High Street and the immaculately kept churchyard of **St Andrew's** is another well known Thameside pub, **The Bull Inn**. This popular 16th-century hotel has low oak beams in its friendly bar.

Three miles (5 km) below Sonning is **Shiplake Lock** and into the weirpool here, the river Loddon joins the Thames. Pass with caution, especially after heavy rains, as the unchecked Loddon causes strong cross-currents where it meets the main stream. Once under the railroad bridge, **Wargrave** comes into view. An attractive village, it has some half-timbered cottages and a handful of Georgian buildings. Closer to the river, the George and the Dragon provides refreshments with a superb view of the waterfront.

The river now weaves through a group of islands with the dramatic rise of **Temple Coombe** woods ahead and to the right. Clearing the islands, a short broad reach approaches **Marsh Lock**, passing the boathouse and manicured grounds of **Park Palace**.

Below Marsh Lock there is a mile to cruise before **Henley Bridge** and the elegant, Edwardian houses which line the bank. On the right bank, upstream of the bridge, is the stylish, modern headquarters and boathouse of the Henley

...and some of the participants.

Royal Regatta. On the left bank is the Angel on the Bridge, one of Henley's many busy pubs. Henley is best known for the annual Royal Regatta, usually held early in July. This event attracts crews from all over the world, competing in all types of racing shells for the coveted trophies. Regatta Week, is one of *the* dates in the British social calendar, drawing thousands of visitors, who come for the sheer spectacle as much as for the racing. Outside Regatta Week and the Art and Music Festival which follows, the town reverts to bustling normality. Henley is strong on architectural conservation and many of its streets haven't changed all that much in a century. But the traffic is heavy and car parking is a nightmare.

On the outskirts of Henley are many historic buildings. On the left, below the town center, stands **Phyllis Court**, a graceful country house now an exclusive club. Beyond and also on the left **Fawley Court**, designed by Wren, stands at the end of an avenue of poplars. As the river curves right toward the lock at Hambleden, the magnificent gardens and topiary of **Greenlawns Management College** come into view.

Hambleden is always a busy lock and, during Regatta, waiting times of an hour or more are not uncommon. Below the lock the white wood boards of the mill can be seen across the expanse of the weir. A short cruise beyond leads to the stage of the old ferry at **Aston**. From moorings here, it is a short walk to the village of Aston and the curious but hospitable Flower Pot Hotel.

There follows another of the most attractive stretches of the river, as it turns past **Culham Court**, above and between small islands to approach **Medmenham Abbey**. Medmenham, once a priory, was reconstructed with ruined, mock Gothic tower, in the 18th century by Sir Francis Dashwood. He lived at nearby **Wycombe Park** and Medmenham became the meeting place for the notorious Hellfire Club.

Winding tortuously between islands again, the river runs beneath the clifftop mansion at Danesfield and curves to- **Clivedon Reach.**

282

ward **Hurley Lock**. Here, from the meadows below the lock, the visitor can walk to the boatyard of Peter Freebody, where all types of traditional wooden craft are built and restored. The ramshackle workshop is a delight to tour, as a dedicated team of craftsmen lovingly shape and finish these classic designs.

From the boatyard a narrow leafy lane leads to **Hurley** itself. A small village green, the tiny Saxon **Church of St Mary**, one street of houses and two pubs are virtually all there is to it. Walk down to the **Tythe Barn** house with its 12th-century dovecote and the tour is complete. However, don't rush through Hurley; leave time for a drink in Ye Olde Bell Hotel. Built in 1135, the Bell claims to be the oldest pub in England and encapsulates the flavor of this very English village.

Temple Lock and its massive weir are next, and below it is a very modern development of fashionable houses around a pool of moorings. Just beyond them, on the right bank, stands **Bisham Abbey**. Now a physical training coaching center for the National Sports Council, these buildings were once the residence of Anne of Cleves, who was given them by King Henry VIII at the time of the decree ordering the Dissolution of the Monasteries. Passing the small Norman-towered church of Bisham, the river runs by the Salter Steamer landing stage at **Higginson Park** and into Marlow.

Marlow needs sufficient exploration time. From the river, the view of the town is dominated by the 19th-century suspension bridge by Tierney Clarke, and the lofty Gothic spire of All Saints Church. The wide High Street contains a good selection of stores and the town has numerous excellent restaurants and pubs. The Compleat Angler Hotel, perhaps Marlow's most famous building, stands between the bridge and the weir. The name commemorates the book by Izaak Walton, written on the river and published in 1653. The poet Shelley is also associated with Marlow where he wrote *Revolt to Islam* in Albion House, West Street.

Below **Marlow Lock** is the Scouts

A typical pub by the Thames.

boating center; the right bank is steeply wooded and perched among the beech trees are some of the most luxurious homes on the river. Soon, however, this view gives way to the humbler dwellings of Little Switzerland, a curious mixture of chalet styles which line the banks as far as Cookham.

At **Cookham** the houses become grander once more, reflecting the status of this prestigious town. In the main street is **Fernlea**, the birthplace of the artist Sir Stanley Spencer (1891–1959), and the old meeting hall which now contains an exhibition of his works. Spencer based many of his unusual paintings on his own vision of Christ preaching at Cookham. He is buried in the churchyard, where he often painted during his turbulent life.

An attractive row of boathouses lines the river, one of which is the office of the Keeper of the Royal Swans – almost every swan in Britain is the property of the Queen.

Passing under the bridge at Cookham, the river divides into four channels; a long cut between two islands leads to **Cookham Lock**. Below the lock is, without doubt, one of the most beautiful stretches of the entire river. **Cliveden Reach** is unspoiled, rural landscape overlooked by the steep hanging woods. Here, perched some 300 ft (100 meters) above the river is **Cliveden House**. Once the home of the Astor family, this grand residence and its grounds are now owned by the National Trust, which has leased the house to a luxury hotel chain. Non-residents can only view certain public rooms on Sundays and Thursdays, but the gardens are open daily to the public. An afternoon's walk by themselves, they're a must for the passing visitor, and the moorings close to the estate also make a perfect overnight stop.

The river follows the Cliveden estate downstream, to the entrance to **Boulters Lock** cut, and **Maidenhead**, an unremarkable town, little more than a dormitory suburb of London. Below the lock are two famous bridges, the late 18th-century **Portland** stone road bridge and Brunel's stunning railroad crossing, which boasts the longest brick-span arch in the world.

Just above **Bray Lock** is the **Waterside Inn**, a gourmet restaurant made famous by the French Roux brothers, but be prepared for high prices. Below Bray Lock the river flows under the tastefully blue painted M4 bridge towards **Boveney Lock**; on the way it passes Bray Film Studios and the **Oakley Court Hotel**, loosely modelled on a Rhineland castle.

At Boveney Lock, the **Windsor racecourse** can be seen to the right, totally surrounded by the waters of the river. Approaching **Windsor** by river gives the visitor the best view of the castle, which overshadows the town from its hilltop position.

No visit would be complete without a tour of the **Castle**, although in the height of the season, crowds turn this into a nightmare. The Castle was conceived by William the Conqueror in the 11th century, and since then, most monarchs have added and altered to produce a blend of styles. The tourist entrance was built by Henry VIII around 1510 as a

Henry VI, the founder of Eton College.

defensive measure: if the castle were breached the invaders would still have a long uphill slog to the heart of the royal residence. The Royal family and State visitors use St George's Gate next to Edward III's Tower (founder of the Order of the Garter), but it's the more photographed George IV's that one sees from the end of the Long Walk (Charles II's contribution).

A tour should start with the Round Tower, with a panoramic view over 12 counties and the famous playing fields of Eton. Off the **North Terrace**, built by the first Queen Elizabeth are the **State Apartments** which contain among many other treasures, a fabulous art collection, plus portraits of the English sovereigns, Queen Mary's Doll's House, and the Art Gallery.

St George's Chapel, named after and dedicated to the Order of the Garter's patron saint, is a superb example of Perpendicular architecture in England. (Henry VII Chapel at Westminster Cathedral and the Chapel at King's College Cambridge are the only other examples in its league). Construction started in 1472, and it was intended by its creator, the York king, Edward IV, to outstrip and outshine the chapel started in 1441 across the river in Eton by the ill-fated Lancastrian Henry VI.

In the choir, the banners of the Garter Knights are hung above the seats they occupy during ceremonies. St George's Chapel is also the burial place of English Royalty: Henry VIII and one of his Queens, Jane Seymour (mother of the boy king, Edward VI), Charles I (the only king to lose his head), George V and his Mary, and the reigning Queen's father George VI (with space reserved for the Queen Mother), plus several lesser family members.

Don't look for Edward VIII's tomb or that of the infamous Mrs Wallis Simpson, later Duchess of Windsor; after the abdication crisis, the family refused her the title Royal Highness, which meant, among other things, that Wallis couldn't join the Royals in eternity. Love, however, knows no bounds, and the Duke, who refused to rule with-

Queen Victoria guards Windsor Castle.

out "the woman I love" beside him, decided the same was true for the after-life, and both are buried in the heart of Windsor Great Park near the very private Royal Lodge.

After the castle, there is excellent shopping, a boisterous nightlife and so many more things to see and do in the most visited of the Thameside towns.

Those wishing to escape the fast pace of Windsor are recommended the short stroll across the footbridge to **Eton**, whose High Street is a quiet backwater compared to Windsor's. The narrow thoroughfare is crammed with antique shops and it seems that every other building is a pub or restaurant.

At the far end of the High Street is **Eton College**, the most famous of the English public (i.e. fee-paying) schools. It was founded in 1440 by the 18-year-old Henry VI, who wanted the school and its chapel to become a monument and pilgrimage center to the Virgin, not the bastion of snobbery it has become. Of particular note in the chapel are scenes from the Virgin's life, and the cloisters are not to be missed. The college is open to visitors daily and members of staff conduct excellent guided tours.

Through **Romney Lock**, the river curves away from Eton, giving a good view of the college buildings. As the bend continues south-eastwards, between the Victoria and Albert bridges, the **Windsor Home Park** comes into sight, with the town and castle in the distance. Below the **Albert Bridge**, New Cut truncates a tight curve, creating **Ham Island** (now a bird sanctuary) before reaching **Old Windsor Lock**. The name Old Windsor at first appears to be a mistake, for the village, built around the site of a Saxon palace, is totally engulfed by modern houses.

Beyond Old Windsor, **Runnymede** appears, virtually the last open meadowland before the buildings which line the banks all the way into London. Runnymede was the site of the signing in 1215 of the Magna Carta, an historic agreement between King John and his knights which gave birth to the English parliamentary system. Runnymede is

Sketching London's canals.

also the site of the **J.F. Kennedy Memorial** and the **Commonwealth Airforces Memorial**, and is owned by the National Trust.

After **Bell Weir Lock** the river passes under the M25 motorway before entering the sprawling commuter town of **Staines**, as ugly as its name with little to offer the visitor. **Penton Hook Lock** creates a horseshoe-shaped backwater, the myriad of flooded gravel pits nearby forming Penton Hook Marina. Opposite, the village of **Laleham** lies almost obscured among the trees. The poet and essayist Matthew Arnold was born here and is buried in the churchyard.

The town of **Chertsey** is uninspiring, barely managing to retain its 18th-century origins except in Windsor Street where the **Curfew House** dates from 1725. To the north is Thorpe Park, England's first theme park, the theme being the country's maritime heritage; it is popular with summer tourists. The next three miles do little to impress the river user, as **Weybridge**, **Shepperton** and **Walton** are quickly passed but in

Sunbury, Thames Street, adjacent to the river, contains some buildings of architectural and historic interest.

From Sunbury to the tideway, the suburban towns run together, cluttering the banks with a miscellany of chalets, houses, smart cruisers and dilapidated houseboats.

The one glorious exception to the mediocre is **Hampton Court**, 3 miles (5 km) from Teddington. It is arguably the greatest secular building in England and worthy of at least a day of any visitor's time. Under the direction of Cardinal Wolsey, work on it began in 1514, but in 1529, King Henry VIII, jealous of his Cardinal's ostentation and angry at his failure to secure a divorce, confiscated the palace and completed it for himself. What resulted is a 1,000-room palace in red brick, now mellowed into subtle splendor. The state apartments, courts and great hall are all open to the public, and many works of art are on display, including the famous *Hampton Court Beauties* by Kneller, and the *Windsor Beauties* by Lely. Outside the

Getting
oriented on
Tower Bridge.

formal gardens include the Great Vine, the Long Water and the notorious **Maze**, where Jerome's friend Harris got hopelessly lost.

After Hampton Court there remains a short cruise before the locks at Teddington passing, on the way, the suburbs of Kingston and Teddington.

Round London by boat: Almost every capital has a major river running through its heart, and although the **River Thames**, which bisects **London**, is small fry in comparison with the great rivers of the world, it has nonetheless played a key role in the life of the capital.

London's other waterways, whether natural or artificial, have all been developed as arteries to the Thames and the great city it served. Once, this was the heart of the British Empire, with an endless flow of ships, some great, some small, bringing fine goods from the Orient, or coals from north-east England to supply the homes and businesses of the capital. Today almost all the commercial craft have gone, to be replaced by hundreds of smaller boats taking advantage of one of the most pleasant ways to see the sights of London.

To experience the best of London's water routes make a long round trip, down the Thames (boat rental permitting), then up through north London, along the **Regent's Canal** and the **Grand Union Canal** *(see page 291)*, before rejoining the Thames again.

Two cautions: mooring is not always easy on the Thames, and those with only basic boating skills would be well advised to leave the driving to others. Sightseeing can be done from one of the many cruisers that ply up and down the Thames from **Westminster pier**.

The tidal lower reach of the Thames begins at **Teddington Lock**, about 12 miles (20 km) west of the Westminster Bridge. Just before **Richmond** there is a magnificent view of the Star and Garter Home on the top of **Richmond Hill** which was built after World War I for disabled and injured veterans. Behind the house is **Richmond Park**, once popular with the kings of England who came down the Thames regularly to go deer hunting. Parts of the town are beautiful, but much has been redeveloped.

On the east bank stands the **Royal Botanical Gardens** at **Kew**. Although Kew's famous tree collection suffered badly from hurricane-force winds in October 1987, the gardens are a must, with exotic collections of plants from all round the world.

Opposite Kew is the entrance to the Grand Union Canal, and **Strand on the Green**, which has two excellent riverside pubs: The Bull, and The Bell and Crown. Beyond Kew is **Mortlake**, and the end of the Oxford-Cambridge Boat Race route, which begins 20 minutes' hard rowing further downstream at Putney Bridge.

From **Putney Bridge**, it's just a short walk to the 16th-century **Fulham Palace**, once the residence of the Bishops of London, and its attractive gardens, which are accessible to the public.

The sights of central London really begin beyond **Wandsworth Bridge**. To the north is **Chelsea**; Kings Road, famous for its punks and fashions, a short distance from **Cheyne Walk** which runs along the Embankment.

Albert Bridge was one of dozens of memorials to Queen Victoria's consort that was built in the later years of the 19th century, and it is probably London's most beautiful and recognizable after Tower Bridge. Beyond Chelsea Bridge looms another famous London landmark, **Battersea Power Station**, built in the 1930s.

After this comes **Vauxhall Bridge**. A few yards further on, to the north, is the **Tate Gallery**, one of Britain's finest, and noted for its collection of paintings by J.M.W. Turner and for its often controversial collection of modern art.

The Thames then passes through Westminster, and right beside the **Houses of Parliament**, which have long waterside terraces. From Westminster Bridge near the Houses of Parliament, it is only a short walk up to Whitehall to **Downing Street**, and the home of Britain's Prime Ministers, and beyond that to **Trafalgar Square** and **Nelson's Column**.

Westminster Abbey, built in the 11th century, is just the other side of Parliament Square; many kings and queens, as well as a large assortment of Britain's most famous historical figures, are buried here. It is also usually the site of Royal weddings and funerals.

On the south bank, opposite the Houses of Parliament, is **Lambeth Palace**, the London home of the Archbishop of Canterbury. A short distance further along is a huge complex of arts facilities, the **South Bank**, which includes the Royal Festival Hall, the Hayward Gallery, the National Theatre and the National Film Theatre. There are limitations on private mooring here; the most convenient places are at the **Festival Pier** by the Royal Festival Hall or at **St Katharine's Yacht Haven** by Tower Bridge.

Entrance to **St Katharine's Dock** depends on the tide level; call the yacht haven before setting off to be certain of getting in without waiting. St Katharine's Dock has become one of London's most popular new tourist sites. The area around the old dock has been extensively refurbished, and several old

Cruising by Regent's Park Zoo.

ships are there, including an old lightship, which was once moored at sea to warn seafarers of rocks ahead.

After this, the river swings eastwards and heads towards the **City of London**, the capital's financial district. On the north bank, *HMS Discovery*, the ship in which Captain Scott sailed on his ill-fated expedition to the South Pole, is moored; visits are possible.

The City has some excellent riverside pubs where financiers and day laborers crowd the sidewalks outside. Just beyond **Southwark Bridge** on the south bank is **The Anchor**. Originally a tiny riverside tavern, it has been enlarged many times, though it's not easy to see what's old and what's new. Close by is the newly built replica of Skakespeare's **Globe Theatre**.

To the north, there are good views of **St Paul's Cathedral**, built by Sir Christopher Wren to replace one destroyed in the Great Fire of 1666, and of the City of London. The tallest building visible is the **National Westminster Tower**.

The crossing of nursery rhyme fame,

London Bridge, is next, but this is not the original structure – that's now a tourist attraction in the Arizona Desert. The old bridge was bought by an entrepreneur in 1969 who, so the story goes, thought he was getting the more spectacular Tower Bridge. The original bridge was replaced because it had narrow piers – so narrow that in winter the Thames used to freeze because the piers so slowed the river's flow.

Tower Bridge, the last on the river, is most famous for its lifting center – although, with the decline in commercial traffic on the Thames, it now opens only occasionally. The bridge is named after the **Tower of London**, almost next to it on the north bank. Among the sights inside the Tower are the Crown Jewels, the White Tower, and the Beefeaters who stand guard. It was here that important people were executed, among them Henry VIII's wife Anne Boleyn, whose ghost is said to haunt the Tower.

Beyond the Tower, the river enters the old dockland areas, now the site of dozens of multi-million pound development of flats and offices. Amid the reconstruction some older parts survive. In particular, look for two pubs, The Angel on the south side in Rotherhithe, and the Prospect of Whitby in Wapping, on the north.

The river then winds round to the south, passing **Greenwich**, site of the famous observatory, on the south bank. The Greenwich Meridian on which Greenwich Mean Time is based comes from here, and until budget restraints brought cutbacks, the clock here was the basis for time around the world. Despite last-minute pleas, the giant clock was allowed to wind down. Here also, preserved in dry dock, is one of the old sailing clippers, the *Cutty Sark*, which is open to the public.

Beyond Greenwich, there is little to see on either bank, though it's worth heading downstream a short distance to look at the **Thames Barrier**, built during the 1970s to remove the danger of flooding. A masterpiece of engineering, in the event of a dangerously high tide, huge sluice gates form a barricade to keep the high water downstream.

To enter **Regent's Canal**, retrace your path back to its entrance which is just to the east of the Prospect of Whitby pub in **Wapping**. The first stage of the canal is singularly unattractive; pass through it quickly and without stopping. In **Bethnal Green** the waterway passes the junction with the Hertford Canal, before heading up through Hackney and on into Islington, and the Narrow Boat Inn before entering the half-mile **Islington Tunnel**. Beyond the tunnel, **Kings Cross** and **St Pancras** railway stations lie to the south. St Pancras is famous for its huge canopy roof, the biggest of its kind in the world.

Camden Lock market, about another half-mile further on, is one of the best known stops on London's waterways. Located just alongside the canal, the market is only fully open at weekends, but the surrounding streets are always full of shops and stalls selling clothes, books, and bric-a-brac. Being located in one of the trendier parts of London, **Camden Town** has a wide variety of ethnic, vegetarian and health food restaurants.

The Duke of Bridgewater Memorial.

The waterway passes via a deep cutting through **Regent's Park**, and London's famous **zoo**, with many cages visible from the canal. It then passes through another tunnel, the 815-ft (250-meter) **Maida Tunnel**, before reaching **Little Venice**, where Regent's Canal meets the end of the Grand Union Canal. This is the most popular area in London for water dwellers, and boasts some extremely luxurious houseboats.

The most attractive part of the canal ends after Little Venice as the **Grand Union** heads west through rather ordinary-looking suburbs. It is 13 miles (20 km) to the junction with the section of the Grand Union Canal that rejoins the Thames, an easy trip with no locks. At **Bull's Bridge junction** in Southall, turn north and cruise up the Grand Union or look south, and head back towards the Thames.

The Grand Union Canal: This vital artery consists of several waterways which cover more than 300 miles (480 km) and link London with such Midlands cities as Birmingham, Leicester and Nottingham. The most important section is generally agreed to be the 135 miles (216 km) between Brentford in London and Birmingham. This section, one of England's leading cruising grounds, meanders through the Chilterns and passes through the counties of Hertfordshire, Buckinghamshire, Bedfordshire, Warwickshire and Northamptonshire. Other than at its extremities, the Grand Union avoids industrial areas and passes mostly through open, verdant, thoroughly English countryside.

You may start out a wimp on a voyage on the Grand Union but, after passing through its 165 unmanned locks (17 less if you voyage only as far as Kingswood Junction where the Grand Union joins the Stratford-on-Avon Canal), you will end up an Arnold Schwarzenegger.

En route, three tunnels have to be navigated. The **Blisworth**, which at 9,170 ft (2,751 meters) long is the second longest navigable tunnel in the British waterways system (it is exceeded only by the Dudley near Birmingham which is 9,516 ft /2,855 meters long). First attempts to construct the Blisworth ended in failure and it was not opened until 1805, more than 10 years after the opening of the canal. Until then boats would be lifted from the water at one end of the tunnel, placed on horse-drawn wagons and replaced in the water at the other end.

The **Braunston Tunnel**, 23 miles (37 km) beyond the Blisworth, is 6,125 ft (1,838 meters) long and, although its construction was plagued by quicksands, it opened in 1796. A miscalculation by the engineers has given this tunnel a slight S-bend. Finally, 22 miles (35 km) further on is the **Shrewley Tunnel** which is just 1,299 ft (390 meters) long and which passes under the village of that name.

Brentford, once the capital of Middlesex and the guardian of the Thames, has fallen on rough times; but don't cast off your mooring until you visit **Syon House** or, according to Sacheverell Sitwell, you will have denied yourself one of the greatest works of art in England. Don't be put off by the unprepossessing exterior: within Syon, Robert Adam has displayed his genius not only

Grand Hall of Syon House.

as an architect but also as a decorator.

If the weather is inclement when you are at Syon Park, visit the **Great Conservatory**, the only place in Britain where coconut palms reach full maturity, and pretend you are in the Tropics. This vast crescent of metal and glass was the first construction of its kind in the world. Also in the grounds are a **Butterfly House** and a **Motor Museum**. The grounds at Syon are the work of Capability Brown, a renowned 18th-century master of landscaping whose imprint can be enjoyed at several other estates on a Grand Union canal voyage.

Also in Brentford is the **Musical Museum**, occupying an old Victorian church which bears the sobriquet St. George's-by-the-Gasworks. It houses an unusual collection of automatic musical instruments, some of which are played during a 90-minute tour.

Three miles (5 km) after Brentford, **Three Bridges** is reached. Standing here in 120 acres (50 hectares) of grassland and ponds is another Robert Adam house. **Osterley** has been called less a

historic house than a museum of Robert Adam's decoration. Adam conceived the rooms at Osterley, and designed the exterior which is a superb example of 18th-century classicism, as complete entities; no detail was too minute for his inventiveness. Horace Walpole thought that the drawing room at Osterley was worthy of Eve before the fall and you might be tempted to carry the astonishing four-poster from the State Bedroom aboard your barge... if only it would fit!

Back on the canal, **Cowley Peach Junction** (9 miles/14 km from Brentford) is soon reached. Already city life has disappeared and the canal has assumed a somewhat rural air, enhanced by numerous houseboats. Look out for **Uxbridge** with an attractive lock cottage in its grounds, which are landscaped to the water's edge, and where there are several excellent pubs.

In the village of **Denham** the parish church of St Mary has a 500-year old mural of the Judgement Day. If you fear ghosts, don't spend the night at **Black Jack's lock** at Harefield, three miles

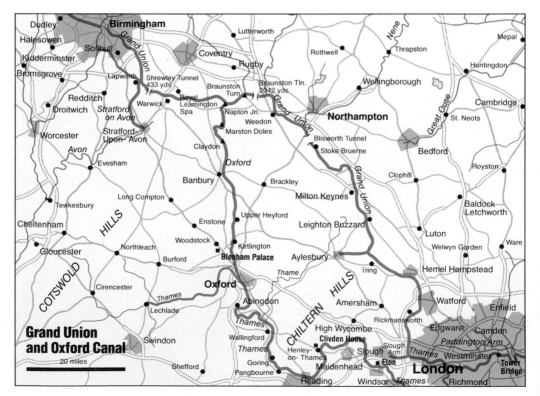

Grand Union and Oxford Canal

20 miles

(five km) further on. Black Jack is said to have been murdered by canal folk because of his thieving ways and his ghost still haunts the lock.

Batchworth and **Rickmansworth** (known to boat people as Ricky) are soon passed. A mile to the east of the latter stands **Moor Park Mansion**, the clubhouse of the exclusive Moor Park Golf Club. Clubhouse and grounds may be visited. The grounds were landscaped by Capability Brown while the Baroque house, which was originally built in the 15th century for the Archbishop of York and then became Cardinal Wolsley's country seat, has superb interior decorations.

The canal now climbs through lovely **Cassiobury Park**, a long stretch of wooded parkland which was, in the 17th century, part of the gardens of the Earl of Essex. Many trees here are more than 300 years old and the avenue of limes was planted in 1672. At the northern end of the park stands **Grove Mill** and a handsome balustrated ornamental bridge which the Earl demanded before he would permit the Grand Union to be dug through his park.

After Cassiobury Park the inclination increases and so does the workload. However, there are several pleasant stretches of cut lined by innumerable excellent pubs and inns. At busy **Berkhamstead** (31 miles/50 km from Brentford) the ruined Norman castle, which has strong associations with William the Conqueror, is immaculately maintained in grounds which are very close to the canal.

And so, 35 miles (56 km) after leaving Brentford, the first summit level of the canal, 400 ft (120 meters) above the Thames, is reached. Relax and enjoy, for after a leisurely passage through the 3-mile (5-km) long sylvan **Tring Cutting**, it will be back to work again. However, before that, canal enthusiasts – especially those with a sense of history – will tie up at **Bridge 135** and proceed eastwards for about a mile to the charming village of **Aldbury** which is built around a village green and pond.

Surrounding this are the timbered

One of the many iron bridges on the Grand Union Canal.

manor house, thatched cottages and other handsome homes. A stone's throw away is the **Church of St John the Baptist** with a tall slender tower and long, low nave. Rambunctious children should be shown the stocks and whipping post on the green.

Immediately beyond the village a steep path through beech woods leads in 20 minutes to a clearing on top of an escarpment where stands a monument to the Third Duke of Bridgewater (1736–1803) commemorating his pioneering of English canals. While making the obligatory Grand Tour of Europe, the Duke was fascinated with France's Canal du Midi. On returning to his estates at Worsley near Manchester, he decided to exploit the coal mines on these estates by building a canal to Manchester. The Bridgewater Canal, the first section of which was opened in 1761, was Britain's first modern canal and inaugurated the Canal Era.

In **Tring**, you might wish to see the world's largest collection of *Siphonaptera* (known better as fleas). **Tring Park**, once owned by the Rothschild family, one of half-a-dozen great mansions here, was gifted to the British Museum. It now houses a superb natural history collection which was collected by Lionel Rothschild.

If the stuffed wildlife at Tring does not satisfy, then **Whipsnade Zoo** is only 3 miles (5 km) to the east. Here ditches take the place of bars and the animals enjoy relative freedom.

Back on the canal, the ubiquitous ducks and geese are joined by grebes and goosanders, mallards and moorhens and sometimes a solitary heron. This is because immediately north of Tring are four reservoirs, all part of a National Nature Reserve, which is sure to delight ornithologists.

Spare a glance for **Bulbourne** at the end of the Tring Cutting, for a group of solid buildings with an Italianate tower. They belong to the British Waterways and it is here, for centuries, that lock gates and paddle gear have been made and maintained.

The canal broadens here and **Mars-**

The Waterways Museum at Stoke Breurne.

BRITISH WATERWAYS MUSEUM

Would you like to know why some canal boats were called "Joshers" and others "Joeys", why some were "Tom Puddings" and others "Flyboats"? The answers can be found in a three-storey building, formerly a corn-mill, which stands on the banks of the Grand Union Canal at Stoke Bruerne and which is now the British Waterways Museum.

In this building are a wide range of canal relics and memorabilia ranging from prints and photographs to boat people's clothing and boat ornaments; from models to boat interiors and from company seals to surveying equipment.

Exhibits on the ground floor trace the evolution from horse power through steam power to diesel. Actually, shire horses continued to be used until the 1960s although paired donkeys, called hanimals, were abandoned much earlier. Here also are models of sophisticated equipment with which barges could be moved from one water level to another.

What are the boards in the corner? A study of photographs shows that when a barge came to a tunnel these boards or wings were fixed to either side of the foredeck. Then the crew members, or specially hired leggers, would literally leg the boats through the tunnel by walking along the tunnel walls while lying on the board.

On the first floor are Joshers and Joeys, Tom Puddings and Flyboats and also steam puffers, Weaver flats and packets and Severn trows: these are different kinds of canal craft. Noteworthy is a Starvationer, possibly the first type of boat built specifically for use on canals. The name derived from the fact that the straight sides of these wooden craft were joined to the flat wooden bottom by a series of wooden ribs.

Here, too, you will learn how canals evolved from contour cuts which avoided changes in level into waterways with locks and tunnels whose construction involved heavy and sophisticated engineering. The visitor is introduced to Brindley and Telford as well as to Rennie, Jessop and Barnes, brilliant canal engineers.

Another exhibit is the gaily decorated interior of a canal boat. Although canal boats with lively decoration and immaculate interiors have almost become the logo of English canals, this is a relatively new development. Until the end of the 19th century, boats were not painted and had all-male crews who were paid enough to take care of their land-based families. However, competition with the burgeoning railways meant that, for the boats to remain viable, costs had to be cut; so boats became homes and families became crew.

It was then that colorful paintings featuring roses and castles came into being. (Compare this with ethnic painting on trucks in Pakistan, jeepnies in the Philippines, fishing boats in southeast Thailand and trishaws in many Asian countries). Two distinctive painting styles are recognizable: the Southern, or Braunston, is more abstract than the Trent and Mersey style.

Exhibits on this floor show the importance of tradition in the life of the boat people. These include dress, especially Sunday garb, and the intricate decoration of ropes used on the boats. Drinking water was carried on the roof in gaily painted cans which, tradition demanded, should be placed just so.

Measham ware is another art form on display invariably associated with boat people. This is heavy, dark brown, highly glazed pottery with white sprigs of flowers and birds. It was made between 1870 and 1910 at Stoke-on-Trent in Staffordshire and at Church Gresly in Derbyshire. The most common item is a giant teapot whose lid is topped with a non-functional tiny teapot. Usually these pieces are inscribed: "Abe's teapot, A present from Catherine". Did boatmen actually take these fragile items aboard their craft? The consensus is that the pieces were gifts given to shore-based friends.

The paraphernalia of carpenters and blacksmiths and of all the others who kept the canal functioning is displayed on the top floor, as is the manner in which law and order were maintained on the waterways. Cargoes were often stolen, with coal being replaced by rocks and stones and wine being replaced with water. And do not believe that toll officials were entirely without blemish: they could be bribed. ∎

worth Junction (39 miles/62 km from Brentford) is reached. This pleasant village with its Norman church, beamed cottages and inglenooked waterside inns, is mentioned in the Domesday Book and is known as "Maffers".

Those with time and strength will enjoy a side-trip on the six-mile (10-km) **Aylesbury Arm**. It has 16 locks which are a mere 7 ft (2 meters) wide, and very narrow bridges and falls steeply away from the Chiltern escarpment. In spite of the canal basin at Aylesbury always being busy with touring and residential craft, the Aylesbury Arm is one of the most remote and peaceful stretches of canal in England.

In **Aylesbury** enter the King's Head Inn through a medieval gateway and, while sipping a refreshment seated in a chair claimed to have been used by Oliver Cromwell in 1651, admire the stained glass windows which are of such exquisite quality that some have been removed to Westminster Abbey and others to the British Museum. Refreshed, visit **St Mary's Square** which is domi-nated by the 13th-century church of that name and off which run delightful narrow Tudor alleyways which pass through courtyards and past 17th-century houses.

Back on the Grand Union, the cut now falls away to **Leighton Buzzard** (47 miles/75 km from Brentford) and the **Ouzel Valley**, leaving the Chilterns behind as a backdrop. Leighton Buzzard is a fairly large, pleasant market town with thatched brick and timber cottages and several excellent old inns. If you happen to be here on 23 May, then do not be too surprised to see a choirboy standing on his head in front of the almshouses while parts of the donor's bequest, made in 1633, are read. This was a stipulation in the will.

Railway aficionados will wish to steal time away from the water and travel on the 3-mile (5-km) stretch of line of the narrow-gauge Leighton Buzzard Railway Society. The rolling stock has some whimsical steam engines.

Not of the canal and yet not to be missed is **Woburn Abbey**, about 5 miles **Charlecote Park.**

(8 km) northeast of Soulbury (51miles/ 82 km from Brentford). Woburn, which is an enormous Palladian palace rather than an ecclesiastical pile, is one of the showpieces of England. The house and its contents are magnificent and include a wonderous series of Canaletto paintings. Here, too, is the fabulous Sèvres dinner service presented to the Fourth Duke by Louis XV of France. Rounding off the Abbey is a complex of 40 antique shops whose frontages were rescued from demolition sites throughout the country.

The **Deer Park**, which covers 3,000 acres (1,250 hectares) is home to nine species of deer which roam freely. The *Père David* is descended from the Imperial Herd of China and it was here at Woburn that this species was saved from extinction. In 1985 the Bedford family made a gift of 22 of these rare animals to the People's Republic of China. If all this is too tame, then lions, elephants, rhinos and giraffe roam free in the adjacent Wild Animal Kingdom.

The canal next wanders gently through the **Ouzel Valley**. Depending on your attitude, you will either rush or dawdle through **Milton Keynes** (55miles/88 km from Brentford), which is Britain's most successful new town. The canal here is extremely well maintained and, if your interest is city planning or shopping, then stay awhile and visit with the pleasant thought that, having passed 80 locks since leaving Brentford, there is only one for the next 16 miles (26 km). Even before reaching that lock, look for the elaborate Gothic bridge, the most handsome on the entire waterway, at the pretty village of **Cosgrove** (66 miles/ 106 km from Brentford).

Six miles (10 km) further on is **Stoke Bruerne**, a delightful typical English village with thatched roofs and sturdy church, which has long been a gathering place for boat people, and which is now home to the British Waterways Museum. Just past the village is the **Blisworth Tunnel**. After it, **Gayton Junction** is immediately reached.

To the right is the start of the **Northampton Arm** which links up with the navigable **River Nene** (*see page 321*)

and thus with Peterborough and the Fens. The narrow Northampton Arm drops steeply for 5 miles (8 km) through 17 locks and a short tunnel to the busy, relatively large county town of **Northampton**, whose market square is reputed to be the largest in England. Nearly all the 17 locks are visible from Gayton, a discouraging sight, and the opening and closing of these and of four unusual wooden bascule drawbridges makes for very hard work.

From **Gayton**, you can proceed by road to Northampton whose **Central Museum and Art Gallery** boasts Europe's best collection of historical footwear. Shoes on display include those worn by Queen Victoria at her wedding and the ballet shoes worn by Fonteyn and Nijinsky. Northampton, a center for leather, also has a **Museum of Leathercraft**, which tells the story of leather's use from Egyptian times to the present.

Also worth a visit are some of the city's many churches, one of which, **St Matthew's**, has modern works of art, including a Crucifixion by Graham Suth-

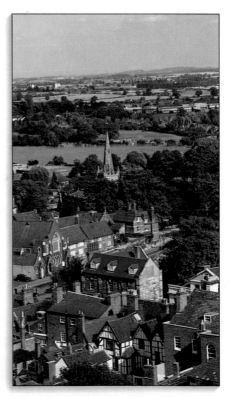

The town of Warwick.

erland and a Mother and Child by Henry Moore. Another church, the **Holy Sepulchre**, is one of only four surviving round churches in England.

Before reaching **Weedon**, 8 miles (13 km) after Gayton Junction, the canal begins to meander and the valley steepens sharply on both sides of the cut. The barracks at Weedon may not be of much architectural or aesthetic interest, but they are of topographic importance. They, together with a Royal Pavilion, were built by George III in 1803, to be used in case of invasion because Weedon is that point in England which is furthest from the sea.

Norton Junction, 5 miles (8 km) past Weedon, is where the Leicester section of the Grand Union branches off to the right. The Grand Union now turns westwards and passes through hilly, wooded country and into the **Braunston Tunnel** before reaching (4 miles/6 km) Braunston and the second summit level. Here the northern arm of the Oxford Canal links with the Grand Union. Five miles (8 km) further on is Napton Junction where the south arm of the Oxford Canal enters.

Stop at **Long Itchington** (103 miles/ 165 km from Brentford) with its tiny village green and pond fringed by poplars and surrounded by timber-framed houses. The **Jolly Fisherman Pub**, which overlooks the green pond and whose juke-box plays period records, faces a half-timbered building in which Queen Elizabeth I stayed in 1575 *en route* to Kenilworth.

Seven miles (11 km) further on is stately **Leamington**, one of England's spas, which was blessed with the royal prefix when visited by Queen Victoria in 1838. You can still taste the bitter waters in the Pump Room, and then cross the road to admire the colorful floral displays in handsome **Jephson Gardens** through which gently flows the **River Leam**. Wide tree-lined avenues bordered by elegant white Regency buildings led Henry James to describe Leamington as: "The core and center of the English world, midmost England, unmitigated England."

Guide playing knight at Warwick Castle.

Leamington imperceptibly merges with **Warwick**, dominated by England's mightiest medieval castle, first fortified in 914 by Ethelfleda, daughter of Alfred the Great. The ghost tower, the dungeon and torture display, and the state apartments are brought to life with wax models of eminent Edwardians enjoying a Royal British weekend. The grounds, through which the **River Avon** flows and where peacocks strut, is another achievement of Capability Brown.

However, there is much more to Warwick, than the castle. Visit the 18th-century **Court House**, the 16th-century **Lord Leycester Hospital**, the **City Gates** and **St Mary's church**, whose pseudo-Gothic tower may be ascended. **Castle Street**, with its **Doll Museum** in a half-timbered house, is a gem.

Immediately after Warwick, the canal climbs nearly 150 ft (45 meters) through the formidable **21 Hatton Locks**. It is a daunting sight, and brings with it the prospect of tiring work, to gaze simultaneously on the white painted balance beams and paddle casings of these locks which form a giant stairway climbing up Hatton Hill.

A couple of miles beyond Hatton, the **Shrewley Tunnel** is entered. Three miles (five km) after the tunnel is **Lapworth** village where a short arm to the left connects with the Stratford-on-Avon Canal at the Kingswood Junction. **Packwood House** in Lapworth, a beautiful example of Tudor architecture, contains a collection of needlework, tapestries and furniture. In its grounds is the famous yew topiary which is said to represent the Sermon on the Mount, with the trees representing Jesus and His disciples. It is believed to date from the reign of Charles II (1630–85).

From Lapworth, it is 17 miles (27 km) and 17 locks through relatively uninteresting and suburban country (except for a splendid moated house at **Baddelsey Clinton**), to the journey's end at Salford Junction in Birmingham.

Join the **Stratford-on-Avon Canal** at **Kingswood Junction** and it is only 13 miles (21 km) to Shakespeare's town. However, on this short stretch of narrow

Warwick Castle.

canal are 35 locks. Observe at some locks the cast-iron split bridges built in two halves and separated by a tiny gap through which the towline could be dropped, thus doing away with the need to disconnect the horse. Observe also the delightful barrel-roofed lock cottages. Most unusual are the three aqueducts. The largest is at **Edstone** (or Bearley) and is about 600 ft (180 meters) long. It consists of a narrow cast-iron trough carried on brick piers and is the second longest iron aqueduct in the country.

Lowsonford is reached soon after leaving **Kingswood Junction**; here nature lovers will enjoy mooring among the weeping willows at the Fleur-de-Lys pub. **Wooton Wawen** has an abundance of timbered houses, the 17th-century Hall and, above all, its church which is three churches in one, and has been called a manual of church architecture. Of special interest and not to be missed is the rare Anglo-Saxon portion and chained library.

Then comes **Wilmcote** and the visitor's first contact with Shakespeare. Visit the timbered house which is believed to have been the home of Mary Arden, mother of the Bard. The house is simply furnished and has a delightful garden with roses and box hedges. Old stone barns at the rear contain many old agricultural implements known as Warwickshire bygones.

The lovely Wilmcote landscape is soon, unfortunately, replaced by the horrors of the industrial 20th-century rubbish dumps and the like, but then the canal enters a secluded corridor and proceeds towards the **River Avon**. It drops steeply through several locks, passes under the lowest bridge of the canal and suddenly emerges into a basin in the middle of Bancroft Gardens. Watching over all is the Bard who sits atop a monument surrounded by Lady Macbeth, Prince Hal, Falstaff and Hamlet which is near the **Shakespeare Memorial Theatre**.

You will wish to join the throngs of tourists and visit, among other sites, the birthplace, a half-timbered 16th-century building; **Holy Trinity Church** where Shakespeare was buried, and the school which he is supposed to have attended. And, of course, one can take in a play at the Memorial Theatre and possibly visit the **World of Shakespeare**, a multimedia entertainment.

However, Stratford has more to offer than Shakespeare. There is **Harvard House**, associated with the great American university; the handsome 14-arched **Clopton Bridge** from the 15th century; the ancient **Guildhall** and the adjoining 15th-century almshouses which are still used today; the **vintage car museum** and much much more.

Slightly further afield (1 mile to the west), is **Shottery**, with **Anne Hathaway's Cottage**; it is, in fact, a thatched house of 12 rooms set in the most beautiful of English gardens. **Charlecote**, 4 miles (6 km) east of Stratford, is also well worth visiting because of the grand Elizabethan house, the grounds which were landscaped by Capability Brown, and the legend which relates that it was here that Shakespeare was caught poaching deer. The story goes that he was birched by the owner – after which, in revenge, he wrote lampoons on Sir Thomas Lucy, and fled to London where he began his career.

The Oxford Canal: The waterway runs from Hawkesbury, near Coventry, to Oxford, a distance of 77 miles (123 km). It's high on the "Top of the Canals" chart and extremely popular, not only with boaters but also with fishermen and strollers. At its northern end it links with the Coventry and Ashby Canals, while at its southern it joins the River Thames.

At both Braunston and Napton, in the heart of the Midlands the Oxford links with the Grand Union and the 5-mile (8-km) stretch of water between these two junctions is designated the Oxford/Grand Union Canal. That part of the Oxford which runs north from Braunston to Hawkesbury, a distance of 28 miles (45 km) and a passage of four locks, is called the North Oxford Canal and will not be considered here.

The canal which runs from Napton and generally acclaimed as one of England's prettiest waterways is called the

South Oxford Canal and covers a distance of 50 miles (80 km). For much of the way it is shallow, narrow and meandering and flows through archetypal English countryside. The canal has 39 locks and 29 charming wooden lift bridges (these are generally open and should be left as found) with very low clearances. Ignore these last three words at your peril.

Leaving **Napton Junction** astern, the Oxford gently swings around **Napton-on-the-Hill**; on top stands a 13th-century church and a restored windmill. The ascent of the hill is worthwhile for glorious vistas of the surrounding, rolling countryside. Especially attractive, although somewhat daunting, is the view southwards of the nine Napton locks which raise the canal to **Marston Doles** and its 11-mile (18-km) summit cut. Visit also the **Museum of Mechanical Music** where occasional concerts are held.

Back on the water and through the locks, the canal makes an almost complete circle: a reminder that the Oxford was originally built as a contour canal. Although the distance by land between Bridges 127 and 132 is less than 3,000 ft (1,000 meters), by water it is almost four times that distance.

After **Fenny Compton** (11 miles/18 km from Napton Junction), the canal makes an acute left turn and travels through the densely wooded **Fenny Compton Tunnel**, about 3,300 ft (1,000 meters) long; having had its head sliced off more than 100 years ago, however, it is no longer a tunnel.

Next are the **Claydon Locks**, a series of five locks marking the end of the summit pound. Observe alongside the third lock the disused red brick buildings; they were stables for horses when barges had horse rather than engine power. **Claydon's Granary Museum** features curiosities from agricultural and domestic life in the "good old days" and has a 19th-century kitchen, a delight for children of all ages.

A further 2 miles (3 km) and, after passing between some high hedges masking the view of open fields beyond

Shakespeare's birthplace in Stratford.

the canal, **Copredy**, on the west bank, is reached. Here the **River Cherwell**, which will keep travelers company nearly until Oxford, first appears. A plaque on **Cropredy Bridge** commemorates the fierce Civil War battle between Royalist Cavaliers and Oliver Cromwell's Roundheads.

Five more miles (8 km) and **Banbury**, renowned for its nursery rhyme, cross and cakes, is entered. Sad to say, civic vandalism has ruined the town which is now better reached on a canal boat than on a cock-horse and whose famous old cross was replaced about 130 years ago. At least the cakes are still baked according to a 300-year old recipe. What makes visitors to Banbury linger are excursions to two nearby stately homes.

Sulgrave Manor, 8 miles (13 km) northeast of Banbury is a gem of an Elizabethan manor and will especially appeal to Americans who might wish to test their knowledge by carefully observing the coat of arms in the main doorway. The three stars and two stripes are said to be the inspiration for the American flag, one of which flies over this house. Sulgrave, completed in 1558 by Lawrence Washington (ancestor of George) and occupied by the Washington family for 120 years, contains much Washington family memorabilia.

Three miles (5 km) southwest of Banbury is **Broughton Castle**, a delightful medieval moated house with interesting Civil War connections.

The canal continues through beautiful, wooded countryside past a string of attractive villages, most of which are somewhat back from the water. After 4 miles (6 km) and half a dozen drawbridges through a relatively straight navigation, **King's Sutton**, whose church steeple has been a landmark for some time, appears. However, rather than making for this difficult-to-reach village, moor on the west bank and stroll the one mile to **Adderbury**.

Stone thatched cottages, an elm-shaded green, and a superb decorated and perpendicular church make a glorious ensemble. The soaring church spire has inspired the tag "Bloxham for length,

Learning to use the tiller.

302

Adderbury for strength, and King's Sutton for beauty." Adderbury's **Manor House** is not without interest. It was once occupied by a profligate Earl of Rochester who courted his insane second wife by pretending to be the Emperor of China. Shoppers will make for the **Waterways Art Gallery** which features works of talented canal artists and canalware.

A mile or two further on and, as the **River Cherwell** decides to flow to the west rather than to the east of the canal, its waters mingle briefly with those of the canal. Immediately after, moor and stroll up the hill to **Aynho** with its pretty ancient stone thatched cottages. Facing these is the classical facade of **Aynho Park**, a 17th-century mansion rebuilt by the distinguished 18th-century architect and collector, Sir John Soane. The canal, now isolated in the middle of open pastureland, meanders merrily along for about 5 miles (8 km) past the villages of **Clifton**, **Somerton**, **Steeple Aston** and **Upper** and **Lower Heyford**. An unusual curiosity at **Somerton** is the

Troy Maze, located at Troy Farm (by appointment only), about a mile east of the village. This turf maze, consisting of ridges and furrows, dates from medieval times and is one of only seven found in England.

At **Lower Heyford**, cross the bridge for a short stroll to an ancient watermill screened by a line of willow trees, which leads to an unusual iron bridge, the only iron drawbridge in England. Continue westwards for about another mile to the 17th-century **Rousham House** where shooting holes in the door are a legacy from the Civil War. The great joy here is the 18th-century garden, a delight of cascades and classical buildings, statues and vistas, and the only surviving example of the work of William Signor Kent. And one cannot fail to see his **Sham Castle Gate** known as the "Rousham Eyecatcher."

Back on the canal, it is 5 more miles (8 km) to thickly wooded countryside and the village of **Kirtlington** where, at the magnificent eponymous Park, polo can be watched. The **Park** is also flanked by

Stratford-on-Avon Basin.

an ancient Roman road over which the canal flows.

The canal widens out and makes a large loop around **Shipton on Cherwell** and its charming waterside churchyard. This is immediately followed by **Thrupp** with its single riparian row of terraced cottages, a canal village virtually unchanged for more than a century.

Moor at Kidlington – not that there is much to view here, but **Blenheim Palace**, the Versailles of England and inexorably linked with the Duke of Marlborough and his descendant, Winston Churchill, is just three miles (five km) away. Blenheim, a massive pile, richly adorned with works of art evokes the lines of Pope:

Thanks, sir cried I, 'tis very fine,
But where d'ye sleep or where d'ye dine?
I find by all you have been telling
That 'tis a house and not a dwelling.

The magnificent grounds, a Capability Brown showpiece, are enhanced by a lake spanned by a handsome bridge from the drawing board of Vanbrugh,

the architect of the house. The lake was formed by damming a small river and induced Brown to remark: "The Thames will never forgive me for this." Across the bridge, a long tree-lined avenue (the trees are said to represent the opposing armies at the Battle of Blenheim, the Duke's memorable victory), leads to a tall victory column with the Duke, to whom a grateful nation gifted this estate, standing on top of it.

On to **Oxford**, 7 miles (11 km) away, founded in the 10th century, that university city of dreaming spires. The canal ends at the **Isis (Louse) Lock**, immediately before Hythe Bridge. It's just a short distance from this unattractive area to the city center and the university which was founded in the 13th century and is enclosed on three sides by water. The **Thames** flows immediately to the west of the canal and the **Cherwell** lies somewhat further to the east. The two rivers join to the south of the university.

Try punting on the Thames (hire at Folly Bridge) or on the Cherwell (Magdalen Bridge). The more attractive Cherwell flows past **Magdalen College**, pronounced *maudlin* and generally agreed to be the most handsome of Oxford's 39 colleges.

Visit Magdalen and **Christ Church**, the largest, richest and most distinguished college; **Merton** with the oldest buildings and **St John's**, **Trinity** and **Worcester**, all of which vie for the honor of having the most beautiful gardens. Visit also the **Sheldonian Theatre**, the work of Wren, and the **Bodleian Library** and its **Radcliffe Reading Room**.

If you have misplaced your copy of this book, the Bodleian is sure to have it: it is one of six libraries entitled to a free copy of every book published in Britain. If you prefer to buy a new copy, cross the road to **Blackwell's**, one of the world's largest single bookshops and a bibliophile's heaven. End the day with a stroll on **the High (High Street)**, architecturally one of the most intriguing and stunning streets you'll ever see.

From Oxford's **Isis lock**, a short passage leads to the Thames where the voyager can turn south or west.

Left, leaving Oxford's Examining School. **Right**, the Grand Union Canal near Tring.

THE NORFOLK BROADS

Slightly more than 100 years have elapsed since a Norwich trio trundled a boat from that city to Wroxham Bridge, 6 miles (10 km) to the northeast. From here they set out on a voyage of discovery through **Broadlands**, a region covering an arc which spreads from Norwich, southeast of Lowestoft and northeast to Stalham. Most of the area lies in East Norfolk, with some of it in East Suffolk.

Little did this trio know of the madness they were about to unleash: of the flood of boatmen who would follow in their wake. Nowadays, it is estimated that approximately 250,000 people a year enjoy a boating holiday in Broadlands, whose waters are home to approximately 13,000 registered craft. Ten thousand of these (about 80 percent) are privately-owned sailboats, and another 3,000 can be hired. Broadlands offers these craft about 150 miles (240 km) of waterways, consisting of seven rivers and a score of broads.

All these figures add up to the fact that, during the summer months, traffic on the waters of **The Broads** begins to equal that on an expressway at the beginning of a summer's weekend. Yet, even in July and August, quiet backwaters can be found where you can enjoy peace, perfect peace.

Basically, a broad is a lake. Other local terms visitors should know are *staithe* (landing stage); *dyke* (a channel which connects a river and a broad); and *fleet* (dyke through a marsh or a shallow pool). None of the broads is large and indeed many cover an area no greater than half a dozen football fields.

Until about 30 years ago the origin of the broads was a mystery. Then, savants looked across the North Sea to Holland and gasped "Eureka". It was obvious that, as in Holland, the broads are artificial and are the result of peat diggings, an activity commemorated in the name of the village of Barton Turf on the River Ant, together with land sinkage and high tides.

Although each of the rivers of the Broads (Ant, Bure, Chet, Thurne, Waveney, Wensum and Yare) has its own character, they are not individual entities but are linked to form a complex network which attempts to unravel itself in **Breydon Water**, an inlet of the **North Sea** rather than a broad, lying immediately to the west of the port of Great Yarmouth. River, rather than road, signs are placed at river junctions to ensure that inexperienced or unwary boatmen do not end up on the River Thurne when they wish to be on the River Burne.

The navigable reaches of the rivers are of no great length; the 30-mile (48-km) Bure is the longest, and the less than 4-mile (6-km) long Chet, the shortest – and, although, considerably wider than most canals, are quite narrow. The narrowness and all of the commercial traffic, found mainly on the Yare, are potential hazards for those under sail. On the other hand, the waters are seldom ruffled. The rivers are tidal and although this produces powerful cur-

Left, sailing on the River Bure. **Right**, taking aim.

rents near their mouths, upstream they are positively languorous.

Other potential hazards, especially for sail boats, are 30 bridges, several of the swinging or lifting variety. More exciting for all craft are the bridges at **Wroxham** (River Bure) and at **Potter Heigham** (River Thurne) which have very low and narrow clearances. Indeed, so tight is the latter bridge that large hire craft are only permitted through when carrying an official bridge pilot. The chain ferry on the River Yare at Reedham should also be treated with circumspect. Although there are a few locks on the Broads, hire craft are not permitted through them.

Most visitors prefer to cruise the northern rivers, Ant, Bure and Thurne, rather than the southern ones; the consensus is that they are more attractive and have less commercial traffic. Another reason is Breydon Water where, with a fresh wind against the tide, the surface can get fairly choppy. The difference between high and low tides on this relatively large southern stretch of water – it is 4 miles (6 km) long and about 3,000 ft (1,000 meters) wide – is great and it is embarrassing to be stranded high and dry on mudbanks. Choose carefully the time to pass, staying in the clearly marked channel, and such a fate need not befall you.

Essentially, the Broads are for lazing and loafing but they also offer an almost infinite variety of activities which will appeal to the nature lover, to those in search of cerebral attractions and to those just looking for fun.

A delightful and varied voyage can be enjoyed by travelling the River Bure from **Coltishall**, the limit of upper navigation, to **Great Yarmouth**, a distance of 30 miles (48 km). Admittedly, few visitors to the Broads are so purposeful: usually they make side-trips.

Even before casting off from Coltishall those who delight in magnificent homes and their grounds, should travel the 7 miles (11 km) northwest to **Blickling Hall**, once the property of King Harold, the last true English King and a true East Anglian. This was the very first property to be taken under the wing of the National Trust, the biggest landowner in Britain, who now have in their care more than 100 stately homes.

Blickling, said to satisfy the most romantic conception of an English country house, has a Jacobean exterior and the interior includes the Peter the Great room with gorgeous Russian tapestries from Georgia. Other attractions are just as lovely, lush grounds, an orangery, a lake and a 200-year-old pyramid mausoleum.

The only other major distinguished home in the Broads is **Somerleyton Hall**, near the mouth of the **River Waveney**. Notwithstanding that the Hall is a hotchpotch of styles, the interior and the gardens are glorious. The maze, one of the best in the country, is an excellent place to lose those unruly children.

From Coltishall, the River Bure makes a gentle curve through marshland and after less than 2 miles (3 km) flows past the village of **Belaugh** with its Norman church of **St Peter**. A deep horseshoe bend to the south now takes the Bure through luxurious woodland for about 4

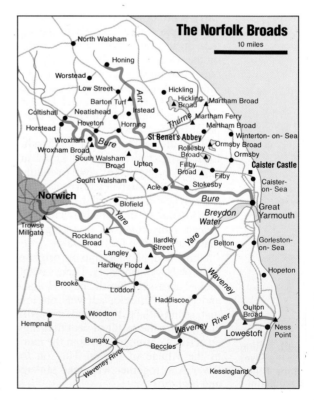

The Norfolk Broads

miles (6 km) to the low bridge at busy Wroxham.

Wroxham actually consists of the towns of **Hoveton** on the north bank of the river and Wroxham on the south. This is the capital of the Broads and is, especially during the summer months, one giant marina. Arrive on a Saturday, which is turn-around day for hire-boats and you will be engulfed by platoons of cleaning women invading returning craft in order to make them ship-shape for the "afternoon lot". Wroxham is the place to be on the Broads if you have forgotten to pack wine or smoked salmon, books, cruising gear or just about anything. **Roy's**, with justification, advertises itself as "The Largest Village Store in the World".

If not intending to visit **Norwich** by boat (the capital of Norfolk stands on the River Wensum and the River Yare), then travel there by road from Wroxham, 6 miles (10 km). It is a different world: Wroxham brash and modern, Norwich old and elegant. Cobbled Elm Hill, situated between the **Castle** and the **Cathe-**dral and a good place for antique hunters, is the best known of Norwich's quaint and attractive streets. The Castle houses a **museum** in the lee of which is a colorful daily, except Sunday, market.

The city, which has a noted university, also has 32 medieval churches, many of which are now secularized. However, pride and joy of Norwich is its wondrous cathedral crowned by the second highest spire and surrounded by the largest **cloisters** in England. The green lawns of its close run down to the **River Wensum** where it is possible to moor immediately opposite **Pull's Ferry**, a 15th-century watergate with a 16th-century ferryman's house. Sir Nikolaus Pevsner, that doyen of English architecture, summed it up succinctly: "Norwich has everything."

The first broad, **Wroxham**, appears soon after leaving town at the start of a large horse-shoe loop in the river, and is one of those few broads which has not suffered excessive engulfment by vegetation in recent years and where the visitor can cruise without any restric-

Below, the River Chet at Lodden. **Right**, Norwich Cathedral.

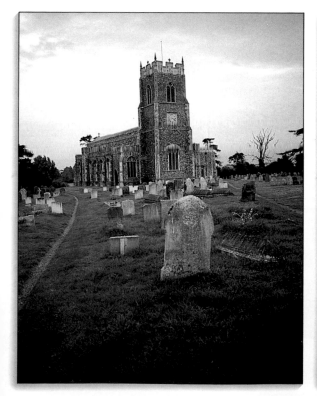

tions. Do not be surprised to see many sails: this is the home of the **Norfolk Broads Yacht Club**.

Return to the river from the south end of Wroxham Broad and soon the non-navigable **Hoveton Great Broad** is passed on the left. However, it is tempting to moor here and to stretch your legs on the half-mile **nature trail** which features natural fenland and various mosses, ferns and lichens, and where a variety of waterfowl are visible from the observation platform.

On the opposite bank is the entrance to the small navigable **Salhouse Broad**. The river next heads north, through flat fens rather than through wooded countryside, to **Horning** 10 miles (16 km) from Cottishall, when it turns back on itself. On route, a small broad stands on either side of the river. **Hoverton Little Broad** (known to locals as **Black Horse Broad**) is on the left and **Decoy Broad** is on the right: the latter is not navigable while the former is, but only during the summer months.

Horning is a popular, beautifully main-tained village where tiny Venetian-like canals lead to thatched boathouses at the bottom of immaculate lawns stretching to spectacular homes. Stop and enjoy a refreshment at one of Horning's attractive pubs or, if feeling the need for a swim (nobody, but nobody swims in the river waters which, although biologically pure, are aesthetically unattractive) try the outdoor or indoor pools of the **Horning Ferry Marina**. (The last ferry was sunk in World War II and has not been replaced.)

Immediately opposite the Horning Ferry landing and linked to the river by a short, non-navigable, *dike* (moor at the river bank) is the small, reclaimed **Cockshoot Broad**, now a nature reserve. Be sure to turn right at the next dike, which appears about two miles (three km) after Horning Ferry. A fence at the end of this 2,400-ft (800-meter) stretch bars entrance to Ranworth Broad, but a left turn permits entry into the busy tree-lined **Malthouse Broad**. From the landing on this broad it is but a short walk to the **Broadlands Conservation**

Feeding swans on the River Yare.

NORFOLK'S VANISHING BROADS

More and more chasing less and less: that's the story of **The Broads** where more and more visitors enjoy themselves on a gradually diminishing water area. In the 19th century there were more than 40 broads, with about 3,000 acres (1,200 hectares); now only 16 navigable broads remain, with less than 1,000 acres (400 hectares).

Nearly all the broads have shrunk. Some have disappeared completely and others are too small or too shallow to be functional. Conservationists and ecologists are worried about this erosion and about how power boats are disturbing the ecosystem. In 1978, in an attempt to control matters, the Broads Authority was established.

The shrinking of the broads is the result of the encroachment of alder carr, a dense shrubby growth which is the nearest thing in Britain to impenetrable jungle, and to changes in the quality of the water. The latter is the result of pollution with sewage effluent phosphates and fertilizer nitrates. These can cause changes in the flora of the water which lead to an oozy mud filling up the beds of the broads.

Good management can control alder carr: legislation can attempt to control pollution. However, the Broads Authority has successfully resuscitated Cockshoot Broad, part of the **Bure Marshes National Nature Reserve**, by building dams and pumping out the ooze. The waters of Cockshoot, where there is now a nature trail, are now as pellucid as in the good old days.

Hickling Broad, part of **National Nature Reserve**, is a place of remarkable beauty illustrating the traditional concept of a broad. This reserve has hides, an observation hut, wader pools whose depth is controlled by sluices and three nature trails. Its most famous trail (booking essential) is the water trail aboard a replica lighter of the type once used to carry out cut reeds. On Hickling today it's even possible to see the Swallowtail, Britain's largest butterfly.

Conservation at work can also be enjoyed at the

Surlingham Broad Nature Reserve (River Yare) and at **How Hill** (River Ant) where **Toad Hole Cottage**, once the home of the local marshman, is an environmental center. Board How Hill's electric boat and travel along their water nature trail.

Windmills and wherries have also engaged the attention of conservationists. The latter, a distinctive sailing craft unique to The Broads, could carry up to 40 tons of cargo. Its design, clinker-built, gaff-rigged and with mast stepped well forward, evolved because of the narrow and shallow waters on which it sailed.

The last wherry was built in 1912 and, by 1949, all had folded up their sails and quietly faded away to end their days in the scrapyard. Just in time the Norfolk Wherry Trust came on the scene and saved the *Albion* – which isn't quite typical in that it is carvel rather than clinker-built. The *Albion*, soon to be joined by a second restored wherry, can usually be seen on the **Rivers Bure** and **Thurne**, and can be chartered by groups who want a special day out on The Broads.

Power, which the sluggish rivers could not offer, was amply provided by the abundant winds which blow over the flat land of The Broads. Indeed, until the middle of the 19th century, the landscape was dotted with hundreds of windmills. These were allowed to fall into desuetude. Today, thanks to the Norfolk Windmill Trust and private individuals, many restored (and some working) windmills are once again part of Broadlands and its heritage.

Open to the public, although privately owned, is the **Sutton Windmill**, near **Sutton Broad** and the River Ant. Originally built in the late 18th century, this distinctive red and blue building is the tallest windmill surviving in Great Britain. Visitors can enjoy a permanent exhibition and then ascend the nine floors for excellent views of the surrounding countryside.

Still on the River Ant can be found the **Turf Fen** at How Hill and **Boardman's**, smaller, yet intriguing working mills.

Down in the southern part of The Broads is the **Berney Arms Mill** (River Yare). It is over 70 ft (21 meters) tall and houses an exhibition that is well-worth seeing. Other restored mills are **Stracey Arms** (River Bure) and **Horsey** and **Thurne Dyke** (River Thurne). ∎

Centre on Ranworth Broad. Here, a wide variety of birds including bitterns, marsh and hen harriers, ruffs and reeves and, on rare occasions, ospreys and avocets can be spotted.

Next, stroll up the hill to **Ranworth Church**, considered by many to be the most magnificent church in Broadlands. The 15th-century screen, delicately painted with saints and swans, ducks and dogs, and lions, has been described as "suggestive of a great initial page of some splendidly illuminated manuscript". The paintings are believed to be the work of German members of the school of Meister Wilhelm of Cologne who settled in Norwich during the 15th century. Having absorbed these man-inspired delights ascend to the flat roofed tower of the church and enjoy an eagle's-eye view of the surrounding countryside.

Return to the River Bure and, after slightly more than one mile, the **River Ant** enters from the left. Those eager to enjoy some of the more remote areas of The Broads will delight in cruising the navigable 8 miles (13 km) of this river which flow past long stretches of reeds and low-lying meadows. However, beware: the Ant is shallow, narrow and twisting.

The Broads are fringed with reeds which are cut not only for local thatching, but for export. However, it is unlikely that the majority of visitors will observe reed cutting for this occurs in winter: rather, one may chance upon the cutting of sedge and marsh litter which takes place in summer.

Almost facing the mouth of the River Ant is the mile-long **Fleet Dyke** which leads to the bipartite tree-surrounded **South Walsham Broad** whose western part is private except to sailboats. **South Walsham** has two churches sharing one churchyard.

Back on the Bure, the shore – especially to the left – is flat and open and here, in splendid isolation, in what looks like a very wet marsh, are the exiguous remains of **St Benet's Abbey**. A *staithe* here permits a stroll to the site, beloved by many painters who visit The Broads. Once, St Benet was one of the most powerful Abbeys in the land and even today the Bishop of Norwich sits in the House of Lords not as the Bishop of Norwich but as the Bishop of St Benet-at-Hulme.

A further 1 mile and the junction of the Bure and the **River Thurne** appears on the left. An acute right turn will keep you on the Bure where, immediately to the left, at the start of a short dike, stands a restored working white windmill which has practically become the logo of The Broads.

It is now less than 4 miles (6 km) to **Acle Dyke**. Midway is **Upton Dyke**, and both streams take off to the right, and after a few hundred yards reach their respective villages of **Acle** and **Upton**. Worthy of a glance is the wherry carved on a gravestone in **St Margaret's** church at Upton. Between the two dikes is **Acle Bridge** which does not constitute a hazard. Not so the bridge which formerly stood here. It was an execution site and guilty criminals were hung from the parapet where they were a hazard to boats passing below the bridge.

Three miles (5 km) northeast of Acle Bridge are the **Trinity Broads**. However, **Much Fleet** which ought to lead you to them is silted up. Still, the three linked broads, **Ormesby**, **Rollesby** and **Filby** are quite beautiful and a magnet for anglers. While enthusiastic fishermen flip and lazy good-for-nothings loll, there is much to interest others. Each member of the trinity has an eponymous village with an artistically distinguished church.

Immediately south of Filby is **Thrigby Hall Wildlife Gardens** which is home to a wide variety of exotic animals including snow leopards and tigers. Two miles (three km) east of Filby and on the east coast is **Caister** with a splendid sandy beach.

However, what attracts visitors to Caister is the 15th-century moated castle from whose 100-ft (30-meter) tower splendid views, both inland and seaward, may be enjoyed. **Caister Castle** was built by Sir John Fastolf, who is buried in St Benet's Abbey, on his victorious return from wars with France.

Yes, his name was sometimes spelled Falstaff and Shakespeare is said to have modelled Falstaff in *Henry IV* on this knight. Before returning to Acle Bridge, consider visiting the veteran and vintage car exhibition at the castle and the nearby, somewhat scanty, **ruins** of an ancient **Roman town**.

And so to **Stokesby** 2 miles (3 km) away, the last good mooring and replenishment point before Yarmouth. From Stokesby, a red-brick picturesque village which stretches along the left bank of the Bure, the river follows a fairly straight course for 5 miles (8 km) to **Mautby Marsh Farm**.

This is the least attractive stretch of the river and, at low-tide, many mudbanks are exposed. The flat skyline is broken by nearly a dozen windmills lining the banks and by the ever-nearer chimneys of Great Yarmouth. **Stacey Arms windmill**, on the right shore, has been fully restored and is worth visiting.

Beyond Mautby Marsh Farm and its working windmill, the Bure makes a large loop to the north before entering **Great Yarmouth** just to the east of **Breydon Water**. The **Haven Bridge**, less than a mile from the seafront, is the limit of navigation for hired boats.

Great Yarmouth is different things to different people. To the avid boatman it is one long marina: to the lover of ancient places it is a town of narrow streets and old buildings, redolent with history, much of it connected with herring; while to the hedonist it offers all the fun of the fair. Great Yarmouth, among Britain's top four resorts, has miles of golden sands, two amusement piers, a maritime museum, a butterfly park and a frenetic nightlife.

Lowestoft, 10 miles (16 km) south of Great Yarmouth and just beyond **Oulton Broad**, is the end of the line for those on the **River Waveney**. It has more of the same, although on a smaller and possibly more upmarket scale. Lowestoft prides itself on its **Transport** and **Maritime Museums** and there are organized tours of trawlers and the fish market. **Ness Point** is the first place in Britain to greet the sun each day.

Somerleyton Hall near Outon Broad.

THE FENS

Mention of The Fens and barging (or cruising) immediately conjures up images of the Great Ouse and the Nene rivers. (Use of the adjective "great" is essential or the traveller will find himself in Yorkshire rather than The Fens. Do not be upset if enquiries about the *Nene* (pronounced as in *keen*) fail to elicit a response; some pronounce it *Nen* (as in *ten*), others *Nyne* (as in *nine*).

Each of the two rivers, which rise 16 miles (26 km) apart in Northamptonshire, flows merrily its own way northeast (160 miles/258 km in the case of the Great Ouse; 90 miles/144 km for the Nene) before debouching, just 7 miles (11 km) from each other into **The Wash**, that wide, shallow inlet of the North Sea.

The Great Ouse is navigable from Bedford to Denver, a distance of 70 miles (112 km). There are junctions with the Cam (for Cambridge), Lark, Little Ouse and Wisney, and each is navigable for about 12 miles (19 km). The Nene is navigable between Northampton, where it joins with the Grand Union Canal (*see page 291*) and Peterborough, a distance of 60 miles (96 km).

The Nene, especially between Wellingborough and Wansford, meanders hither and thither through wide, lush, grazing meadows and is quintessentially English. The Great Ouse flows more directly through a similar, but somewhat busier, landscape until Honeywell (33 miles/53 km from Bedford), then the landscape becomes flat, treeless and low-lying. Both rivers are not infrequently spanned by handsome, multi-arched, medieval bridges and flow past picturesque villages and small towns with occasional watermills and innumerable churches which will delight even agnostic Philistines.

The navigable stretch of the Great Ouse has 17 locks with nearly all on the upper-third of the river; the shorter Nene has 37. However, the consensus is that navigation on the Great Ouse is more tricky than on the Nene. All locks on the

Nene and most on the Great Ouse are of the guillotine type and must be left as found which involves raising and lowering. All the locks are singles, so working them is not too exhausting until the lock at Little Paxton on the Great Ouse: it requires 500 turns as opposed to the more usual 100.

Linking the lower reaches of the Great Ouse and the Nene, and cutting through some of the most typical stretches of Fenland are the **Middle Level Navigations** (MLN). Built for drainage rather than for navigation, these long, straight ditches were first cut by the Romans, then by the Dutch and finally the English had their turn.

Barging the MLN has all the feeling of barging the waters of the Netherlands, a similarity which is accentuated when passing the merging towns of Upwell and Outwell where thousands of tulip bulbs have been planted. The landscape is endless: the skyscape is infinite. If you are a flat-earth nutter then this is the place for you: if you suffer from agoraphobia then best avoid it. MLN is para-

Left, sunset behind Ely Cathedral. **Right**, punting on the Cam.

dise for ornithologists, especially in winter, when thousands of waterfowl rest here. These stretches are also beloved by fishermen. Even in mid-summer it can be cuttingly cold when the wind blows but there are always welcoming inns.

The customary route linking the Great Ouse and the Nene covers about 30 miles (48 km) and involves passing through seven locks called sluices. Leave the Nene by way of Stanground Sluice from where King's Dyke is entered. Then proceed via the Whittlesey Dyke to March on the Old River Nene. This river joins with the eight-mile (13-km) long Well Creek passing the towns of Upwell, Outwell and Nordelph and then enters the Great Ouse via Salter's Lode Lock and the Denver Sluice.

Only narrowboats may make this voyage and permission is usually not given to hire-craft. If barging the MLN appeals, then best charter a steel narrowboat at **March**. Before leaving March, the Grand Central Station of the MLN, be sure to visit the church of **St Wen-**dreda** and feast upon the host of carved angels whose home is the double hammerbeam roof. Voyages on the MLN pass through Hereward the Wake country, home to many legends associated with that great Saxon warrior who held out against Norman invaders.

The Great Ouse: Bedford, a town of 75,000, believes in accentuating the positive, and has created the delightful **Priory Marina Park** around the Great Ouse which flows through the town. The park, bordered on the north side by a handsome esplanade, is entered by a 100-year old **Chinese footbridge**, and has several areas of water set aside for different recreational purposes.

John Bunyan lived here from 1655 until his death in 1688 with about one-third of that time being spent in prison. Walk the **Bunyan Trail** and visit the great reformer's **statue**, the **Bunyan library**, and the **Bunyan Meeting House**. Observe at the last, now a **museum** filled with Bunyan memorabilia, the bronze doors which depict scenes from the *Pilgrim's Progress*.

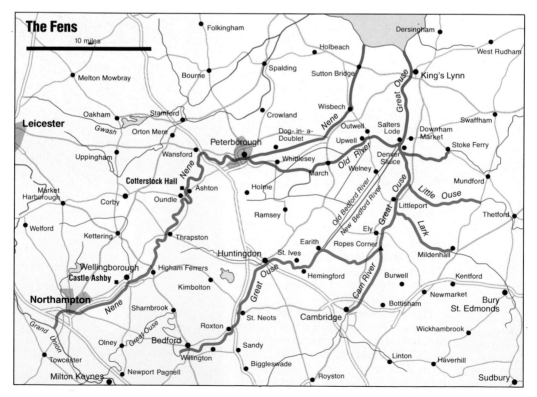

Enthusiasts will, before leaving Bedford, stroll south for about one mile to **Elstow**, Bunyan's birthplace and where he spent his childhood. **Moot Hall** is a museum of 17th-century rural England.

Cast off, and Bedford is soon left astern as the river makes a deep horseshoe curve to the south followed by an equally deep, but wider, arc to the north. En route, **Cardington Lock** and **Castle Mill Lock** are passed. Clearly seen to the south of the former are enormous hangers where airships were built in the 1930s and where they are now being built again. A halt at **Willington**, on the south bank of the river about 5 miles (8 km) from Bedford, offers the opportunity to view a dovecote, a great barn-like building with a stepped facade and 1,500 nesting boxes, a reminder of times when pigeons and their eggs were favourite foods. Here, too, are the outlines of a channel and harbor cut by invading Danes. The latter could accommodate 25 longships, and had two slips for repairs.

The river soon passes **Roxton** (10 miles/16 km from Bedford) where a rush-roofed chapel with a verandah made of trees will arouse more interest than the 14th-century church. **Eaton Socon**, 5 miles (8 km) further on, was an early coaching town. Visit its **White Horse Inn**, parts of which date from the 13th century, and you will be following in the footsteps of Samuel Pepys and Charles Dickens who mentioned it in *Nicholas Nickleby*.

The river next flows through the heart of **St Neots** but search as you will, there is no trace of the monastery which gave it the name. Rather, look for the 15th-century perpendicular **St Mary the Virgin church** whose glory is the interior of the roof which is delightfully carved with myriad angels, birds and animals. **St Neots Lock**, north of the town, is actually in **Little Paxton** where you might wish to stretch your legs and scramble up **Paxton Hill**, to the east, from where there are delightful views of rolling downs to the east, and thick woods and the river to the west. Better do this before passing through the lock

The River Nene at Fotheringay.

which requires 500, rather than the customary 100, turns to raise and lower.

Two miles (3 km) further on is **Great Paxton** whose **Holy Trinity church**'s exterior belies a magnificent Saxon cruciform interior. Soon, the spire of the church of **Offord Darcy**, one of two merging villages, the other being **Offord Cluny**, comes into view and then **Brampton Lock** (23 miles/37 km from Bedford). The lock with its working waterwheel is charming and rural but the passage is difficult.

Attractive **Brampton** is about one mile west of the lock. Immediately on entering the village is the home of Samuel Pepys' family. Legend claims that Pepys buried his money here when a Dutch invasion appeared imminent. Visit **St Mary's Church** and then, after a refreshment in the garden of the 300-year-old **Black Bull Inn**, walk eastwards for about 10 minutes on the A41 to **Hinchingbrooke House**. This handsome home was built around the ruins of a nunnery by Oliver Cromwell's prosperous great-grandfather. It is now a school but may occasionally be visited.

After Brampton the river turns and meanders eastwards for a delightful 10 miles (16 km). At **Godmanchester** (2 miles/3 km beyond Brampton) it flows through gentle meadows one of which, **Port Holme Meadow**, extends for 365 acres (153 hectare) and is the largest single hay meadow in England. Leave this charming area by crossing a Chippendale **Chinese footbridge**, and one is in small, attractive Godmanchester with its varied architecture.

Godmanchester is practically a suburb of the market town of **Huntingdon** and can be expediently reached by crossing a superb medieval bridge. (Alternatively, excellent moorings are available in Huntingdon.) Oliver Cromwell was born here and baptized in **All Saints Church**. Both he and Samuel Pepys attended the grammar school, now a **Cromwell Museum** with much interesting memorabilia. During the Civil War Huntingdon was the headquarters of Cromwell and later of Charles I. The **George Inn**, once owned by Cromwell's great-grandfather, is one of the few inns in England with an inner galleried courtyard. Plays are occasionally performed here during summer. **The Falcon Tavern** claims secret passageways, used by Cromwell, which connect this inn to the river and to **Hinchingbrooke House**.

Immediately on leaving Huntingdon a phalanx of church spires marks the merging villages of **Wyton** and **Houghton** on the north (left) bank and the two **Hemingfords**, **Abbots** and **Grey**, on the south (right) bank. **Houghton Lock**, with a profusion of flowers, a mill pond and a working mill which houses a milling exhibition, is mentioned in the Domesday Book and is sheer delight. Both the Hemingfords have many magnificent timber framed, thatched houses and Hemingford Grey boasts the oldest inhabited house in England. The upper part of this village's church spire was destroyed in a 1741 hurricane and is believed to lie at the bottom of the Great Ouse.

St Ives now comes into view and very attractive it looks with its tall church spire, old houses and public gardens bordering a tree-lined back-water at the west end of the town. At the east end the river is spanned by a superb early 15th-century six-arched stone bridge with a small **chapel** in the middle: one of only three such churches in England.

The St Ives lock is tricky but, having passed through it, there are 3 miles (5 km) of peaceful meadows before reaching the village of **Holywell** and its glorious thatched houses, which lies north of the river. Ye Ferry Boat Inn on the riverfront vies with the Trip to Jerusalem in Nottingham for the honor of being the oldest licensed house in England. Not unexpectedly, the Inn is haunted and the ghost is most likely to be seen on St Patrick's Day.

And now the Great Ouse changes its nature. No longer is it a natural river, flowing through meadows and countryside, but rather, until its mouth, it is a fenland river, bullied in its course by man, and flowing on flat land between raised banks. The river now courses through an inverted V which covers 8 miles (13 km). **Earith**, with its large marina, stands at the apex of this inverted V and from here, stretching northeast, straight as a die, flow two man-made channels, closed to hire-boats, the **New** and **Old Bedford Rivers**. Not to worry: the most interesting part of the river, now called the **Old West**, turns and flows southeast to **Aldreth Bridge** where the inverted V ends.

The Old West continues eastwards for a further 4 miles (6 km) to **Twenty Pence Bridge** after which it widens and the chimney of the old Stretham engine and the tower of Ely Cathedral become major landmarks.

Lovers of preserved steam will delight in the **Stretham engine** which first pumped water from the Fens in 1831 and was last used in 1941. It sits in mint condition in an immaculate engine house on the river's right bank. The house also contains a collection of peat and bog oak samples and fragments of Roman pottery dug from The Fens.

The Cam: Another 2 miles (3 km) to the northeast is **Popes Corner** where the Old West is joined by the **River Cam** and becomes the **Ely-Ouse**. Turn right for Cambridge but stop first and relax at the lively Fish and Duck. Ardent naturalists, and others, rather than rushing to reach Cambridge will enjoy entering and exploring one or more of the *lodes* (channels) which join the east (left) bank of the Cam. At **Upware**, 3 miles (5 km) from Popes Corner, enter the **Reach Lode Lock** and then cruise up the **Burwell Lode** and/or its side-arm **Reach Lode**.

Another side-arm, the **Wicken Lode** is navigable but very narrow. However, **Wicken Fen**, which it borders, is the oldest nature reserve in Britain, and an excellent example of a fen before drainage was introduced. The windmill comes from Burwell and has the unusual function of keeping Wicken Fen wet rather than dry. Wicken Fen has a unique flora and fauna including the Swallowtail, the largest butterfly in Britain. **Wicken village** contains the grave of Henry Cromwell, Oliver's son.

Houses at **Burwell**, have landing stages and, in days gone by, this very inland hamlet was a busy port. The

Near
Holywell.

upper section of the tower of Burwell's **St Mary's church** is clearly inspired by Ely, and Pevsner, that doyen of architectural taste, suggests that it is the most perfect example in the county of the Perpendicular of the glasshouse.

Back on the Cam the river passes through **Bottisham Lock** and **Baits Bite Lock** and, 14 miles (23 km) after leaving Popes Corner, arrives at **Jesus Lock** in **Cambridge**. This is the limit of navigation in summer, but from October 1 until March 30 craft are permitted through this lock and can cruise along that part of the willow-lined river which runs past the *backs* (green lawns) of several major Cambridge colleges. If there be heaven on earth then this might be it. (During summer, when Jesus Lock is closed, the backs can be enjoyed from a punt, either trying your skill or making use of student hire services.)

Enough frivolity: explore at least a couple of the colleges. From Jesus Lock it is a hop, skip and jump to **Magdalene College**, pronounced *maudlin* and the last Oxbridge male bastion to be pene-

trated by female students. At Magdalene, devotees of the diarist Samuel Pepys (1633–1703) can visit his library, kept exactly as it was during his lifetime.

Another magnet for bibliophiles is the magnificent baroque **Trinity College** library designed by Christopher Wren. Treasures here include a Gutenberg Bible (the first printed book) and a first folio Shakespeare. Trinity College is the largest Oxbridge college and includes among its alumni Isaac Newton (of apple-on-head fame), Francis Bacon (was he Shakespeare?), Nehru (first Prime Minister of India) and the present Prince of Wales. Lord Byron, whose Trinity days were notable mainly for his athletic pursuits, and a bear which he led on a chain, wrote of his unfortunate tutor: "*Unlucky Tavell Doomed to daily care by pugilistic pupils and by bears...*" And here too, at Trinity, that infamous gang of spies, Burgess, McLean, Philby and Blount, were fellow students.

In the gardens of **Christ's College** the tree supposedly planted by the poet John Milton (1608–74) still stands. The Great Court at **Trinity** is the world's largest university quadrangle. Behind **St John's**, along the river, is the 1831 **Bridge of Sighs** modeled on its Venice namesake.

Summer or winter, the navigable portion of the Cam ends at **Mill Lane** in Cambridge. However, punts are always for hire for a delightful 2-mile (3-km) meander through quintessential English countryside to **Grantchester**, a village made famous by Lord Byron and Rupert Brooke. Stroll to Byron's pool, much less attractive than the land leading to it, where the poet swam.

Back at Popes Corner rejoin the Ely-Ouse and after 4 miles (6 km) reach **Ely**. The splendor of Ely Cathedral, completed in 1351, lies in its unusual situation, perched on top of what used to be called the Isle of Eels (after the staple diet of the villagers). Excellent moorings are available in the lee of the cathedral and close to the riverside Maltings, an old converted brewery building, where concerts are held. Climbing the hill in **Abbey Park**, with the cathedral on the right looking like some vast ship

St John's College, Cambridge.

riding the waves, contemplate that this was once an island surrounded by marshes. The cathedral, the adjacent Kings' School (it was founded by three kings, not one) and the grounds are superb, and the Georgian market town where Oliver Cromwell once lived is interesting.

Beyond Ely the river flows due north for 17 miles (27 km) past Lilleport towards **Denver Sluice**, at the northern end of the **New Bedford river**, and then on to **King's Lynn** and, beyond this, the Wash. (Denver Sluice is the limit for hire boats.) Between Ely and Denver, the river is joined from the east, by three of its tributaries. First is the **Lark**, navigable for 13 miles (21 km) to **Jude's Ferry**; then the **Little Ouse** (or Brandon), navigable for 13 miles (21 km) before reaching a series of disused locks at **Brandon Staunch**; and finally the **Wissey** which can be cruised on until **Stoke Ferry** (10 miles/16 km).

The Nene: Urban **Northampton** *(see page 296)* is soon replaced by countryside which, unfortunately, for the first few miles of the course of the **Nene River**, is scarred with gravel pits. Four miles (6 km) from town, adjacent to the **Billing Lock**, is the **Billing Aquadrome** and, for those less active, a **Mill Museum**. Three miles (5 km) beyond this is **White Mills Lock** from where, 2 miles (3 km) south stands solid **Castle Ashby**, a splendid 16th-century stately home whose wooded grounds bear the imprint of Capability Brown, the renowned 18th-century landscape architect.

From White Mills Lock the Nene flows for about 4 miles (6 km) to **Wellingborough** after which it commences its tortuous meanderings. Slake your thirst at the 400-year-old Golden Lion, or at the somewhat younger Hind Hotel. The former boasts a minstrels' gallery, while Oliver Cromwell, Sir Winston Churchill and Charles de Gaulle all visited the latter.

The soaring 170-ft (51-meter) spire of **St Mary's** church at **Higham Ferrers** announces the village (15 miles/24 km from Northampton) long before it is reached, but first a somewhat tricky low

Hotel bargees at St Ives.

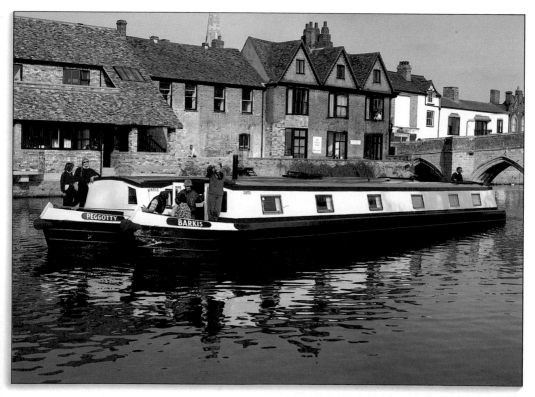

bridge must be negotiated. Higham Ferrers, mentioned in the Domesday Book, has many splendid buildings including the church which has twin naves and lovely brasses. Observe one with angels, holding over the head of a priest his soul wrapped in cloth. Retire for a refreshment at the **Green Dragon** and admire its 300-year-old dovecote.

Immediately to the north but on the west, rather than on the east, bank is **Irthlingborough** where, from the top of the bell tower of **St Peters**, magnificent views of the river and surrounding countryside can be savored.

Eight miles (15 km) further on the river flows under an irregular arched medieval bridge past, to the west, the small town of **Thrapston** and, to the east, the smaller community of **Islip**. The latter's **St Nicholas** church will appeal to those with American connections. The chancel screen was donated by the descendants of Mathia Nichol, mayor of New York in 1671, and a tablet is dedicated to Mary Washington, great-aunt of George.

Titchmarsh Lock, 3 miles (5 km) further north, is the first of several places on the river associated with John Dryden, England's outstanding 17th-century poet. Dryden, who was born at **Aldwincle**, 1 mile to the north, spent his childhood at Titchmarsh. A bust of the poet stands in the church of **St Mary the Virgin** in Titchmarsh, unusual in that its boundary is marked by a *ha-ha*, a ditch preventing cattle from entering, a device more often associated with stately homes (there is one at Castle Ashby) than with churches.

The river now loops, first right and then left, before proceeding northwards to **Oundle** (33 miles/53km from Northampton), a gem of a small town with splendid 17th and 18th-century houses. Moor at **Lower Barnwell Lock** and stroll up the hill to the town. This part of England has many public (fee-paying) schools and a visit to Oundle offers the opportunity, if not to enter the classrooms, at least to wander through one of England's major public schools.

One mile east of Oundle but about 3 miles (5 km) by river from the **Barwell**

Locks is **Ashton**. Your instincts are correct if you sense something different. The cottages in this model village, which was built in 1900 by Charles Rothschild and given to his wife as a wedding present, were much ahead of their time: they had gardens, bathrooms and electricity, and all the wires in Ashmont are underground. Rothschild, who was an enthusiastic entomologist, chose Ashton because it was the habitat of the rare Chequered Skipper butterfly. Try to visit Ashton on the second Sunday in October for the world's conker championships.

Immediately beyond Ashton to the west of the river is **Cotterstock Hall**, a 17th-century manor house in whose attic Dryden wrote his fables. Two miles (3 km) beyond this, moor at **Fotheringhay** in the lee of the magnificent church of **St Mary and All Saints** which is supported by flying buttresses. A superb octagonal tower takes the place of a spire. Visit also the miserable ruins of the castle in whose banqueting hall Mary, Queen of Scots, was executed in 1587. Richard III was born in the same infamous hall. Spare a tear for the Scottish thistles in the grounds: Mary is said to have planted them during her imprisonment. Fotheringhay has lovely stone thatched cottages which rival those of the Cotswolds.

Immediately east of Fotheringhay but 3 miles (5 km) by river is **Elton Hall**, a hotchpotch of architectural styles. Its owners have been avid collectors with the result that you can enjoy a splendid library, which includes Henry VIII's prayer book and a glorious collection of paintings.

At **Wansford**, 47 miles (85 km) from Northampton the river which, until now, in spite of its many meanderings, has been flowing practically due north, passes under yet another irregular medieval bridge and turns east for Peterborough. Wansford is the terminal for the **Nene Valley Railway**, one of those railways in aspic so dear to the heart of the British. The track runs for 5 miles (8 km) to **Orton Mere** but the great excitement for enthusiasts are the locomotives from all over Europe. Relax, as did

Mary, Queen of Scots and Queen Victoria, at the **Haycock Inn**, a 17th-century coaching inn alongside the bridge.

The Nene now flows straight, but not for long, to **Water Newton Lock**. Impossible to believe that this blissful spot with church, lock-keeper's cottage and watermill is so close to a bustling highway. A couple of miles further on is **Alwalton** where, even if you lack a Rolls-Royce, you might wish to visit the churchyard which contains the remains of Henry Royce, who was born here.

The Nene now turns north and loops around attractive **Merry Meadow Country Park**. This is a splendid place at which to dock, especially for those with children, as the activities are many. Outstanding are the water sports including board and dinghy sailing, canoeing and rowing. Also available is horse-riding, fishing and golf and, for the less active, there are nature trails.

Three miles (5 km) before Peterborough is **Longthorpe Tower** which was part of a 13th-century manor house. Here, half a century ago, a remarkable set of medieval wall paintings, the best in England, were uncovered below layers of whitewash.

And so to **Peterborough**, 59 miles (94 km) from Northampton, where a long, immaculately maintained embankment, rich in trees, provides ample mooring. Immediately north of the embankment is the breathtaking **cathedral** with its beautiful 13th-century western front, one of the most notable Norman buildings in England.

Catherine of Aragon and Mary Queen of Scots, were buried in the sanctuary, the oldest part of the cathedral. However, James I had his mother's body removed to Westminster Abbey. Also worth visiting are the 17th-century **Guildhall** and the 14th-century **church of St John the Baptist**.

The Nene is navigable to hire boats for five uninteresting miles (8 km) beyond Peterborough to the **Dog-in-a-Doublet Lock**. One mile beyond Peterborough is **Stanground sluice** which leads to the Middle Level Navigations, and ultimately, to the Great Ouse.

Daffodils decorate the lawns of Cambridge University.

THE MIDLANDS

The **Cheshire Ring**, birthplace of Britain's canal system, is still one of the country's most popular and varied waterways. During its 125-mile (200-km) run, the Ring flows west from Manchester through the center of Cheshire along the Bridgewater Canal, then south on the Trent and Mersey Canal before turning north to traverse the east side of the county along the Macclesfield, Peak Forest and Ashton Canals, ending where it started.

The various parts were built to promote the industrialization of the Midlands. The Bridgewater, England's first wholly artificial waterway, was constructed during the 1750s and 1760s as the link between Manchester and the sea. The Trent and Mersey Canal helped Josiah Wedgwood and his counterparts make Stoke-on-Trent the pottery center of the world, and the Macclesfield *et al* shortened the distance between Manchester and Birmingham.

Some of Britain's most famous engineers worked on the waterways. The Bridgewater was the brain child of Francis Egerton, Third Duke of Bridgewater, who wanted a cheap, fast and easy way to carry coal from his mines north of Manchester into the town, and then to Liverpool.

One of the Duke's main engineers on the project, James Brindley, also built the Trent and Mersey Canal, which linked the Duke's canal with the River Trent and the Midlands, and was part-sponsored by the Wedgwood family, who also wanted a cheap, fast and safe way to get raw materials in and the finished product out (a smoother water passage meant fewer pieces of cracked china and still greater profits).

One of the other great engineers, Thomas Telford, was responsible for the Macclesfield Canal, which opened in 1831 and rises higher than 500 ft (150 meters) above sea level and passes through some of the most beautiful countryside on the canal system.

The first stage of the Cheshire Ring begins at the old **Castlefield Basin**, near the heart of Manchester and site of the Duke of Bridgewater's original wharf for unloading coal in the 1760s. Today the basin is partially derelict, although considerable restoration efforts are going on in the vicinity, and Castlefield has become Manchester's most important tourist area.

In Roman times, Castlefield was the site of Manchester's military garrison and, within walking distance of the canal, parts of the old walls have been rebuilt. Nearby is Manchester's **Air and Space Museum**, and its **Museum of Science and Industry**, constructed on the site of the Old Liverpool Road Station. The station was the terminus for the Liverpool and Manchester Railway, Britain's first passenger route, and the railway on which George Stephenson made his name with his steam locomotive, the *Rocket*.

At the top of the canal basin is a short stretch of canal and a lock linking into the **River Irwell**, and from it the Manchester Ship Canal. It is possible to take

Left, Little Morton Hall at night. **Right**, a kayak needs steadying.

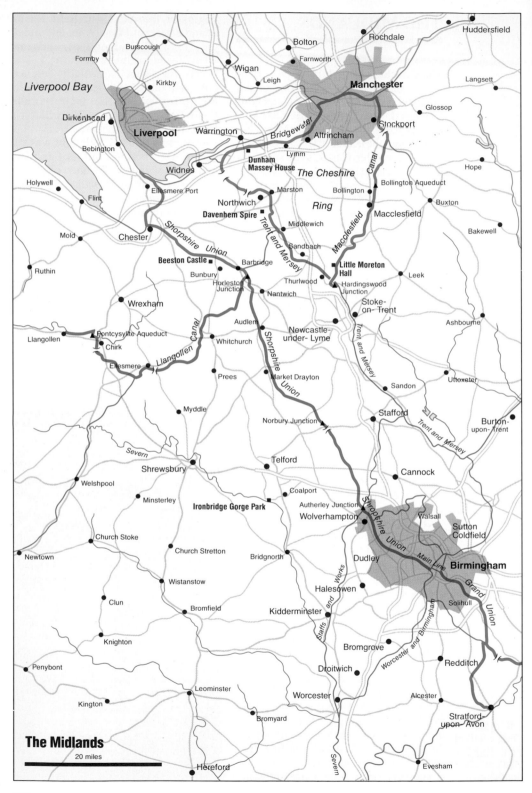

The Midlands

20 miles

a boat for a short distance up the Irwell, but the bleakness of the view makes dull traveling. There is another junction into the short stretch that survives of the old **Rochdale Canal**, which links Castlefield with the return leg of the Ring.

From Castlefield the canal passes through industrial areas of Manchester, before dividing at a junction known as **Water's Meeting**. To the right, it follows the original line of the Bridgewater Canal and then joins the Leeds-Liverpool Canal (*see page 343*). The Ring takes the left turning, down the old route to Liverpool. There is very little to be seen until after Altrincham when the canal heads past one of Cheshire's most attractive stately homes.

Dunham Massey, the home of the Earls of Stamford, is on the south side of the canal about 2 miles (3 km) beyond Altrincham. It is owned by the National Trust, and its grounds and deer parks are particularly appealing. The house contains a fine collection of 18th-century furniture, Huguenot silver and some superb paintings, including a famous portrait of Lady Jane Grey who was Queen of England for less than a week in 1553. (She ended up being beheaded after Mary Tudor successfully contested her claim to the throne.)

The canal crosses **Dunham Park** on a huge embankment, and goes over the **River Bollin** on a stone aqueduct which collapsed in 1971, causing extensive damage and blocking the canal for two years. To the north are views of the **Manchester Ship Canal**, once one of Europe's busiest waterways but now used only by a handful of ships.

Beyond Dunham the canal flows through the edge of the town of **Lymm**, which has two marinas for supplies. On the opposite side of town, the waterway passes quite close to the Ship Canal, and both are crossed by an impressive viaduct carrying the M6 motorway.

Daresbury, about 9 miles (15 km) beyond Lymm is the birthplace of Charles Lutwidge Dodgson, better known as Lewis Carroll, creator of *Alice in Wonderland*. His father was rector of the village church, which now has stained glass windows depicting scenes and characters from Carroll's books. A short distance beyond Daresbury is the village of **Preston Brook**, and the junction with the Trent and Mersey Canal.

The Bridgewater Canal continues its run on to **Runcorn**, where it used to connect with the Manchester Ship Canal and the River Mersey, via two flights of locks. The locks are now derelict, and mostly destroyed. The completion of the link from Manchester to the Mersey in 1776 proved to be a momentous turning point in the history of Manchester, already a growing industrial center, but the canal opened new opportunities and after the new link was opened, the town rapidly grew into an economic powerhouse.

The **Trent and Mersey Canal** does not actually begin at the Preston Brook junction, but a short distance to the south at the start of the 3,700-ft (1,140-meter) **Preston Brook Tunnel**. The driving force behind the Trent and Mersey was a relative of the Duke of Bridgewater, the Marquis of Stafford, although the Duke was himself closely involved in planning the route.

The idea was to create a link between the River Trent in the Midlands, and the Bridgewater Canal, and hence to the River Mersey and Liverpool. It opened a year after the Duke's canal, in 1777, and the close coordination of the plans for the two routes explains the fact that the Bridgewater diverts south to meet the Trent and Mersey before heading on towards Liverpool.

About 6 miles (10 km) south, the canal traverses through two more tunnels in close succession, the **Saltersford** (1,270 ft/390 meters) and the **Barnton** (1,715 ft/528 meters). These tunnels can be an eerie experience for the novice: they were some of the earliest dug in Britain, and aren't quite straight, so that for a short distance the opposite end isn't visible. Don't look for towpaths through the tunnels; the horses walked over the hill-top, and some of the paths still survive.

Once past Barnton tunnel, the canal skirts the town of **Northwich**; the **Salt Museum**, detailing the story of the Cheshire salt industry from Roman days to the present, is within bicycling distance of the water. The canal is cut into the hillside overlooking the River Weaver and ICI's huge complex.

At the point where the Trent and Mersey and the River Weaver pass closest together is one of the seven wonders of the British waterways system, the **Anderton boat lift**. Built in 1875 to take barges up and down the 50 ft (15 meters) between the two waterways, the lift was originally powered by a steam engine. In 1903 it was converted to electricity, but the lift is no longer operational, though it is being refurbished and should soon return to service.

About 2 miles (3 km) beyond the boat lift is the village of **Marston**, once a major center of the salt industry. The Tsar of Russia is said to have dined in the mines under the light of thousands of candles when he visited Britain in 1844. The canal was re-routed here in the 1950s after an old salt shaft collapsed, taking the waterway with it. The canal now passes along what is known as the **Marston New Cut**.

Alongside the canal is one of the most

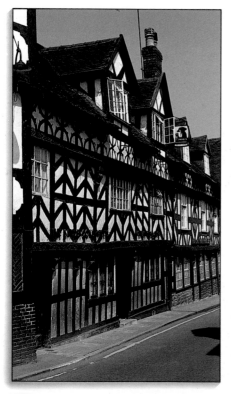

famous of Cheshire's salt factories, the **Lion Salt Works**. Until recently it still produced salt, and there are now plans to convert it into a working museum.

Sitting on this quiet dock, it's hard to imagine that this was once an important transhipment point of salt: brought here by barge, it was loaded onto wagons for transport into Northwich, and then to the Weaver River for shipment elsewhere. When the Anderton boat lift was completed, Broken Cross lost its importance, settling into obscurity.

The canal now runs south through the **Billinge Green Flashes**, an area providing evidence of the collapse of land caused by salt mining. The collection of abandoned and mostly derelict boats, some now rescued and refurbished, has yielded one treasure: the only existing Bridgewater Tug.

On the opposite bank, a little further along, looms one of Cheshire's best-known monuments. It is said of **Davenham Spire** that if Cheshire was turned on end, it would spin on the church steeple. Although the current church is Victorian, the spire dates to the mid-1600s. The Italianate building glimpsed through the trees was originally built in 1755, and modified several times to its present look; more interesting are the views along the escarpment toward the River Dane as it meanders through the rural countryside. The **Coxton Aqueduct**, rebuilt after a flood destroyed it in 1930, crosses the river, and the canal passes the Big Lock Pub as it heads into the town of Middlewich.

Middlewich was the site of a brief skirmish during the English Civil War; bullet holes from the battle are said to be still visible in the church. The town is good for waterside services, and the shops are easily available.

Little remains except a few buildings, now converted to other purposes, of the once-flourishing salt trade. From here, the loose salt was packed into cloth bags and shipped throughout the world. There are three tricky locks rising a total of 32 ft (10 meters) to negotiate before the junction with the Middlewich arm of the Shropshire Union Canal (*see page 331*); after the first two is an immediate

Market Drayton is filled with "Black-and-White" houses.

right angle turn, then the third lock. In the reach before **Kings Lock**, the Shropshire branches off, and a line of old canal houses (originally used by boatmen who did not have their families on board) appears.

After Middlewich, watch for the dip in the old towpath under **Bridge 165** where the A533 crosses the canal; it was designed to give the horses extra room.

The canal then skirts the market town of **Sandbach**, famous for two stone Anglo-Saxon crosses; they are reputed to have been built to commemorate the conversion of a Saxon prince to Christianity. After Wheelock, the canal climbs a flight of eight locks. Originally, there were two side-by-side flights, but many are now in ruins. After a short distance the canal passes the village of **Hassall Green**, with a pub with the unusual name of The Romping Donkey.

Thurlwood, 2 miles (3 km) further, has a unique steel lock that was built in the 1950s to replace one of stone that had subsided. It is difficult to operate, and many boatmen prefer to use the second original lock which is still intact. Watch out for the village of **Church Lawton** a mile further on, with its Norman church built on a rocky hilltop and 17th-century Gothic hall.

About a mile on, the Trent and Mersey passes the Red Bull pub, then it reaches the rather unusual flyover linking it to the **Macclesfield Canal**. This waterway which leaves the west side of the Trent and Mersey at **Hardingswood junction**, and then is carried back to the east side by an aqueduct.

Before heading back over the aqueduct, it is worth cruising a short distance further down the Trent and Mersey, and going through the famous **Harecastle Tunnel**. It is 8,690 ft (890 meters) long, and at some points is as little as 6 ft (2 meters) high. The existing tunnel was built in the 1820s by Thomas Telford. Alongside it, is the original, now derelict, tunnel built by James Brindley half a century earlier.

Beyond Harecastle Tunnel, the canal passes through **Stoke-on-Trent**, a rather unattractive town, but famous both for

Entering Harecastle Tunnel.

its china and as a setting for the novels of Arnold Bennett. The **potteries** are worth a visit, particularly the **Wedgwood factory** and **museum**.

Back at the junction with the Trent and Mersey, the Macclesfield Canal heads northwards towards the mill towns of Congleton and Macclesfield. Look for the village of **Scholar Green**, on the left, and the Bird in Hand pub, a lovely old inn, where the beer is still brought up from the cellar by the jugful. Also keep on the lookout for **Bridge 86**. Stop here, and walk up a track to **Little Moreton Hall**, one of England's most beautiful Tudor manor houses. It was begun in 1480 by the Moreton family, who had become powerful local landlords by building up extensive estates in the aftermath of the Black Death. The hall is quite superb, and totally crooked, and surrounded by a small moat and attractive gardens.

As the canal heads towards Congleton, it passes **Mow Cop**, a National Trust home sited on a rather rugged hill a mile away to the east. On the top is a folly, built in the 1750s to give the local landowners a better view of the surrounding area. The canal passes **The Cloud** (National Trust), and crosses an aqueduct over the River Dane before skirting **Congleton**, an old market town once noted for silk weaving. Today's tourist will enjoy the 18th-century **St Peter's church** and a superb collection of 17th-century black-and-white timbered houses.

Although Congleton is convenient for the **Peak District National Park**, any would-be ramblers are better waiting until Macclesfield, from where it is quite easy to get up into the hills. Between Congleton and Macclesfield, the canal passes through some particularly attractive countryside, with lovely views of the Peak hills away to the east. It also climbs 110 ft (34 meters) in only a mile, up 12 locks near **Bosley**.

Macclesfield was originally a medieval market town whose charter was given in 1261, but is better known as a silk center. By the 18th century, its mills were famous for the quality of their work, and one of them, **Paradise Mill,** has been renovated as a working museum. Queen Eleanor founded **St Michael's Church** in 1278; it's been restored several times, but the **Savage Chapel** (1501) and Leigh Chapel (1601) are original. The town also has good boatyards and provisioning shops.

If canal life begins to bore, catch a bus to the spa town of **Buxton**, 12 miles (20 km) across the moors. In the 19th century it was a popular resort (even earlier, too, since Mary, Queen of Scots once visited the spa), and still has numerous huge hotels along its main streets. The road between the two towns passes the Cat and Fiddle, the highest pub in England at 1,600 ft (470 meters).

From Macclesfield, the canal heads almost due north, passing through the middle of **Bollington**, before joining the Peak Forest Canal at Marple. In Bollington the canal passes by a local tourist attraction, the old **Adelphi Mill**.

Before getting to Marple, stop by **Bridge 15**, and make the 2-mile (3-km) walk to **Lyme Hall**, a huge Elizabethan mansion which has 18th and 19th-century additions and is set in a large park. During one period of her captivity, Mary, Queen of Scots was in residence. The red deer which roam the park are indigenous, having been bred over the centuries by the Legh family.

The **Peak Forest Canal** was traditionally part of the same network as the Macclesfield and the Ashton Canal which links them to Manchester. Since the 19th century, the three have been under the same ownership. The Macclesfield and the Peak Forest meet in the town of **Marple**, 521 ft (190 meters) above sea level, the highest point on the British canal network.

To the right, the Peak Forest runs to the town of **Whaley Bridge**, where it originally linked up with a tramway which crossed over the Cromford Canal on the other side of the hills. From Marple, a pretty town set on the hillside, the Cheshire Ring follows the Peak Forest back towards Manchester.

The first part of the route is particularly attractive. The canal goes down through a flight of 16 locks, before crossing the spectacular **Marple Aque-**

duct over the Goyt Valley, with the **River Goyt** 100 ft (30 meters) below. The views of the Goyt Valley are lovely, and one of the prettiest parts of the Peak District. The cutting beyond the Marple Aqueduct used to be a tunnel (it was opened out in 1820 after several collapses). A short distance on, though, there are two in close succession. This stretch of the canal was disused until the early 1970s, and was restored after great public pressure.

As the canal goes back into the outskirts of Manchester, the scenery becomes more mundane. At **Dukinfield** the Peak Forest Canal becomes the **Ashton Canal**, a 6-mile (10-km) waterway which takes it back into the center of Manchester. where the Ashton links up with the only navigable stretch of the **Rochdale Canal**. Once it ran from Manchester over the Pennines into Yorkshire, but is now mostly derelict.

This last stretch of the Cheshire Ring, back to Castlefield, is mostly hidden behind buildings and walls, although there are good views of the vast canopy of the **Old Manchester Central Railway Station**, now converted into an exhibition center. The canal then descends through the last of its locks, back into the Castlefield Basin.

The Shropshire Union: Through the rolling green meadows of Cheshire and the rugged cuttings of Shropshire, past the site of medieval battles and markets, along stretches of water haunted by the ghosts of the past, and eventually leading into the web of water in and around Britain's second city, the **Shropshire Union** has something for every holidaymaker. Leading from the end of the Dee estuary, a short distance from Liverpool and the River Mersey, it winds through the heart of England along what was once one of the nation's key industrial arteries.

The Shropshire Union was developed not as a single canal but as a series of waterways built over the course of 60 years between 1774 and 1835. The original stretch linked the old salt town of Nantwich to the River Dee at Chester which was subsequently extended to

Along the Macclesfield Canal.

join the River Mersey at Ellesmere Port.

Only in the 1830s, though, was Thomas Telford hired to extend the waterway southwards to link up with the canals of the Midlands. The canal was never particularly successful in attracting industry; as a result, much of the route runs through open countryside.

Ellesmere Port, where the Shropshire Union begins, is a classic example of a waterway town. Before the canal was built, it was a small village called Whitby. But with the arrival of the waterway it grew into a thriving trading center, acquiring its new name because of the canal connection with the town of Ellesmere. It acquired even greater importance at the end of the 19th century with the construction of the Manchester Ship Canal, which is linked to the Shropshire Union.

The old canal center is now run-down, but part of it has been converted into a **Boat Museum**, housing one of the best collections of traditional canal barges and equipment in Britain. Observe particularly the old steam barges, and the examples of traditional canal art on utensils and the boat panels.

From Ellesmere Port the canal heads toward **Chester**, one of the most attractive cities in England and worth an extended visit. The canal passes close to the center, making it easy to moor at the **Tower Wharf** and walk into the city. Chester is an old Roman town, and traces of that era can be seen. Look for the largest **Roman Amphitheater** in Britain, and remains of the Roman harbor wall near the racecourse.

Chester is rare in having its old **city walls** almost intact, making it possible to almost walk the circumference. There are some lovely old houses, particularly down by the **River Dee** and most notably along the lines of galleried shops known as **The Rows** where some splendid half-timbered black-and-white houses sit. These latter are two-tiered buildings, with ground floor and upper-floor shops reached by flights of wooden stairs from the road.

Chester is full of antique shops, and has numerous good pubs and fine res-

Boats can accommodate lots of people.

taurants, notably the Lock Vaults. For an extravagant evening,, try the Grosvenor Hotel .

Beyond Chester, the Shropshire Union heads out into open country. Just after the village of **Waverton** is the site of the 1645 Battle of Rowton Manor, one of the decisive engagements of the Civil War, when King Charles I's troops were defeated by the Roundheads. About 9 miles (14 km) after leaving Chester, and a 20-minute walk from **Bridge l08**, the canal passes close to **Beeston Castle**, which was built by the Earl of Chester around 1220. It is now in ruins, having been destroyed in the Civil War, but what's left is open to the public. Moor alongside the Shady Oak pub, and walk up to the castle.

On a neighboring hill stands **Peckforton Castle**, which is medieval-looking but is in fact a 19th-century folly built by Lord Tollemache, a local landowner, to look older than it is.

Beyond Beeston, the canal passes **Bunbury**, an attractive community set around a medieval church. The village was once a freight depot for the canal and many of the old warehouse buildings remain intact along the waterway.

A good pub, the Davenport Arms in **Calveley**, arrives before reaching **Barbridge**. The canal then branches in three directions. To the west lies the Llangollen canal, to the east is the Shropshire Union's **Middlewich Arm**, which links up with the Trent and Mersey Canal and the Cheshire Ring.

Just down the Middlewich is the village of **Church Minshull**, worth a detour if only to visit the Badger Pub. The low building at the junction of the main line and the Middlewich arm used to be a church for boatmen.

South of Barbridge the canal skirts **Nantwich** (the suffix *wych* means "brine spring"), an attractive old salt-producing center. Look for the half-timbered houses, particularly **Churche's Mansion**, a magnificent house built in 1577. The mansion is open to the public except during winter, and part of it has been converted into a restaurant. In the church, notice the elaborately carved choir stalls and the octagonal center tower.

Six miles (9 km) beyond Nantwich is the village of **Audlem**. At the foot of a flight of 15 locks, the **Canal Craft Center** has traditional hand-painted canalware for sale. Next to it, the Bridge Pub offers nourishment before tackling the long flight upward, or a thirst-quencher after a downward journey. In the village itself, there is an attractive 12th-century church, and several half-timbered houses.

Leaving Audlem Locks, the canal crosses the Cheshire/Shropshire border between **Bridges 73 and 74**. Once in **Shropshire** the character of the canal route begins to change. The Cheshire countryside is very green, and relatively flat with huge dairy farms lining the banks. The Shropshire landscape is more contoured, with the canal passing through regular cuttings, some quite magnificent. One of the early cuttings, at **Betton Coppice** near **Bridge 67**, is said to be haunted, and in the past bargemen and their families refused to spend the night there.

Market Drayton, a medieval market

town offering all necessary services for passing boats, is the next town of any size. It is full of attractive half-timbered buildings; its weekly market dates to the 13th century and attracted people from a wide area, even as far away as the Welsh hills. Robert Clive, later Clive of India (of East India Company fame), started scaling the heights of greatness early when he climbed to the top of the gargoyles of **St Mary's Church** when he was at school locally.

South of Market Drayton, the canal passes through enormously varied scenery: at times it runs high above the countryside with lovely views, then it disappears into cuttings. Of these, **Woodseaves Cutting**, a little over a mile beyond Market Drayton, is the most beautiful. Building this stretch of the canal proved to be one of the most difficult attempted by the canal engineers, and it is said that pressure brought on by difficulties in completing the route contributed to the death of Thomas Telford in 1834.

After passing a condensed milk factory at **Knighton**, the canal goes through another series of cuttings before reaching **Norbury Junction**, 10 miles (16 km) south of Market Drayton. On this stretch, the Anchor Inn at **High Offley** is well worth visiting.

Norbury Junction was originally the connecting point to the Shrewsbury and Donnington Wood Canals. Part of this network, now closed, ran to the town of Ironbridge (now part of Telford) named for its great iron bridge, the first constructed entirely from iron and built across the River Severn in 1779. The structure is no longer approachable by water but forms part of the **Ironbridge Gorge Park** (best visited by taxi from Wolverhampton).

But the bridge is only one part of the whole, a valley more than 3 miles (5 km) long, through which the Severn flows, a monument to Shropshire's importance in the development of England as the world's first industrial nation. An open-air museum in the truest sense of the word, many of the sites have been renovated and rebuilt where they originally stood.

At **Coalbrookdale** (near Ironbridge), observe the blast furnace where in 1709, iron was first smelted with coke instead of charcoal; the nearby **Museum of Iron** tells its history in layman's and technical terms. Also preserved are the homes of ironmasters and five iron blast furnaces at Bedlam.

Beyond the celebrated bridge, near the gorge's end, is **Coalport**, whose factories produced some of the world's most delicate chinaware. Although production ceased in 1926, the old workshops have been turned into a **Museum of Porcelain**. To complete the atmosphere, a new village is under reconstruction above Coalport which will have actors recreating the life of a Shropshire coal village.

From Norbury Junction, the Shropshire Union heads south towards **Wolverhampton** – though, despite the proximity of the west Midlands conurbation, the route still passes through some attractive countryside. At **Gnosall**, 2 miles (3 km) beyond Norbury, there's a long cutting with a short tunnel in the middle.

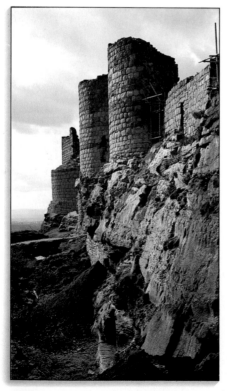

Ruins of Beeston Castle.

Originally Telford planned the whole length as a 2,100-ft long (645-meter) tunnel, but much of the bore crumbled, and the route had to be dug out.

This stretch of the canal is particularly well-endowed with pubs, one of the most popular is the Bridge Inn at **Brewood**. Just to the north of Brewood the canal crosses an aqueduct built by Telford over his own London to Holyhead road. Beyond Brewood the route reaches **Autherley Junction**, the end of the Shropshire Union and the link with the Staffordshire and Worcestershire Canal. Look for a full-service marina just near the junction.

Although the Shropshire Union ends at Autherley, it is well worth continuing to a predetermined end-point somewhere on the **Birmingham Canal** Navigations. Before sailing on, however, make sure detailed maps of Britain's most complex network of canals are on board. Out of an original network of a 160 miles (256 km) of canals around the Birmingham area, there are 100 miles (160 km) remaining, and, though some of the routes pass uninspiring industrial landscapes, the network is full of fascinating relics of the days of industrial canals.

Although it is better for visiting canal enthusiasts to plan their own route according to time and interest, there are several highlights not to be missed. At the heart are two main routes into and through Birmingham, and both involve a tunnel. The 1,080-ft (332-meter) long **Coseley Tunnel** is just before the **Factory Junction and Locks**. Once in the city, Birmingham is linked to the Grand Union Canal *(see page 291)* and the south via the Birmingham and Fazeley Canal.

The best place to visit in the Birmingham network is the town of **Dudley**. This is probably the most attractive part of what is, because of its grimy industrial past, known as the Black Country. Dudley has a Norman castle set on a hill above the town, a well-known zoo, and the **Black Country Museum**, a must for those who didn't make it to the Ironbridge Museum.

Coalbrookdale celebrates the Industrial Revolution.

Dudley Tunnel, which passes for 9,515 ft (2,928 meters) under the hill, was one of three enormous tunnels on the original network. The other operational one is the 9,080-ft (2,794-meter) **Netherton Tunnel**, on a branch that flows east of Dudley.

Also in Dudley, look for the Boat Inn to the south. Its bar is half a disused narrow boat, and it serves Cow Pie, of the kind eaten by the British cartoon character Desperate Dan, and a full meal for the most immense appetite.

The center of **Birmingham**, Britain's second city, isn't particularly inspiring nor attractive, though it has improved much in recent years. Sights of particular interest on the waterway include a huge cavern underneath the old Snow Hill station, containing a lock, and above this, a sprawling, intricate motorway interchange known as "Spaghetti Junction".

Unknown to most of the motorists who drive overhead are two other forms of transportation below the maze of roads: a railway, and the **Birmingham and Fazeley Canal**.

The focal point of the city waterways is the **Gas Street** basin, close to **Farmers Junction** where the routes from Wolverhampton and Dudley link up with the Birmingham and Fazeley and other routes. The dock here is the best place to moor and explore Birmingham, and it is a focal point for narrow boats from around the country, including some which are permanent homes.

In central Birmingham, look out for the **Bull Ring**, a fortress-like city center complex, as well as a number of typical Victorian municipal buildings including the **Council House** and the **Town Hall**. The city is mainly a business center and has a massive exhibition complex.

Above all, the way to enjoy the Birmingham Canal navigations is to explore. There are endless branches and nooks and crannies to be discovered, remembrances of the time when this was one of the busiest industrial waterways serving one of Britain's biggest industrial centers. The scenery may not be very bucolic, but there is no shortage of interesting places.

An artist creates a bucket for a narrowboat.

NARROWBOAT DECORATION

The 17th-century canal engineer James Brindley, regarded as the father of the English canal, set out the dimensions of bridges, tunnels and locks, and in doing so determined the size of the vessels that were to use them. Commercial pressure, to carry as much cargo as possible at the speed that a horse could tow, determined the final design, and the narrowboat was born.

With the advent of this revolutionary new transport system came the rapid growth of the canal companies, the boat owners, and the formation of a small, close-knit community: the bargees. These two groups became a powerful influence on the decoration of the barges but the origin of much of their inspiration is obscured in folklore.

A logical requirement of the canal companies was to develop distinctive livery, by which their craft could be instantly recognised, particularly by a community which could neither read nor write. The desire of the individual boatmen was to assert their own identity within a framework of company regulations and strict tradition.

The bargees had added motivation to brighten up their austere and very cramped living and working spaces. The task of producing the final effect was left to the skippers and the canal boatyard painters.

The narrowboats were working craft, in the main drab and functional, there were few places where decoration could be applied. One large area was the cabin sides, which carried the company name, yard of registration and registration number. Background colors were always dark; red, blue, green or maroon being the most common. The lettering was imposed boldly, in blocked letters often with a dropped shadow or exotic, curling serifs. The whole was edged in a band of light, contrasting color. The effect was bright and powerful but never gaudy.

The top bends (around the bow, the stern and the rudder post) were the other areas to receive attention, again with light color on dark in a bold pattern. These designs consisted of circles, diamonds, crescents and stripes again with the light border edging each panel. Some experts believe that these designs allude to the shields carried along the hulls of Viking longboats, similar patterns also occur in Dutch and Danish fishing boats where the decoration is known as *prinswerk*. The bold bow decoration in the manner of the oculus, or eyes of the ship tradition are well documented from the time of the Ancient Greeks.

The dominant features of the paintwork that remained to be embellished was largely given over to the bargees and the canal fraternity. The designs that resulted are today referred to as "Roses and Castles". To appreciate these designs, it is necessary to consider the lives and backgrounds of those people who worked the canals.

At the start, canal journeys were short and there was no need for crews to stay with their boats overnight. As the canal system developed the trips took longer and took the bargees further from home. Most skippers eventually moved on board their barges, bringing families with them. Many of these family crews were Romanies, the menfolk having labored on canal construction naturally settled into the itinerant life of the barges. The style of "Roses and Castles" bears close resemblance to the imagery found in gypsy art and the castle scenes may well symbolize their Carpathian homelands.

It is also possible that the simple designs owe their origins to the booming industries of the period, particularly furniture, pottery and tinplate. Each manufacturer employed artists to finish their products, the fashion of the day being for inlaid designs in wood and ornately enamelled or glazed tin and pottery. Whether the artists came from industry to the canals or the art developed in parallel amongst the boatmen is a matter for conjecture. What resulted, was the establishment of a group of narrowboat decorators, each with his own distinctive style.

Over the 200-year history of the canal narrowboat, these designs have survived with little outside influence. Few working boats still remain, but those that are left, and an increasing number of pleasure craft built on narrow boat lines, retain the bold simplicity and color of this unique skill. ■

WALES

Acrophobics will not enjoy parts of the 46-mile (73-km) **Llangollen Canal**: it crosses several of the country's highest and most awesome aqueducts during its run into the Welsh hills. To compensate, and as a bonus, it also passes through some of Britain's most spectacular scenery.

Cruising this sleepy backwater from its beginning at a junction with the Shropshire Union Canal at **Hurleston**, near Nantwich in Cheshire, to the end at a waterfall on the River Dee, just beyond **Llangollen**, it's hard to realize the canal was once a key part of an ambitious plan to link three of Britain's biggest rivers.

The route was intended by the men who built it (led by two of England's most prominent canal engineers, William Jessop and Thomas Telford), as just one part of a route that would join the Rivers Dee, Severn and Mersey. The aim was to link the Shropshire Union, and hence the river connections with the Dee at Chester and the Mersey at Ellesmere Port, with the River Severn at Welshpool, down the Llangollen Canal and the now disused Montgomeryshire Canal.

The latter part of the route is now closed, and the Llangollen itself only survived because it was a primary source of water for the more important Shropshire Union Canal.

From **Hurleston Junction**, the Llangollen heads southwest through the Cheshire countryside past the villages of **Swanley** and **Wrenbury**, which has an attractive hall now owned by the local authorities. The Cotton Arms Pub is a short distance from the canal and is a good place to take a break before the next locks.

Almost all the locks are in the first few miles, and after a flight of six just before Whitchurch, there are only two more on the way to Llangollen. **Whitchurch** is an attractive market town, and although once linked directly to the canal by a short waterway, its less than a 2-mile (3-km) walk away. Look for the Old Eagles with good beer and a pleasant atmosphere.

After Whitchurch, the route passes through a huge area of peat moss. Part of it has been cut and taken away by commercial peat producers, though much is quite untouched. The next place of particular interest is **Ellesmere**, about 12 miles (20 km) beyond Whitchurch. Just before it, the canal, however, briefly enters the Welsh county of **Clwyd**, before re-emerging into Shropshire.

On the outskirts of Ellesmere, the waterway passes a series of nine tree-lined lakes, used for boating and fishing by local people. After a short cutting comes a junction, from where a short arm leads into the town center. The old canal maintenance yard, with some fine examples of old waterway buildings and equipment, is just by this junction. With several easy moorings along the towpath, it's easy to wander round this attractive old market town. The White Hart Inn is said to be the oldest pub in this area of the country – and it certainly looks the part.

Left, rolling Welsh hills. **Right**, typical stone houses.

About 4 miles (6 km) beyond Elles-mere, at **Welsh Frankton**, is the junction with the **Montgomeryshire Canal**. The old route to Welshpool has been a target for restoration enthusiasts for years, though the obstacles in their way seem insurmountable. There is an excellent canalside bakery at **Bridge 33**, about 4 miles (6 km) beyond Welsh Frankton. The Llangollen is now approaching the Welsh hills and by the time it nears the town of **Chirk**, there are views of the mountains.

Just before Chirk is the first of the huge aqueducts that have made the Llangollen famous (or infamous). The **Chirk Aqueduct** with its stunning vistas is a huge stone construction carrying the canal 70 ft (21 meters) above the River Ceirog, alongside an even bigger and more impressive railway viaduct. There are easy moorings at Chirk just beyond the aqueduct, and its 14th-century **castle** is open to the public during the summer months.

Beyond Chirk, the canal traverses a 1,375-ft (423-meter) tunnel, then through a shorter one, before passing close to the historic earthwork, **Offa's Dyke**, built in the 8th century as a fortification against the Welsh. The dyke, well signposted, is just a short walk from the canal.

The canal then runs down the **Dee valley**, before reaching its most famous point, the **Pontcysyllte Aqueduct**. One of Thomas Telford's most spectacular achievements, this quite remarkable feat of design and engineering took a total of six years to build between 1799 and 1805.

Essentially an iron trough, the half-mile aqueduct runs 121 ft (37 meters) above the ground and is supported by a series of arches. The journey across it looks precarious enough to weaken the nerves of most travelers, especially those with a fear of heights. On one side, the top of the trough is only a short distance above the water level; there is no rail of any kind between its users and a very long drop into the River Dee. The acrophobic can only take a deep breath, close the eyes (letting someone else do

Floating along the Llangollen Canal.

the steering) and think of lovely, lovely solid earth until the change in wind pitch indicates the crossing has been well and truly completed.

The last stretch of the canal into Llangollen was designed more as a water feeder for the rest of the route than as a waterway. It was intended to be navigable, though only with care and not by heavy volumes of traffic. The canal can be extremely shallow round here, so check boating charts before venturing into this part of the waterway. The scenery, particularly where there are views over the Dee, is lovely and one reason for the popularity of this part of the Llangollen for holiday craft.

Llangollen itself is a charming town; nestling in the hills with plenty to see. Apart from the canal, which at its top end has horse-drawn boat trips, the town has a steam railway and craft center and is easily placed for walks. From the canal wharf, it's a short walk up the hillside to **Castell Dinas Bran**, a medieval castle just outside the town.

Llangollen has an annual musical festival, the Eisteddfod, in July. Observe the old bridge over the River Dee, which dates back to the 14th century. There are many lovely pubs and restaurants, but try in particular the Jenny Jones on Abbey Road.

Beyond the wharf, the Llangollen is not navigable; but **Horseshoe Falls**, the head of the canal, is a pleasant walk from town. Here, part of the River Dee is diverted through a narrow chamber and provides the water supply for the route to Hurleston Junction. This part of the Dee is particularly beautiful: it falls 120 ft (40 meters) between Horseshoe Falls and Llangollen and is popular for canoe slalom.

Llangollen is not always the easiest place to moor for any length of time, and so it's perhaps best to avoid it in the height of the tourist season. Fall is a particularly lovely time to visit: the trees are turning rich golds and reds giving a glow to the entire countryside. But the trip from the Shropshire Union is one that no canal enthusiast should miss no matter when one can visit.

Looking down on the Pontcysyllte Aqueduct.

THE LEEDS TO LIVERPOOL CANAL

It is often almost impossible to imagine the waterways of Britain as key industrial supply routes, filled with dirty and heavy barges laden with coal, clay, iron and steel to supply factories often hundreds of miles away. On parts of the trans-Pennine route from Leeds to Liverpool, one could be forgiven for imagining that the canal's industrial heritage was just a myth. As the canal winds through the edges of the Yorkshire Dales, with lovely views of moorlands on all sides, and as it passes through old stone market towns, industrial Britain seems a world away.

Yet within miles, the situation is reversed. On the embankment high above **Blackburn**, or on the wharf at **Wigan Pier**, the visitor could easily forget that, only a short distance before, the canal was up in the moors. The Leeds to Liverpool Canal is one of stark contrasts, and that, more than anything, makes it a popular holiday route.

It took forever to build the route from Yorkshire across the divide between the Red and White Roses into Lancashire, and on over to the River Mersey and Liverpool. Forty years after the first stretch was dug, the engineers were still working away to conquer the geographical problems posed by the route.

Parliament first gave approval to the canal in 1770. Only in 1816 was it finished, delayed by periodical lack of interest and money and engineering difficulties. Like many of the early canals, only when traffic was flowing on a stretch (and toll money flowing in) could the next part be paid for. Sometimes construction was delayed for years while engineers tried to work out how to cross the next barrier.

The city of **Leeds**, where the canal begins at a junction with the **River Aire**, is of little intrinsic interest, except for a few attractive municipal buildings. But the canal rapidly moves on, and two miles beyond the junction the canal passes **Armley Mills**, an industrial museum built in an early 19th-century tex-

tile mill, with a wide range of relics of Britain's Industrial Revolution. About half a mile on, and a short walk down the hill on the banks of the River Aire is the Bridge Inn.

About 3 miles (5 km) out of Leeds the canal passes the village of **Kirkstall**, noted for its beautiful 12th-century Cistercian abbey. Although little known, **Kirkstall Abbey** is one of the finest and most intact abbeys of its kind in Britain. Though part is fenced off, it's possible to walk round much of the site. Opposite the abbey is a well-organized **folk museum**, which has, among other exhibits, reconstructions of Victorian shops and streets.

Throughout this stretch of canal there are numerous hand-operated swing bridges. Although many of them have roads passing over the top, don't be daunted: just push, they move easily under pressure.

From Kirkstall, the canal heads up the Aire valley, past the village of **Rodley**, and the town of **Shipley**. **Saltaire**, the next village on the canal, is a classic

Left, exterior of Skipton Castle. <u>Right</u>, some of the castle's many exhibits.

example of a number of model towns built by enlightened employers in the 19th century to improve the lives of their workforce. Here, the benefactor was Sir Titus Salt, a Bradford textile manufacturer who decided in the 1850s to move his factory and his workers out of that town.

The result was Saltaire, a very regimented little town built around the huge 550-ft (170-meter) mill. In all, Salt built a total of 820 houses, as well as municipal buildings and schools. But also in keeping with the strict ethics of the Victorians, there are no pubs.

After Saltaire, the canal enters a long wooded cutting, before passing over an aqueduct above the River Aire and entering **Bingley**. Although of little interest, the town boasts one of the wonders of the British waterway system, the **Bingley Five-Rise Locks**.

A remarkable feat of engineering, and a nightmare for the inexperienced boatman, the locks raise (or lower) the canal by almost 60 ft (18 meters). They differ from most staircases of locks in that

there is no breathing space between each lock in the flight. Instead, leaving one lock chamber, the boat immediately enters the next. Trying to get one boat up and another down at the same time is a feat of planning, but there is a permanent lock-keeper to supervise.

From Bingley, the canal heads off with magnificent views od the moors, along a 16-mile (25-km) non-lock stretch to **Skipton**. To the north is **Ilkley Moor**, famous for the old folk song *On Ilkley Moor Baht 'At*. About three miles (five km) beyond Bingley the canal skirts the town of **Keighley**, where the short steam train up into Brontë country originates.

Watch out, also, on the way into Keighley for the rather attractive 17th-century **East Riddlesden Hall**, set alongside a small lake a few yards from the waterway and now owned by the National Trust. Near the Hall, is the Marquis of Granby pub.

To visit the land of the Brontës, there is a regular train service at weekends, and daily in summer on the preserved **Keighley and Worth Valley Railway**.

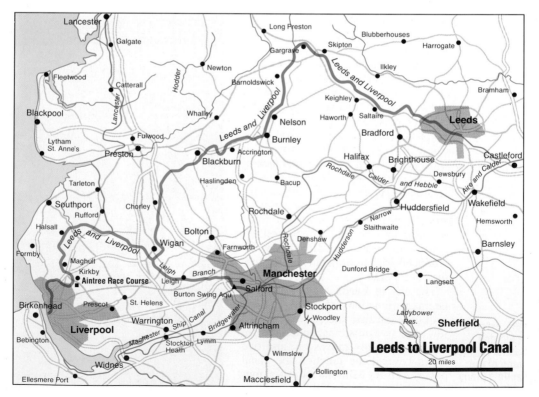

Leeds to Liverpool Canal

20 miles

Get off at **Haworth**, and walk up to the top of the hill to **Haworth vicarage**, where Emily, Charlotte and Anne were brought up. It was here that classics like *Wuthering Heights* and *Jane Eyre* were written, and much of the bleak Yorkshire countryside in which they were set lies just to the north of Haworth. The vicarage is now preserved as a **Brontë museum**, and is full of relics of the family's time there, including the sofa where Emily died. It gets crowded.

Beyond Keighley there are even better views of the moors. One of the prettiest towns in Yorkshire, **Skipton** ("Sheep Town" in Anglo-Saxon) is 5 miles (8 km) from Keighley, and is an old market town dating to medieval times, and the late medieval **castle** is well worth a visit, especially its dungeon. Near the castle is a corn mill, dating to 1200.

The first meeting of the canal company was held in the Black Horse Hotel; there is a chandlery on the main quayside, with all necessary services, and shops are only a short distance from the towpath. From the center, a now redundant, half-mile canal runs under the castle walls to an old freight depot; don't try going up it in a narrow boat, you may not be able to turn around.

Use Skipton as a jumping off point to spend a short time in the **Yorkshire Dales**. Take a train up into the heart of some of the most beautiful moorland. Indeed, the train journey, along the famous **Settle to Carlisle line**, is one of Britain's most famous tourist attractions. (The schedule is irregular. Check with BritRail in Skipton for departure times.) The railway is a stupendous example of the skills of Victorian engineering, climbing right over the hills and affording some breathtaking views. Head for some of the highest stations, such as **Dent** or **Ribblehead**, famous for its spectacular and famous Victorian railway viaduct which spans a lovely moorland valley.

Returning to the waterway, the 10 miles (18 km) or so beyond Skipton are probably the most attractive part of the canal, with good views of the moorland

The Brontë sisters' home in Haworth.

on either side. **Gargrave**, which lies at the western end of this stretch of water, is a lovely village on the edge of the Dales. The Anchor Inn, just outside Gargrave, is a good canalside pub.

Only a short distance from Gargrave by either bus or taxi is the village of **Malham**, and its cove, a rare geological formation which has become one of the Dales' most popular sites. **Malham Cove** is a rather bizarre limestone cliff with a huge stone terrace above it. From the top, which is easily accessible, there are spectacular views of the area.

After Gargrave, the canal turns south and away from the heart of the Yorkshire Dales, and moves off into **Lancashire**. Though less attractive than the previous stretch, the canal passes through some pleasant countryside; even some of the more industrial parts of the route are backed by views of moorland. Most of the towns on this stretch of the Leeds-Liverpool are old Lancashire textile centers, and remain grimy and depressed with the decline of their factories and mills.

At **Foulridge**, 12 miles (20 km) beyond Gargrave, there is a one-mile tunnel which takes the canal through the hillside before passing a group of reservoirs that provide it with much of its water supplies. Legend has it that a cow swam the entire length of Foulridge Tunnel earlier this century, before being revived with a large quantity of brandy. A photograph on the wall of the Hole in the Wall Inn, in Foulridge village, appears to substantiate the tale.

The canal then climbs a flight of seven locks and skirts the town of **Nelson** before heading into Burnley, once the most prosperous textile center in Lancashire. To the north, look for views of the **Calder Valley**, and of **Pendle Hill**, one of Britain's best-known witchcraft areas, with a long tradition as the site of many magical rites. In the Middle Ages there were witch-hunts here, and in one particularly brutal purge in 1612, many local women were executed after being accused of having practised magic.

For the waterway enthusiast, though, **Burnley** is more remarkable for its long canal embankment, which is acclaimed as one of the seven wonders of the waterway network. It runs in an almost exact line for 1 mile across the edge of the town, with a chimney-top view of the grey slate roofs. As recently as 1955 this was a flourishing stretch of commercial waterway, carrying around a million tons of freight each year. That traffic is now gone.

On the far side of Burnley, the canal passes through another short tunnel, and follows the line of the M65 motorway towards the town of Blackburn. At **Clayton-le-Moors**, the Dunk Inn, a small manor house converted into a restaurant and inn, sits on the bank. Though the local authorities in **Blackburn** have begun to re-landscape the canal's route through town, much of the area remains unattractive and often derelict. After Blackburn, happily, the canal flows through pleasant countryside and at **Wheelton** there is a cruising center with all amenities.

At the bottom of the seven-lock flight at Wheelton is the junction with the now disused **Walton Summit** branch of the canal. Originally this 3-mile (5-km) route linked the Leeds-Liverpool to the Lancaster Canal, via a tramway route across the Ribble Valley.

Indeed, the original plan was to link the two via a huge aqueduct, which, had it not been rejected as totally uneconomic, would certainly have been one of the finest sights on the canals of Britain.

For the 12 miles (20 km) beyond Wheelton, before the canal reaches **Wigan**, it runs close to the line of the **River Douglas**, passing through a steep cutting in the rock. Although Wigan, like Blackburn and Burnley, was a major industrial and coal mining center which has now become somewhat run down, it has much to offer the canal enthusiast, chiefly thanks to the work of the author George Orwell. His novel *The Road to Wigan Pier* has given the town a fame which it would certainly not have otherwise enjoyed.

Originally **Wigan Pier** was a local joke: it was nothing more than a wharf from which the daily passenger service down the canal to Liverpool ran before the arrival of the railways. But the notoriety of its pier has been used to create a remarkable tourist attraction in the old warehouses and buildings around the site of the original pier.

The thriving **museum** and **heritage center** has displays giving a fascinating insight into the industrial history of the town. Of special interest is the recreation of a Victorian classroom where visitors can experience for themselves the harsh teaching and discipline of the era that produced Dickens's famous Dotheboys Hall. The museum has several unemployed actors on its books at a time, and they can be found throughout the complex offering dramatic portrayals of past Wigan characters. Together with a range of cafés, restaurants and pubs, the area is a must.

In Wigan the canal forks, with the main line heading on westwards towards Liverpool, and the Leigh branch turning to the south-east, where it links up with the Bridgewater Canal leading into Manchester. The route towards Liverpool is of less interest, though it passes close to the sea and past **Aintree Race-**course where the Grand National is held. The last stage into **Liverpool** is in poor repair, and flows through some of the less attractive parts of the city.

A better cruising route is down the **Leigh branch** and then on into Manchester down what was Britain's first canal, the Bridgewater. The journey is unusual in that it has no locks, and has much to offer the enthusiast. Follow the canal towards the village of **Worsley**, about 13 miles (20 km) by water from Wigan as it passes through the heart of the South Lancashire coal fields.

Although most of the mines are now closed, their effects are clear to see. Many of the old black slag heaps have been relandscaped, and do not impose on the landscape in the way they once did. But the results of subsidence, caused by the collapse of old mine shafts, is evident all around. For much of this part of the route, the canal runs along a raised embankment; but in fact, the canal is at its original level, it is the fields alongside it that have sunk.

A few miles from Worsley the canal

The Yorkshire Dales.

begins to turn orange. This bizarre phenomenon is caused by iron deposits seeping into the water from the huge network of underground mines at Worsley, which was the heart of the Duke of Bridgewater's industrial enterprises. He began his first canal in the 1760s to carry coal from his mines in the area into Manchester.

The water for the canal was ingeniously taken from the water supplies that seeped into the mine workings, by tunnelling deep into the hillside to create a channel for it to run out of. The remains of the old workings can still be seen in Worsley, just after the canal runs under the M62 motorway.

There is a small basin a few yards from the main canal route, and it was from here that the original water supply channels were built. Not only did the tunnels supply water for the route to Manchester and Liverpool, but they also served as an underground water access route to the coal faces. Much of the output from the Bridgewater collieries was shipped out of the hillside in long, low boats, before being transhipped to Manchester.

There are some lovely old half-timbered houses close to the canal, as well as The Bridgewater, a great pub. About 20 minutes' walk away is **Worsley Old Hall**, home of the Duke of Bridgewater, and now a restaurant and banquetting center.

From Worsley, the canal heads south into **Manchester**, passing another of the wonders of the waterway system, the **Barton Swing Aqueduct** over the Manchester Ship Canal. The plan caused mirth when it was mooted, and amazement when it opened in 1761, but its original aqueduct's successor, built in the 1890s, is, if anything, a still more remarkable feat of engineering. When in use, an entire section of the aqueduct is sealed and then swivels to allow ships to pass along the canal below.

At **Water's Meeting**, a junction about 2 miles (3 km) beyond the aqueduct in **Stretford**, fork off to the left and head into Manchester and the end of the route.

Right, wending through the Midlands.

348

SCOTLAND

The 60-mile (100-km) long **Caledonian Canal**, which provides a link between the Atlantic on the west coast and the North Sea on the east, is sheer bliss for those in search of a waterways vacation. The canal, which runs northeast to southwest, takes advantage of four lochs, **Dochfour**, **Ness**, **Oich** and **Lochy**, which lie in the heart of the **Great Glen**, "Glen Mohr", a giant geographical gash through the heart of the Highlands.

In 1822, after 19 years of labor, Thomas Telford linked these lochs by 22 miles (35 km) of man-made cuttings. At its southern end the canal enters Loch Linnhe at Fort William while at its northern end it debouches into the Moray Firth near Inverness. The canal was never a commercial success for its opening coincided, more or less, with the coming of steam and the building of ships larger than the 500 tons maximum permitted in the canal.

Those wishing to cruise its entire length (terms of hire do not permit boats to exit from it) have to negotiate 17 manned locks and eight swing bridges. Observe the chains in front of some of the lock gates. They are reminders of the days when sailing ships used the canal and the chains stopped them from colliding with the lock gates. At its southern end the canal crosses four small aqueducts over four small rivers.

The canal, especially in the lochs, is much wider than other British canals and might more appropriately be called the Caledonian Waterway, especially when force four or five winds funnel down the Great Glen and the waters of mile-wide Loch Ness become rough. Do not, on such occasions, make for the shore, but proceed to the man-made sections at either end of the loch. Three lighthouses assist those who stray from the straight, and not so narrow.

Vacationers have the canal pretty much to themselves, although they are occasionally joined by fishing boats or small naval vessels which use the canal to escape the rigors of Cape Wrath and the Pentland Firth at the north of Scotland. The region through which the canal runs is intimately associated with clan battles, the Jacobite rebellion and the deeds of the romantic Jacobite leader, Bonnie Prince Charles Edward Stuart, whose House of Stuart supporters attempted to overthrow the Hanoverian monarchy.

Inverness, the capital of the Highlands, is a delightful county town with excellent shopping; the **River Ness**, where anglers cast for salmon, flows through it. The town is dominated by its **Castle**, a relatively modern affair, which occupies the site of older edifices. Superb views of the surrounding countryside can be enjoyed from **Castle Hill**. Other important buildings are the **Museum** and **Art Gallery**, the **Town House** and the **Mercat Cross**.

Five miles (8 km) after leaving Inverness, boats pass through the lock at **Dochgarroch** and enter small **Loch Dochfour**. Seven miles (11 km) later **Bona Light** is passed to the right and Loch Ness is entered. Bona is the only manned

lighthouse on the British inland waterway. Another unique claim is that the *Scot II*, which makes excursions from Inverness during the summer is, in the winter, the only ice-breaker on a British inland waterway. Its services are required only about once a decade when Loch Oich freezes over.

Twenty-two-mile (35-km) **Loch Ness**, although not as large as Loch Lomond, has the largest volume of water of any British loch (or lake) and, in parts, is more than 800 ft (240 meters) deep. And hidden in this depth is Nessie – or is it? If you fail to encounter the fabled monster then the evidence, both pro and con, is fairly presented at the Loch Ness Center at **Drumnadrochit**, a village 14 miles (22 km) south of Inverness and on the north shore of the loch. Although sceptics dismiss Nessie as a tourist gimmick, its first sighting goes back to the 6th century when St Columba is reported to have driven back a raging beast which was attacking a villager on the shores of the loch. Unproven, that peculiar verdict held in Scottish law courts (Scots law is different from English), is currently the answer to the existence of the monster. Whatever the truth, Nessie has been good to Hollywood.

Two miles (3 km) beyond Drumnadrochit, the shell of **Urquart Castle**, one of the most photographed castles in all Scotland, stands on Strone Point. In the 13th century, Robert the Bruce of Scotland and Edward I of England fought for its possession during the Wars of Independence. Then, in 1689, government troops held out against Jacobite forces; when they left in 1692, they blew up the castle so that it could not be used by the Jacobites.

Immediately south of Urquart Castle stands a monument to Sir John Cobb, killed in 1952 when attempting to break the world water-speed record on Loch Ness. Did his jet-boat, *Crusader*, overturn because it hit the monster?

Further south (22 miles/35 km from Inverness) is **Invermoristone**, a tiny town at the end of **Glen Moriston**. About 15 miles (24 km) west of the town at the head of the glen is a cave where Prince Charlie hid after his defeat at Culloden. A cairn here marks the spot where a young Edinburgh lawyer, Roderick McKenzie, a bodyguard who bore a striking resemblance to the Prince, was killed by government troops. As he lay dying he murmured: "You have murdered your Prince." Tempted by the £30,000 ransom on the Prince's head, the soldiers believed McKenzie; their mistake was not discovered until the Prince had escaped.

Over on the other side of the loch are **Inverfarigaig** and **Foyers**, which have good moorings and are pleasant places to stretch one's legs. The former has a Forestry Commission **exhibition center** showing how forest plantations are developed, what species of trees are grown and what animals and birds live in these plantations. Several forest walks from here offer splendid views of Loch Ness. About 1 mile from the Foyers pier the **Falls of Foyer** tumble through an attractive setting.

And so to **Fort Augustus** at the foot of Loch Ness. It stands about midway between Inverness and Fort William. A

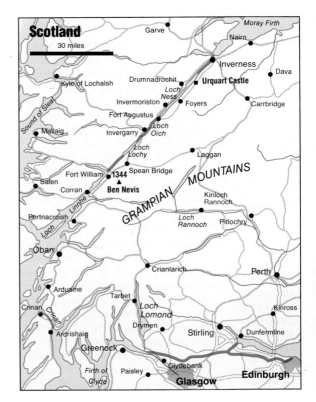

series of five locks in the heart of the town is the focal point. Before entering the locks you might wish to moor in the short stretch of canal and visit the town about which Johnson wrote, five years after his great Highland jaunt with Boswell: "The best night I have had these 20 years was at Fort Augustus."

Fort Augustus received its name in 1715 when a fort was built after the Jacobite uprising of that year. General Wade enlarged it in 1730 and built a road, parts of which can still be seen, linking Fort William and Inverness. Other roads built by Wade are seen on the south bank of the canal and a splendid bridge which he built still stands at **Whitebridge**. The site of the fort is now occupied by an abbey, overlooking Loch Ness, which is home to Benedictine monks and the boys who attend their school. Visitors are welcome. Also worth visiting is the **Great Glen Heritage Exhibition**, which charts the history of the region and the canal.

After Fort Augustus comes the most secret part of the canal. For 5 miles (8 km) it runs alongside the River Oich far away from the road and its bustling traffic. **Cullochy Lock** leads to the 4-mile (6-km) long **Loch Oich** which, at 106 ft (32 meters) above sea-level, is the highest point on the canal. It is the shallowest of the lochs.

Ruined **Invergarry Castle**, burned down by the Duke of Cumbernauld in the harrying of the Highlanders which went on after Culloden, stands on the north side of the canal. Just after this is a monument with inscriptions in English, Latin, Gaelic and French (the Scottish Rosetta Stone?) which records a most sanguine event. **The Well of Heads** remembers the decapitation of seven brothers; their heads were washed here before being presented to the chieftain whose two sons they were alleged to have murdered.

On leaving Loch Oich, the canal passes through the long, almost straight, tree-lined **Laggan Cutting** before entering an 8-mile (13-km) canal section linking this loch with the sea at Corpach. However, immediately before this, and be-

Ben Nevis, Britain's highest mountain.

yond the limits of boat hire, is **Neptune's Staircase**, which may well be the most remarkable lock flight in all Britain. A flight of eight locks descends through 64 ft (19 meters). From here there are superb views of **Ben Nevis** which at 4,406 ft (1,321 meters) is the highest peak in Britain.

Fort William, at the head of **Loch Linnhe** into which the canal flows, is a busy touring center. From here it is possible to climb to the summit of Ben Nevis. Climbing equipment is not needed but it is an exhausting full day's outing. In the town visit the **West Highland Museum** which contains much memorabilia associated with Prince Charlie and the Jacobite uprising.

While passing through the canal, bird-watchers should keep an eagle eye for the Golden ones; nesting osprey can also be observed. Roe and red deer are most common on the section which joins Loch Ness and Loch Oich, and otters are also frequently spotted. Good salmon and trout fishing can be enjoyed in the waters of the canal and, indeed, the

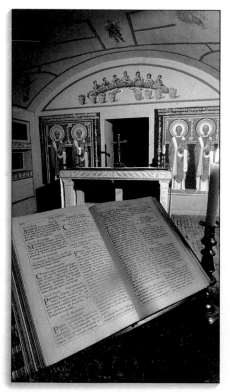

largest brown trout ever caught in Britain was landed from Loch Oich.

Two excursions, one from either end of the canal, involve the ubiquitous Prince Charlie. **Culloden**, 5 miles (8 km) east of Inverness, is a sacred shrine to died-in-the-wool Scots. Here, on the grim battlefield where the ambitions of the Stuarts finally perished, is a memorial to those who died along with a comprehensive Visitors Center.

At **Fort William**, train aficionados will thrill to what is possibly the most picturesque railway journey in all Britain. The destination is **Mallaig**, the end of the song-writer's *Road to the Isles*. From there it is a short ferry trip to the island of **Skye**. The train journey takes two hours and is on the only normal gauge British Rail line which still, on occasions, uses a steam locomotive. During the summer months some trains have an observation car. En route, **Glenfinnan** is passed, where stands a prominent monument marking where the clansmen rallied to the banner which Prince Charlie unfurled in 1745. Or does it? Recent research suggests that the rallying cry was uttered about 800 meters to the north.

Loch Lomond: Some may take the low road and some may take the high, but visitors to Loch Lomond, queen of the Scottish lochs, might prefer to charter a motor cruiser at **Inverbeg** or at **Ardlui**. This is the most peaceful way to enjoy Loch Lomond. The waters are seldom busy and rare is the day when they are visited by as many as 1,000 boats, the vast majority of which keep to the southern end. And, although the winds may blow, rare also, is the day when the waters of the loch are ruffled by waves.

Loch Lomond, the largest loch in Great Britain, sits just 18 miles (29 km) north of **Glasgow**. The loch, 24 miles (38 km) long and 630 ft (189 meters) at its deepest point, consists of a long narrow pipe-like portion (about a mile wide) at the northern half which expands into a bulbous southern half which is 5 miles (8 km) at its widest. Dotted about the waters of the southern section are 30 small islands.

Inchmurrin (Island of Spears), the

Abbey Church in Fort Augustus.

most southerly and largest of the islands (large is a purely relative term with no island covering more than a couple of square miles) has several attractions, including the meagre ruins of **Lennox Castle**, a ruined monastery believed to have been founded in the 6th century by the Irish missionary St Mirren, and, in the north corner of the island, a nudist colony. Visitors who are more modest, but wish to brave the cold waters (beware the steep shelving) might make for the sandy **Bikini Beach** of **Inchmoan** which is near Inchmurrin.

The yew trees on **Inchlonaig**, the most northerly island, have historical interest, as it is from these trees, or their forefathers, that Robert the Bruce's men cut their bows before defeating the English at the Battle of Bannockburn in 1314, a date known to every Scottish schoolchild. (The yews on **Eilean Vow**, one of the very few islands in the northern part of the loch, are said to have been planted by Bruce so that his descendants might have powerful bows.)

Several islands near the eastern shore of the loch constitute a nature reserve. Visitors who clamber to the summit of **Inchcaillon**, the largest, will be straddling the **Highland Line**, a geological fault running from nearby **Helensburgh** on the west coast to **Stonehaven** on the east and which demarcates the Highlands and the Lowlands.

All these islands can be visited by the public who, however, will not be welcomed on **Inchconnachan** or on **Inchfad**. The former belongs to Lady Arran who holds the world's water speed record for women (set on Lake Windermere), while the latter's is owned by Ted Toleman who, with the entrepreneur Richard Branson, attempted in 1986 to establish a record Atlantic crossing (their boat sank).

Visitors should not be conned into thinking that they have seen Loch Lomond monsters if they observe strange animals swimming around **Bantry Bay** in the southwest corner of the loch. These are not Loch Lomond's answer to Nessie but a species of white deer, not albinos, swimming between the islands in search of food. Red deer also graze on

these islands and wild goat are seen on **Ben Lomond**. Golden eagles can be spotted at the northern part of the loch, while some of the islands are breeding grounds for capercailles, the largest of all British game birds. More mundane bird inhabitants of the loch are kestrel and ptarmigans.

Balloch, at the south end, is the busiest spot on the loch, attracting those in search of fish and chips or ice-cream, and those wishing to board the *Countess Fiona* for half and full-day excursions. When Dr Johnson and Boswell stayed at Cameron House near Balloch in 1772, the doctor thought little of the countryside. Nor did William Wordsworth on his first visit: he found that the proportion of diffused water was too great. Nevertheless, he was inspired to write several poems including *To a Highland Girl*. (Perhaps he liked women better than water?)

Balmaha, around the corner from Balloch on the eastern shore, has good moorings and great fishing.

Luss on the west shore and 7 miles (11 km) from Balloch is an absolute

Loch Ness, where a monster may lurk.

picture-book village which featured in the long-running British TV series *Take the High Road*. Five miles (8 km) past this is **Inverberg** which has an art gallery featuring the work of international artists. Sympathize, especially if it's dark, with the inhabitants of Culag Farm, just south of Inverbeg. The farm occupies a tiny no-man's land between the grids of two electricity suppliers.

Five miles (8 km) beyond Inverberg is **Tarbet** which is separated from **Arrochar** at the head of **Loch Long**, a sea loch, by a 2-mile (3-km) isthmus. In 1263 invading Norsemen dragged their longboats across this isthmus before pillaging and killing the inhabitants of Loch Lomond.

At the top of the loch is **Ardlui** where pleasure craft can venture up the **River Fallon** for about two miles (three km). From here a canal, still visible but not navigable, was cut when Queen Victoria wished to visit **Inveranan Inn**, about a mile away. A dram still awaits those who make the journey on foot.

Over on the east shore of the loch,

facing Inverbeg, is **Rowardennan**, behind which towers the mass of 3,192-ft (958-meter) **Ben Lomond**. Magnificent views can be enjoyed from the summit: allow five hours for an easy ascent and descent. Five miles (8 km) to the north of Rowardennan is **Inversnaid** and immediately beyond this is **Rob Roy's cave**. Strange that the cave should bear his name for almost 400 years before Rob Roy was born in 1671! Robert the Bruce, King of Scotland, is reputed to have hidden here.

Could the cave have gained its eponymous name because of the power of the pen? The famous freebooter, immortalized by Sir Walter Scott in his novel *Rob Roy*, was a kind of Scottish Robin Hood and Al Capone rolled into one. In return for payment of meal (cattle feed) Rob Roy offered protection to farmers. These payments became known as blackmeal and thus originated the word blackmail – another first for the Scots. Like Loch Ness, Rob Roy was rediscovered by Hollywood in 1995; he ended up looking uncannily like Liam Neeson.

Loch Dochfour, part of the Caledonian Canal.

From Inversnaid, a steep 4-mile (6-km) road leads inland to **Loch Katrine** in the heart of the Trossachs. This lovely stretch of water, also immortalized by Scott in *Lady of the Lake*, can best be enjoyed by boarding a delightful steamer which is, not unexpectedly, called *Sir Walter Scott.*

Loch Lomond, Britain's largest freshwater lake, 23 miles (37 km) long and 5 miles (8 km) across at its widest point, is a delight for fishermen, with both brown and sea trout, and coarse fish in the shape of perch, roach, eel and pike. The last named are enormous and the world's largest, Tommy Morgan's, which weighed 48 lbs (22 kg) was caught at the mouth of **Endrick Water** near Balmaha. Then there are powan, small freshwater herring found only in one other Scottish loch and in some Welsh lochs, whose presence suggests that in prehistoric times Loch Lomond was linked to the sea.

Across the loch is **Ben Lomond**, one of Scotland's 277 "Munros" – mountains which rise to more than 3,000 ft (900 meters) and offer a perenniel challenge to outdoors types from all over the world who set out to climb every one of them.

The Crinan Canal: This 9-mile (14-km) long canal on the west coast is Scotland's only other fully functional canal. It will scarcely attract those in search of an inland waterway or a barging holiday. Rather, the canal, with its 15 locks (the entrance ones are the only manned ones) and seven manned road bridges, offers yachties a short cut between **Loch Fyne** on the Firth of Clyde and cruising grounds on the west coast, and saves the long and often tempestuous voyage around the Mull of Kintyre.

Two miles (3 km) after entering at **Ardrishaig**, the canal passes above the pretty little white-washed town of **Lochgilphead**, the county town of Argyll. **Crinan**, at the west end of the canal, is a place of enchantment with its hotel, recommended restaurant and well-maintained boat basin. From the hotel's bar and restaurant splendid views can be enjoyed, especially at sunset, of **Duntrune Castle**, one of Scotland's oldest inhabited castles.

The Crinan Canal.

Atlantic

Ocean

ULSTER

NORTHERN IRELAND

Belfast

Lough
Neagh

Lower
Lough
Erne

Erne Waterway

Upper
Lough
Erne

Castle Coole

Lough
Allen

CONNAUGHT

EIRE

Irish

River Shannon

Lough
Ree

Royal Canal

Clonmacnois Abbey

Grand Canal

Clogham Castle

Birr Castle

Lough
Derg

River Shannon

LEINSTER

Naas Line

Japanese Gardens

Milltown Feeder

National Stud Farm

Dublin

Barrow Navigation

Sea

MUNSTER

Irish Canals
30 miles

Dunglow
Letterkenny
Londonderry
Coleraine
Strabane
Maghera
Ballymena
Glencolumbkille
Donegal
Omagh
Cookstown
Balyshannon
Belleek
Boa Island
Bundoran
Garrison
Dungannon
Ballycastle
Easky
Manorhamilton
Enniskillen
Lurgan
Sligo/ Sligeach
Belcoo
Armagh
Newcastle
Dowra
Monaghan
Keadew
Drumshanbo
Belturbet
Newry
Charlestown
Boyle
Carrick- on- Shannon
Castleblayney
Castlebar
Cavan
Carrickmacross
Claremorris
Ballymoe
Longford
Virginia
Dundalk/
Dun Dealgan
Tuam
Roscommon
Lanesborough
Slane
Galway/
Gaillimh
Athlone
Mullingar
Naul
Drogheda/
Driochead Atha
Ballinasloe
Kinnegad
Rush
Loughrea
Edenderry
Innfield
Maynooth
Gort
Shannon
Harbour
Tullamore
Lowtown
Sallins
Clondalkin
Portumna
Banagher
Droichead Nua
Naas
Bray
Scarriff
Monasterevin
Kildare
Ennis
Portlaoise
Nenagh
Roscrea
Athy
Laragh
Killaloe
Durrow
Carlow
Rathdrum
Limerick/
Luimheach
Milestone
Tullow
Carnew
Rathkeale
Urlingford
Kilkenny
Arklow
Rath Luirc
Cashel
Borris
Courtown
Caher
New Ross
Mitchelstown
Wexford/ Loch Garman
Mallow
Waterford/
Port Láirge
Dungarvan
Dunmore East
Cork/ Corcaigh
Bandon

362

IRELAND

Even when the Troubles in the northern part of the island were at their height, it was never too difficult to find havens of tranquility. Often, such escapes involved water – an easy enough commodity to find in Ireland, whether it is cascading from the sky or forming lakes and rivers filled with compliant fish. A journey along Ireland's waterways is a magical affair – a journey through a land of legends, poets and ancient castles, and some of the most beautiful, unspoiled lakes and rivers in Europe.

There's no better way to savor the country's great, green beauty than from a boat meandering along the River Shannon or the lakes of the River Erne, or cruising the Grand Canal. Gentle hills sloping to the water's edge, meadows filled with sheep, and small, dark forests with moss-covered trees line the waterways. There's excellent fishing throughout for everything from eel to trout, and plenty of coves and inlets for those who seek solitude.

History is here, too, for Ireland is bursting with the ruins of castles, medieval monasteries and ancient stone fortresses. Many of these ruins are on tiny islands in the lakes and rivers, accessible only by boat. There are also villages to explore where famous poets and novelists lived and worked: places that inspired men such as Oliver Goldsmith, William Butler Yeats and Anthony Trollope.

Lively pubs, many with traditional music, towns with tennis, golf and swimming facilities, and nature trails through wildlife preserves all are within easy reach of the water-borne traveler.

Preceding pages: Lough Ree on the River Shannon; upper Lough Erne in Northern Ireland.

THE IRISH REPUBLIC

Ireland's principal recreational waterways are the Shannon River, the Grand Canal and the Barrow Line in the Republic of Ireland, and the Erne River which flows north from the Republic into Northern Ireland.

The Shannon: Mention Ireland's longest river and immediately the image of green, rolling hills and placid waters is conjured into the mind. Although the river is that, it is more. Geographically, it divides the country's eastern and western halves, and the biggest river in Ireland cuts a long swathe down the center of the country for 214 miles (342 km). It played an important role in the country's ancient history, bringing both conquerors and settlers to its shores: Vikings from Scandinavia, Celts from northwest Spain and France, and monks who preserved learning during Europe's Dark Ages.

The river also served as a trade route, as a major line of defence against invaders, and as a means of gaining access to the country's interior, for both welcome and unwelcome visitors.

While much of the Shannon has been navigable since ancient times, it was not until the mid-18th century that it was opened as a continuous route for barges. In 1860, during Ireland's Great Famine, the navigation was further improved as part of a plan to relieve the famine.

In a land steeped in folklore, it should come as no surprise that the Shannon takes its name from a mythical princess, Sinann. Legend has it that Sinann, in pursuit of mystic knowledge, plunged into the well where the salmon of wisdom swam. The well suddenly boiled up into a raging flood and created the River Shannon, forever keeping her memory alive.

The Shannon is as beautiful and gentle as Ireland itself. From its source in County Cavan, to where it joins the Atlantic Ocean near Limerick City, the Shannon flows through 15 lakes and nine locks. It is navigable for 132 miles (211 km), from **Acres Lake**, near Bat-

tlebridge, County Leitrim, to the estuary at **Limerick City**. In addition, it has a network of tributaries, canals and lakes that give the Shannon system a total of more than 1,100 navigable miles (1,760 km), and a lack of industrial works along the river ensures clear water and unpolluted skies.

Occasionally, however, the skies of Ireland weep too much for even the Shannon's swollen arteries, and the brown waters spill out over the bogs, the pastures and farmland. Not surprisingly, fishing and boating dominate the region's attractions.

So gentle is the Shannon that from **Lough Allen**, near its source, to **Killaloe**, the southernmost point of most recreational boating, it drops only 60 ft (18 meters) in 187 miles (299 km), and passes through seven locks. The river's remaining two locks are south of Killaloe in a stretch of river that's off-limits to rental boats.

Shannon Pot, a tiny, swirling spring in the Cuilcagh Mountains, 500 ft (150 meters) above sea-level, about a half-

Left, Birr Castle. Right, feathered friends.

hour's drive from Carrick-on-Shannon, is the river's source. It's easy to find, but take along rubber boots or plan to go barefoot because the area is very muddy, especially after a rain.

The Shannon flows into Ireland's two largest lakes: **Lough Ree**, covering 40 square miles (109 sq. km) and **Lough Derg**, 50 sq. miles (128 sq. km). The Ree is in the center of Ireland, near Athlone, while the Derg is in the lower Shannon, with Portumna at its northern tip, and Killaloe at its southern.

Harbors and mooring sites are scattered throughout the Shannon system, many with fishing and boating facilities. Seven of these have boating centers with companies offering cabin cruisers for rent on a weekly basis. These are Carrick-on-Shannon, Athlone, Ballykeeran, Portumna, Banagher, Williamstown and Killaloe.

Fishing is excellent throughout, and there's an abundance of wildlife to enjoy. Swans, waterhens, ducks and many types of birds will come up to your boat and feed from your hand. The woods along the shores hide foxes, badgers, otters and weasels, which can sometimes be spotted in the evenings.

You might even see mink, for the woods of the upper and middle Shannon and the Grand Canal are full of wild mink. Why mink? Around 1985 they either escaped from a mink farm or were turned loose by animal rightists, nobody knows for sure. But mink, like most rodents, proliferate quickly, and there are now thousands of them living in the wild.

Carrick-on-Shannon, northern gateway to Shannon cruising, is the capital of County Leitrim, Ireland's least populated county. It is surrounded by some of Ireland's most beautiful lake country and is both a fishing and boating center.

In ancient times, Vikings and others frequently crossed the river at Carrick to pillage and plunder. In 1613 the town was incorporated by King James I of England, and was fortified and garrisoned for protection. Today the ancient walls are gone and the town of nearly 1,900 people welcomes invaders of an-

Looking down on Lough Derg.

366

other sort: those who come to enjoy boating, fishing, miles of nature walks, and an old-fashioned Irish town.

Few buildings from Carrick's past survive: the **Court House** and **Protestant church** from the 1820s are just about it. The **Bush Hotel** is one other landmark building, with the distinction of being Ireland's oldest continuously-operated family hotel. For 200 years, the Maher family have run it, and Thomas and Rosaleen Maher, the current proprietors, are the sixth generation. Friday nights in July and August, the **Bush Pub** offers Irish Nights, traditional Irish music that fills the pub with both locals and visitors. Irish Nights are popular in pubs all along the waterways and are a wonderful way to meet local people and fellow boaters.

Just across the river is something older: the 15th-century ruins of **Creevelea Abbey**. Founded by the Franciscans in 1508, a church and cloister remain, and among the well-preserved carvings is one of St Francis preaching, with birds and other wild animals around him.

You've seen the Shannon Pot, you've rented a cabin cruiser at Carrick-on-Shannon, you've had your lessons and you're ready to go. But don't go south; head north to **Battlebridge** and to the **Lough Allen Canal**, a waterway 4½ miles (7 km) long, with two locks, leading to Lough Allen, the Shannon's third largest lake. A popular fishing spot, the lake is 7 miles (11 km) long and 2 miles (3 km) wide, and has many secluded coves and inlets. The village of **Drumshanbo**, at the southern end of the lake, is an angling resort and home of **Paddy Mac's**, a lively and popular pub when on weekends and in the summer season, music resounds from the building.

Also north of Carrick is **Lough Key**, near the town of **Boyle**. Considered by many to be the most beautiful lake in the entire Shannon system, the Key is reached by cruising 8 miles (13 km) up the Boyle River, a tributary of the Shannon. Filled with 32 heavily wooded islands and a tiny harbor on the west shore, the lake is part of Lough Key **Forest Park**, a nature preserve with

Monuments abound near Clonmacnois.

walking trails, bog gardens, a deer enclosure, and camping facilities. Many of the lake's islands contain ruins of ancient stone buildings.

Back in Carrick, the Upper Shannon is entered, and just south of Carrick is **Jamestown**, a 17th-century village founded by King James I of England with a small portion of its original fortified walls still standing. Because the arched Jamestown Bridge is low, boats must detour on to the **Jamestown Canal**, about 2 miles (3 km) long, with a lock at the lower end. From here, the Shannon forms a loop and it's possible to go up river a short way to the village of Drumsna, or downstream into a series of lakes.

Drumsna is a quiet, country village where the novelist Anthony Trollope (1815–82) once lived during the years he spent in Ireland as a postal surveyor. Near the ruins of his house is an old cemetery, burial place of Thomas Heazle Parke, who accompanied the explorer Henry Morton Stanley to Africa.

Heading south on the loop you'll enter the tiny, pristine lakes of **Lough Tap** and **Lough Boderg**, both quiet spots, ideal for fishing or swimming. From here, there's another slight detour southwest down the placid mountain river, past reed beds and rocky banks to three more small, secluded lakes: **Carnadoe**, **Grange** and **Kilglass**. All three are noted for the privacy they afford those wanting solitude.

Cruise north again to the Shannon and enter **Lough Bofin**, site of **Derrycarne**, a wooded promontory on the lake's northern tip, where a skirmish took place between the Roman Catholic troops of James II and the Protestant troops of William of Orange. Further south, still on the Bofin, is the village of **Dromod**, once noted for its ironworks. Today it proudly displays signs announcing that it has been named County Leitrim's Tidy Town winner several times.

The Shannon emerges from Lough Bofin at the village of **Roosky**, which has excellent berthing facilities, restaurants, grocery stores, and pubs. A popular and not very expensive restaurant here is The Crews Inn.

Just beyond Roosky is a lock, and slightly further south is **Lough Forbes**, a lake with good trout fishing. At the southern tip of Lough Forbes sits **Termonbarry**, a village named after St Barry who died in 595. Legend has it that he transformed a boulder into a boat and crossed the river in it. Observe the rock at a church in **Whitehall** village.

Just beyond the village on the left, the **Royal Canal** (only partially open) swings in and the Shannon continues its lazy meander southward for 6 miles (10 km), flowing past woodlands and shores lined with beds of high reeds, to Lanesborough.

Lanesborough is the northern entrance to Lough Ree, one of Ireland's two great lakes. The town is also gateway to Goldsmith Country, where the Anglo-Irish writer Oliver Goldsmith, author of *The Vicar of Wakefield* and *She Stoops to Conque*r, was born and wrote some of his major works. **Ballyleague**, where the tour of Goldsmith Country begins, is less than a mile from Lanesborough. The poet was born in 1729 in the nearby village of **Pallas**. All the places associated with Goldsmith's life and poetry are well marked and easy to find, including the "decent church that topped the neighboring hill", "the never-failing brook" and "the busy mill".

Enter **Lough Ree** with caution. One of Europe's most magnificent stretches of water, the Ree (Lake of the Kings) has few safe moorings and is big enough to whip up waves that make crossing in a storm dangerous. Even in mild weather, novice boaters should cruise in the company of other craft.

Once in, the magic of its many islands take over. In the distance, often shrouded in mist, loom ruins of ancient castles and monasteries that seem to rise directly out of the lake, from islands so tiny they look as if they'll sink from the weight of the ruins.

One of the most interesting is **Saint's Island**, which had a flourishing Augustinian monastery during the 14th century. Another, **Inchcleraun**, also called Quaker Island after some 19th-century inhabitants, is where the sister of Queen Maeve, Clothra, was supposedly killed by a stone hurled from the shore. It also has the ruins of a 6th-century monastery, several old churches, including one dating to the 13th century, and a number of early Christian gravestones.

Athlone, County Westmeath, known in poem and song as "the center station of this Irish nation", comes honorably by this description. Sitting at the southern tip of Lough Ree, it is near the geographical center of Ireland, and is the midpoint in the navigable section of the Shannon. The town of almost 10,000 people is about a 10-minute walk from the Jolly Roger Marina, a full-service harbor and leisure complex.

The ancient Gaelic name for Athlone was Ath Moir, (Great Ford), and through the centuries it endured many invasions because of its strategic location on the river. Brian Boru, High King of Ireland, met here with his troops in 1001. In the early 1200s Anglo-Normans occupied Athlone and built a wall to guard the river crossing.

The Shannon at Killahoe. Today visitors can see some of the historic areas on a 45-minute walking tour, outlined in a booklet offered free by the local tourist office. The tour starts at **King John's Castle**, Athlone's most famous historic landmark. It was built in 1210 by the Bishop of Norwich for King John of Magna Carta fame, and inside is an interesting **museum**. The stained-glass windows of the 1930-ish **Saints Peter and Paul church** depict well-known people of the area, including the tenor John McCormack (1884-1945). Locally born, he's further honored with a plaque on the house in **The Bawn** where his life began, and a bust on the walk by the river.

There's a wide variety of land-based sporting facilities in Athlone: an 18-hole golf course, all-weather tennis courts, a heated, indoor swimming pool, plus disco bars and plenty of old-fashioned pubs. (The best ones are found on the winding streets leading to the river.) It's also an excellent shopping town, with three supermarkets, two shopping centers and many boutiques and craft shops which make the quarter-mastering job easier.

Ballykeeran is 5 miles (8 km) from Athlone, on the shores of the Inner Lakes of Lough Ree. It's home to SGS Marine, another extensive boating center, and the pub here resounds on Friday and Saturday nights with traditional Irish music and entertainment.

A short walk from the marina, Ballykeeran is a typical country village, surrounded by stone fences, bramble bushes and winding roads, where sheep and cows have the right of way. It's another good starting point for the Poets' Country of Oliver Goldsmith and John Keegan Casey.

Both Athlone and Ballykeeran are good bases for local touring, but if bicycles don't appeal, try local taxis.

About 11 miles (18 km) south of Athlone, on the banks of the Shannon, is one of Ireland's most famous historical sites: the ruins of **Clonmacnois**, a monastic community founded by St Ciaran in 548. There's a jetty for mooring at the entrance, the monuments include a cathedral, eight churches, two round towers, three sculptured high Celtic crosses and parts of two others, more than 200 monumental slabs, and the remains of a castle.

Created to be a center for education as well as piety, as its scholastic reputation grew, Clonmacnois became a magnet, attracting the most talented and learned. The scriptoria was especially renowned, and the *Book of the Dun Cow* and *Annals of Tighernach* were among the many manuscripts produced here. Artisans were also valuable members of the community, creating beautifully crafted religious artifacts which decorated the churches.

Although Clonmacnois was the object of many plundering raids, the Vikings in the 9th century and Normans 400 years later caused the most damage. The monastery flourished until Henry VIII's break with the Catholic church in the 1530s, and his subsequent edict ordering the dissolution of all monasteries. In 1552 the English troops garrisoned at Athlone, taking Henry at his word, reduced the settlement to rubble. A final sacking 100 years later by

Ireland is in their faces, fishing is in their blood.

Cromwell's forces completed the devastation, and the site remained deserted until 1955 when it came under the aegis of the National Trust. The result is the magnificent ruins on view today.

Sitting high above the Shannon, Clonmacnois is laid out in a pattern familiar to most Irish monastic settlements: a fortified stone wall encloses a cathedral at its center, with several smaller churches dotted about the site.

At the front of the **cathedral** is one of the best-preserved crosses in Ireland, **The Cross of the Scriptures**. Carved in the 10th century, it contains stories from the Bible mixed with local figures and events. On the east face, look for a scene showing King Dermot and St Ciaran laying the church cornerstone.

Other noteworthy remains include the minute 9th-century **Oratory of St Ciaran** which probably contains the founder's tomb, **Temple Finian** whose 12th-century round tower is 56 ft (17 meters) tall, and **O'Rouke's Tower**, which is 4 ft (1.5 meters) higher. The **Nuns' Church** is a short distance away

from the compound. Although in ruins, the entrance doorway and choir arch are in good shape with beautifully executed carvings. Some flavor of the monastery's rich past is remembered every 9 September when the faithful gather to celebrate the feast day of St Ciaran with an open air service held under a canopied altar.

Shannonbridge, just downstream, was named for the 16-arched span that crosses the river, and has a sheltered mooring that is overshadowed by the ruins of a suitably grim Napoleonic fort. Four miles (6 km) from Clonmacnois is **Shannon Harbour**, where the Grand Canal joins the Shannon. From here it's less than 3 miles (5 km) from **Banagher**, County Offaly, an area with many old castles and interesting towns. The harbor is adjacent to a seven-arch bridge built in 1840 during the reign of Queen Victoria.

Banagher is another town where Anthony Trollope once lived. He wrote his first novel here in the 1840s, *The Macdermots of Ballycloran*.

A good catch.

Several castles dot the area, including **Birr Castle**, 8 miles (13 km) south of Banagher, home of the Earl and Countess of Rosse. It has gardens filled with 1,000 trees and box hedges that, according to that bible of banality, *Guinness Book of World Records*, are the world's tallest. **Birr town**, a market center, should not be missed: many fine 17th and 18th-century buildings are located throughout, with some of the best on Oxmantown and St John's Malls.

Other interesting visits near Banagher include **Cloghan Castle**, Ireland's oldest inhabited castle; and **Gallen Priory**, a convent that was once a monastery founded in 492 by St Gallen.

On a more modern note, Banagher has squash and tennis courts, an outdoor swimming pool and a local pottery factory. The town also has one of the most popular pubs on the Shannon, Hough's Irish Singing Pub.

This part of the Shannon has large deep pools for pike, perch and bream fishing, and the **Little Brosna River**, a tributary south of Banagher, has excellent trout fishing.

The next port of call is **Portumna**, County Galway nearly 16 miles (26 km) south of Banagher. Between Banagher and Portumna the river flows past reed beds, flat, wooded areas and a series of channels with islands. The bridge at Portumna is low and must be opened for all craft except rowboats. Sound horn, and slow down in case the keeper is not immediately available.

Portumna, a fishing and outdoors center, has a small harbor and the village is within walking distance of it. On the edge of town is a beautiful walking area and a photographer's dream: **Portumna Forest Park**, a 1,000-acre (400-hectare) wildlife sanctuary bordering Lough Derg. A magical place, its nature trails wind through forests where the trees seem to glow from their moss blankets.

Lough Derg, the largest and most southerly of the Shannon lakes, ranks with Lough Ree as one of the most unspoiled and beautiful lakes in all of Europe. It has its own share of ruin-strewn islands that are accessible only by boat, and a vastness that guarantees solitude and privacy.

Although easier to navigate than the Ree because of its many safe moorings, the same weather cautions apply here. The moorings on the shores of the lake include tiny **Williamstown** and **Dromineer**, a colorful harbor town on Lough Derg, boasts a marina and sailing club with boats grouped around the ruins of 16th-century **Dromineer Castle**. Good trout fishing abounds, and children will enjoy the swimming and picnic areas.

Inland, about 6 miles (10 km) southeast of Dromineer, **Nenagh**, County Tipperary, has a well preserved 13th-century castle. For a spot of exercise, try climbing one of the tower stairwells. The views from the roof of the surrounding countryside are superb, but be prepared for a good workout. The towers are 100 ft (30 meters) high and the stairwells dark and steep; its always locked, so stop at the local tourist office for a key.

Killaloe, County Clare, where the lower Shannon emerges from Lough Derg, is on the southernmost shore of the lake, 13 miles (21 km) from Limerick. The Killaloe marina, with 200 berths, is the largest inland marina in Ireland, and the headquarters of Ireland's only luxury cruise ship, the *Shannon Princess*, owned and operated by Ronnie Kearsley.

Rental boats are not allowed south of Killaloe and only experienced sailors with seaworthy vessels should attempt to navigate the remaining 18 miles (28 km) of river. Below Killaloe is a two-rise staircase lock, with a rise and fall of 110 ft (33 meters). Even the fish get a little help: salmon trying to swim upstream to their spawning ground have their own lock which takes three hours to raise them to the upper canal. The entire procedure is fascinating; if time permits make the trip to the locks.

Killaloe is connected to the village of **Ballina**, County Tipperary, by a stone bridge with 13 arches that spans the Shannon. Both towns have plenty of hotels, bed and breakfast places, pubs and restaurants. Only an an hour's drive from Shannon Airport, those renting boats at Killaloe can usually arrange to be met and driven to the marina.

The Grand Canal: The other main recreational waterway in the Republic was excavated in the 1750s. It cuts across the center of the country, from the Liffey River in Dublin to the Shannon River at Shannon Harbour, County Offaly, 80 miles (128 km) to the west. It took 54 years to build the canal – from 1751, when construction began in Dublin, to 1805 when the Grand Canal reached Shannon Harbour. By the mid-1800s, the canal was a major shipping route, filled with barges transporting nearly 400,000 tons of goods annually to and from Dublin. By 1950, annual tonnage had dropped to 100,000 and in 1959 commercial traffic was withdrawn.

Wending its way through an unspoiled section of rural Ireland, the Grand Canal also travels through towns and villages that were thriving commercial centers during the glory days of barge travel. It also passes vast expanses of bogland where some farmers still cut turf by hand and carry it off by donkey cart to be

used as local fuel. There are long stretches of woodlands, and isolated villages with ruins of ancient castles and old monasteries.

Beginning with sea locks at the tidal River Liffey in Dublin, there are 36 locks on the Grand Canal, with the last one at Shannon Harbour. Branching off from the Grand is a network of smaller navigable canals with more locks, including the Barrow, Milltown Feeder, and Naas Lines.

Individual boat owners be warned: although the canal is navigable straight through to Dublin, Celtic Canal Cruisers, the only boat rental company on the canal, has made the area near Dublin off-limits to their barges because of vandalism within the city limits. (The nation's capital might be better left for a pre or post barge trip.)

Cruising west from Tullamore to Shannon Harbour, you'll pass a whiskey distillery, one of **Tullamore**'s best-known industries and one that made this town a busy center for canal traffic in the 18th and 19th centuries. Castles are

In springtime, yellow "blankets" cover Irish fields.

everywhere and an excursion to them is another way of getting to know local people. Those in the neighborhood include the ruins of **Shra Castle**, built in 1588, and **Ballycowan Castle**, built in 1626. Ruins of others, such as **Kilcolgan Castle** and **Coole Castle**, are within 2 miles (3 km) of the canal between Locks 31 and 32.

Between Locks 33 and 34 is **L'Estrange Bridge**. It was built, along with a military barracks, in the early 19th century to meet the threat of a French invasion. Within walking distance is **Clonony Castle**, which has a tower dating to the 16th century, and gravestones bearing the names of some of the family of Anne Boleyn, mother of Elizabeth I, and the first of Henry VIII's wives to be beheaded.

At **Shannon Harbour**, Locks 35 and 36 are larger than the others on the canal because they were built to accommodate steamers that once used the waterway. The town itself is a pretty, but sleepy village with a pub, general store and post office.

Cruising east from the 24th Lock, the scenery on the far side of Tullamore includes an 8-mile (13-km) stretch across bogland, from Lock 20 to Lock 19. This section of the canal was the most difficult to construct in the entire system, taking 10 years to complete because a series of drains had to be built across the soggy bogs then recrossed by transverse drains. Material was then excavated, dried, and wheeled to the canal to form embankments.

The Barrow Line: One of the important small canals branching south from the Grand Canal begins near Lock 19 at Lowtown, Country Kildare, the Barrow flows 28 miles (45 km) south to Athy. There it joins the River Barrow which continues another 42 miles/67 km to the sea at Waterford, and below Athy, the river is wild and beautiful, and for experienced boaters only (some rental agreements forbid passage on it). Opened to traffic in 1790, the canal served barges transporting goods from malt refineries in Athy and from mills, sugarbeet factories and refineries in Carlow, a town on

All ages participate when the music begins.

the Barrow River 12 miles (19 km) below Athy.

Halfway down the Barrow is the town of **Kildare**, one of Ireland's great horse-breeding and training centers. Kildare is on the western edge of **the Curragh**, a flat, grassy area stretching over 6,000 acres (2,400 hectares), where many of Ireland's top racing horses are trained. Visitors can walk or drive through the Curragh, and watch stablehands ride thoroughbreds across the vast plain. It's a dramatic sight: horse and rider silhouetted against the sky, with vivid green grass stretching as far as the eye can see. The Curragh racetrack hosts many races, including the Irish Derby.

The village of **Tully**, on the outskirts of Kildare, is home of the **National Stud Farm**, which has produced some of the world's great race horses. Open to the public from March through October, grooms will often lead a spirited stallion out of its stall and parade it around for visitors to admire. Especially beautiful to watch are the mares in the springtime, grazing in the meadows

with their foals. Even those only a few hours old are out, their mothers gently nudging them to try their wobbly, spider-like legs.

Across the road from the National Stud are the **Japanese Gardens**, designed by the well-known Japanese landscape designer Eida in 1906. They are open year-round, with guided tours available.

A good place to eat in Kildare is **Silken Thomas**, a restaurant and pub named after Lord Thomas Fitzgerald, a local aristocrat nicknamed Silken because of his love for silk clothes. A member of the Geraldines, a group of Irish aristocrats who rebelled against English rule, Silken had less than a smooth ending when he was beheaded on orders from Henry VIII in 1537. In addition to excellent food, the restaurant offers a brief glimpse of the area's history through oil portraits of the Kildare and Fitzgerald families and paintings of County Kildare as it existed in the 15th and 16th centuries.

Other points of interest on the Barrow

Recalling when cargo ran by water.

Line include **Monasterevan**, once the center of several thriving industries, including a distillery that operated from 1784 to 1934; **Vicarstown**, with friendly pubs on both sides of the canal, and flocks of mallards which are reared at the water's edge; and **Dunrally Castle**, one of many in this area. Slightly south on the canal, at Ballymanus Bridge looms **Castle Reban**, built in the 13th century on the site of an ancient town which was recorded on Ptolemy's map of the second century.

Athy, where the Barrow Line ends, is County Kildare's largest town, with a population of nearly 5,000. An important crossing point on the Barrow River, it was the site of many battles, dating back to the 11th century. The town's main attraction is a striking fan-shaped Dominican Church (1963–65). Two interesting castles to visit here are **White's Castle**, built in 1506, to protect the bridge (which carries the name "Crom-a-Boo" from the Desmonds' family war cry) over the Barrow and the 13th-century **Woodstock Castle**.

Other Irish waterways: The Milltown Feeder, branching south of the Grand Canal, again near the 19th lock, is the Grand's main source of water. Eight miles (13 km) down the Feeder is a beautiful and interesting geological phenomenon: **Pollardstown Fen**, a wetlands filled with the type of vegetation that was widespread in Ireland 5,000 years ago. Today it's a nature preserve filled with rare plants and waterfowl. Near the Fen is **Seven Springs**, a small pool of bubbling water pure enough to drink. There are 36 springs in the area, producing the lime-rich alkaline water that saved the vegetation centuries ago and kept the fen from turning into bogland.

A third interesting waterway off the Grand Canal is the **Naas**, which joins the main line near the 16th Lock, by the town of **Sallins**. The canal flows south for 2½ miles (4 km), past woodlands and lines of beech trees. This being Ireland's main horse-breeding area, the town of Naas, County Kildare, has two racetracks, one for flat racing and the other for steeplechases.

The Grand Canal and its tributaries are filled with fish, including bream, rudd, roach, pike, perch and carp. The most popular fishing areas are between the 16th and 18th Locks; the section from the Bord na Mona Bridge at Allenwood near the 20th Lock; and the sections between the 32nd and 34th Locks at Clonony Bridge.

The **Royal Canal**, another link between Dublin and the Shannon, enters the river further north near Termonbarry. Although never as heavily used for commercial traffic as the Grand, it was still a vital artery. The Royal is also younger: construction did not start until 1792 with completion to the Shannon 25 years, 90 miles (150 km) and 47 locks later. The mid-1800s brought the railroads, and a lessening of freight tonnage. When a railroad finally bought the canal and built a track along it, traffic became non-existent and in 1961 the canal was officially closed. Now its function is purely as a historical monument and it's only partially open for recreational traffic. The fishing is great.

Left, lost in music. Right, Lough Derg.

NORTHERN IRELAND

One hundred minutes westward by road from Belfast and the visitor is in boating paradise. Ireland's third boating center is in Northern Ireland on the **River Erne**, one of the world's few large rivers that flows north instead of south. Its source is in the Republic of Ireland and it enters Northern Ireland through County Fermanagh.

Comprised primarily of two large lakes, **Upper Lough Erne** and **Lower Lough Erne** which meet at Enniskillen, the Erne Waterway System encompasses more than 300 sq. miles (780 sq. km) of island-studded lakes and rivers. The region is filled with prehistoric monuments, stone carvings, and ruins of ancient castles and churches. In all, one-third of County Fermanagh, the most westerly of the six counties of Northern Ireland, is covered by this glorious body of water.

Although a waterway of Northern Ireland, its end as well as its beginning is in the Republic: the river rises in County Cavan, the same county where the source of the Shannon is located, and enters the sea near Ballyshannon in County Donegal. In between, the Erne flows north by northwest for 52 miles (84 km) in Northern Ireland's County Fermanagh, through some of the wildest, most beautiful and desolate lakeland in the British Isles. **Belturbet**, on the border at the river's southern (upper) end, is a tiny fishing and boating center. **Belleek**, on the northern (lower) end, where the river leaves the lough and Northern Ireland for its short run of less than two miles to the sea, is known for its fine chinaware.

Dominating is **Lough Erne**, upper and lower, which divides County Fermanagh in two and which extends from one end of it to the other. This magnificent waterway, the second largest in Ireland, has only one lock to negotiate, and is choc-a-bloc with over 150 small islands. Some have intriguing historical remains; others are nature reserves, and many are still covered by virgin woodland which shelters an abundant amount of wildlife.

Although boats are available from seven charter companies, the Erne Waterway must be the most under-used waterway in all Europe. It is estimated that, even on a busy weekend, each and every boat has its own 3 sq. miles (8 sq. km) of territorial imperative and the absence of open water because of the many islands, especially on the upper lough, enhances the feeling of privacy. For those who seek total solitude, the Erne is one answer.

The **Upper Lough**, crammed with islands, is more like a meandering river than a lake and brings to mind the Amazon or the Danube Delta in Romania. However, here in County Fermanagh, unlike in the Danube Delta, the islands do not float although, as in Romania, their reedy shores abound with nesting ducks and grebes.

The **Lower Lough**, a more open body of water, has little natural current. When the wind rises the waters are rough, and novice boaters should take particular care when on the lake.

For a hawk's eye rather than a duck's eye view of the region, berth at **Magho**

Left, farmers and their horses are a familiar Irish sight. **Right**, ancient stones on White Island.

jetty at the west end of the south shore of the Lower Lough (not suitable for overnight stops) and take the steep mile-long path to the top of the mighty cliffs of **Lough Navar Forest**. The views of almost the entire Lower Lough and of the surrounding mountains of Tyrone, Donegal, Leitrim and Sligo are immense. (Camera enthusiasts should note that this is a morning shot.) Trails in the Lough Navar Forest provide pleasant walks.

Enniskillen, the county capital, sitting on its own island around which swirls the River Erne, separates the two loughs. The only lock on the waterway is here; although seldom needed since the difference in water levels is not great, a keeper is in attendance.

In the center of the town, which is best enjoyed on Thursday, its market day, is **Enniskillen Castle**, which has two small museums, one devoted to pre-history and the other to military paraphernalia. The castle's handsome 16th-century water-gate, cathedral and French-style Catholic church are also interesting. Enniskillen's Portora Royal School was attended by both Oscar Wilde and Samuel Beckett. Like many cozy Ulster market towns, Enniskillen is rich in small bakeries and butcher's shops, and there's a gossipy atmosphere as farmers mix with townspeople over a pint.

Also in town, at the edge of the river, is an excellent recreation-sports complex. Immediately to the south, and with commanding views of the River Erne as it enters the Lower Lough, is the handsome **Ardhowen Arts Center** which presents a mixed bag of entertainment through the year.

The fishing, both for coarse fish (bream, roach, eel, pike, gudgeon and some rudd) and for game fish (brown and sea trout and salmon) is magnificent. Fishing festivals held here often result in new world records and 100 lbs (45 kg) per angler per day is kids' stuff. (If not wishing to bring your own rod and reel, local firms have gear for rent. Be prepared, however, to leave a large deposit against its safe return.)

Those who prefer to lounge on a sandy beach will find their pleasure at several **The beach at Knockninny.**

380

places, the outstanding being **Knock-ninny** on the Upper Lough. And who knows – you might be offered a drop of fiery *poteen* (alcohol made illegally from barley, sugar, yeast and water). But beware: bad poteen can blind you.

Approaching **Belleek**, on the Lower Lough, the ruins of **Castle Caldwell** stand on a promontory which protrudes into the lake. A misty morning evokes memories of dragons and knights and fair maidens needing rescue.

The avid fisherman will temporarily abandon his boat (but not his tackle) at Belleek, the western limit for cruisers on the waterway, and proceed southwards by road for 5 miles (8 km) to the anglers' mecca of **Garrison** on **Lough Melvin**. This water contains three of the most unusual species of trout: the gillaroo, the sonaghan and the ferox. All three species, although small, are fiery fighters.

The visitor is well advised when fishing Lough Melvin to carry a passport. The Lough straddles the border between Northern Ireland and Eire, and if a gillaroo or a sonaghan bites in the North

it could well be that it will not be landed until you are in the South.

Non-anglers might prefer a 30-minute tour of the renowned **Belleek pottery** where ornaments with Irish designs, and looking like woven baskets are made from Norwegian felspar.

To cruise the Lower Erne is to pass islands with some of oldest ruins in the British Isles. Mysterious pagan statues, early Christian gravestones and ancient monastic settlements are on many of its 97 islands. Typical is **Devenish**, or Ox Island, at the southern end of the Lough (good mooring); it boasts the most extensive remains in Ireland of a medieval Christian settlement founded in the 6th century by St Molaise. These include parts of a 6th-century monastery, 15th-century abbey, a museum and a splendidly preserved 81-ft (24-meter) high round tower which can be ascended.

A row of eight enigmatic stone figures standing along one wall of the ruined 12th-century church on **White Island**, further up the Lough, has aroused much controversy. Are they Christian

Getting directions.

or pagan? If, as has been suggested, seven of them represent the deadly sins, what about the eighth?

The problem appears to have been resolved on **Boa Island**. Said to be the last place in Ireland where the Druids practised their rites, this small island at the very top of the Lough has a free-standing Janus statue in the Caldragh Burial Ground with carvings on both sides: one is claimed to be Christian; that on the other to be pagan.

Less interesting ruins consisting of a 6th-century monastic site and a unique undecorated Celtic cross can be seen on **Inishmacsaint Island**, in the southwest corner of the Lough.

On the Upper Lough, two 18th-century stately homes, full of rare furnishings and rich in paintings and decorative work, are well worth visiting. The recently restored and renovated **Castlecoole**, southeast of Enniskillen, is but a few hundred yards from the mooring at the Ardhowen Arts Center. The well-landscaped grounds of this "Mansion in the Meadow", which is a delightful example of late Georgian architecture, are famous for their greylag geese, introduced 300 years ago.

Florence Court, about 5 miles (8 km) from the northwest corner of the Upper Lough, has a striking classical exterior. It stands in extensive, immaculate gardens containing a famous yew tree which is claimed to be the progenitor of all yew trees throughout the world.

The small towns of **Lisnaskea** and **Newtown Butler**, a couple of miles from the northeast corner of the Upper Lough, are not without interest. Noah's grandson, not Noah, is claimed to have landed in his own ark just beyond Lisnaskea (local legend has him arriving where the ruins of Balfour Castle stand) while eye-witnesses at Newtown Butler report having seen a leprechaun which cynics and spoilsports suggest was actually fireflies dancing over the water. Not to be outdone, **Irvinestown**, a few miles to the east of the Lower Lough, claims to have seen the "Lady of the Lake" floating on the water's surface.

Right, Ireland is known for fresh seafood.

382

INSIGHT GUIDES
Travel Tips

FOR THOSE WITH MORE THAN A PASSING INTEREST IN TIME...

Before you put your name down for a Patek Philippe watch *fig. 1*, there are a few basic things you might like to know, without knowing exactly whom to ask. In addressing such issues as accuracy, reliability and value for money, we would like to demonstrate why the watch we will make for you will be quite unlike any other watch currently produced.

"Punctuality", Louis XVIII was fond of saying, "is the politeness of kings."

We believe that in the matter of punctuality, we can rise to the occasion by making you a mechanical timepiece that will keep its rendezvous with the Gregorian calendar at the end of every century, omitting the leap-years in 2100, 2200 and 2300 and recording them in 2000 and 2400 *fig. 2*. Nevertheless, such a watch does need the occasional adjustment. Every 3333 years and 122 days you should remember to set it forward one day to the true time of the celestial clock. We suspect, however, that you are simply content to observe the politeness of kings. Be assured, therefore, that when you order your watch, we will be exploring for you the physical—if not the metaphysical—limits of precision.

Does everything have to depend on how much?

Consider, if you will, the motives of collectors who set record prices at auction to acquire a Patek Philippe. They may be paying for rarity, for looks or for micromechanical ingenuity. But we believe that behind each $500,000-plus

bid is the conviction that a Patek Philippe, even if 50 years old or older, can be expected to work perfectly for future generations.

In case your ambitions to own a Patek Philippe are somewhat discouraged by the scale of the sacrifice involved, may we hasten to point out that the watch we will make for you today will certainly be a technical improvement on the Pateks bought at auction? In keeping with our tradition of inventing new mechanical solutions for greater reliability and better time-keeping, we will bring to your watch innovations *fig. 3* inconceivable to our watchmakers who created the supreme wristwatches of 50 years ago *fig. 4*. At the same time, we will of course do our utmost to avoid placing undue strain on your financial resources.

Can it really be mine?

May we turn your thoughts to the day you take delivery of your watch? Sealed within its case is your watchmaker's tribute to the mysterious process of time. He has decorated each wheel with a chamfer carved into its hub and polished into a shining circle. Delicate ribbing flows over the plates and bridges of gold and rare alloys. Millimetric surfaces are bevelled and burnished to exactitudes measured in microns. Rubies are transformed into jewels that triumph over friction. And after many months—or even years—of work, your watchmaker stamps a small badge into the mainbridge of your watch. The Geneva Seal—the highest possible attestation of fine watchmaking *fig. 5*.

Looks that speak of inner grace *fig. 6*.

When you order your watch, you will no doubt like its outward appearance to reflect the harmony and elegance of the movement within. You may therefore find it helpful to know that we are uniquely able to cater for any special decorative needs you might like to express. For example, our engravers will delight in conjuring a subtle play of light and shadow on the gold case-back of one of our rare pocket-watches *fig. 7*. If you bring us your favourite picture, our enamellers will reproduce it in a brilliant miniature of hair-breadth detail *fig. 8*. The perfect execution of a double hobnail pattern on the bezel of a wristwatch is the pride of our casemakers and the satisfaction of our designers, while our chainsmiths will weave for you a rich brocade in gold *figs. 9 & 10*. May we also recommend the artistry of our goldsmiths and the experience of our lapidaries in the selection and setting of the finest gemstones? *figs. 11 & 12*.

How to enjoy your watch before you own it.

As you will appreciate, the very nature of our watches imposes a limit on the number we can make available. (The four Calibre 89 time-pieces we are now making will take up to nine years to complete). We cannot therefore promise instant gratification, but while you look forward to the day on which you take delivery of your Patek Philippe *fig. 13*, you will have the pleasure of reflecting that time is a universal and everlasting commodity, freely available to be enjoyed by all.

Should you require information on any particular Patek Philippe watch, or even on watchmaking in general, we would be delighted to reply to your letter of enquiry. And if you send us

fig. 1: The classic face of Patek Philippe.

fig. 4: Complicated wristwatches circa 1930 (left) and 1990. The golden age of watchmaking will always be with us.

fig. 6: Your pleasure in owning a Patek Philippe is the purpose of those who made it for you.

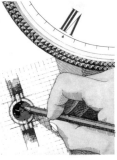

fig. 9: Harmony of design is executed in a work of simplicity and perfection in a lady's Calatrava wristwatch.

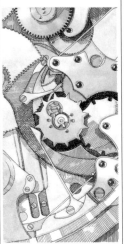

fig. 2: One of the 33 complications of the Calibre 89 astronomical clock-watch is a satellite wheel that completes one revolution every 400 years.

fig. 5: The Geneva Seal is awarded only to watches which achieve the standards of horological purity laid down in the laws of Geneva. These rules define the supreme quality of watchmaking.

fig. 7: Arabesques come to life on a gold case-back.

fig. 10: The chainsmith's hands impart strength and delicacy to a tracery of gold.

fig. 11: Circles in gold: symbols of perfection in the making.

fig. 3: Recognized as the most advanced mechanical regulating device to date, Patek Philippe's Gyromax balance wheel demonstrates the equivalence of simplicity and precision.

fig. 8: An artist working six hours a day takes about four months to complete a miniature in enamel on the case of a pocket-watch.

fig. 12: The test of a master lapidary is his ability to express the splendour of precious gemstones.

PATEK PHILIPPE
GENEVE
fig. 13: The discreet sign of those who value their time.

your card marked "book catalogue" we shall post you a catalogue of our publications. Patek Philippe, 41 rue du Rhône, 1204 Geneva, Switzerland, Tel. +41 22/310 03 66.

You close your laptop and adjust your footrest. A taste of Brie. A sip of Bordeaux. You lean back and hope you won't be arriving too soon.

That depends on how far you're going.

The fact that Lufthansa flies to 220 global destinations comes as a surprise to some. Perhaps we've been too busy with our award-winning service to tell everybody that we are one of the world's largest airline networks. A network that can offer you fast and convenient connections to anywhere. A network that offers rewards with Miles and More, one of the world's leading frequent flyer programmes. And above all, a network that makes you feel at home, however far you're going. So call Lufthansa on 0345 252 252 and we'll tell you the full story.

Lufthansa

Getting Acquainted

Time Zones

Most of Europe is within the Central European Time Zone which is Greenwich Mean Time (GMT) plus one hour and US Eastern Standard Time plus six hours. All countries observe Summer Time setting their clocks one hour ahead in April and back again in October. Continental Europe and Ireland/ England do not always change their clocks at the same time. Check locally.

Planning the Trip

What to Bring

Electricity

The electric current in most of Europe is 220 volts alternating current, with the exception of part of Southern France where 110 volts is still in use. A 220v appliance in a 110v socket will not function very well, but a 110-volt appliance in a 220-volt socket will cause a short circuit. Adaptors are needed if you wish to use 120-volt appliances. Two-pin round plugs and sockets are general except in Britain, which has three-pin square plugs.

Entry Regulations

Visas and Passports

A valid passport is necessary for all non-European Union citizens traveling into and around Continental Europe. EU citizens require a National Identity Card. Visa regulations change from time to time so travelers would be advised to check on the current rules at the Embassy of the country to which they wish to travel. At present citizens of Australia, Canada, New Zealand and the United States do not require a visa for stays of less than six months in Britain and three months for most other European countries.

Animal Quarantine

Dogs and cats are subject to quarantine regulations in Great Britain and Ireland but in Continental Europe they require a veterinary certificate of health translated into the language of the host country and certified by an official translation agency or Embassy. Please check. Animals taken from Great Britain to the Continent will be subject to a six-month quarantine on their return.

Customs

In general visitors over 17 are allowed to import the following items duty-free: toiletries; photographic equipment and film; camping and sports equipment; jewelry provided it is intended for personal use and will be re-exported; food required in transit; souvenirs, gifts and personal purchases provided their total value does not exceed the limitations of the host country; 400 cigarettes or 200 small cigars or 100 cigars or 500 gm of tobacco or proportionally equivalent mixed amounts; 1 liter spirits containing more than 22 percent alcohol and 2 liters still or other wine; 50 gm perfume; 0.25 liter toilet water; coffee, depending on the country, 250–500 gms or 100–200 gm coffee extract; 100 gm tea extract.

There are no Customs checks for those traveling between two EU states.

Health

Inoculation certificates are not normally required for entry into Europe unless you have traveled from an area which is a designated risk. These areas include Africa, India, and South America. Check if in doubt.

Generally speaking, the tap water provided at boat docks is drinkable. If in doubt check with the dock master and drink only certified bottled water or buy water purifying tablets. Be careful to wash fruit and vegetables in purified water and mix drinks with ice cubes made from purified water.

Always use sterilized water for cleaning teeth and it is useful to carry a medicine to treat mild upset stomach or diarrhoea.

Insects and pests: Be prepared with insect-repellant liquid and insect-repellant sprays to discourage bites from mosquitoes and flies, and anti-histamine creams to reduce swelling and irritation if bitten. Antihistamine tablets for severe allergies to insect bites may be handy.

Sun protection: It can get very hot on a boating trip and sunburn is a hazard. The sun is at its hottest between 11am and 3pm so keep heads covered. Bring witch-hazel to treat sunburn, and plenty of good suntan cream or a sunblock to protect the skin.

Some rental boats carry a basic first-aid kit, but make up a travel first-aid box including such items as anti-septic wipes, dressings, plaster.

Insurance cover is strongly recommended as medical treatment can be expensive. Citizens of Great Britain should apply for form E111 from a DHSS office a month or so before going to the Continent. This gives entitlement to free or reduced-cost emergency treatment in countries of the EU.

For a boating trip casual clothes and comfortable shoes are necessary. Several layers of light clothing will be infinitely better than thick cumbersome clothes; sweat shirts and a warm sweater over slacks or shorts are best. Waterproofs will be essential as dry weather can never be guaranteed at any time of the year. If intending to visit churches or shrines, remember to take suitable clothing for the surroundings; shorts and sundresses may be frowned upon.

Currency

Most countries of Europe have no limitations on the amount of currency brought into or taken out. However, changes do occur and it is wise to check with a travel agent beforehand. Traveler's checks are an easy and safe way of carrying money while on the move.

Credit cards are accepted in most hotels and large shops and may be used to withdraw cash in many banks. In larger cities, most banks have cash dispensers outside so that money can be withdrawn outside banking hours. Currency can be exchanged at most banks in even the small towns along the canals.

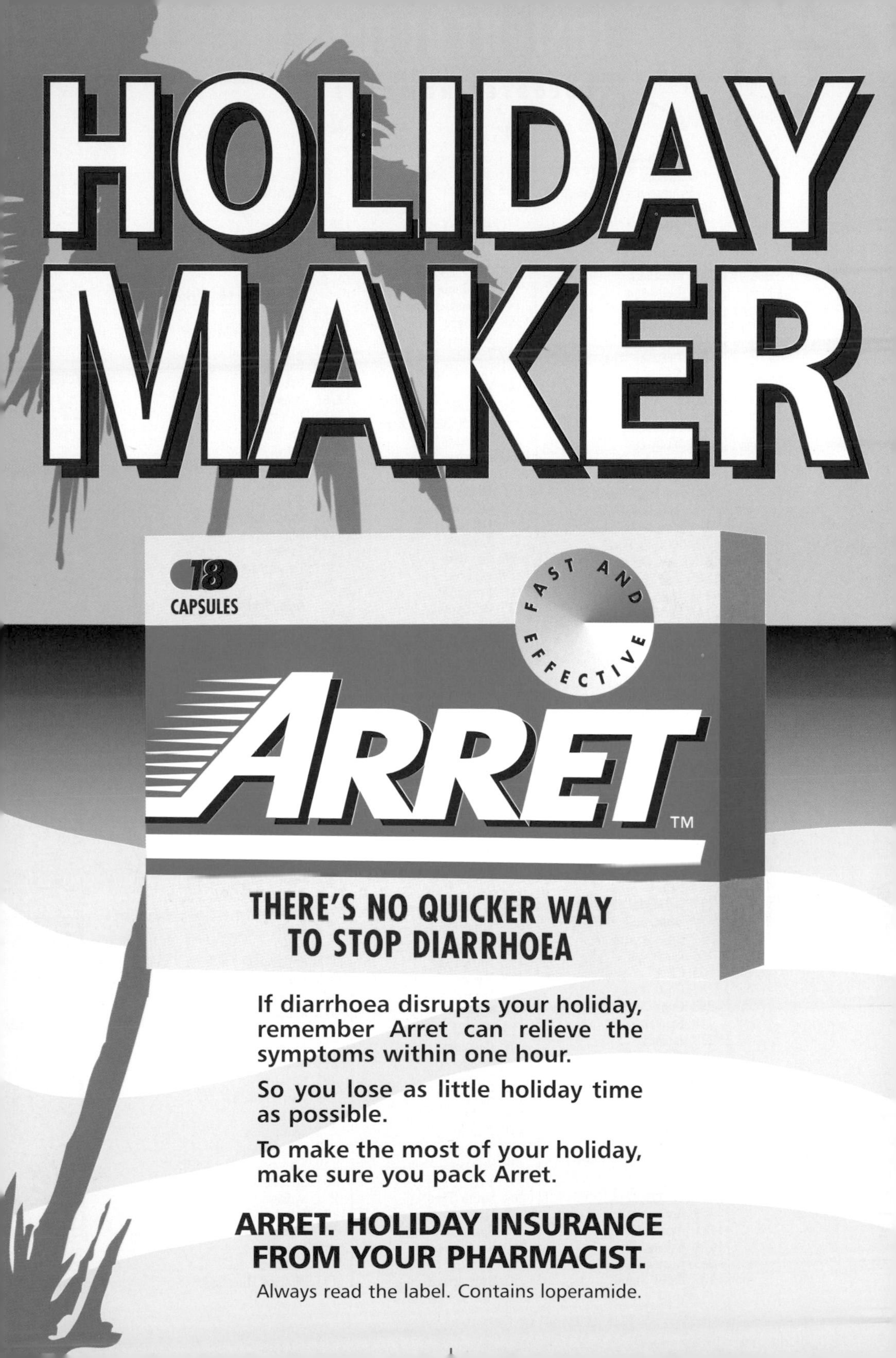

HOLIDAY MAKER

18 CAPSULES

FAST AND EFFECTIVE

ARRET™

THERE'S NO QUICKER WAY TO STOP DIARRHOEA

If diarrhoea disrupts your holiday, remember Arret can relieve the symptoms within one hour.

So you lose as little holiday time as possible.

To make the most of your holiday, make sure you pack Arret.

ARRET. HOLIDAY INSURANCE FROM YOUR PHARMACIST.

Always read the label. Contains loperamide.

INSIGHT GUIDES

COLORSET NUMBERS

These vary from country to country but those that apply throughout are:

New Year's Day – January 1st
Easter Monday
Whit Monday
Christmas Day – December 25th
Boxing Day – December 26th

Getting There
By Air

Most visitors to Europe travel by air and international airlines fly regular, sometimes daily, flights to all the major airports: London (Gatwick and Heathrow), Brussels (Zaventem), Paris (Charles de Gaulle and Orly), Amsterdam (Schiphol), and Dublin. All the major European airlines have daily flights out of London.

By Sea

There are daily ferries and hovercraft crossings from ports on the English coast to European ports. The shortest crossing is Dover–Calais. The Channel Tunnel offers an alternative means of transport for passengers and cars.

Special Facilities
Lock Passage

Locks are simple devices and are generally easy to operate. The few rules that exist do so merely to ensure safety and to conserve water. Although locks differ slightly from region to region, essentially the operation is the same, whether on an English canal or a major European waterway

Principally a lock consists of a chamber enclosed by two walls at the sides and two gates, or pairs of gates at either end. The lock separates two stretches of water, of different levels, which the boat must cross.

A crew member is usually landed to prepare the lock for entry. If going up through the lock, first drain it by opening the paddles in the lower gates. The paddle rack and pinion are operated by a windlass (usually provided by the boat operator at the time of rental).

After draining the lock, open the gates by leaning on the balance beam. This will cause the water on both sides of the gates to reach the same level, thus releasing the pressure which held

the gates shut. Steer into the lock, then close the gates and the paddles.

Fill the lock by opening the top ground paddles, which open sluices in culverts either beneath or to the sides of the top gates. Make sure the boat is firmly secured as the surge of incoming water can easily force it into the bottom gates. As soon as the water levels are the same, open the top gates by moving the balance beams.

On clearing the lock, assuming there is no traffic moving down, close the top gates and shut all paddles.

When going down through a lock reverse this procedure, filling the lock, if necessary, before entry and draining before exit. The single but important difference from going up through the lock is that when coming down, leave the boat unsecured while in the lock. Otherwise the boat may "hang" as the water falls away beneath it.

Care should also be exercised with the paddle windlasses: remove the windlass as soon as the paddles are in position. Otherwise the windlass may fly off as the ratchet slips, sending the windlass to the bottom of the lock, or worse, injuring a bystander.

On larger locks, such as those found on the River Thames, the gate and paddle operations are aided by hydraulic power, and the boater is assisted by the lock-keeper. This is usually the case in Continental Europe, where locks can vary considerably both in size and design.

European locks range from the small, manual English type, already described, to massive river locks capable of holding vessels of 2,000 tons or more. In the smaller ones a lock keeper will usually help the boater into the lock, expecting her crew to lend a hand to complete the operation. At larger locks, typically of 500 to 700 ton capacity, the lock-keeper will operate the system mechanically, give direction and even assist with the lines.

Some large European locks are entirely automatic and often a series of locks will be in the charge of one official. In such cases the traffic flow is controlled by visual signals or traffic lights and the gate operations can be halted, in an emergency, by pulling a cord or lever. The larger locks frequently have a greater rise and fall than those on English canals, vertical movements of 90 ft (30 meters) are

quite common. In locks with such a drop the mooring fixtures float with the lock water, thus allowing the vessel inside to remain secured at all water levels.

Other European differences likely to be encountered include inclined planes, where vessels are carried up and down in huge tanks, called *caissons*, mounted on wheels, and water slopes, where a barge is pushed up a slope by a giant blade, floating in a 'V' shaped wedge of water before the blade.

Despite all of these variations the underlying principle remains the same and the guidance of lock-keepers, other boat users and bystanders is usually freely given.

Useful Addresses
US Operators

Operators offering barge and river tours in Europe include:

Abercombie & Kent, 1420 Kensington Rd, Suite 111, Oak Brook, Ill. 60521. Tel: 800-323-7308, 312-954-2944.
Argosy Tours, 133 E. 55th St, NY 10022. Tel: 800-635-81, 212-223-3177.
Bergen Line, 505 Fifth Ave, NY 10017. Tel: 800-3-BERGEN, 212-986-2711.
Buddy Bombard's Great Balloon Adventures, 6727 Curran St, McLean, Va, 22101-3804. Tel: 800-862-8537, 703-448-9407.
DER Tours, 11939 Wilshire Blvd, Los Angeles 90025. Tel: 800 037 1234.
Esplanade Tours, 581 Boylston St, Booton 02116. Tel: 800 343 7104, 617-266-7465.
Exprinter Danube Cruises, 500 Fifth Ave, NY 10110. Tel: 800-221-1666, 212-719-1200.
Floating Through Europe, 211 Madison Ave, NY 10018. Tel: 800-221-3140/1, 212-685-5600.
Gaona Travel Corp, 11145 Tampa Ave, Suite 28, Northridge, CA 91326. Tel: 800-225-5668, 800-341-6294.
Globus-Gateway, tel: 800-221-0090 east, tel:.800-556-5454 west.
Hapag-Lloyd Tours, 159 Great Neck Rd, Great Neck, NY 11022. Tel: 800-33-HAPAG, 516-466-1262.
Horizon Cruises, 16000 Ventura Blvd, Suite 200, Encino, California 91436. Tel: 818-906-8086.

Insight International Tours, PO Box 10247, Irvine, California 92713. Tel: 800-582-8380, 800-792-7209.

International Cruise Center, 250 Old Country Rd, Mineola, NY 11501. Tel: 800-221-3254, 516-747-8880.

Jet Vacations, 888 Seventh Ave, NY 10106. Tel: 800-JET-0999, 212-247-0999.

KD German Rhine Line (Rhine Cruise Agency), 170 Hamilton Ave, White Plains, NY 10601. Tel: 800-346-6525, 914-948-3600.

Lindblad Travel, PO Box 912, One Sylvan Road North, Westport, Conn. 06881. Tel: 800-243-5657, 203-226-8531.

Love Holidays, 15315 Magnolia Blvd, Sherman Oaks, California 91403. Tel: 818-501-6868, 213-873-7991.

Maupintour, tel: 800-255-4266, 913-843-1211.

Quiztour (B & D de Vogue Travel Service), 1830 S. Mooney Blvd, Suite 113, PO Box 1998, Visalia, California. Tel: 800-338-0483, 209-733-7119.

Romantik Travel & Tours, 14178 Woodinville Duvall Rd, Woodinville, Wash. 98072. Tel: 800-826-0015.

Smolka Tours, 1 Cantonah St, Ridgfield, Conn. 06877. Tel: 800-722-0057, 203-431-9612.

Trafalgar Tours, 21 E. 26th St, NY 10010. Tel: 800-854-0103, 212-689-8977.

Travcoa World Tours, 4000 MacArthur Blvd, Suite 650 E. Newport Beach, California 92660. Tel: 800-992-2003, 800-992-2004.

UK Waterways (BOAT/US Yacht Charters), tel: 800-BOAT USA.

Wagon-Lita International, 928 Broadway, Suite 1001, NY 10010-6008. Tel: 800-247-5434, 212-475-2120.

Waterline Inc, Carlton Plaza, 26 Strawberry Hill Ave, Suite 20, Stamford, Conn. 06902. Tel: 800-433-9883, 203-323-4411.

William B. Buckman's Travel Time, 17 N. State St, Chicago 60602. Tel: 800-621-4725, 312-726-7197.

World Balloon Tours Ltd, 2501 W. 134th Circle, Broomfield, Colo. 80020. Tel: 303-469-1243.

Practical Tips

Weights & Measures

Some useful conversion rates

1 gram = 0.04 ounce
1 kilogram = 2.2 pounds
100 grams = 3.5 ounces
1 ounce = 28 grams
1 pound = 0.45 kilos
1 liter = 1.76 pints
1 meter = 3.28 feet
1 cm = 0.39 inches
1 kilometer = 0.62 mile
8 kilometers = 5 miles
1 mile = 1.6 kilometers

Media

Newspapers

English and American newspapers and magazines will be found at major news-stands, hotels, airports and railway stations, though current issues may not always be available, and prices would almost always be higher than those at home. Current issues of the *International Herald Tribune*, because it is published in Europe, will be found more easily and at a more convivial price.

Radio

BBC World Service and British and American Forces Network stations are the most listened to English-language broadcasts, and they broadcast regular news and current affairs programmes.

Postal Services

These vary and will be found in detail under individual countries. Many large cities have post offices close to the railway station which operate longer hours than smaller offices.

Getting Around

Orientation

All European countries have tourist information services, and their local offices in your home country will provide you with useful information before a trip. The tourist offices in the host country are the best places to obtain maps, brochures, sightseeing guides, hotels, etc. Lists of the addresses of these offices appear under individual countries in this Guide and from these can be found information regarding any trip you contemplate taking.

Shopping

General

Many stores in Europe display signs which indicate that travelers from non-EU countries can receive a refund of VAT (Value Added Tax) or TVA (Tax Valeur Ajoutée) on any taxed purchase when leaving the country, or by mail afterwards. You need to fill out a tax reclaim form at the place of purchase.

This can amount to as much as 25 percent of the purchase price, depending on the local VAT rate and so is well worth the effort. This does not apply to tax-free shopping at airports, etc.

Language

Boating Terms

The following glossary gives a list of useful terms likely to be encountered while boating in Europe and they are given where possible in the three main European languages, i.e. English, French and German.

English/*French*/German

Ait (Eyot)/*Ilot*/Klein Insel
A small island between the banks of a river.

Abaft/*Sur l'arrière*/Achtern
Closer to the stern of the vessel.

Abeam/*Par le travers*/Querab
Right angles to the length and directly opposite the centre of the vessel.

Aground/*Echoué*/Gestrandet
Stranded with the keel of vessel on the riverbed.

Ahead/*En avant*/Voorn
Beyond the bow of the vessel.

Aqueduct/*Pont aqueduc*/Aquadukt
Bridge carrying one waterway over another.

Backwater/*Bras de Décharge*/Durchwasser
Area of standing water out of the main stream.

Bale/*Ecoper*/Ausshoffer
To empty the vessel of water by means of a hand-held scoop.

Ballast/*Lest*/Ballast
Weights added to vessel to increase the draft and/or stability.

Barge/*Chaland*/Schute
Large, flat-bottomed vessel purpose-built for navigation on inland waterways.

Basin/*Bassin*
An area of water for mooring which gives access between tidal and non-tidal waters.

Bateau Mouche
Vessel designed for pleasure trips on French waterways.

Bargee/*Batelier*/Schutenschiffer
One of the professional crew of a barge.

Beam/*Travers*/Breite
The width of vessel at its widest point.

Bilge/*Bouchain*/Bilge
Lowest internal spaces within a vessel usually kept free of water by operation of bilge pump.

Boathook/*Gaffe*/Bootstange
Long pole with a hook at one end used to hold on whilst mooring or to push off when aground.

Bollard/*Bitte*/Poller
Strengthened post of wood or metal fixed to the deck of a vessel or a dock, around which mooring lines are secured.

Bow/*Avant*/Bug
Foremost part of vessel where the two sides meet in a sharp, vertical joint.

Branch/*Derivation*/Gabellung
Section of canal, particularly a spur leading from a major canal system.

Broads
Local name for series of shallow, navigable lakes, interconnected by rivers, in the East of England, which form a popular tourist area.

Calor Gas/*Butagaz*
Name for bottled Propane gas sold in steel bottles.

Canal/*Canal*/Kanal
Manmade waterway originally constructed to allow barge navigation.

Canal bridge/*Pont canal*/Kanalbrücke

Chamber/*Chambre*/d' écluse
Interior of a lock, the space contained by the two pairs of lock.

Chandler/*Chandelier*/Kerzenzieher
Merchant specialising in supply of stores and equipment to the marine consumer.

Chomage
Closure of waterway for maintenance.

Cleat/*Cambrion*/Klampe
A deck fitting, particularly in smaller vessels for securing mooring lines.

Cut/*Derivation*/Gabellung
Another name for branch; or man-made section of river constructed to straighten a bend.

Diesel Oil/*Gasoil*/Deisol
Marine diesel oil. In France legislation has now banned the use of Gasoil domestique in pleasure craft.

Dinghy/*Canot*/Beiboot
Small boat propelled by sail, oars or motor.

Downstream/*Avalant*
Boat going downstream.

Dredger/*Drageur*/Baggerarbeiter
A vessel designed to excavate material from the bottom of a waterway.

Draught/Zug
The distance from the waterline of a vessel to the lowest point on the keel.

Elsan
English name for a chemical used in boats' portable lavatories.

Fairlead/*Margouillet*/Fuhrungsring
A deck fitting through which a line can be led to take it clear of obstacles.

Fender/*Bourelet*/Fender
A device to hang between the hull of a vessel and the dock to prevent damage by scraping.

Flood/*Onde*/Flut
The state of a river when it is swollen by rain or meltwater.

Ford/Furt
A shallow point in a river where it is possible to cross by vehicle or on foot.

Freeboard/*Francbord*/Freibord
The part of the hull of vessel between the waterline and the gunwhale.

Gaff/*Gaffe*/Meist
Another name for boathook or a pole as part of the rigging of a vessel.

Galley/*Galère*/Galleere
Kitchen of a vessel in nautical parlance.

Gangplank/*Planche à Débarquer*/Landungsbrücke
Bridging construction placed between boat and dock to enable personnel to walk ashore.

Gunwhale/*Platbord*/Schandeckel
Topmost edge of the hull of a vessel or the walkway outboard of vessel's deckhouse.

Halyard/*Drisse*/Fall
Line rigged up mast of vessel for hoisting sail or flags.

Headwater/Oberlauf
Upper reaches of river or depth of water above a river lock.

Headroom/*Encrombrement*/Lichte Hone
Vertical clearance between waterlevel and an obstruction above, such as a bridge arch.

Helm/*Barre*/Helm
Apparatus by which vessel is steered or the position from which steering is effected.

Inboard/*Interieur (moteur)*
Within hull of vessel, with particular reference to position of an engine.

Junction/*Embranchement*/Zusammenfluss
The confluence of two or more canals.

Keel/*Larene*/Kiel
Longitudinal beam forming the centreline of bottom of hull and sometimes projecting beneath.

Lay-by/*Gare*/Beiseite
Waiting station before a lock, usually having a jetty or piles for mooring.

Lift/*Suite de biefs*
Series of locks where the lower gates of one become the upper gates of lock below. Alternatively mechanical device to lift vessels from one level to another.

Line/*Corde*/Lein
Any length of rope or cordage used for mooring a vessel.

Lock/*Ecluse*/Schleuse
Means by which vessel is able to navigate up and down 'hill' by water. It consists of a chamber enclosed by two pairs of gates fitted with sluices to enable the lock to be flooded or drained.

Log/*Loch*/Log
Mechanical or electrical instrument for measuring vessel's speed through the water.

Manivelle
French name for manual operating handle for lock gates and sluices.

Marina/*Port de Plaisance*/Marina
Purpose-built harbor area offering a range of facilities to the boater.

Mooring/*Amarrage*/Ankerplatz
Designated place for securing vessels, often an unprepared stretch of bank.

Navigation/*Navigation*/Schiffsvekehr
The act of conducting a vessel's passage upon a waterway. In England also a name given to a canal system, e.g. The Trent Navigation.

Narrowboat/*Perrichon*/Lastkahn
A canal boat designed particularly for the British canals, having maximum dimensions of 6 ft beam and 70 ft length.

Overtaking/*Trématage*
Act of passing another vessel travelling in the same direction.

Outfall/*Deversoir*/Uberlaufen
Discharge into a waterway, usually from an industrial, cooling process, often marked. They may present a hazard to navigation.

Paddle/*Vanne*
Device within a lock gate or weir to control flow of water through it. Resembling a dinghy paddle, it is usually inserted and withdrawn by hand.

Paraffin/*Petrole*/Kerosin
Kerosene.

Passing/*Croisement*
Act of sailing past another vessel travelling in the opposite direction.

Péniche
Traditional French canal barge, usually of around 60 tons and 60 ft in length.

Petrol/*Essence (Benzine)*/Benzin

Petrolier
French canal gasoline tanker.

Pier/*Quai*/Kai
Structure jutting into the water for tying up vessel, loading and offloading.

Pilot/*Pilote*/Lotse
Waterway official guiding vessels through complex or hazardous sections, sometimes used to describe any barge helmsman.

Pile/*Pieu*/Pfahl
Large vertical timber driven into the bed of waterway to facilitate mooring.

Pontoon/*Pont Flottant*/Ponton
Floating structure either in midstream or tethered to the bank, used for mooring and landing.

Port/*Sabord*/Backbord
Nautical term for left side of a vessel or direction to left of centreline.

Portage/*Portage*/Beforderung
Act of carrying boats or marine stores from one waterway to another or the charge levied for such a service.

Punt/*Bateau Plat*/Stechkahn
Long, narrow, flat-bottomed boat usually propelled by long pole carried in the stern.

Pump out/*Pomper*/Auspumpen
Facility provided at marinas and elsewhere for emptying sewage holding tanks. (On most European waterways it is prohibited to discharge any liquids overboard).

Race/*Raz de courant*/Stromung
Area of fast moving and often turbulent water associated with an outfall, millstream or meeting of moving and static water.

Railway bridge/*Pont de chemin de fer*/Eisenbahnbrücke
Bridge over which railway lines run.

Reach/*Bief*/Wasserhaltung
Stretch of inland waterway, particularly that between two prominent points such as locks or bends.

Regatta/*Regate*/Regata
Race meeting for sailing or rowing boats.

Dangerous rocks/*Roches dangereuses*/Gefärlicher Felsen
Rocks hidden under the water.

Rudder/*Gouvernail*/Ruder
Steering apparatus of vessel, consisting of a vertical plate at stern, projecting underwater and moved by the operation of the helm.

Sandbank/*Sable*/Sandbänke

Screw/*Helice*/Schranke
Another name for propellor of vessel.

Scupper/*Dalot*/Speigatt
The deck edge where it joins hull or the holes cut into it to facilitate deck draining.

Sheet/*Ecoute*/Schot
Lines attached to the sail corners which control the trim of the sail.

Sill/*Radier d'écluse*
Lock structure directly beneath the closed gates which forms the bottom seal. Its position is usually marked to prevent accidental bottoming of locking vessels.

Skiff/*Esquif*/Skiff
Small boat propelled by oars, sail or motor.

Slip(way)/*Cale de mise a l'eau*
Area of the bank designed to allow trailered boats to be put into or taken out of the water.

Sluice/*Vanne*/Schleusentor
Large openings within bottom of the lock gates, the operation of which can fill or drain the lock.

Spate/*Encrue*
The state of a river in flood after heavy rain or snow melting.

Starboard/*Tribord*/Steuerbord
Nautical term for the right side of vessel or the direction to right of the centerline.

Stay/*Etai*/Stag
Part of a vessel's rigging which supports or braces the mast.

Step/*Collet*
Act of erecting the mast of vessel, or device into which the mast stands.

Stern/*Arrière*/Heck
The aftermost part of a vessel.

Stop gate/*Ecluse de garde*/Schleuse
Usually a blocked off or closed canal barrier.

Tabernacle/*Pied de Mat*
Apparatus at the base of stepping mast.

Tender/*Navire*/Tender
Dinghy or small boat carried or towed by a large vessel and used to run to the bank or access shallow water.

Tideway/*Lit de la Marée*/Priel
That part of a waterway that is influenced by the rise and fall of the ocean tide.

Thwart/*Transversalement*/Ruderbank
Transverse member in a boat, often forming a seat in a small rowboat.

Tiller/*Barre*/Ruderpinne
Means of steering, the bar connected to the rudder by which it is moved.

Towpath/*Halage*/Treidelweg
Track alongside a waterway originally for the draught animals used to tow barges.

Tow train/*Rame*/Abschleppen
Line of motorless vessels under tow.

Tug/*Toueur*/Schleppen
Purpose-built vessel with a powerful motor for towing barges.

Upstream/*Montant*
Boat going upstream.

Wake/*Brassage*/Kielwasser
Disturbed water left by the passage of a vessel.

Warp/*Grelin*/Schleppleine
Line used to secure a vessel or to assist in turning vessel around.

Weir/*Barrage*/Wehr
Damming arrangement, usually associated with a lock. Moving tackle within the weir allow the water levels and rates of flow to be controlled

Further Reading

General

Art & Architecture in Medieval France, by Whitney Stoddard. Harper & Row.
Guide to the Wines and Vineyards of France, by Alexis Lichine. Alfred a Knopf.
Languedoc-Roussillon, by Neil Lands. Spurbooks Ltd.
The Canal du Midi, by Odile de Roquette-Buisson. Editions Rivage.
The Country Life Picture Book of the Thames, London, by Gordon Winter. Country Life Books.
The Thames Valley and Oxford, by Kenneth L. Lowther & Reginald Hammond. Ward Lock, London.
The Thames Valley Heritage Walk, by Miles Jebb. Constable, London.
Through France to the Med, by Mike Harper. Cadogan Books, London.
Two Towns in Provence, by M.S.K. Fisher. Vintage Books, Division of Random House.
Where to go in The Thames and Chilterns, Various authors. The Thames & Chilterns Tourist Board.
The River Shannon. A Boater's Guide, by Bernadette Tipper. Town House, Dublin.
Inland Waterways – Maps and Guides to 3,000 miles of Waterways. Brittain Publications in association with the Inland Waterways Association.

For a more complete list of books, maps and charts (including the French *Carte Guides*) covering Europe's inland waterways, write to: **Shepperton Swan Ltd**, The Clock House, Shepperton, Middlesex, England TW17 8RU. Tel: (01932) 783319. Their 80-page catalogue is available upon request.

For more information about other Insight Guides, see page 415.

FRANCE

The Place

France is a Republic, with a predominantly Roman Catholic population in excess of 55 million. It is the fifth largest economic power in the world and is a major producer of wine, agricultural products and steel.

The country covers an area of about 360,000 sq. miles (930,000 sq. km) and stretches about 600 miles (965 km) east to west and north to south.

The capital of the country and seat of Government is Paris, which contains more than 16 percent of the country's population.

Planning the Trip

Entry Regulations

Visas and Passports

All visitors are required to have a valid passport, except for citizens of the EU for whom a National Identity Card is sufficient. Visa regulations do change from time to time so check before you travel.

Health

Health certificates are not normally required for entry into France, unless visitors have traveled from an area which is a risk. Check to make sure.

Pharmacies normally open daily except Sunday 9am–12pm and 2pm–7pm. There will often be a bell on the door to ring in an emergency should the pharmacy be closed. Check with the harbor-master who will probably know the pharmacy rota.

The telephone number of the Ambulance service is: 15.

Currency

The currency of France is the French franc (Ffr.) which is divided into 100 centimes. Coins in use are 5, 10, 20, 50 centimes, and 1, 2, 5 and 10 francs. Notes are in denominations of 10, 50, 100 and 500 francs.

Traveler's checks are the safest way to carry money around but if taking cash, anything more than Ffr.5,000 in foreign currency should be declared. You will then be required to fill in a currency declaration form which must be shown upon departure.

Banks are open Monday to Friday 9am–4pm except on public holidays. However, in small towns they usually close for lunch.

Credit cards are accepted in most establishments, including American Express, Diners Club and Visa.

Tipping is almost a way of life in France, and you will normally be expected to pay 15 percent to a waiter or taxi driver, and about Ffr.5 to anyone who has rendered a service including porters, guides and toilet attendants. Look for the words *service compris* on the bill. Strictly speaking, this should mean that the tip is included but even so, it would be considered incorrect not to add a little something.

Public Holidays

The following days are celebrated as public holidays in France:
January 1: New Year's Day
Easter Monday
May 1: Labor Day
Ascension Day
Whit Monday
July 14: Bastille Day
August 15: Assumption Day
November 1: All Saints Day
November 11: Armistice Day
December 25: Christmas Day

Getting There

By Air

France is well served by its national airline, Air France, as well as most other foreign airlines, including American, Air Canada, and British Airways. Its two main airports are Roissy–Charles de Gaulle, which is about 15 miles (23 km) northeast of Paris, and Orly, which is 9 miles (14 km) away. The addresses of the major airline companies in Paris are:
Air Canada: 24 Capucines, tel: 320-14-15.
Air France: 119 Champs-Elysées, tel: 535-61-61.
British Airways: 91 Champs-Elysées, tel: 778-14-14.

By Sea

Britain is well served with frequent ferry links to Ireland and many European ports. The quickest and busiest route from the Continent to Britain is between Calais and Dover which takes just 1½ hours by ferry and only 35 minutes by hovercraft (Hoverspeed, tel: 01304-240241). In an attempt to compete with the Channel Tunnel, Hoverspeed introduced in 1991 the impressive SeaCat service which can travel at speeds of over 40 knots. It is the world's first car carrying catamaran and is capable of carrying 80 cars and 450 passengers. This service travels between Dover and Calais/Boulogne. Other popular routes from France are Boulogne to Dover/Folkestone, Dieppe to Newhaven, and Le Havre or Cherbourg to Portsmouth.

If you plan to bring a vehicle over by ferry it is advisable to book in advance, particularly during peak holiday periods. If traveling by night on a long journey it is recommended also that you book a sleeping cabin in advance.

By Channel Tunnel

The Channel Tunnel opened in late 1994, providing Eurostar passenger services by rail to Paris Nord (3 hours) and Brussels Midi (3 hours 15 minutes) from London's Waterloo Station. UK bookings, tel: 01233 617575. Vehicles are carried by train through the tunnel from Folkestone in Kent to Nord-Pas de Calais in France. Bookings not essential; just drive up. Enquiries in UK, tel: 01303-271100.

Special Facilities

Boating Tips

On most of the rivers and canals of France hire companies can be found from whom to obtain information about hiring craft. Cruisers range from 2-berth cabin cruisers to much larger craft for 10 or more passengers.

Some of the larger companies will meet visitors from plane or train and transport them to the point of hire.

An up-to-date list of cruiser hire firms can be obtained from :
Le Syndicat National des Louers de Bateaux de Plaisance, Port de la Bourdonnais, Paris 7. Tel: 555-10-49.
French National Tourist Office, 610 Fifth Ave, NY City 10020. Tel: (212) 757 1125.
French Tourist Office, 178 Piccadilly, London W1V 0AL. Tel: (0171) 491 7622.

AUTOMATIC LOCKS

It is essential to study your maps and watch for approaching automatic locks. They will be operated by radar which is installed a short distance (approximately 900 ft/270 meters) either side of the lock. Watch your speed and approach the locks slowly. Do not stop once your boat has passed the radar, nor inside a chain of automatic locks, as the boat will have triggered off the mechanism.

Traffic lights on these locks are of two types. Generally speaking the red light (one or sometimes two of them) means wait. One yellow light or sometimes one red and one green light together (sometimes flashing) means that the lock is preparing for your entry but still wait. One or sometimes two green lights mean that you can enter.

Proceed as follows:
1. Wait until the light is green before entering the lock.
2. Wait 20 seconds beside the radar, or push the entrance bar for 10 seconds.
3. Moor tidily inside the lock.
4. Wait for at least one minute then lift the BLUE pull cord for 5 seconds which will close the lock gates, open the sluices and fill/empty the lock.
5. The gates will open automatically when the cycle is complete. Do not leave the lock if the warning bell rings or if the light remains red.
6. As your boat moves out slowly the bell will ring and the gates will close behind you.

Should an accident occur, hold the RED cord down for five seconds and this will interrupt the cycle. The sluices will then close and not resume their operation until manually operated by the lock-keeper.

Automatic Locks with Entrance and Exit Bars
The procedure is almost the same without the radar control.

A heavier boat will push the bar back against the side of the lock as it passes and this will activate the sluice gates. However, should your boat not be heavy enough, stop beside the swing bar and push it back against the side of the lock with a boat hook for ten seconds.

To tip or not to tip the lock-keeper is a matter for your discretion but it is customary if he has been helpful to you, and most are.

During the locking manoeuvre leave the engine running but put it in neutral gear.

Please note that commercial traffic always has priority.

Mediterranean to Atlantic

The Petit Rhône: This river is restricted to small pleasure-craft with a draught of less than two ft (three quarters of a meter) and headroom of less than eight ft (two and a half meters).

Commercial traffic is not allowed.

Before starting off ask the lock-keeper at St Gilles about navigating conditions.

Pay particular attention to the buoys which mark submerged obstacles, and stay in the center of the channel.

As the water level may drop considerably during the night it is advisable not to moor close to the bank. Be prepared with a gangplank.

The speed limit on this section is 9 miles (15 km) per hour. The channel is marked by buoys which it is very important to watch because of mud banks.

Canal du Rhône à Sète: There is one lock in the section from St Gilles to the Étang de Thau and one on the Beaucaire branch, the operating hours of which are:
1–28 February 7am–6pm
1–31 March 7am–7pm
1 April–30 September 6.30am–7.30pm
1 October–30 November 7am–6pm
1 December–31 January 7.30am–5.30pm

The locks are closed from 12.30–1.30pm. Please check the opening hours of the mobile bridge at **Frontignan** at the bridge office, tel: (67) 480020 or at the **Navigation Of-**

fice, tel: (67) 486529.
When sailing along stretches with large lakes on either side be careful of the strong wind and current and stay in the center of the canal under bridges.

There are moorings for 85 boats at Aigues-Mortes. For enquiries, tel: (66) 51-01-96.

To open the bridge at Grau du Roi please contact the bridge-keeper between 7.30am–12.30pm and 1.30–6pm, tel: (66) 619186.

The bridge remains closed during all holidays.

It is impossible to enter the Rhône via the Beaucaire lock.

Useful telephone numbers
Navigation Office, Frontignan, tel: (67) 486529.
Navigation Office, Sète, tel: (67) 748820.
Navigation Office, Aigues-Mortes, tel: (66) 510166.
Navigatio Office, Beaucaire, tel: (66) 591004.

Canal du Midi: There are 65 locks on this section which are often double or triple.

Please allow commercial barges priority at all times, including entry to the locks.

Operating hours of locks on this section:
1–28 February 7.30am–6.30pm
1–31 March 7am–9 pm
1 April–30 September 6.30am–7.30pm
1 October–30 November 7.30am–6.30pm
1 December 31 January 7.30am–5.30pm

Locks are closed all day on all public holidays except Easter Monday, 8 May, Ascension Day, and Assumption day (15 August).

When passing through a lock it is customary for the lock-keeper to telephone ahead to warn the next lock-keeper of your impending arrival, and he will then empty/fill the lock to prevent a delay at his lock. Therefore, if intending to moor between locks it is courteous to inform the last lock-keeper.

There are very few petrol pumps on the Canal but diesel fuel is available at some of the ports. It would be useful to carry a jerrycan on the boat.

Navigation Office, tel: (61) 540707.
Bureau Navigation Toulouse, tel: (61) 525322.
Ste Girone Plaisance, tel: (61) 735572.
Navigation Office, Castelnaudary, tel: (68) 230020.
Navigation Office, Carcassonne, tel: (68) 250150.
Lock-keeper TPE Béziers, tel: (67) 761301.

At Béziers ask the lock-keeper for the upstream or downstream Inclined Plan which is progressively replacing seven locks. The lock-keeper TPE at Bézier who controls the seven locks of Fontserranes, tel: (67) 284644. Keep clear of commercial barges which may have to cut corners in the many beds.

Canal de la Robine: Before crossing the Aude river into this canal check on the conditions with the lock-keeper as moving sand can make crossing difficult. There are 13 locks on this section. Passing can be difficult due to its narrow width, and overtaking impossible. There is a 3.5 ft (1.5 meters) draught limit on the whole of the canal.

Useful telephone numbers
Navigation Office, Narbonne, tel: (68) 320235.
Tourist Information Office, tel: (68) 651560.
Canal Service, Port-la-Nouvelle, tel: (68) 480171.

Canal Latéral à la Garonne: There are 53 locks on this section, most of which are automatic with traffic light control. Follow the procedure set out at the beginning of this chapter with the following exception:

When the lights turn to red and green to signify that the lock is ready for you, turn the rod which hangs above the canal a quarter of a turn to the right.

When both lights turn to green edge forward to the start of the lock.

When the light on the lock wall turns green enter and put a crew member ashore to tie up. The locking cycle is controlled by a lever on the quayside.

At the end of the locking cycle move the handle and when the gates open you have three minutes to move out of the lock before the gates start to close again.

Useful telephone numbers
Service Maritime, tel: (56) 630113.
Service des Canaux, tel: (56) 610509.

The Garonne: This section has no locks at all in its 34-mile (56-km) length. When entering the river ask for the time of the tides and try to leave during high tide to avail yourself of the current. Mooring at night is not recommended due to variations in the water level.

La Charente

From Angoulême to the Atlantic: The locks between Angoulême and Port du Lys are unmanned. Your boat hire company will have made the necessary requests for lock passage but if not, application must be made 48 hours in advance. Address for requests: **Service Hydrologique de la Charente**, 46 rue de Québec, Angoulême. Please make sure the lock gates and sluices are closed behind you.

Between Port du Lys to Tonnay-Charente the locks are manned by lock-keepers and open:
1 May–30 September 8am–6pm
The locks close at midday from noon–2pm.

There is a bridge at Montrou and if the boat has more than 6½ ft (2 meters) headroom you must wait for it to be raised. This takes place one hour before and after high tide during the following time schedule:
March, April, October 6am–8pm
May to end September 5am–9pm
November to end February 7 am–9pm
The river will be closed to all traffic if the water level rises above a certain level at different sections. Please watch the signs or call, tel: (46) 99-37-36 for a recorded message.

Alsace-Lorraine

Canals of the Marne au Rhin: Operating hours at the locks:
1 December–31 January 7.30am–5.30pm
1–28 February 7 am–6pm
1–31 March 7am–7pm
1 April–30 September 6.30am–7.30pm
1 October–30 November 7 am–6pm

The **Mauvage Tunnel** is one of the few remaining tunnels operated by an electrically driven tug. It takes an hour and a half to go through and there are two trips per day in each direction. Check the operating times at a passing lock, but the timetable is normally as follows:

DEMANGE (MAUVAGES)
1 December–31 January 6.30am–12.30pm, 9.30am–3.30pm
2–28 February 6.30am 1pm, 9.30am–4pm
1 March–30 September 6.30am–1.30pm, 9.30am–4 30pm
1 October–30 November 6.30am–1pm, 9.30am–4pm

The **Foug Tunnel** has single-lane traffic and is operated by a traffic light. At the entrance there is a rod which must be pushed against the bank for five seconds before entering.

The two **Arzviller Tunnels** are also single lane operated by traffic lights which are controlled by a waterways officer. The tunnels are 1½ miles (2,300 meters) and a third of a mile (475 meters) long.

For procedure at automatic locks please see section at the beginning of this chapter.

Between Dombasle and Rechicourt are lights to help you operate the automatic locks. The orange light flashes when the radar has detected your boat. If it fails to flash, push the button on the radar post.

Locks 12, 13, 14, 15, 16, 17 are equipped with loop detectors which work a little less efficiently. The system works well for heavier commercial barges but lighter boats may fail to activate the mechanism. In this case you must hold metallic screens in front of the loop detector for 10 seconds or so. The screens are handed out to each boat and taken back again at locks 11 and 18.

Canal de Toul à Nancy: This section stretches almost 9 miles (14 km). You must obtain permission 24 hours in advance to travel on the Embranchement de Nancy.

The Canal de l'Est is closed on Sundays.

Navigation in Strasbourg: Between June and September a River Tourist Office operates from an old tugboat moored at Quai des Pecheurs.

If wanting to make a water tour of the city in your own boat, double-check headroom against current water level; during the rainy season, levels can fluctuate rapidly causing height restrictions when going under some of the fixed bridges.

Hire craft are not allowed onto the Rhine River.

Le Canal du Rhone au Rhin: All navigation on the waterway is governed by the general waterway traffic regulations which are published (in French only) every year in the Vagnon Waterway Code. These laws are also supplemented by the local laws which became effective at the end of 1974 which stipulate the following:

1. Navigation must not exceed:
a. six miles (10km) in river sections.
b. in lock areas or canal sections, five miles (eight km) for pleasure craft of less than 20 tonnes and four miles (6 km) for all other vessels.
2. The wearing of life jackets is obligatory when moving on parts of the boat where there is no protection against the risk of falling overboard.
3. It is forbidden for pleasure craft to anchor or moor to stakes in the navigable channel.
4. In the restricted passages and tunnels which are not controlled by lights, the vessel proceeding downstream has the right of way.
5. It is forbidden for craft to navigate when coupled abreast.
6. A lifeboat is required on board cargo vessels and large boats of more than 20 tonnes.
7. If no other boat has reached the lock after a wait of 20 minutes, "small boats" will be permitted through either individually or in groups.

In general, lock opening times and dates and automatic operation are the same as for Le Canal de La Marne au Rhine. Most locks have their own keeper, but some men look after two. Between L'Ilse-sur-Doubs and Mulhouse (locks 2 to 39), however, the lock-keepers work in shifts with three teams which will escort the yachtsman while locking through (team one: locks 2–15; two: 16–27 and three: 28–39). For this reason, it is most important to phone the day before (going upstream,

tel: 89-44-48-25 between 7.30am and noon; downstream: 84-23-34-22 during the same hours) to make a locking-through appointment. It is possible to not make the entire passage in one "go", but the first team encountered must be informed of your travel plans.

In the Doubs River section, pay strict attention to channel markings; fixed masonry weirs which are almost invisible run across the river, and there is an ever-present danger the yachtsman may be drawn into danger. Locks on this stretch are not connected by telephone; blow the boat's horn loudly and steadily for approximately 10 seconds to attract the keeper's attention.

As always, commercial barges have the right of way.

ALSACE-LORRAINE USEFUL ADDRESSES

Service de Navigation de Nancy, Direction Regional, 28 Boulevard Albert ler, 54000 Nancy. Tel: 83-96-66-21.
Service de Navigation de Strasbourg, Direction Regionale, 25 Rue de la Nuee, 67081 Strasbourg Cedex. Tel: 88-32-49-15.

Local Service de Navigation offices are found in Vitry-le-Francois, Bar-le-Duc, Toul, Saverne, Mittersheim, Sarreguegmines, Mulhouse, Belfort, Montbeliard, Besancon and Dole.

Burgundy

Canal de Bourgogne: Operating hours at the locks are:
1–31 January 8am–5.30pm
1–28 February 7.30am–6pm
1–15 March 7am–7pm
16 March–15 April 6.30am 7.00pm
16 April–31 August 6.30am–7.30pm
1–last Sunday in September 7am–7.30pm
last Monday in September–31 October 7am–6 pm
1–30 November 7.30am–5.30pm
1–31 December 8am–5.30pm

The locks do not normally open on the following days: New Year's Day, Easter Sunday, 1 May, 8 May, Whitsunday, 14 July, 15 August, 1 November and Christmas Day.

During the tourist season from mid-March to the end of October, the locks are normally closed on a Wednesday. Outside these months, the locks are closed on Sunday and *no* locking through is possible.

On Sundays and holidays on which

the locks are open, the locks are only open from 9am–noon and from 2–6pm.

To pass through on a Wednesday when the locks are normally closed, also on 8 May, Whitsunday, or 15 August, boats can be accompanied by a Navigation Office personnel at the price of 400 Ffr. per boat. Notice must be given to the appropriate staff person in accordance with transport notices Nos. 9 and 10 of March 1985. Boats with an overall length of less than 48 ft (15 meters) can join the lock passage at a reduced fee, and no special notice is required.

Those on boats of less than 65 ft (20 meters) are permitted to go through the following locks without waiting for a keeper to help. They are 1–9 and 11 and 12 south of the Pouilly tunnel. Instructions are given in four languages and a waterways official usually patrols this stretch in case of problems.

Passing through the Pouilly Tunnel: Only boats with a headroom less than 10 ft (three meters) in the axix and eight ft (2.2 meters) by the board are permitted to enter. They must also have sufficient lights, a loud horn, a bucket for hauling water, a fire extinguisher, and one life jacket per person. The passage is free and is operated by the boat's crew.

The River Yonne: Operating hours at locks on this section are:
I October–30 November 7am–6pm
I December–31 January 7.30am–5.30pm
I–28 February 7am–6 pm
1–31 March 7am–7pm
1 April–30 September 6.30am–7.30pm

Locks are closed at midday from noon–12.30pm and are open at 9am on Sundays and public holidays unless otherwise stated.

Canal du Nivernais: On this section locks are open from 8am–noon and 1–7pm. The canal is closed from I November to 31 March. Please keep to the authorised channels crossing the summit reach. There is one-way traffic here which is controlled by the Baye and Port Brulé locks. Please report at the lock upon departure so that the tunnel can be reserved for you.

Les Canaux du Centre: Operating hours at the locks on these canals are:
1 October–30 November 7am–6pm
1 December–31 January 7.30am–5.30pm
1–28 February 7am–6pm
1–31 March 7am–7pm
1 April–30 September 6.30am–7.30am

Make sure to inform the lock-keeper on this section of your expected time of arrival so as to facilitate the flow of traffic on the Briare to St Mammes section and to minimise delays.

It is suggested that you moor your boat on the towpath side of the canal but please keep all boating paraphernalia off the path. Do not attach lines to trees.

On the section between locks 11 and 31 the locks are controlled by traffic lights and linked by telephone. There will always be an official at hand in case of difficulty but if the procedure given at the beginning of this chapter on negotiating automatic locks is followed there should be no problem.

A very good boat harbor at Chalon sur Saône, near the center of town, has all facilities. The office is open from 9am–9pm and for information, tel: (85) 48-83-38.

Canal de Roanne a Digoin: The locks are closed all day on Sundays.

The Mayenne and Sarthe

The operating hours of the locks on the Bassin de la Maine (Sarthe to Oudon) section are:
Beginning of Easter holidays–30 September 9am–8pm
1 October–1 November 9am–6.30pm
2 November–day before Easter holidays 9am–5.30pm
The locks close from 12.30–2pm.

There is no fee for locking. Notify the lock-keeper of your arrival by sounding your horn, and wait for the gates to open. This section is a favourite spot for angling so please slow down and do not moor close enough to interfere with the fishing.

Brittany

Except for the period from 15 June to 15 September locks are closed on the first Sunday of the month and on all other weeks on Tuesdays on the whole of this section. Additional periods of closure are listed.

Operating hours of the locks on the Canal d'Ille et Rance:
1 April–30 September 8 am–7.30pm
1 October–31 March 8.30am–7 pm
The locks close at midday from 12.30–1.30pm.

Except for the period from 15 June to 15 September with the exception of the first of the month, locks are closed on this section all day on Wednesday

Passage takes place on the hour every hour through locks 21 and 29 in the Rennes direction and through locks 15 and 20 in the Dinan direction.

The speed limit on this section is 6 km per hour.

Operating hours of the locks on the Vilaine and Canal de Nantes à Brest section from Redon to Hennebont:
1–28 February 7am–6pm
1–31 March 7am–7pm
1 April–30 September 6.30am–7.30pm
1 October–30 November 7am–6pm
1 December–31 January 7.30am–5.30pm
The locks close from 12.30–1pm.

Please keep strictly to the navigation channel on the river Blavet from Pontivy to lock 29 as the boat could go aground straying from the marked channel.

The section from lock 29 to Hennebont is tidal and the downstream side dries out at low water.

Operating hours of the locks on the Canal de Nantes a Brest from Redon to Quiheix:
16 February–31 March 8.30am–6pm
1 April–30 September 8.30am–12.30pm, 1.30–8pm
1 October–15 November 8.30am–6pm
16 November–15 February Closed
Watch the depth on the Canal d'Ile et Rance and the Vilaine.

To negotiate the locks in the Rance barrage, the boat must be there 20 minutes before the hour, as passage takes place every hour on the hour. If a passage between 8pm and 4.30am is desired, telephone the lock-keeper (tel: 46-21-87) two hours in advance.

Ile de France

The Marne River: There are 18 locks on this waterway, the operating times of which are as the Oise. Except for the automatic locks, and locks 1 to 17, they all close at midday, usually from 12.30–1pm. They are closed all day on 1 January, Easter Sunday, Whitsunday, 1 May, 14 July, 1 November, 11 November and Christmas day. On Sundays and other public holidays the opening hours of locks 1 to 9 are 7.30am–5.30pm. It is compulsory to wear a life jacket when passing through a lock.

In accordance with the Bye-laws objects used as fenders must be able to float as there is a danger of the lock gates being blocked. Therefore if tyres are used they must be inflated otherwise they are forbidden.

The speed limit for pleasure boats is 9 miles (15 km) per hour unless otherwise shown.

Persons under the age of 16 years are not permitted to pilot a motor boat.

Please note that it is compulsory to carry a blue flag of at least three and a half square feet (one square meter). Pleasure boats must comply with this regulation. When a large boat or barge is forced to cross the middle of the channel to negotiate a bend, he must signal his intention to do so by showing a blue flag, and if possible flash a white light. Any approaching craft must acknowledge this signal by showing a blue flag for a few moments. Upstream-going craft should yield to downstream-going craft when passing and to keep to the right of the river. At all times commercial craft has priority.

Canal de l'Aisne à la Marne: This waterway is 40 miles (58 km) long with eight locks, the operating times of which are as Canal Latéral.

The summit reach runs through the Mont de Billy tunnel which is 7,500 ft (2,302 meters) long and operated on a one way system. There can be a wait of up to an hour here. Please watch the access lights.

The lock ladder between locks 17–24 is closed to access three and a half hours before the normal closing time on the day before holidays. Boats are not allowed to remain within the lock ladder.

Canal Latéral à l'Aisne: This canal has eight locks which operate at the following times:
1–28 February 7am–6 pm
1–31 March 7am–7pm
1 April–30 September 6.30am–7.30pm
1 October–30 November 7am–6pm

1 December–31 January 7.30am–5.30pm

They are closed at midday from 12.30–1pm and all day on 1 January, Easter weekend, Whitsun weekend, 1 May, 14 July, 1 November, 11 November and Christmas Day. On Sundays and public holidays when there is not much traffic, locks 5 and 5 are operated by an itinerant lock-keeper.

The Aisne River: There are eight locks on this river, the operating times of which are the same as on the Canal Latèral à l'Aisne. It joins its lateral canal at Celles-sur-Aisne and continues down through Soissons to the Oise just north of Compiègne.

Just north of Soisson at Pont Gambetta until Vauxrot (lock 10) the speed limit is three miles (five km) per hour and mooring on the south bank is not allowed except at Pont des Anglais.

At Vic-sur-Aisne (lock 12) please keep to the east bank and do not attempt the little detour which is not allowed.

The Oise River: The operating hours of the locks on this canal are as follows:

1–28 February 7am–6pm
1–31 March 7am–7pm
1 April–30 September 6.30am–7.30pm
1 October–30 November 7am–6pm
1 December–31 January 7.30am–5.30pm

All locks close between 12.30 and 1pm.

They are also closed all day at Easter, 1 May, 14th July, 11 November and Christmas Day.

This waterway links Northern France and the Paris region. It has 11 locks between Conflans-Ste Honorine and Chauny which is the beginning of the St Quentin canal. It is a busy waterway for commercial traffic, which must always be given priority.

The locks at Pontoise, l'Isle d'Adam and Boran can be passed through at night under the regulation system except for the following periods, when they close completely:

All day on Easter Sunday and Monday, 1 May, 14 July, 11 November, from 5.30pm on 24 December to midnight on Christmas Day, and from 5.30pm on 31 December to 7.30pm

on 1 January.

It is important to inform the lock-keeper of your intended time of arrival, by telephone during normal working hours. If this is impossible telephone the **Regulation Center**, tel: (34) 740175 or (34) 741518. There is a toll fee which may be paid only by cheque at each lock.

At Pont de Chaponval beware of convoys going up or downstream. In view of their difficulty negotiating the bend, try to keep out their way and allow them priority.

Seine River: The regulations given above apply to this section also as both are covered by the same authority.

Pleasure-craft require no special permission to navigate on the Seine, but third party allowed in the channel nor in places reserved for commercial craft. Please ask permission before mooring alongside private property.

Except for the Port-à-l'Anglais lock which is opened from 7am–7pm throughout the year, the operating times of the locks are the same on all sections of l'Ile de France, as follows:

1–28 February 7am–6pm
1–31 March 7am–7pm
1 April–30 September 6.30am–7.30pm
1 October–30 November 7am–6pm
1 December–31 January 7.30am–5.30pm

Locks 1 to 9 (Conflans to Jaulnes) are closed at midday noon–12.30pm.

On Sundays there are variable times. Locks 1 to 4 remain closed, locks 5 to 9 operate from 7.30am–5.30pm, all other locks operate as usual.

The locks are closed on the following public holidays, (except La Grande Bosse and Marolles which remain open on 1 January, Whitsunday and 15 August,) 1 January, Easter Sunday, Whitsunday, 1 May, 14 July, 15 August, 1 and 11 November, 25 December.

There is a regulation service in operation from Varennes to Port à l'Anglais which is the same system described at the beginning of the l'Ile de France section. This means that by informing the lock-keeper in advance during normal working hours it can be arranged for boats to pass through locks at night. There is a toll fee which may be paid only by cheque at each

lock. Telephone the Regulation Center, tel: (3) 4740175 or the individual locks in question.

All locks have traffic lights controlling their operation and commercial craft has priority.

The regulation regarding articles used as fenders being able to float applies equally on the Seine. Motor tyres may be used as long as they are inflated.

Please remember to use the blue flag. Slowing down or stopping to take photographs when boating through Paris is forbidden. Mooring is possible at Port de la Concorde and the Port de Paris, both of which have water and electricity, toilet and washroom facilities.

PORT OPENING HOURS

1 April–31 May 9am–7pm, Sunday 9am–8pm
1 June–15 September 8am–9pm
16 September–15 October 9am–7pm, Sunday 9am–8pm
16 October–31 March 9am–6pm

The speed limit on the waterway in Paris is 11 miles (18 km) per hour, excepting between Pont des Invalides and Passerelle Solférino, and Pont Sully and Pont Neuf, when it is 3.7 (six km) upstream and five miles (eight km) downstream.

Useful telephone numbers
Navigation Service of the Seine, tel: (1) 5786192 or (3) 4742288 for recorded information.
Port Autonome de Paris, tel: (1) 5786192.

For information about trips around the canals of Paris, tel: (1) 42391500. Cruise 1 takes three hours and goes from the Parc de la Villette to the Paris-Arsenal marina, crossing the Crimée bascule bridge, four twin locks, two turning bridges, and under the Bastille vault. Two trips per day at 9.15am and 2.30pm. Cruise 2 takes one whole day and sails from Paris to the Brie countryside. Departure 8.30am daily except Wednesday. This cruise is not recommended for children.

Cruise 3 takes two hours and covers the highest lock in the Ile de France, La Villette Parc, the industrial Ourcq canal, and the Pantin harbor.

La Somme

OPERATING HOURS AT THE LOCKS

1 October–30 November 7am–6pm
1 December–31 January 7.30am–5.30pm
During February 7am–6pm
During March 7am–7pm
1 April–30 September 6.30am–7.30pm

Locks close between 12.30 and 1pm on the Somme canal, the Sambre, the Oise-Sambre canal, the Oise-Aisne canal, and the Aisne side canal, with the exception of tunnels and automated locks and lock ladders, where traffic is non-stop.

The locks on the Oise, the Oise side canal, the St Quentin canal, the Canal du Nord, and the Somme are closed during Easter and on May 1, July 14, November 11, and Christmas Day.

Additionally, locks on the Somme are closed on Sundays between September 1 and May 9.

The locks on the Sambre, the Oise-Sambre canal, the Oise-Aisne canal, and Aisne, and the Aisne side anal, are closed on January 1, during Easter and Whitsun, and on May 1, July 14, November 1, November 11, and Christmas Day.

Useful Addresses
Canal Cruises

Horizon Cruises, Ltd, 16000 Ventura Blvd, Encino, CA91436 USA. Tel: (818) 906-8086, toll free: (800) 252-2103 (within California), (800) 421-0454 (USA), (800) 367-8075 (Canada) offer a wide variety of hotel barges in France for individual travel or group charter. In Burgundy, *Nenuphar* and *Horizon II* have a 12-passenger capacity; *Liberte* carries 10, and the *De Hoop* and *Sara Jane* each offers six people accommodations on a for-charter basis only. On the Canal du Midi, the six-passenger *Alouette* is also only for charter use. The *Esprit*, which carries 18, travels the waterways of Alsace-Lorraine.
Lady A Tours, B.P. 52, 21002 Dijon Cedex, France.
Chemins Nautiques Breton, Lyvet, La Viconté sur Rance, 22690 Pleudihen. Tel: (96) 832871.
Argoat Nautic, Port de Betton, 35830 Betton. Tel: (99) 557036.
Blue Line Bretagne, Port de Plais-ance, 35480 Messac. Tel: (99) 346011.
Comptoir Nautique de Redon, 2 quai Surcouf, 35600 Redon. Tel: (99) 714603.
Bretagne Plaisance, Quai Jean-Bart, 35600 Redon. Tel: (99) 721580.
Breiz Marine, Zone Portuaire, 56190 Arzal. Tel: (97) 450354.
Agera, 1 rue de Capitaine Carhumel, 44000 Nantes. Tel: (40) 205725
Air et Soleil Mutualité, 2 quai St George, 44390 Nort-sur-Erdre. Tel: (40) 295629.
Breton Leisure Cruisers, Base nautique de la Daufresne, 56140 Malestroit. Tel: (97) 751957.
Le Ray Loisirs, 14 rue de Caradec, 56120 Josselin Tel: (97) 756098.
Rohan Plaisance, B. P. 19, 56580 Rohan. Tel: (97) 389866.
S. B. D. M. Nautique, Port de plais-ance de Penn Ar Pont, B. P. I. 29119 Chateauneuf du Faou. Tel: (98) 732534.
Maine Anjou Rivières, Madeleine and René Bouin, Le Moulin, Chenillé-Changé 49229 Le Lion d'Angers. Tel: (41) 951083, (41) 951098.
Quiztour, 19 rue d'Athenes, 75009 Paris. Tel: (1) 48747530.
Flot Home S.A.R.L., 1 rue de la Corderie, B. P. 151, 34302 Agde Cedex. Tel: (67) 949420.
Loisirs Accueil Loire-Atlantique, 34 rue de Strasbourg, 44000 Nantes. Tel: (40) 895077.
Maine Reservations, B. P. 2207, 49022 Angers Cedex. Tel: 41) 889938.

BRITISH COMPANIES OPERATING CANAL HOLIDAYS IN FRANCE

SFV Holidays, 68 Harpes Road, Summertown, Oxford OX2 7QL. Tel: (01865) 57738.
Flot Home UK Ltd, 22 Kingswood Creek, Wraysbury, Staines, Middlesex. Tel: (0178481) 2439.
European Canal Cruises, 79 Winchester Road, Romsey, Hants SO51 8JB. Tel: (01794) 514412.
Hoseasons Holidays Abroad Ltd, Sunway House, Lowestoft, Suffolk NR32 3LT. Tel: (01502) 500555.
Abercrombie and Kent Travel, Sloane Square House, Holbein Place, London SW1W 8BS. Tel: (0171) 730-9376.
Blakes Holidays, Wroxham, Norwich, Norfolk NR12 8DH. Tel: (016053) 2141. (Blakes' agent in France: 17 rue du Fbg, Montmartre, 75009 Paris. Tel: (1) 452-35151.)
UK Waterway Holidays Ltd, Penn Place, Rickmansworth, Herts WD3 1EU. Tel: (01923) 770040. (UK Water-way's agent in France: **Europ' Yacht-ing**, 7 rue Saint Lazaire, 75009 Paris. Tel: (1) 452-61031.)

Practical Tips

Postal Services

Post offices are open during normal working hours and are usually closed from noon to 2pm. The main post office in Paris is open day and night. Post boxes are yellow and easily recognisable.

Telecoms

International telephone calls can be made at post offices throughout the country. For direct international calls dial 19, wait for the second dialling tone, then dial required number. The number to call for international information, tel: 19-33-33. Calls are cheaper between 8pm and 8am. Telephone calls are available in Ffr.40 and Ffr.120 units.

Tourist Offices

The French Tourist Office in Paris is at the following address:
Service des Etrangèrs, Prèfecture de Police, Place Louis-Lepine, 75004 Paris. Tel: 4-277-11-00.

Tourist Information Offices abroad can be found at the following addresses:
Canada: 372 Bay St. Suite 610, Toronto, Ontario M5H 2W9. Tel: (466) 361-16-05.
1840 Ouest, rue Sherbrooke, Montreal 109. Tel: (514) 931-38-55.
Great Britain and Ireland: 178 Piccadilly, London W1V 0AL. Tel: (0171) 491-7622.
USA: 610 Fifth Ave, New York 10020. Tel: (212) 757-1125.

645 North Michigan Ave, Chicago, Ill.60611. Tel: (312) 337-6301; 360 Post Street, San Francisco, CA94180. Tel: (415) 272-2661; 9401 Wilshire Blvd, Beverly Hills, CA90212. Tel: (213) 271-6665.

Consulates & Embassies

Canada: 35 Ave. Montigne. Tel:723-50-15.
Great Britain: 35 rue du Faubourg Saint-Honore. Tel: 266-91-42.
Ireland: 12 Ave. Foch. Tel: 500-20-87.
USA: 4 Ave. Gabriel. Tel: 296-12-02/261-80-75.

Eating Out
Where to Eat
Restaurants

CANAL DU RHÔNE À SÈTE

Le Chalut, 38 quai Gen. Durand, Sète. Tel: (67) 748152.
Mireille, 2 pl. St Pierre, Arles. Tel: (90) 937074.

CANAL DU MIDI AND LE CANAL ROBINE

France, rue République, Villefrance de Lauragais. Tel: (61) 816217.
Palmes, 10 rue Mar. Foch, Castelnaudary. Tel: (68) 230310.
Languedoc, 32 Allée d'Iéna, Carcassone. Tel: (68) 651474.
Méditerranée, bd. Front de Mer, Port-la-Nouvelle Tel: (68) 480308.
Midi et Restaurant La Rascasse, 13 rue Coquille, Beziers Tel: (67) 491343.
Les Trois Sergents, Hôtel St Clair, Agde. Tel: (67) 267313.

CANAL LATÉRAL À LA GARONNE

Capricorne, Marmande. Tel: (53) 644142.
Ibis, 105 bd Carnot, Agen. Tel: (53) 473123.
Moulin de Moissac, pl. Moulin, Moissac. Tel: (63) 040355.
Notre Dame, pl. Jean-Jaurès, Montech. Tel: (63) 647745.
Relais des Garrigues, tel: (63) 673159.

Brasserie Beaux Arts, 1 quai Daurade, Toulouse. Tel: (61) 211212.

LA GARONNE

Grangousier, 2 rte d'Auros, Langon. Tel: (56) 633050.

Côte d'Argent, Castets. Tel: (58) 894033.

LA CHARENTE

St Antoine, 31 rue St Antoine, Angoulême. Tel: (45) 683821.
La Ribaudière, Jarnac. Tel: (45) 813054.
Le Coq d'Or, 33 pl. Francois Ier, Cognac. Tel: (45) 820256.
Relais du Bois, St Georges, rue Royan, Saintes. Tel: (46) 935099.
La Corderie Royale, rue Audebert, Rochefort. Tel: (46) 993535.

LES CANAUX DU CENTRE

Grand Hotel, 18 cours République, Roanne. Tel: (77) 714882.
Merle Blanc, Digoin. Tel: (85) 531713.
Gd. Hotel Commerce, 1 pl. Champ de Foire, Decize. Tel: (86) 250531.
Loire, quai Medine, Nevers. Tel: (86) 615092.
Host. Canal, 19 Quai Pont Canal, Briare. Tel: (38) 312254.
Climat de France, ave. Antibes, Montargis. Tel: (38) 982021.
Trois Faisans, Royal Hotel, 8 rue Port Villiers, Chalons-sur-Saône. Tel: (85) 481586.
Auberge de la Marine, St Jean de Losne. Tel: (80) 290511.

L'YONNE ET CANAL DU NIVERNAIS

Host. de la Poste, 9 pl. E. Sola, Clamecy. Tel: (86) 270155.
Les Clairions, av. Worms, Auxerre. Tel: (86) 468564.
Modern'H Frères Godard, av. Robert Petit, Joigny. Tel: (86) 621628.
Paris et Poste, 97 rue République, Sens. Tel: (86) 651743.

CANAL DE BOURGOGNE

Altea Château Bourgogne, 22 bd.Marne, Dijon. Tel: (80) 723113.
Host du Château, Chateauneuf. Tel: (80) 492200.
Ecu, 7 rue A. Carre, Montbard. Tel: (80) 921166.
Abbaye St Michel, Tonnerre. Tel: (86) 550599.

CANAL DE NANTES À BREST

Pullman Beaulieu, Ile Beaulieu, Nantes. Tel: (40) 471058.
Port, 6 quai Surcouf, Blain. Tel: (40) 790122.
Gare Relais du Gastronome, Redon, Tel: (99) 710204.
Chateau, 1 rue Gen. de Gaulle, Josselin. Tel: (97) 222011.
Martin, 1 rue Leperdit, Pontivy. Tel: (97) 250204.
France, 17 av. Libération, Hennebont. Tel: (97) 362182.

LA MAYENNE

Voyageurs, Le Lion d'Angers. Tel: (41) 953008.
Host Mirwault, Château Gontier. Tel: (43) 071317.
St Pierre, 95 ave. R. Buron, Laval. Tel: (43) 530610.

LA VILAINE ET CANAL D'ILLE ET RANCE

Deux Magots, La Roche Bernard. Tel: (99) 906075.
Gare, Messac. Tel: (99) 346104.
Altea Parc du Colombier, 1 rue Cap. Maignan, Rennes. Tel: (99) 315454.
D'Avaugour, 1 pl. du Champ Clos, Dinan. Tel: (96) 390749.
Central, 6 Gde. Rue, St Malo. Tel: (99) 408770.

CANAL DE LA MARNE AU RHIN

Gare, 2 pl. République, Bar-le-Duc. Tel: (29) 790145.
Syracuse, 29 r. Etats-Unis, Ligny-en-Barrois. Tel: (29) 784870.
La Belle Epoque, 31 ave. Victor Hugo, Toul. Tel: (83) 432371.
La Toisson d'Or, 11 rue R. Poincare, Nancy. Tel: (83) 356101.
Berceaux, 13 rue des Berceaux, Epernay. Tel: (26) 552884.
St Eloi, 27 ave. Soissons, Château-Thierry. Tel: (23) 830233.
Climat de France, 32 ave. Victoire, Meaux. Tel: (64) 331547.
Nogentel, 8 rue Port, Nogent sur Marne. Tel: (48) 727000.

LA SOMME

Le Bresilien, 3 pl. du 8 October, St.Quentin. Tel: (23) 627762.
St Claude, 42 pl. Cdt. L. Daudre, Peronne. Tel: (22) 844600.
Condé, 14 pl. Liberation, Abbeville. Tel: (22) 240633.

LE CANAL DU RHONE AU RHIN

L'Alsace, 4 Place Général de Gaulle,

Mulhouse. Tel: 89-46-01-23.

Wir, 1 Porte de Bâle, Mulhouse. Tel: 89-56-13-22.

Bistro au Boeuf, 1 Rue General LeClerc, Montbéliard. Tel: 81-91-18-37.

La Cremaillère, Route Nationale 83, Hyevre-Paroisse. Tel: 81-84-07-88.

Le Chaland, Promenade Micaud, Besançon. Tel: 81-8061-61.

Restaurant de la Terrasse, Avanne. Tel: 81-52-18-43.

Hotel de la Marine, Ranchot. Tel: 84-71-13-26.

Restaurant des Roches, Rochefort-sur-Nenon. Tel: 84-70-60-01.

Le Clemenceau, 62 Bis rue des Arenes, Dole. Tel: 84-79-16-47.

Auberge de la Marine, St-Jean-de-Losnes. Tel: 80-29-05-11.

Attractions

Things to Do

Sightseeing

Many tourist sites and attractions are closed between noon and 2pm. Most National Monuments are closed on Tuesday. Please ask at the local tourist office for up-to-date times.

Museums

Canal de Berry: Museum at Reugny, near Montluçon. Items include a complete *berrichon* barge.

Canal du Midi: Centre Pierre-Paul Riquet. Aire de Port Lauragais, near Castelnaudary. Situated between Ecluses 16 and 17 at the A61 autoroute service area. Devoted to Riquet and his Canal du Midi.

Canal du Nivernais: Musée de Clamecy. Contains relics of timber rafting on the River Yonne.

River Loire: Musée de la Marine de la Loire, Châteauneuf. Part of the museum at Cosne, contains material on Loire traffic.

River Rhône: L'Association des Amis de la Batellerie du Rhône is attempting to preserve the steam tug *Ardèche* as the center of an open air

museum. Details from M. Tracol, 5 rue Pasteur, 26000 Valence. Chapelle-Musée, Serrières (between Tournon and Vienne), relics of Rhône boats and boatmen.

River Seine: Musée de la Batellerie, Conflans Ste-Honorine. The leading French collection with models, a large archive of prints and photographs, several portions of actual commercial craft, and various artifacts, tel: (3) 972-58-05.

River Saône: Musée Derson, Chalon-sur-Saône. Some exhibits recall freight traffic on the river. At the Ecluse de Couzon, there is a waterways exhibition by the lockside.

Shopping

Shopping Areas

France is renowned for lace (Chantilly and Breton), antiques, perfumes, china (Limoges and Sèvres).

Most businesses including market stalls close for lunch and then open again until 7pm. However, in the warmer parts of the south you may find establishments closed until 4pm and they will normally remain open longer in the evenings. You may find shops closed on Mondays. It is best to check from town to town.

BELGIUM

The Place

Size

Belgium has a predominantly Catholic population of almost 10 million who occupy an area of 11,730 sq miles (30,380 sq km). It has two linguistic zones, with Flemish spoken in the north and French in the south. Brussels is a bilingual city where all official notices and street names are in both French and Flemish. The country is divided into nine provinces.

The Economy

Belgium is one of the world's leading exporters of cut and industrial diamonds and sheet glass, and Antwerp is known as the City of Diamonds in its role as the cutting and trading centre of the world's diamond industry.

The Government

Belgium is a monarchy, with King Baudouin the Head of State. The capital of the country is Brussels which is the residence of the king and Queen Fabiola, the seat of Government, the European Economic Community and NATO.

Planning the Trip

Entry Regulations

Visas and Passports

The rules and regulations governing entry into Europe in General apply to Belgium. You must have a valid passport or for the citizens of the EU, a National Identity Card. Visas are not required for visits of up to three months from citizens of North America and Canada.

Currency

The currency is the Belgian franc which is divided into 100 centimes. There are coins of 50 centimes, 1, 5, 10 and 20 francs, and notes of 50, 100, 500 and 1,000 and 5,000 francs.

Banks are normally open 9am–noon and 2–4pm, while some of the larger branches remain open at midday.

Most of the major credit cards are accepted in banks, post offices, restaurants, and shops which display the sign outside the premises.

Public Holidays

The following days are celebrated as public holidays in Belgium:
January 1: New Year Day
Good Friday
Easter Monday
Ascension Day
Whit Monday
July 21: National Day
Assumption Day
November 11: Armistice Day
December 25: Christmas Day
December 26: Boxing Day

Getting There

By Air

Most international airlines fly daily to Brussels Airport (Zaventem). Among these are Belgian national airline Sabena, American, Air Canada, British Airways.

By Sea

From England there are daily services from the ports of:

Hull to Zeebrugge: Services run by North Sea Ferries, tel: (0482) 796145.

Dover to Ostend, Dover to Zeebrugge, Felixstowe to Zeebrugge: Services run by P and O European Ferries, tel: (0304) 223000.

By Rail

Belgium is linked by train with the rest of the Continent by means of the Trans-Europe-Express (TEE) and with Great Britain via the Channel Tunnel (see page 392).

By Road

Belgium has an excellent system of motorways and is accessible by means of a network of roads linking it to Holland, France and Germany. Distances are short (212 miles from south-east to north-west) and there are no toll charges to pay.

Special Facilities

Boating Tips

Although Belgium's land area is relatively small, the country has one of the densest networks of navigable waterways in the world. Access to the North Sea is provided by the ports of Nieuwpoort, Ostend, and Zeebrugge.

There are more than 1,864 miles (3,000 km) of waterways winding through Belgium passing through Limburg, the plains of Flanders and the Meuse valley.

All these waterways are accessible to pleasure craft except for shallow sections such as the Ourthe, the Dijle, the Nèthe and Démer, which can only be used by dinghies and canoes.

Pleasure boats of non-Belgian origin sailing on the navigable waterways of Belgium must adhere to the same regulations as Belgian boats. However, they do not need a registration plate but on arrival in Belgium must report at the first navigation tax office where an entry declaration will be issued. On departure the same in reverse, the last navigation tax office must be visited where a declaration of exit should be signed.

For visits of more than two months a registration plate, which costs Bf.360, is required.

Fees for the use of the waterways are normally paid when passing through a lock but payment can be made in advance by applying at the first navigation tax office on entering Belgium where the fee will be calculated on the tonnage of the boat.

All foreign vessels must carry a first aid kit, rockets, life jackets, pump, fire extinguishers, compass, navigation lights, anchors, engine tools and the ship's papers.

The maximum cruising speed is seven knots along the whole network of waterways unless otherwise stated, i.e. local regulations or high speed sections.

Pleasure boating on the canal from Brussels to the Rupel is governed by the conditions laid down by the public company which owns it.

The busiest sections of the waterways are the section from Terneuzen to Ghent, the Sambre between Charleroi and Namur, and the Albert canal from Antwerp to Liège.

It should be noted that pleasure craft of less than three tons are only permitted on canals and canalised rivers at official discretion, and that as a general rule, locks do not operate on public holidays, and on a limited basis on Sunday.

Insurance against third party risks and cover for the cost of rescue, assistance, and salvage, is a legal requirement and this insurance should be taken out before you leave home and should cover all Western European countries. When hiring a boat in Belgium check that the insurance documents are sufficient to cover all legal requirements. A book entitled *Inland Waterways of Belgium* by E.E. Benest and published by Imray, Laurie, Norie & Wilson is strongly recommended as it describes in detail all the legal requirements laid down by the Belgian authorities.

Most clubs and official harbors supply water and electricity, but fuel is not always available. For information on the availability of fuel contact any branch of the Royal Belgian Yachting Federation (RBYF), tel: (02) 512-3426.

Most of the facilities of the affiliated branches of the RBYF or branches of the Vlaamse Vereniging Voor Watersport, tel: (031) 19-2207 are available to foreign boat owners. In addition, mooring is allowed at any site designated for commercial boats provided no obstruction to other river users is caused. These moorings are very popular and fill up quickly.

The procedure for passing through automatic locks:
1. Wait until the green light is on before entering the lock.
2. Wait 20 seconds beside the radar or push the entrance bar for 10 seconds.
3. Moor tidily inside the lock.
4. To start the lock cycle, lift the BLUE pull cord for 5 seconds and do not touch it for at least one minute after activating the lock entrance detector. The lock gates close automatically, the sluices open and the lock fills or emp-

ties. When the cycle is complete the gates open automatically.

5. Leave the lock slowly, waiting 20 seconds beside the radar detector (or pushing the entrance bar for 10 seconds). As you leave a bell will ring and the gates will close. It is strictly forbidden to leave the lock while the red light on the gate is on or if the warning bell rings.

If an accident occurs hold the RED pull cord down for five seconds which will interrupt the cycle. The sluices will close and not resume until operated by the lock-keeper. Please note that commercial traffic has priority.

Automatic locks with entrance and exit bars:

The procedure is almost the same without the radar control.

With a heavier boat, i.e. barge, the bar is pushed back against the side of the lock as it passes and this activates the sluice gates.

However, should your boat not be heavy enough, stop beside the swing bar and push it back against the side of the lock with a boat hook for ten seconds.

A detailed map of the entire waterways system is available from Service d'Exploitation des Voies Navigables, and all information regarding the waterway network is available from Ministère des Travaux Publics, Service S.E.V.N., Administration des Voies Hydrauliques, The address of both bodies is:

Rue de la Loi 155, 1040 Brussels. Tel: (02) 733-9670.

Brussels Port Authority, Place des Armateurs 6, Brussels.

In the case of any major difficulty of a technical nature consult:

Conseil Supérieur de la Navigation de Plaisance et des Loisires Aquatic, Ave. Charles-Quint 345, 1080 Brussels. Tel: (02) 466-1514, 466-1572.

(Blakes' agent in Belgium: **British Reservation Centre**, Rue de la Montagne 52E, B.1000 Brussels. Tel: (02) 5112386.)

Floating Through Europe, 271 Madison Ave, New York City, NY 10016. Tel: (212) 685-5600, (800) 221-3140 operates *Lys*, a 10-passenger barge, which makes weekly cruises through the tourist highlights of Belgium.

Hoseasons Holidays, A38 Sunway House, Lowestoft, Suffolk NR32 3LT Tel: (01502) 500555. (Hoseasons agent in Belgium: **Travel Agency Wirtz**, Shell Building, rue Ravenstein 66, B.1000 Brussels. Tel: (02) 5137630.)

Practical Tips

Pharmacies close on Saturday afternoons and all day Sunday. In an emergency look for the notice in the pharmacy window which shows a list of pharmacies remaining open and their addresses.

Post offices are open daily 9 am–6pm and 9am–12pm on Saturdays. Smaller branches may be closed on Saturdays.

The telephone service is automatic throughout the country and telephone offices are open day and night in the larger cities, although in smaller towns they close at the same time as post offices.

The Belgian Tourist Office can be found at the following places abroad:

Canada: 5801 Ave.Monkland, Montreal H4A 1G4. Tel: (514) 487-3387.

Great Britain: 38 Dover Street, Lon-

don W1X 3RB. Tel: (0171) 499-5379.

USA: 745 Fifth Ave. New York. Tel: (212) 758-8130.

In Belgium, detailed information can be obtained from the Brussels Tourist Board which can be found at rue du Marché-aux-Herbes 61, tel: (02) 513-9090 or (02) 513-8940. Their office is open in summer 9am–8pm daily and 9am–7pm at weekends.

For information at the airport when you arrive, look for the National Tourist Bureau desk at the airport. Consulates and Embassies in Brussels:

Canada: 6 rue de Loxum. Tel: (02) 513-7940.

Great Britain: 28 rue Joseph II. Tel: (02) 219-1165.

Ireland: 19 rue du Luxembourg. Tel: (02) 513-6633.

USA: 27 blv. du Regent. Tel: (02) 513-3830.

Shopping

As a general rule shops are open 9am–6pm but in many towns stores stay open until 8 or 9pm one evening per week, this day quite often being Friday.

Belgium is renowned for its handmade lace from Bruges, Brussels, Binche and Mechelen and its tapestries from Mechelen, St Niklaas, Brussels and Ghent.

Most of the towns and art centers can be reached by water and have one or more mooring places where you can leave your boat and explore. This applies particularly to Antwerp, Ghent, Bruges, Brussels, Tournai, Liège, Huy, Namur and Dinant.

NETHERLANDS

The Place

The Netherlands (Holland) is a constitutional monarchy with Queen Beatrix of Orange as its Head of State. The capital of the country is Amsterdam with the seat of government in The Hague (Den Haag).

With a population of 14 million people occupying an area of just under 16,000 sq. miles, the Netherlands is a densely populated country. More than half of its total area lies below sea level, most of which was reclaimed from the North Sea, and the size of the country grows as the Dutch get better and better at reclaiming the land. This reclamation has culminated in the gigantic Ijsselmeer *polders* (the former Zuiderzee) in the world famous Afsluitdijk and in the Delta works in Zeeland.

It is said that the Dutch are a nation of sailors and sailing is in their blood. Holland is known throughout the world for its wide network of waterways. The total length of main Dutch rivers (Lek, Waal, Neder Rijn, Gelderse Ijssel and the Maas) totals about 680 miles (1,100 km). There is a network of about 3,700 miles (6,000 km) of rivers and canals and it is ideal for a boating holiday.

There are many religious denominations and church services are held at set times, differing from place to place. There are often foreign language services held in larger churches at weekends.

Planning the Trip

Entry Regulations

Visas and Passports

Generally speaking, the regulations laid out in the Europe in General section apply. Visitors need a valid passport or a National Identity Card (citizens of the EU) but at the time of going to press no visas were demanded of citizens of Australia, Canada, Great Britain, Ireland, New Zealand and the United States for a visit of less than three months.

Children under the age of 16 years require no passport if they are traveling with an adult on whose passport they are entered.

Health

Inoculation certificates are not normally required for entry into Holland unless traveling from a risk area. Check if in doubt. Foreign tourists and their families have the right to medical assistance in accordance with the Dutch Health Service law in the following cases:

1. When they originate from a country with which the Netherlands has concluded a treaty on this subject.
2. When care cannot be delayed until the subject returns to his own country.
3. An international insurance form is given to the doctor, chemist or hospital.

Always carry with you copies of forms which entitle you to medical assistance: without them you would have to make immediate payment for medical treatment.

Further details can be obtained from the foreign affairs department of the Health Service: **Afdeling Buitenland van het Ziekenfonds ANOZ**, P.O. Box 9069, 3506 GB Utrecht. Tel: (030) 618881.

Currency

There are no import/export restrictions of money or foreign exchange in the Netherlands, whose unit of currency is the guilder (florin) which is written as Dfl. and is divided into 100 cents. The cent coin was recently withdrawn from circulation and existing coins are 5 cents (stuiver), 10 cents (dubbeltje), 25 cents (kwartje), Dfl.1 (1 guilder or 100 cents) and Dfl.2.50 (2 guilders 50 cents or rijksdaalder). Existing notes are Dfl.5, Dfl.10, Dfl.25, Dfl.50, Dfl.100, Dfl.250 and Dfl.1000.

Banks are open Monday to Friday 9am–4pm and sometimes also one evening in the week. (Check locally). Most banks will exchange your currency and traveler's checks. There are exchange offices (Grenswisselkantoren) at major frontier crossings, which are sometimes open at weekends.

Most international credit cards are accepted in banks, post offices, restaurants, and shops which display the sign outside the premises.

Public Holidays

The following days are celebrated as public holidays in the Netherlands:
January 1: New Years Day
Good Friday (most shops open)
Easter Monday
The Queen's Birthday (April 30, all shops closed)
Ascension Day
Whit Monday
December 25: Christmas Day
December 26: Boxing Day

Getting There

By Air

Royal Dutch Airlines (KLM) and many foreign airlines fly regularly to Schiphol, Amsterdam. Bus and rail services link Schiphol with other major destinations throughout Holland.

By Rail

Holland is linked by direct train services to most countries in Western Europe and to most other European cities by Trans-Europe-Express (TEE).

By Sea

Holland is reached by ferry from England from the following ports:
Dover to Zeebrugge, daily services

Netherlands

operated by P&O European Ferries, Box 12, Dover, Kent, CT16 1LD, tel: (0304) 223000.

Dover to Ostend, daily services operated by P&O European Ferries as above.

Harwich to Hoek van Holland (The Hook), two sailings daily. Takes approximately six to seven hours day crossing, seven to eight hours night crossing. Service operated by Sealink/ Zeeland Steamship Company, tel: (01) 8348122 or (0255) 508439.

Hull to Rotterdam, nightly service crossing 14 hours. Service operated by North Sea Ferries, King George Dock, Hedon Road, Hull, North Humberside, HU9 5QA, tel: (0482) 795141.

Sheerness to Vlissingen, (Flushing) two sailings daily. Day crossing seven hours, night crossing eight hours. Service operated by Olau Line (UK) Ltd, tel: (0795) 666666.

Great Yarmouth to Scheveningen, three sailings daily Monday to Friday, two sailings daily Saturday. Day and night crossings eight hours. Freight service operated by Norfolk Line, taking a limited number of passengers, tel: (0493) 856133.

There are excellent motorways and good E routes from Holland into Belgium and from there into France.

Special Facilities
Boating Tips

No frontier documents are required at present for any boats which are to be used for tourist purposes including privately owned boats, but upon arrival and departure you must report to the nearest Customs harbor office. You will be asked to provide some data about your vessel and your itinerary, and you will be given a document which must be produced whenever you are asked for it.

Please check with the rental company that all the legal requirements have been met. It is normal for rental companies to attend to all these matters but it is best to double check.

The Dutch Government is considering bringing in compulsory sailing certificates for those in charge of certain categories of vessel. As far as pleasure-craft are concerned this would be obligatory for skippers of vessels 50 ft (15 meters) or more in length, and

motor boats less than 50 ft (15 meters) long but capable of more than 12 miles (20 km) per hour. This legislation will probably be decided upon in the near future.

There are very few restrictions in the form of licences or legal formalities unless your boat is capable of traveling in excess of 10 miles (16 km) per hour, even if you do not intend to travel at this speed. In such cases the boat must be registered at a post office for the sum of Dfl.47.50. (This amount is subject to change.) A registration number will be issued which must be produced when required. There is also a compulsory insurance with a minimum value of Dfl.250.000.

As the import, export, transit or possession of all weapons in the Netherlands is banned, you must be sure to obtain the necessary papers if you plan to carry or use signalling pistols or signalling equipment of any description. If the signalling pistol can be heard plainly by other shipping there are specific requirements to be met and for further information about these contact the following:

Cabinet for the Queen's Commission in the Province of Utrecht, Achter Sint Pieter 200, 3512 HT Utrecht, tel: (030) 582448.

They will want to see your licence so be prepared. Dutch yachts almost always use smoke and light signals in distress, and radio for emergencies. Speedlimits for canals are clearly signposted along the banks and range from four to nine miles (six to 15 km) per hour depending on the size of the canal. The current speed limit is up to a little over one mile (two km) per hour on the Maas, four miles (seven km) on the Waal and the first part of the Gelderse Ijssel. Depth can vary with the tide to a level of about five ft (1.5 meters).

There is a vast amount of shipping traffic on the Waal which is called the motorway of rivers because of its heavy Rhine traffic to Rotterdam. In Limburg the speed limit ranges between a maximum of about six to 10 miles (10–16 km) per hour.

Speed limits in operation on the canals and lakes are from about 4 miles (six km) through towns and on very small canals, to about seven miles (12 km) on the larger canals and rivers. On a number of busy canals and

rivers, there is a rule that yachts have to keep starboard quay so that they may not steer a middle course.

The *Inland Waters Police Regulations* and the *Almanac for Water Tourism II* are useful cruising companions.

BRIDGES AND LOCKS

Most of the bridges are controlled by traffic lights. Two red lights signify that the bridge is closed. If one red light is shown, give three blasts on the horn. When the lights change to one red and one green prepare to proceed. When there are two green lights you are free to proceed. If the bridge opens and two red lights remain lit, traffic is approaching from the opposite direction so wait until the green lights appear.

Some bridges close altogether on Sundays or open less frequently so this must be borne in mind.

It would be useful to note the height of your boat as there are many low bridges to negotiate, and the height is usually displayed on them. If your boat is unable to pass beneath some of the swing, lifting and tilting bridges you will need to note the operating times and arrange your itinerary accordingly. Some of these bridges are free but at others the bridge-keeper will lower a wooden clog (klomp) on the end of a fishing line into which you will be required to place a moderate sum ranging from 50 cents to Dfl.2.50. You will find the prices listed on a board affixed to the bridge.

Locks are not so numerous as they are in France or Belgium because of the very minor variations in land level. Most locks are operated by friendly lockkeepers and are nearly always situated in pretty countryside.

There are 19 locks on the 70-mile (112-km) channel from Maastricht to Utrecht.

Commercial traffic always has priority at bridges and locks and pleasure-craft has to wait its turn. The river Waal is especially busy as it is a route to the Rhine.

Useful Addresses
Hire Operators

Horizon Cruises Ltd, 16000 Ventura Blvd, Encino, CA91436, USA. Tel: (818) 906-8086, toll free: (800) 252-2103 (within California), (800) 421-0454 (USA), (800) 367-8075 (Canada), operates the *M.S. Rembrandt*, an 18 passenger barge, which cruises between Amsterdam and Bruges between April and November with special Tulip departures during blooming season.

Floating Through Europe, 271 Madison Ave, New York City, NY 10016. Tel: (212) 685-5600, (800) 221-3140, operates the *Juliana*, an 18 passenger barge which makes a circle tour around Holland.

Swan Hellenic operate cruises to the bulbfields aboard the *Victoria Regia*, which takes 70 passengers. The trip includes Volendam, Hoorn, Aalsmeer, Gouda, Delft, Rotterdam and Amsterdam.

Hoseasons Holidays Abroad, A38 Sunway House, Lowestoft, Suffolk NR32 3LT. Tel: (01502) 500555. *Their agents in Holland*

Reisorganisatie Boot and Co, Meent 75, NL-3011 JE Rotterdam. Tel: (10) 113260.

UK Waterway Holidays Ltd, Penn Place, Rickmansworth, Herts WD3 1EU. Tel: (01923) 770040. *Their agents in Holland:*

Thalassa Travel, John Huizingalaan 86, 1065 JD Amsterdam. Tel: (020) 173011 and 173012.

Yachtcharter Panorama, Wolvenjacht 2, 8064 PB Swartsluis Holland. Tel: (05208) 67108.

H. B. Bies, Rijkstraatweg1, 8468 BG Haskerdijken, Holland. Tel: (01031) 5139212.

Practical Tips

Most restaurants and cafès have a service charge included and this will be stated on the bill. Otherwise it is usual to add a tip of 10 percent. It is customary to give tips to guides, cloakroom attendants, porters, and taxi drivers. As a guide, the usual tip for a cloakroom attendant would be 25–50 cents and a porter should be given Dfl.2.50 per suitcase.

Post offices are generally open Monday through Friday from 8.30am to 5pm and some also open on Saturdays until 12pm.

The telephone system is fully automatic. International calls can be made from some telephone booths and from post offices. For information about Dutch telephone numbers dial 008. For operator assisted calls within Europe call 0010, and outside Europe call 0016. Cheap rate calls are from 6pm to 8am and weekends. For calls outside Europe, the code is 09, then the country code (Canada and the United States 1) followed by the number.

Great Britain: J. Vermeerstraat 7, Amsterdam. Tel: 764343.
USA: Museumplein 19, Amsterdam. Tel: 790321.

Getting Around

You will find NBT Offices (Netherlands National Bureau for Tourism) in New York, Chicago, San Francisco, Toronto, London, Sydney and Tokyo. In Holland their offices will bear the sign VVV (Vereniging Voor Vremdeling Verkeer), sometimes with the words i-Nederland beneath. The head office is at Bezuidenhutseweg 2, 2594 AV Den Haag, tel: 070-814191.

The following is a list of their representatives overseas:
Australia: Suite 302, 5 Elizabeth Street, Sydney NSW 2000. Tel: 02-276921.
Canada: Suite 710, 25 Adelaide Street East, Toronto M5C 1Y2. Tel: (416) 363-1577.
Great Britain and Ireland: 25–28 Buckingham Gate, London SW1E 6LD. Tel: (0171) 630-0451.
Japan: No. 10 Mori Bldg. 1-18-1 Toranomon, Minato-ku, Tokyo. Tel: (03) 508-8015/16.

USA Eastcoast: (21st floor), 355 Lexington Ave, NY 10017. Tel: (212) 370-7367.
USA Westcoast: Room 401, 605 Market Street, San Francisco, Calfornia 94105. Tel: (415) 543-6772.
USA Midwest: Suite 326, 225 N. Michigan Ave. Chicago, Ill. 60601. Tel: (312) 819-0300.

Shopping

Shops are usually open Monday to Saturday from 8.30am to 6pm, closing at 5pm on Saturday. In holiday resorts you will find shops open in the evenings and on weekends also.

Most tourists collect dolls in costume, wooden clogs, and Delft blue pottery. Visit Dutch flower bulbfields and arrange a shipment through the dealer to your home. Tulips, hyacinths, daffodils and crocuses are in bloom from the end of March to mid-May. Bulbs can only be taken out of the country if accompanied by a health certificate issued by the Plant Disease Service.

GREAT BRITAIN

The Place

The British Isles, which is made up of England, Scotland, Wales and Northern Ireland, has a population of more than 56.6 million, 9 million of whom live in the London conurbation. The Church of England is the established church, but religious services are also conducted by other denominations and religions.

It is in Greenwich, Kent, at longitude 0°, where Mean Time for the meridian of Greenwich is calculated. All zones west of Greenwich calculate their time from Greenwich Mean Time (GMT) minus and east of Greenwich GMT plus. Standard time on the West Coast of the United States is eight hours earlier than Greenwich and in Western Australia eight hours later.

Planning the Trip

Entry Regulations

Visas & Passports

Passport holders of most European countries, North America, South Africa, Japan and many Commonwealth countries do not generally require a visa to enter the UK for a short stay. If in doubt check with the British Embassy in your home country.

Customs

If you enter the UK directly from another European Union country, you need make no declaration to Customs for goods brought in for personal use. However, if you're found bringing in more than 800 cigarettes or 10 litres of spirits or 110 litres of beer, you may be asked to prove that they're for per-sonal use (e.g. you're a hopeless addict or there's a family wedding coming up). Cars, boats and planes do attract duties.

On entering the UK from non-EU countries, those carrying goods within two categories of duty-free allowances may pass through the **nothing to declare** channel (green) where there are spot checks. Those with goods over the limits should go through the **goods to declare** (red) channel.

(a) Goods which have been obtained outside the EU or duty and tax free within the EU:
200 cigarettes/or 100 cigarillos/or 50 cigars/or 250g of tobacco; 2 litres still table wine; 1 litre spirits (over 22 percent by volume)/or 2 litres fortified or sparkling wine/or a further 2 litres still table wine; 60 cc/ml of perfume; 250 cc/ml of toilet water; £32 worth of gifts, souvenirs or other goods..

(b) Goods obtained duty and tax paid in the EU:
300 cigarettes/or 150 cigarillos/or 75 cigars/ or 400g of tobacco; 5 litres still table wine; 1.5 litres spirits/or 3 litres fortified or sparkling wine/or an additional 3 litres still table wine; 90 cc/ml perfume; 375 cc/ml toilet water; £265 worth of gifts, souvenirs or any other goods.

It is illegal to bring animals, plants, perishable foods, certain drugs, firearms and obscene material into the country without prior arrangement. But any amount of currency can be brought in.

For further information contact **HM Customs and Excise**, Dorset House, Stamford Street, London SE1 9PS, tel: 0171-620 1313.

Export Procedures

VAT (value added tax) is a standard sales tax of 17.5 percent which is added to all goods except food and books. Most large department stores and smaller gift shops operate a scheme to refund this tax to visitors, but often require that more than a minimum amount (usually £50) is spent. To get a refund you will need to fill in a form from the store, have it stamped by customs when you leave the country and then post it back to the store. Provided you leave the country with the goods within three weeks of purchase you will be refunded the tax less an administration fee.

Animal Quarantine

Dogs and cats are subject to very strict quarantine restrictions and all animals must remain under guarded quarantine for six months. There are no exceptions to this rule, even if the animal has received all its inoculations so it would be unwise to bring any pets on a boating trip.

Health

Inoculations or vaccinations are not required for entry into Britain unless traveling from a country which is known to be at risk, notably Asia, Africa, South America.

In a medical emergency go to the nearest hospital. Under the National Health Scheme you may receive immediate treatment without charge for emergencies such as accidents, infectious diseases, but you will be charged for any other treatment and admittance to a hospital. Be cautious and take out an insurance to cover such costs while abroad.

Currency

The British pound sterling (£) is a decimal currency divided into 100 pence (p). Coins come as 1p, 2p, 5p, 10p, 20p and £1. Notes come in £5, £10, £20 and £50. Scotland issues its own notes, which are not technically legal tender in England and Wales, though some shopkeepers will accept them. English notes, however, can be used anywhere in Scotland.

General banking hours are between 9.30am and 3.30pm Monday to Friday. A few banks are open until 4.30pm and on Saturday mornings. In rural Scottish areas banks may close for lunch. Branches of the major national banks – Lloyds, Barclays, Midland, National Westminster, Royal Bank of Scotland and the Bank of Scotland – can be found on most high streets and tend to offer similar currency exchange rates. They charge no commission on travellers' cheques presented in sterling or for changing a cheque in another currency if the bank is affiliated with your own back home. However, there will be a charge for changing cash into another currency or for giving cash against a credit card. Proof of identity is usually required. Most banks have automatic machines where international credit or cashpoint cards can be used in conjunction with a personal number to withdraw cash.

Money may also be changed by travel agents, such as Thomas Cook, and at some large department stores and hotels, but bear in mind that banks tend to offer the best rates. There are numerous bureaux de change throughout towns and cities in Britain, but you should be wary of changing money at these as they may offer low rates and charge high commissions. Look out for the British Tourist Authority's (BTA) code of conduct sticker.

International credit cards are widely accepted in shops, hotels and restaurants, although there are a few exceptions. Eurocheques are also widely accepted.

Public Holidays
England and Wales
January 1: New Year's Day
Good Friday
Easter Monday
First Monday in May: May Day
Last Monday in May: Bank holiday
Last Monday in August: August Bank holiday
December 25: Christmas Day
December 26: Boxing Day

Scotland
January 1: New Year's Day
First Monday in January: Bank holiday
Good Friday
First Monday in May· May Day
Last Monday in May: Bank holiday
First Monday in August: August Bank holiday
December 26: Boxing Day

Getting There
By Air
ENGLAND
Although your most likely destination when flying to Britain will be one of London's five airports, the regional airports of Birmingham, Manchester, Glasgow, Prestwick and Cardiff also receive international flights.

London is served by the large major international airports of Heathrow, 15

miles (24 km) to the west receiving mainly scheduled flights, and Gatwick, 28 miles (45 km) to the south, receiving a mixture of scheduked and charter flights. North of London, Stansted is now London's third major airport.

From **Heathrow** the easiest way to reach central London is the 45-minute Tube journey on the Underground's Piccadilly Line, costing about £3 (depending on destination). By coach you can take the London Regional Transport red double-decker Airbus (A1 to Victoria or A2 to Euston) which picks up from all terminals at half-hourly intervals between 6.30am and 10.15pm. It stops off at major hotels en route and costs £5 one-way, £8 return. For 24-hour Airbus information, tel: 0181-668 7261. Alternatively, Green Line provides the more comfortable Flightline 767 coach service to Victoria with on-board washrooms and a luggage loading service for the same price. A ride in a black cab will cost upwards of £22 to central London.

Gatwick Airport is served by the main-line Gatwick Express train service and also by regular coach services, both running to and from Victoria. The train leaves every 15 minutes between 5.30am and 10pm, and there is an hourly service during the night. Taking 30 minutes, it costs £8.50 one-way. Flightline 777 coaches leave from both the North and South terminals and take about 70 minutes to reach Victoria. A single fare is £6 (US and Canadian dollars accepted), £8 return.

National Express runs a coach service connecting Heathrow, Gatwick, Stansted and Luton airports with each other and Victoria railway station. Enquiries, credit card bookings, tel: 0171-730 0202.

For those heading elsewhere in Britain other than London, there are regular Railair bus links to nearby British Rail stations.

Manchester International Airport is 10 miles (16 km) south of the city and caters for flights to 160 destinations around the world. A shuttle bus service runs half-hourly to Manchester Piccadilly and Victoria main-line stations and to Chorlton Street coach station. The airport is currently being expanded to include a rail link to the city centre.

Birmingham International Airport hosts over 100 international airlines and is being expanded to include a

new passenger terminal. Trains run every 15 minutes from the airport's station to Birmingham New Street station 9 miles (14 km) away.

SCOTLAND
As a result of recent changes in UK air regulations, airports at Edinburgh, Glasgow and Prestwick all now receive transatlantic charter flights. Before these changes, all scheduled international flights to Scotland landed at Prestwick only.

Glasgow Airport has been extended to cope with this increased traffic. Situated 8 miles (13 km) west of the city, it is connected to the centre by a half-hourly coach service running to Anderston and Buchanan Bus stations. Journey time: 25 minutes.

Edinburgh Airport lies 8 miles (13 km) west of the city. Airlink runs a bus service to the city which takes about 30 minutes.

Airport Information:
Birmingham, tel: 0121-767 5511
Gatwick Airport, tel: 01293-535353
Heathrow Airport, tel: 0181-759 4321
Manchester, tel: 0161-489 3000
Stansted Airport, tel: 01279-502380
Edinburgh, tel: 0131-344 3136, 333 1000
Glasgow, tel: 0141-887 1111

By Sea
The cross-channel ferries are the most usual mode of transport to and from Britain, Ireland, and the Continent of Europe. There are daily and frequent sailings out of many different British ports but for further information consult the section of the Guide which deals specifically with the country to which you wish to sail.

From **North America** you could arrive in style on the Cunard Steamship Company's *Queen Elizabeth II* luxury cruiser, the world's only superliner. Operating between April and December, she takes five days to cross the Atlantic. For information, tel: (718) 361 4000 in the US, 0171-839 1414 in the UK.

Special Facilities
Boating Tips
The British Waterways Board are the authority for a network of almost

2,000 miles of canals and rivers plus 90 reservoirs throughout England and Wales, the majority of which are enjoyed by millions of tourists each year.

In addition to the seven areas into which they are divided for administrative purposes in England and Wales, they also administer five waterways in Scotland.

But the British Waterways Board are not the only controllers of the waterways and the addresses of the Board's Area Offices plus other important authorities are listed at the end of this section.

It is compulsory for all pleasure craft to carry a Pleasure Boat Licence which must be displayed at all times, preferably on the port side. The licence can extend for any period from seven days to one year. However, if you intend to sail only on rivers and exclude all the canals the licence fee is cheaper. Hired boats need a Hire Boat Licence or River Registration (Hire) Certificate so check before taking to the water.

If fishing from the boat is intended a valid licence issued by the Regional Water Authority is required.

On inland waterways keep to the right when approaching another boat. Overtake on the left side of another boat unless specifically requested to overtake on the right by, say, a larger boat which needs to stay in the deep channel in the center.

The speed limit is normally four miles per hour on rivers and six miles per hour on canals unless otherwise stated.

Always give priority to commercial traffic and allow them to overtake if they wish to.

Be cautious when approaching tunnels and wait until they are clear before entering, always switching on headlights and sounding the horn. There may be a tunnel which operates a one-way system, and if so consult the times displayed at the entrance and obey them.

There are no locks on the Norfolk Broads or the Ashby, Bridgewater and Lancaster Canals. Many of the other locks will be manned by lock-keepers but if not, they are not difficult to operate alone.

If you have to open or close a gate or moving bridge to go through, please leave it as was when you arrived as it may be a crossing or a farm track, and an accident could result if you don't.

Water, rubbish bins and 'sanitary stations' are provided at intervals along the route, and keys to open padlocks on locks, swing bridges or gates are obtainable in advance from most boatyards.

Useful Addresses

British Waterways Board Headquarters, Melbury House, Melbury Terrace, London NW1 6JX. Tel: (0171) 262-6711.
British Waterways Board Craft Licensing Officer, and Fisheries Officer, Willow Grange, Church Road, Watford, WD1 3QA. Tel: (01923) 26422.

British Waterways Board Area Leisure Officers

Birmingham: Reservoir House, Icknield Port Road, Birmingham B16 0AA. Tel: (0121) 454-7091.
Castleford: Lock Lane, Castleford, West Yorkshire WF10 2LH. Tel: (01977) 554351.
Gloucester: Dock Office, The Docks, Gloucester GL1 2EJ. Tel: (01452) 25524.
London: 53 Clarendon Road, Watford, WD1 1LA. Tel: (01923) 31363.
Northwich: Navigation Road, Northwich, Cheshire CW8 1BH. Tel: (01606) 74321.
Nottingham: 24 Meadow Lane, Nottingham NG2 3HL. Tel: (01602) 862411.
Wigan: Swan Meadow Road, Wigan, Lancs WN3 5BB. Tel: (01942) 323895.
Scotland: Canal House, Applecross Street, Glasgow G4 9SP. Tel: (0141) 332-6936.

Other Useful Addresses

Anglian Water Authority, Diploma House, Grammar School Walk, Huntingdon, Cambridgeshire PE18 6NZ. Tel: (01480) 56181.
Association of Pleasure Craft Operators, The Wharf, Norbury Junction, Woodseaves. Tel: (978) 574578.
Associated British Ports, Kingston House Tower, Bond Street, Hull HU1 3ER. Tel: (01482) 27171.
Associated British Ports, East Parade, Goole, N. Humberside DN14 5RB. Tel: (01405) 2691.
Inland Waterways Association Lim-ited, 114 Regents Park Road, London NW1 8UQ. Tel: (0171) 5862556.
Linton Lock Commissioners, c/o M.D. Oakley, I Wheelgate, Malton, North Yorkshire YO17 0HT. Tel: (01653) 3639.
Lower Avon Navigation Trust Ltd, Mill Wharf, Mill Lane, Wyre Piddle, Pershore, Worcestershire WR10 2JF. Tel: (01386) 552517.
Manchester Ship Canal Company, Trafford Road, Manchester M5 2XB. Tel: (0161) 872-2411; Great Jackson Street, Manchester M16 4NG. Tel: (0161) 8344436.
National Trust Canal Office, Lapworth, Solihull, West Midlands B94 5RB. Tel: (0156 43) 3370
Ouse and Foss Navigation Trust, Guildhall, York YO1 2EU. Tel: (01904) 59881.
Port of London Authority, London Dock House North, Thomas Moore Street, London E1 9AZ. Tel: (0171) 481-4887.
Rochdale Canal Company, 75 Dale Street, Manchester M1 2HG. Tel: (0161) 236-2456.
Thames Water Authority, Thames Conservancy Division, Nugent House, Vastern Road, Reading, Berks. RG1 8DB. Tel: (01734) 593-387.
Upper Avon Navigation Trust, Avon House, Harvington, Evesham, Worcestershire WR11 5NR. Tel: (01386) 870-526.

Hire Operators

RIVER THAMES

Key

H	Boats for hire
DH	Craft for day hire
R	Refuse disposal (garbage)
S	Elsan sewage disposal
W	Water hose
P	Petrol (gasoline)
D	Diesel
PO	Pump out (sewage)
G	Gas (propane)
C	Chandlery, maps, etc.
M	Moorings

Riverside Lechlade, Farringdon 52229. Facilities: H, DH, W, P, D, G.
Thames Cruises, Clanfield 313. Facilities: Scheduled trips, private charter.
Ferry Inn Bablock, Oxford 882207. Facilities: R, W, D, G, M.
Medley Boat Station, Oxford 511660. Facilities: DH, R, W, D, PO, G.

Salter Bros, Oxford 243421. Facilities: H, DH, W, P, D, G. Scheduled trips
Abingdon Boat Centre, Abingdon 21125. Facilities: H, DH, W, P, D, G, PO, C.
Red Line Cruisers, Abingdon 21562. Facilities: H, R, S, W, P, D, PO, G, C.
Benson Cruisers, Wallingford 38304. Facilities: H, DH, R, S, W, P, D, G, PO, C, M.
Jones Boatyard, Wallingford 38005. Facilities: H, DH, G, C.
Maidboats, Wallingford 36163. Facilities: H, R, S, W, D, PO, G, C.
Sheridan Line, Cholsey 652085. Facilities: H, DH, S, W, D, PO, C, M.
Reading Marine, Reading 27155. Facilities: W, P, D, G, C, M Services.
Pipers Island Boats, Reading 471539. Facilities: H, R, W, D, PO.
Salter Bros, Reading 52388. Facilities: H, W, D, PO. Scheduled services.
Bridge Boats, Reading 590346. Facilities: H, R, S, W, D, PO, G, C.
Caversham Boats, Reading 54323. Facilities: H, DH, R, S, W, D, PO, G Services.
John Bushell, Wargrave 2161. Facilities: R, S, W, D.
Swancraft, Wargrave 2577. Facilities: H, DH, R, W, PO, G; Wargrave 2485. Facilities: W, P, D, G.
Hobbs & Sons, Henley 572035. Facilities: H, DH, W, P, D, C.
Alf Parrott, Henley 572380. Facilities: H, DH, G.
Harleyford Marine, Marlow 71361. Facilities: R, S, W, G, C, M.
Bourne End Marine, Bourne End 22813. Facilities: H, DH, R, S, W, P, D, PO, G.
Turks Boat Yard, Bourne End 20110. Facilities: H, DH, W, G, M.
Bushnells, Maidenhead 24061. Facilities: H, DH, S, W, P, D, PO, G, C.
Bray Boats, Maidenhead 37880. Facilities: H, DH, W, PO, G. 2 large tripboats for charter.
Bray Marina, Maidenhead 23654. Facilities: S, W, P, D, G, C, M.
Windsor Marina, Windsor 53911. Facilities: S, W, P, D, PO, G, C.
Race Course Yacht Basin, Windsor 51501. Facilities: R, S, W, P, D, G, C.
Windsor Boats, Windsor 862933. Facilities: regular trips up river from Windsor, also private charter.
John Hicks, Datchet. Slough 43930. Facilities: H, S, W, PO, D, G, C.

Crevalds Services, Windsor 60393. Facilities: R, S, W, P, D, G, C.
Salter Bros, Windsor 65832. Scheduled passenger service to Marlow, Reading, Staines.
French Bros, Windsor 51900. Windsor to Hampton. Court passenger service.
Runnymede Boatyard, Egham 62914. Facilities: H, R, W, D, PO.
J. Tims & Sons, Staines 52093. Facilities: H, DH, R, S, W, D, PO, G.
Chertsey Marine, Chertsey 62145. Facilities: H, R, S, W, P, D, PO, G, C, M.
Harris Boatbuilders, Chertsey 63111. Facilities: H, R, S, W, D, PO, G.
W. Bates & Son, Chertsey 62255. Facilities: H, DH, R, S, W, P, D, PO, G.
DBH Marine, Walton 28019. Facilities: H, DH, R, W, D, G.
Turks of Sunbury, Sunbury 82028. Facilities: H, DH, R, S, W, D, PO, G, C.
Brian Ambrose Marine, tel: 01-979-3447. Facilities: H, R, W, P, D, PO, G, C.
T.W. Allen & Sons, tel: 01-979-1997. Facilities: H, DH, R, S, W, D, PO, G.
Maidboats, tel: 01-398-0271. Facilities: H, R, S, W, D, PO, G.
Turks of Kingston, tel: 01-546-2434. Facilities: H, R, S, W, D, PO, G.

Holiday Companies

OVERSEAS

Horizon Cruises Ltd, 16000 Ventura Blvd, Encino, CA91436, USA. Tel: (818) 906-8086, toll free: (800) 252-2103 (in CA), (800) 421-0545 (USA), (800) 367-8075 (Canada), operates the 10-passenger *Barkis & Peggotty* along East Anglia's Great Ouse River.
Calypso Charters International, 1237 Clyde Ave. West Vancouver V7T 1E6. Tel: (604) 9263938.
Blakes Bare Boats, 4939 Dempster Street, Skokie Il. 60077. Tel: (312) 5391010.
Skipper Travel Services, 210 California Ave. PO Box 11277, Palo Alto, California 94306. Tel: (415) 32 Wichita, KS67208, (316) 6851118.
Camp Coast to Coast, 860 Solar Building 1000 16th Street NW, Washington DC 20036. Tel: (202) 4666377.
Pavlik Specialised Tours & Travel Ltd, 2221 Panorama Drive, North Vancouver, BC. V7G 1V4. Tel: (604) 9297011.
Dial Travel, PO Box 1033, Hunt Valley, Maryland 21030. Tel: (800) 4249822.

IN THE UK

Actief Barge Cruising Holidays, Abercrombie & Kent, Sloane Square House, Holbein Place, London SW1W 8NS.
Blakes Holidays, Wroxham, Norwich NR12 8DH. Tel: (016053) 2141.
Hoseasons Holidays, A38 Sunway House, Lowestoft, Suffolk NR32 3LT. Tel: (01502) 500555.
The Boat People, 2 The Woodlands, Mkt. Harborough, Leics. LE16 7BW. Tel: (01733) 313770.
Hobo Holidays Ltd, 1 Port Hill, Hertford SG14 1PJ. Tel: (01992) 550616.
Inland Cruising Co Ltd, 59 High St, Braunston, Daventry, Northants NN11 7HS. Tel: (01788) 890465.
Inland Waterway Holiday Cruises Ltd, Preston Brook, Runcorn, Cheshire WA7 3AL. Tel: (019286) 376.
Mersey Navigation Co, 2 Berkeley Drive, Chester CH4 7EL. Tel: (01244) 678160.
Narrow Boat Cruising Ltd, 39 Church St, Weedon, Northhants NN7 4PL. Tel: (01327) 41997.
Narrowboat Hotel Co, 26 Mount Ave, Bebington, Merseyside L63 5RF. Tel: (01836) 600029.
Rushbrooke Narrow Boats, 21 Bibbey St, Rode Heath, Stoke-on-Trent ST7 3RR. Tel: (019363) 78652.
Trent Valley Cruising Hotel, 27 Aidan's Road, Sheffield S2 2NG. Tel: (01742) 21542.

Charter Services

LONDON CANALS

Colne Valley Passenger Boat Services, Adelaide Dock, Endsleigh Road, Southall, Middlesex UB2 5AR. Tel: (0171) 571 4428.
Jasons Trip, Opposite 60 Bloomfield Road, Little Venice, London W9. Tel: (0171) 286 3428.
Lady Rose of Regents, Mr. Julian Rimmer, Rosamund the Fair, Marston Vicarage, Oxford OX3 0PR. Tel: (01836) 581 361.
The Floating Boater, North Wharf Road, London W2 1LA. Tel: (0171) 724 8740.
London Waterbus Company, Camden Lock, London NW1 8AF. Tel: (0171) 482 2550.
Jenny Wren, 250 Camden High Street, London NW1 8QS. Tel: (0171) 485 4433 or (0171) 485 6210.
Broxbourne Boat Centre, Lee Valley

Regional Park, Old Nazeing Road, Broxbourne, Herts EN10 7AX. Tel: (01992) 462 085.
Atlas Leisure Tours, 58 Roundmoor Drive, Cheshunt, Herts. Tel: (01992) 34234.
Lee Valey Narrowboat Co Ltd, The Lock Cottage, Stanstead Abbots, Near Ware, Herts SG12 8DR. Tel: (01920) 870 068.
Stort Cruises, 50 London Road, Bishop's Stortford, Herts. Tel: (01279) 410 129.
Highline Yachting Ltd, The Boat Yard, Mansion Lane, Iver, Bucks. Tel: (01753) 651 496.
Broxbourne Boat Centre, Lee Valley Regional Park, Old Nazeing Road, Broxbourne, Herts EN10 7AX. Tel: (01992) 462 085.

SHROPSHIRE UNION AND LLANGOLLEN CANALS

Shropshire Union Cruisers, The Wharf, Norbury Junction, Staffs. Tel: (0178-574) 292.
Holidays Afloat, Market Drayton, Shrops. Tel: (01630) 2641.
Welsh Canal Holiday Craft, The Wharf, Llangollen, Clwyd. Tel: (01978) 860702.
C. Hardern and Co, Beeston Castle Wharf, Beeston, Cheshire. Tel: (0182-93) 2595.

THE CHESHIRE RING

Russwell Canal Boats Ltd, 7 Princes Drive, Marple, Cheshire. Tel: (0161) 427 5121.

MACCLESFIELD CANAL

Dyecraft Ltd, The Marina, Kent Green. Scholar Green, Stoke-on-Trent. Tel: (017816) 5700.
Peak Forest Cruisers Ltd, The Wharf, Buxton Road, Macclesfield, Cheshire. Tel: (01625) 24172.
Andersen Boats, 11 Wych House Lane. Middlewich, Cheshire. Tel: (0160684) 3668.
Black Prince Narrowboats, Bartington Wharf, Acton Bridge, Northwich, Cheshire. Tel: (0194872) 420.
Clare Cruisers Ltd, Uplands Road, Anderton, Northwich, Cheshire. Tel: (01606) 77199.
I.M.L. Waterway Cruising Ltd, Bank Newton, Gargrave, Skipton, Yorkshire. Tel: (0175678) 492.
King Line Cruisers, Kings Lock Boatyard, Booth Lane, Middlewich,

Cheshire. Tel: (0160684) 3234.
Middlewich Narrowboats, Canal Terrace, Middlewich, Cheshire. Tel: (0160684) 2460.
Peak Forest Cruisers, The Wharf, Buxton Road, Macclesfield, Cheshire. Tel: (01625) 24172.
Russwell Canal Boats, 7 Princes Drive, Marple, Cheshire. Tel: (0161) 4275121.

LEEDS TO LIVERPOOL CANAL

Pennine Cruisers, 19 Coach Street, Skipton, N. Yorkshire. Tel: (01756) 5478.
Yorkshire Canal Cruisers, 24 Canal Wharf, Leeds, Yorkshire. Tel: (01532) 456 195.
Egerton Narrow Boats, The Old Boatyard, Worsley, Manchester. Tel: (0161) 793 7031.

LOCH LOMOND

Loch Lomond Cruisers, Inverbeg Inn, Luss, Loch Lomond, Dunbartonshire G83 8PD. Tel: (0143) 686678. (Bookings through **Hoseasons Holidays**, Box 353 Lowestoft, Suffolk NR23 3LT, tel: (01502) 62211.)
Lomond Charters, Loch Goil Cruisers, Lochgoilhead, Argyll, Scotland. Tel: (0130) 13382. (Bookings through **Blakes Holidays Ltd**, tel: (016053) 3221.)

Practical Tips

Postal Services

Post offices are open Monday to Friday 9am to 5.30pm and on Saturday 9am to 1pm. Some of the smaller post offices may close from 1–2pm and on Wednesday afternoon.

Telecoms

International calls can be made from post boxes throughout the country by dialling the IDD (International Direct Dialling) number listed in the International Telephone Guide. IDD calls are cheaper from Monday to Friday and all day Saturday and Sunday 8pm to 8am.

To call the United States and Canada dial 00-1, then the area code followed by the telephone number. For help in placing a call dial 100.

Getting Around

Orientation

The following are information offices for the different regions of Britain which you can write to or telephone for information. Unless otherwise stated, they are administrative offices only and therefore cannot be visited in person.
English Tourist Board/British Tourist Authority: Thames Tower, Black's Road, London W6 9EL. Tel: 0171-730 3488.
London Tourist Board and Convention Bureau: 26 Grosvenor Gardens, London SW1V 0DU. Tel: 0171-730 3450.
East Anglia Tourist Board: Toppesfield Hall, Hadleigh, Suffolk IP7 5DN. Tel: 01473-822922.
South East England Tourist Board: The Old Brewhouse Warwick Park, Tunbridge Wells, Kent TN2 5TU. Tel: 01892-540766.
Southern Tourist Board: 40 Chamberlayne Road, Eastleigh, Hampshire SO5 5JH. Tel: 01703-620006.
West Country Tourist Board: 60 St David's Hill, Exeter, Devon EX4 4SY. Tel: 01392-76351.
Heart of England Tourist Board: Woodside, Larkhill Road, Worcester WR5 2EF. Tel: 01905-763436.
East Midlands Tourist Board: Exchequergate, Lincoln LN2 1PZ. Tel: 01522-531521.
Yorkshire & Humberside Tourist Board: 312 Tadcaster Road, York, North Yorkshire YO2 2HF. Tel: 01904-707961.
Northumbria Tourist Board: Aykley Heads, Durham DH1 5UX. Tel: 0191-384 6905.
North West Tourist Board: Swan House, Swan Meadown Road, Wigan, Lancashire WN3 5BB. Tel: 01942-821222.
Scottish Tourist Board: 23 Ravelston Terrace, Edinburgh EH4 3EU. Tel:

0131-332 2433.
Wales Tourist Board: Brunel House, 2 Fitzalan Road, Cardiff CF2 1UY. Tel: 01222-499909.

LONDON

The following **tourist boards** deal with written, personal and telephone enquiries:
Scottish Tourist Board: 19 Cockspur Street, London SW1Y 5BL. Tel: 0171-930 8661.
Wales Information Bureau: British Travel Centre, 12 Regent Street, London SW1. Tel: 0171-409 0969.
British Travel Centre: 12 Regent Street, London SW1. Tel: 0171-730 3400. Personal callers only. Represented here in addition to the British Tourist Authority are British Rail, American Express and Room-Centre offering a booking service for rail, air and sea travel, sightseeing tours, theatre tickets and accommodation throughout Britain. There is also a currency exchange bureau. Open: 9am–6.30pm Monday–Friday, 10am–4pm weekends.

Eating Out
Where to Eat
Waterside Restaurants

RIVER THAMES

Rose Revived, Newbridge, Standlake, Oxon. Tel: (0186 731) 221.
Head of the River, Folly Bridge, Oxford. Tel: (01865) 721600.
Barley Mow, Clifton Hampden, nr. Oxford. Tel: (0186 730) 7847.
Swan Hotel, Shooter's Hill, Pangbourne. Tel: (017357) 3199.
Caversham Bridge Hotel, nr. Reading. Tel: (01734) 53793.
White Hart Hotel, Sonning-on-Thames. Tel: (01734) 692277.
St George and the Dragon, Wargrave. Tel: (0173 522) 3852.
Little White Hart Hotel, Henley-on-Thames. Tel: (01491) 574145.
Compleat Angler Hotel, Marlow. Tel: (016284) 4444.
Boulters Lock Inn, Maidenhead. Tel: (01628) 21291.

Thames Riviera Hotel, Maidenhead. Tel: (01628) 74057.
Monkey Island Hotel, Bray. Tel: (01628) 23400.
Donkey House, Windsor. Tel: (01753) 860644.
Sir Christopher Wren's House, Windsor. Tel: (01753) 861354.
Bells of Ouzeley, Old Windsor. Tel: (017535) 62758.
Runnymede Hotel, Egham. Tel: (01784) 36171.
Thames Court Hotel, Shepperton. Tel: (01932) 221957.
Magpie Hotel, Sunbury-on-Thames. Tel: (01932) 782024.
Three Pigeons (Raj), Richmond. Tel: (0181) 940 0361.
London Apprentice, Isleworth. Tel: (0181) 560 1915.
Ye Olde Swan, Thames Ditton. Tel: (0181) 398 1814.
Prospect of Whitby, Wapping Wall, London. Tel: (0171) 481 1095.

OXFORD CANAL

Boat Inn, Newbold-on-Avon, Rugby. Tel: (01788) 76995.
Boatman Hotel and Steak House, Braunston. Tel: (01788) 890313.
Napton Bridge Inn, Napton. Tel: (0192681) 2466.
George and Dragon, Fenny Compton. Tel: (0129577) 332.
Wise Alderman, Kidlington. Tel: (018675) 2281.
Rock of Gibraltar, Bletchington, Oxford. Tel: (0186983) 223.

GRAND UNION CANAL

Black Horse, Canalside, Greenford. Tel: (0181) 578 1823.
Fox, Hanwell Flight, Hanwell. Tel: (0181) 567 3912.
Hambrough Tavern, Southall. Tel: (0181) 574 8295.
Old Oak Tree, Southall. Tel: (0181) 574 1714.

Royal Cricketers, Bethnal Green. Tel: (0171) 980 3259.
Fishery Inn, Boxmoor, Hemel Hempstead. Tel: (01442) 61628.
Black Horse, Great Linford, Milton Keynes. Tel: (01908) 605939.
New Inn, New Bradwell, Milton Keynes. Tel: (01908) 312094.
Red Lion, Fenny Stratford Lock, Blethley. Tel: (01908) 72317.
Narrow Boat, Stowe Hill Marina, Weedon. Tel: (01327) 40536.

SHROPSHIRE UNION CANAL

Bridge Inn, Chester. Tel: (01244) 25260.
Barbridge Inn, nr. Nantwich. Tel: (0127073) 266.
Boat Inn, Gnosall, Stafford. Tel: (01785) 822208.
Shroppie Fly, Audlem. Tel: (01270) 811772.
Wharf Tavern, Goldstone, Market Drayton. Tel: (01630) 063086.

THE BROADS

Berney Arms, Great Yarmouth. Tel: (01493) 700303.
Hotel Wroxham, Wroxham, nr. Norwich. Tel: (016053) 2061.
Anchor Inn, Coltishall. Tel: (01603) 737214.
Duke's Head, Somerleyton, Oulton Broad. Tel: (01502) 730281.
King's Head Hotel, Wroxham Bridge. Tel: (016053) 2429.
Pleasure Boat, Hickling Broad. Tel: (0169261) 211.
Rising Sun, Coltihall. Tel: (01603) 737440.

GREAT OUSE

Bridge House Beefeater, St Neots. Tel: (01480) 72044.
Pike and Eel, Needingworth, St Ives. Tel: (01480) 63336.

RIVER NENE

Grain Barge, Quayside, Peterborough. (No telephone: this is a floating restaurant)
Bull and Butcher, Northampton (moorings close). Tel: (01604) 35904.

CHESHIRE RING MACCLESFIELD CANAL

Bull's Head, High Lane Bridge, Stockport. Tel: (016636) 2070.
Fools Nook Inn, Sutton, Macclesfield. Tel: (012605) 2254.
Miners Arms, Adlington, nr. Higher Poynton. Tel: (01625) 872731.

TRENT AND MERSEY CANAL

Stanley Arms, Anderton Boat Lift, Northwich. Tel: (01606) 75059.
Barton Turn, Barton Lock, Barton-under-Needwood. Tel: (0128371) 2142.
Bridge Inn, Branston, Burton-on-Trent. Tel: (01283) 64177.
Rising Sun, Stone Top Lock, Stone. Tel: (01785) 813494.
Ash Tree, Rugeley. Tel: (018894) 78314.

Tavern, Hardingwood, Kidsgrove. Tel: (01782) 775382.

LEEDS TO LIVERPOOL CANAL

Kirklees Hall Inn, Top Lock, Wigan. Tel: (01942) 42821.
Bridge House Hotel, Hapton, nr. Burnley. Tel: (01282) 72473.
Red Lion, Scarisbrick, nr. Ormskirk. Tel: (01704) 840317.
Ring o' Bells, Bridge 34, Latham. Tel: (01704) 893157.
Anchor, Gargrave, Skipton. Tel: (0175678) 666.
Cross Keys, nr. Bridge 161, East Marton. Tel: (01282) 843485.
Bay Horse, Snaygill, Bradley, Keighley. Tel: (01756) 2449.
Marquis of Granby, Granby Swing Bridge, Keighley. Tel: (01535) 607164.

CALEDONIAN CANAL

Drumnadrochit Hotel, nr. Temple Pier, Loch Ness. Tel: (014562) 218.
Glengarry Castle Hotel, Loch Oich. Tel: (018093) 254.
Letterfinlay Lodge Hotel, Loch Lochy. Tel: (01397) 81622.

CRINAN CANAL

Cairnbairn Inn, nr. Lochgilphead. Tel: (01546) 2488.
Crinan Hotel, Crinan. Tel: (0154683) 261

Restaurant Boats

The Lace Plate, Opposite 60 Blomfield Road, Little Venice, London W9. Tel: (0171) 286 3428.
The Chinese Floating Restaurant, Opposite 15 Prince Albert Road, Cumberland Basin,1 London NW1. Tel: (0171) 485 8137.
My Fair Lady, 150 Camden High Street, London NW1 8QS. Tel: (0171) 485 4433 or (0171) 485 6210.
Hazlemere Marine, Highbridge Street, Waltham Abbey, Essex. Tel: (01992) 768 013.

Attractions

Things to Do

The National Waterways Museum is open daily between 10am and 6pm throughout the summer and 10am–4pm Tuesday to Sunday in the winter. For information and group bookings contact Llanthony Warehouse, Gloucester Books, Gloucester GL1 2EH. Tel: (019452) 25524.

Gloucester is 106 miles (171 km) from London and 51 miles (82 km) from Oxford, fast rail and coach links connect with many major cities.

The Boat Museum, Ellesmere Port, Cheshire, houses a unique collection of commercial boats plus craft workshops and numerous other attractions. Opening from April to end October, 10am–5pm daily. From November to end March open daily 10am–4pm, Fridays by appointment only. Closed during the Christmas period.

Waterways Museum, Stoke Bruerne is beside the Grand Union Canal in Northamptonshire. An exhibition covering two generations of working life on a boat, the men and their families. Opening from Easter to October, from 10am–6pm daily including Bank Holidays. From October to Easter Tuesday–Sunday 10am–4pm. Closed during the Christmas period.

Shopping Areas

Most shops are open from 9am until 5.30pm with one late shopping evening in larger towns. Many will accept the major credit cards.

IRELAND

The Place

Ireland has a total area of 32,000 square miles (82,880 sq. km) and is divided into four provinces, Connacht, Leinster, Munster and Ulster. The six counties of the province of Ulster (Antrim, Armash, Londonderry, Down, Fermanagh and Tyrone) form the the province of Northern Ireland which is part of the United Kingdom.

The Republic of Ireland is a sovereign independent democratic state, with a population of about 3,500,000, 94 percent of which is Roman Catholic. Dublin is the capital. The predominantly Protestant population of Northern Ireland (with Belfast as capital), accounts for a further 1,600.000, making a total population throughout Ireland of about 5,100,000.

English is spoken all over the island, although the old Celtic language (also called Irish, Erse or Gaelic) is, jointly with English, an official language of the Republic.

Planning the Trip

Entry Regulations

Visas and Passports

Visitors are required to have valid passports, or national identity cards in the case of citizens of the United Kingdom and members of the EU. British citizens require no passports or identity cards to travel to Northern Ireland, or to the Republic if they are traveling direct from Britain. No visas are required for visits of up to three months.

Animal Quarantine

Dogs and cats are subject to very strict quarantine restrictions and all animals must remain in quarantine for six months. There are no exceptions to this rule and it follows, therefore, that it would be unwise to take a pet on a boating holiday.

Customs

Visitors are allowed to take into the Republic of Ireland personal clothing, sports equipment and items for personal use, and there are the usual duty free allowances on gifts, cigarettes, alcohol. As the Republic is a member of the EU the customs regulations are similar to those listed for Europe in General. There are no customs barriers between Northern Ireland and the rest of the UK.

Travel between Northern Ireland and the Republic is subject to passport control and customs clearance.

Health

Inoculations or vaccinations are not required for entry into Ireland.

Any visitor from an EU country would receive emergency medical treatment in Ireland under a reciprocal arrangement but visitors from Britain should obtain form E111 before they leave home so that matters can run more smoothly. Visitors from non-EU countries would be advised to check on their health insurance.

For any medical emergency dial 999 or go to the nearest hospital or pharmacy.

Currency

There are no restrictions on the import of foreign currency or Irish currency. You may export any amount up to the equivalent of £500 or the amount declared when you entered the country. Irish currency of up to £100 may be exported in denominations no higher than £20.

The currency of the Irish Republic is the Irish pound (punt) which is divided into 100 new pence. Coins in circulation are 1, 2, 5, 10 and 50 pence, and notes are of Pounds 5, 10, 20, 50 and 100.

Banks are open in the Republic Monday to Friday 10am to 12.30pm and 1.30 to 3pm. In Dublin they remain open until 5pm on Thursdays. Banks do not open on Saturdays, Sundays, or public holidays, with the exception of some international airports.

In Northern Ireland banks remain open until 3.30pm.

Most banks will exchange currency and traveler's checks and accept many of the major credit cards.

Public Holidays

The following are Public Holidays:
January 1: New Year's Day
March 17: St. Patrick's Day
Good Friday
Easter Monday
December 25: Christmas Day
December 26: 2nd Christmas Day

In addition to the above; in the Republic:
First Monday in June: Whitsun Holiday
Last Monday in August: August Weekend
Last Monday in October: Autumn Bank Holiday

In Northern Ireland:
First Monday in May: May Day
Monday in late May: Spring Bank Holiday
July 12: Orange Day
Monday in late August: Summer Bank Holiday

Getting There
By Air

Dublin airport handles flights from Europe whilst transatlantic flights arrive at Shannon airport. There are frequent flights to both airports and considerable competition between the airlines, including the Irish carriers Aer Lingus and Ryanair. It is well worth shopping around for low-cost fares and fly/drive packages.

Aer Lingus serves Dublin, Cork, Galway, Kerry, Shannon and Sligo. Its Irish flights connect with Boston, New York, London Heathrow, Manchester, Edinburgh, Paris, Dusseldorf and Frankfurt. Manx Airlines flies from London and Luton to Waterford and the new Kerry Airport, serving Ireland's south east and south west.

Competitive prices are available on all UK–Ireland routes. Virgin offers a smooth flight from London City Airport to Dublin, matched by British Midland flights from London Heathrow and British Airways flights from London Gatwick. Ryanair offers good economy flights from London Stansted to Dublin, Knock and Cork. From Dublin, the Airlink bus connects with the city centre, bus and rail stations.

There are flights from most main British airports, as well as Paris and Amsterdam, to Belfast International Airport (at Aldergrove) in Northern Ireland; there's a frequent shuttle service between Aldergrove and London's Heathrow. Belfast Harbour Airport, close to the city centre, handles flights to Scotland and England.

By Sea

Irish Ferries runs services between the UK port of Holyhead on the Isle of Anglesea and Dublin North Wall, and also between Pembroke and Rosslare, on the southeast coast. Stena Line operates between Holyhead and Dun Laoghaire, just south of Dublin and between Fishguard and Rosslare. Irish Ferries also offer three sailings a week between Rosslare and the French ports of Le Havre and Cherbourg.

For Northern Ireland, Stena Line operates a service from Stranraer in Scotland to Belfast, the same route plied by the faster SeaCat Scotland service. P&O Ferries runs between Cairnryan in Scotland and Larne, and Norse Irish Ferries between Liverpool and Belfast. Belfast is also served from the Isle of Man by Douglas Isle of Man Steam Packet.

Special Facilities
Boating Tips

Ireland's extensive waterways are open to everyone, and permits or boating licences are not needed. The three main areas for holiday cruising: In the Republic, the Shannon, and Lough Erne in Northern Ireland.

Ten major boat rental companies operate in the Republic of Ireland, and seven on the Erne River in Northern Ireland. Rentals are available from March through October, weather permitting. Most of the companies on the Shannon and Erne offer cabin cruisers, with two to eight berths, fully stocked with supplies. The only stipulation made is that the person in charge of the boat should be over 21 years of age and that at least two people on board should understand how the boat works. The rule of the river is to keep to the right, and to keep all buoys to the left of your boat.

All of the boating companies provide lists of scenic and historic sites along the waterways, and booklets to guide you to the best fishing, the pubs with traditional Irish entertainment, and interesting things to see and do in the towns and villages along the way. Bike rentals are available for those who want to combine boating with cycling, and arrangements can be made to take visitors by taxi or bus to nearby towns or tourist attractions. Guided motorcoach tours are also available.

The Shannon, Grand Canal and the Erne are so easy to navigate that previous boating experience isn't necessary. Rental companies present a half-hour videotape on boating basics, give hands-on instruction in the harbor, and go over maps that show the locations of the locks, shallow and rocky areas, and potential danger spots. Boaters are sent on their way well-armed with maps, and onto carefully marked waterways.

The only fees on the Shannon and the Grand Canal are small payments made directly to lock-keepers when a lock is used (l7p on the Shannon and 30p on the Grand Canal). There are no fees on the Erne which has only one lock.

The operating hours of the six locks and the moveable bridges on the Shannon are:

Dates (Weekdays, Sundays)

March 25–April 15 (9am–6pm, 11am–5pm)
April 16–29 (9am–7pm, 11am–5pm)
April 30–May 19 (9am–8pm, 10am–6pm)
May 20–August 12 (9am–8.30pm, 9am–6pm)
August 13–26 (9am–8 pm, 9am–6pm)
August 27–September 9 (9am–7.30pm, 9am–6pm)
September 10–23 (9am–7pm, 9am–6pm)
September 24–October 14 (9.30am–6pm, 9.30am–6pm)
October 15–March 24 (9.30am–12.30pm, 10am–12.30pm)

THE SHANNON RIVER

Emerald Star Ltd, 37 Dawson Street, Dublin 2, Ireland. Tel: (01) 718870/718725/718569.
Carrick Craft, P.O. Box 14, Reading, RG361A, England. Tel: (0734) 422975.
Flagline Ltd, Shancurragh, Athlone, Co. Westmeath, Ireland. Tel: (0902) 72892.
Athlone Cruisers Ltd, Shancurragh, Athlone, Co. Westmeath, Ireland. Tel: (0902) 72892.
SGS (Marine Ltd), Ballykeeran, Athlone, Co. Westmeath, Ireland. Tel: (0902) 85163.
Derg Line Cruisers, Killaloe, Co. Clare, Ireland, Tel: (061) 76364.
Silverline Cruisers Ltd, Banagher Co. Offaly, Ireland. Tel: (0902) 51112.
Shannon Castle Line, Dolphin Works, Ringsend, Dublin 4, Ireland. Tel: (01) 600964/600588.
Horizon Cruises Ltd, 16000 Ventura Blvd, Encino, CA 91436, USA. Tel: (818) 906-8086, toll free: (800) 252-2103 (in California), (800) 421-0454 (USA), (800) 367-8075 (Canada), operates the 12-passenger *Shannon Princess* which makes weekly cruises along the Shannon River.

THE GRAND CANAL

Celtic Canal Cruisers Ltd, Tullamore, Co. Offaly, Ireland. Tel: (0506) 21861.

Northern Ireland Boating Companies

THE ERNE

Lochside Cruisers Ltd, Tempo Road, Enniskillen, BT74 6HR, Northern Ireland. Tel: (01365) 24366/22625.
Erne Marine, Bellanaleck, Enniskillen, Northern Ireland. Tel: Florencecourt (0136582) 267.
Lakeland Marina, Muckross, Kesh, Co. Fermanagh, Northern Ireland. Tel: Kesh 31414.
Manor House Marine, Killadeas, Co Fermanagh, Northern Ireland. Tel: Irvinestown 03656.
Aghinver Boat Company, Lisnarick, Co. Fermanagh, Northern Ireland, Tel: Kesh 31400.
Carrybridge Boat Company, Lisbellaw,

Co. Fermanagh, Northern Ireland, Tel: Lisbellaw 87651.
Crannog Cruising, Bellanaleck, Enniskillen, Co Fermanagh, Northern Ireland. Tel: (0136582) 349.

Practical Tips

This is a common custom and a service charge of 10 to 15 percent may be added to the bill in hotels and restaurants. Otherwise a tip of around 10 percent is recommended.

Post offices are open from 9am to 6pm remaining open at lunchtime in all but the smaller branches. International calls can be made by direct dialling in any of the larger towns: otherwise, go to a post office.

Canada: 65 St. Stephen's Green, Dublin 2. Tel: (01) 78-19-88.
United Kingdom: 31 Merrion Road, Dublin 4. Tel: (01) 269-52-11.
United States: 42 Elgin Road, Ballsbridge, Dublin. Tel: (01) 68-87-77.
United States Consulate General: Queen's House, 14 Queen Street, Belfast BT1 6EQ. Tel: (01232) 328329.

Getting Around

Northern Ireland is represented by the Northern Ireland Tourist Board and the Republic by the Irish Tourist Board.
In the UK: Northern Ireland Tourist Board, 11 Berkeley Street, London

W1X 5AD, tel: 0171-355 5040, fax: 0171-409 0487; Irish Tourist Board, 150 New Bond Street, London W1Y 0AQ, tel: 0171-493 3201, fax: 0171-493 9065.

In the US: Northern Ireland Tourist Board, 276 Fifth Avenue, New York, NY 10001, tel: 212-686 6250, fax: 212-686 8061; Irish Tourist Board, 757 Third Avenue, New York, NY 10017, tel: 212-418 0800, fax: 212-371 9052.

In Ireland: Northern Ireland Tourist Board, 59 North Street, Belfast BT1 1NB, tel: 01232-231221, fax: 01232-240960; 16 Nassau Street, Dublin 2, tel: 01-679 1977, fax: 01-679 1863; Irish Tourist Board, 53 Castle Street, Belfast, tel: 01232-231221; Dublin Tourism, Suffolk Street, Dublin 2, tel: 01-6057799.

Eating Out

Where to Eat

Restaurants on the Shannon

Gastrognomes, Killaloe. Tel: (061) 76566.

Peter's Restaurant, Killaloe. Tel: (061) 76162.

Derg Hotel, Mountshannon. Tel: (0619) 27162.

Waterside Hotel, Dromineer. Tel: (067) 24175.

Gurthalougha House, Kilgarvan. Tel: (067) 22080.

Derg Inn, Terryglass. Tel: (067) 22037.

Clonwyn House, Portumna. Tel: (0509) 41012.

Shannon Hotel, Banagher. Tel: (0902) 51306.

Prince of Wales Hotel, Athlone. Tel: (0902) 72626.

Royal Hoey Hotel, Athlone. Tel: (0902) 72924.

Jolly Mariner, Athlone. Tel: (0902) 72892.

Glassan Village Restaurant, Bally-an. Tel: (0902) 85001.

Hotel, Lanesborough/Bally-l: (043) 21115.

Pub and Restaurant, Grange

Lake. Tel: (078) 33152.

Percy French Hotel, Strokestown. Tel: (078) 33040.

Strokestown House, Strokestown. Tel: (078) 33013.

Shannon Lodge, Drumsna. Tel: (078) 20706.

Bush Hotel, Carrick-on-Shannon. Tel: (078) 20014.

Ruttledge's Old Coach Inn, Carrick. Tel: (078) 20032.

Forest Park Restaurant, Lough Key. Tel: (079) 62214.

Forest Park Hotel, Boyle. Tel: (079) 62229.

Royal Hotel, Boyle. Tel: (079) 62016.

Shopping

Shopping Areas

Shops are open from 9am–5.30pm, sometimes 6pm, except on Wednesday which is early closing day in most places. Many will accept the major credit cards and if purchasing something expensive remember to check if the store operates the VAT refund system described in the Europe in General section of this Guide. Things to buy in Ireland are hand-knitted sweaters, hand-woven tweed, Irish linen and lace.

Further Reading

Other Insight Guides

To read in more detail about any of the areas covered in *Waterways of Europe*, there's no better or more comprehensive resource than the 350 books that make up three distinct Insight series.

Insight Guides, the companions to the present volume, cover all the major European nations and cites, providing an in-depth cultural background and extraordinary photography.

Insight Compact Guides are ideal reference guides. Inexpensive and highly portable, they are designed to be read on the spot, with text, maps and pictures all cross-referenced. Excellent coverage of European cities.

Insight Pocket Guides contain a local host's specific recommendations on how to make the best use of your time on a short trip. Each comes with a full-size fold-out map. Good coverage of European cities and regions.

Index

420

U – V

W

Y – Z

A
B
C
D
E
F
H
I
J
a
b
c
e
f
g
h
i
j
k
l